The Eye of the Storm

Bishop John William Colenso and the Crisis of Biblical Inspiration

edited by
Jonathan A. Draper

This paperback edition has been published by arrangement with the publishers of the hardback edition, T&T Clark International, an imprint of the Continuum International Publishing Group Ltd, 11 York Rd, London, SE1 7NX, United Kingdom. The hardback edition, which bears the same title, appears as volume 386 of T&T Clark International's *Journal for the Study of the Old Testament* Supplement Series.

The photograph collage on the cover is taken from the following: a printed and signed photograph of Colenso by J.E. Mayall printed in 1864 reversed; other photographs are of William Ngidi before the Mission Chapel at Ekukhanyeni with converts (PAR-C109/2), Zulu Warriors (PAR-C108/20), and Isandlwana after the battle (PAR-C113). The photo on the Frontispiece is of Bishop Colenso c. 1853 (PAR-108/3).

ISBN 1-875053-39-5

First published in 2003

Published by Cluster Publications
P.O. Box 2400
Pietermaritzburg 3200
South Africa
Tel. & fax: (033) 345 9897
E-mail: cluster@futurenet.co.za
Internet: http://www.hs.unp.ac.za/theology/cluspub.htm

Cluster Publications is a non-profit publishing enterprise of the Pietermaritzburg Cluster of Theological Institutions, aiming to produce good scholarship and accessible and inexpensive resources for contemporary theology.

Typeset and copy-edited by Forthcoming Publications (www.forthcomingpublications.com)

Printed by Interpak Books (Pty) Ltd., Pietermaritzburg, South Africa

Bishop John W. Colenso

CONTENTS

Part I
BIBLE

Part II
THEOLOGY

Part III
EKUKHANYENI

Part IV
FAMILY AND SOCIETY

Part V
BIBLIOGRAPHY

Archbishop Njongonkulu W. Ndungane

In some ways, the history of South Africa has been a microcosm of the collision between Western expansionism and the stubborn resistance of the indigenous peoples. The history of the Anglican Church in Southern Africa is almost as convoluted and conflicted as the history of the relationship between colonialism and empire. From the very beginning, it was dogged by controversy and ambiguity. Bishop John William Colenso stands at the heart of this history. The conflict between Colenso and his metropolitan, Bishop Robert Gray, gained notoriety for the South African Church and polarized opinion in England itself. The majority applauded the stand taken for orthodoxy and autonomy taken by Gray, but key figures in the English Church, such as Tait, the Bishop of London and later Archbishop of Canterbury, and Thirlwall, Bishop of St David's, recognized the significance of Colenso's contribution even then.

In some respects, Colenso was a child of his time, a product of the Enlightenment and a creation of Empire. After all, he held Letters Patent from the British Crown, trusting to them in defence of his right to freedom of thought, and he opposed the emerging autonomy of the Church of the Province of South Africa, with its Synods, Canons and Courts. Here the future clearly lay with Gray's energetic construction of a truly independent local African church, with the right to make its own choices. In other very important respects, though, Colenso represents the possibilities for creative dialogue and fusion between the indigenous culture of the colonized people and the emerging global culture of the West. His openness to the value of African religious experience and culture, his defence of justice and freedom for the Zulu people, his defence of religious tolerance and his study of the Bible, have been vindicated by history also. The bitter struggle between Gray and Colenso is thus, in some respects, the epitome of the ambiguity of the cultural exchange between Africa and the West.

The occasion of the 150th Anniversary of the Consecration of Bishop John William Colenso and the creation of the Diocese of Natal is a celebration of the rich heritage of the Church of the Province of Southern Africa. Today we can proudly claim the contributions of both Colenso and his adversary, the Metropolitan of the South African Church, Bishop Robert Gray, visionary Christian leaders as our own, sorrowing for the scandal, pain and suffering caused by their division, but rejoicing in the creative diversity which is the hallmark of the Anglican communion and is so characteristic of our Province. I commend this collection of essays published on this Anniversary not only to members of our modern Anglican Church of the Province of Southern Africa, but also to students of history and to all who are fascinated, as I am, by this complex and visionary man, Bishop John William Colenso.

LIST OF CONTRIBUTORS

Fiona Bell
Lecturer in Information Studies, University of Natal, South Africa

Gwilym Colenso
A relative of Bishop Colenso and an independent researcher, London,
United Kingdom

Ian Darby
Rector of St David's Church, Prestbury, Pietermaritzburg, South Africa

Philippe Denis
Professor of the History of Christianity, University of Natal, Pietermaritzburg, South Africa

Jonathan A. Draper
Professor of New Testament, School of Theology, University of Natal,
Pietermaritzburg, South Africa

Mandy Goedhals
Professor of History, University of Durban-Westville, South Africa

Jeff Guy
Professor of History, University of Natal, Durban, South Africa

Eric A. Hermanson
Assistant General Secretary: Text Processing, Bible Society of South
Africa

Cornelius Houtman
Professor of Old Testament, Theological University, Kampen, Netherlands

David Jobling
Professor of Old Testament Language and Literature, St Andrew's College,
Saskatoon, Canada

Patrick Kearney
Diakonia Council of Churches, Durban, South Africa

Vukile Khumalo
University of Michigan, United States of America

Timothy Larsen
Associate Professor of theology at Wheaton College in Wheaton, Illinois,
United States of America

Abraham Mojalefe Lieta
Lecture in History of Christianity, University of Natal, South Africa

Iain S. Maclean
James Madison University, New York, United States of America

Gordon Mitchell
Professor Religious Education, University of Hamburg, Germany

Njongonkulu Ndungane
Archbishop of Cape Town, Metropolitan of the Church of the Province of
Southern Africa

Livingstone Lubabalo Ngewu
College of the Transfiguration, Grahamstown, South Africa

Ronald B. Nicolson
Acting Deputy Vice-Chancellor, University of Natal, South Africa

John W. Rogerson
Professor of Old Testament Emeritus, University of Sheffield, United
Kingdom

Maarman Sam Tshehla
Lecturer in New Testament, School of Theology, University of Natal,
Pietermaritzburg, South Africa

INTRODUCTION

Philippe Denis

The significance of Bishop Colenso not only as a key missionary figure but as a major protagonist in South African colonial history is now widely recognized. This, one should note, is a relatively new development in South African historiography. Until the publication of Jeff Guy's ground-breaking book *The Heretic* in 1983, the prevalent view, to quote Peter Hinchliff, the author of a biography published two decades earlier, was that the Bishop of Natal 'cannot be regarded as a great figure in the history of English theology', and that, if he were to be tried again today, he 'would probably be found guilty on half the charges against him' (Hinchliff 1964: 2, 137). Guy's interpretation of Colenso's life had a profound impact on subsequent research. While not ignoring the Bishop of Natal's work as a missionary and a theologian, he chose a different approach. He described Colenso as an imperialist who despite his love for his country, managed to gain insights into the colonial world as it was perceived by the colonized (Guy 1988: 358) and, on the basis of this information, attempted to change the system from the inside. On two important occasions he openly defied the authorities of the Natal Colony: at the trial of the Hlubi chief Langalibalele in 1873 and after the invasion of Zululand in 1879. Even though he succeeded in alerting public opinion in Britain, he failed to prevent the dismantling of the Zulu kingdom. He died in a situation of forced isolation in 1883. Yet his memory is treasured by the African people who call him 'Sobantu', the father of the people. The bishop's relationship with William Ngidi, with Magema Fuze, the Zulu writer, and with the other Ekukhanyeni students, significantly influenced his thought and his action.

Guy argued that one cannot separate Colenso the pastor and theologian from Colenso the social reformer and political campaigner. The Bishop of Natal was condemned as a heretic by his peers. He retained his see against the wish of the Anglican Church but was *de facto* marginalized in his own diocese. In his later years, the political apparatus rejected him in the same way, starting with Theophilus Shepstone, his erstwhile friend. Church and State alike found his views unacceptable.

Twenty years after the publication of *The Heretic* the time has come to re-examine Colenso's life and work. The advances made in areas such as biblical hermeneutics, historical theology, cultural anthropology and African linguistics warrant the need for a new book. Hence this collection of essays whose authors come from a variety of backgrounds. Several of them are black South Africans.

Another reason for proposing to the public a new book on Colenso is that the Anglican Church has changed its position regarding the bishop's orthodoxy. As Ron Nicolson points out in this volume, many contemporary Anglican theologians, including himself, would subscribe to the theological positions which the highest Church authorities declared heretic in the nineteenth century. In fact, if we follow Jonathan Draper's analysis, the trial was seriously flawed. Colenso was not judged fairly. This is now publicly recognized. In September 2002, the Provincial Synod of the Church of the Province of Southern Africa (CPSA), voting by houses, passed a resolution to lift the condemnation by an overwhelming majority.

This book only laterally touches Colenso's career as a political activist. This may be the topic of another study. The present collection of essays primarily focuses on Colenso's work as a reader of the Bible, as a Christian thinker and as an educationist. They show that the Bishop of Natal developed a distinctly novel approach to biblical scholarship, soteriology and missionary work. His familiarity with Zulu society, epitomized by his famous dialogue with Ngidi on the plausibility of the Pentateuch's stories, transformed not only his understanding of the faith but also his social practice. As David Jobling argues in this volume, the most important reason why Colenso's biblical work was controversial was that it originated in the colonies. The Bishop of Natal fed back African scholarship from the periphery to the centre.

Should we, for this reason, regard Colenso as a liberation theologian *avant la lettre*? Certainly not. Neither should we see him as an anti-colonial hero. He was an imperialist (Etherington 1997: 95) and remained so until the end. He objected to the policies of the Natal government because he thought that they would bring the British Empire into disrepute. The Bishop of Natal marked his times because of his strong views and his indomitable energy. But one should not hasten to describe him as a unique person. Several contributions to this volume show that he was less isolated in his enterprises than one would think. As Iain Maclean demonstrates, for instance, his views on polygamy and *ukulobola*, controversial as they may have been, were not fundamentally different from those of Rufus Anderson, the secretary of the American Board of Commissioners for Foreign Missions.

Colenso was good at networking, as one would say today. His indebtedness to F.D. Maurice, who broke off contact with him after the publication of *The Pentateuch*, and to the Christian socialist movement at the beginning of his career has long been noted. But he had many other connections. More research is needed to understand his intellectual milieu. Authors like Timothy Larsen, who finely chronicled the Pentateuch affair in 1862 Britain, or Cornelis Houtman, who analyzes the 29 letters from Colenso to Abraham Kuenen, the Dutch biblical scholar, at the Leiden University Library, show the way. One should also look at the Bishop of Natal's American connections. Some of his views on the universality of salvation were shared across the Atlantic Ocean, where his *Commentary on Romans* was published in 1863 and enjoyed considerable popularity, judging by the number of surviving copies (Draper 2003: ix). Likewise Colenso's translation work was not done in a vacuum. Eric Hermanson's paper has the merit to locate the bishop's pioneering work against the background of other, equally innovative translation practices. And one should not forget, as Sam Tshehla reminds us, that Colenso was, as he says, an 'outsider-translator'. The fact that he was an Englishman does matter. Translation is a political as much as a theological affair. The Bishop of Natal's legacy needs to be re-evaluated from an African point of view. In this respect, a paper like that of Vukile Khumalo, which examines the intellectual production, mostly in Zulu, of the Ekukhanyeni students, is very revealing.

Colenso's most effective network, if one may use that word, was his family. The contributions offered by Mandy Goedhals and Jeff Guy, which close this volume, highlight the extraordinary importance in his life of the women who composed his family: his wife Frances and his three daughters. They also confronted imperialism but, being women in a fundamentally patriarchal society, they suffered even more, especially Harriette and Agnes who continued the struggle until an advanced age.

Part I

Bible

COLENSO'S FIRST ATTEMPT AT BIBLE TRANSLATION IN ZULU

Eric A. Hermanson

Records suggest that about two decades before Bishop Colenso first visited Natal, members of the Church of England had been involved in translating passages from the Bible into Zulu.

During 1835, Captain Allen F. Gardiner, who had applied to the Church Missionary Society, journeyed through Natal attempting to spread the gospel to the Zulu population (Gardiner 1836). In a lengthy letter written from the Gloucester Hotel, Piccadilly, on 1 March 1836, he says:

> Some progress has already been made in translating the New Testament into the Zulu tongue; Mr Fynn, the only competent person in South Africa, having kindly undertaken that work, and I trust that there will soon be a considerable portion prepared for publication. (CMS Mission Book C A4/M1, pp. 1-3)

Whether or not Henry Francis Fynn did actually translate any of the New Testament into Zulu is not clear. If he did, as Gardiner's letter asserts, it seems certain that nothing of it was ever published. Ries (1957: 4) suggests that certain copies of Matthew, Mark, Luke, John, Acts and Jude published in 1836 and now in the Natal Society Library in Pietermaritzburg may be his translation because the word 'Erini', to which Ries adds in parenthesis (perhaps Henry Fynn?), is on the title page. This suggestion is totally erroneous, however, as the publications in question are in Xhosa, not Zulu, and were translated by various missionaries such as William B. Boyce and William Shaw (Luke, 1833 and 1837), W.J. Shrewsbury (Matthew and John, 1836), R. Haddy (Mark, 1837), John Ayliff (James, 1-3 John and Jude, 1837) and Henry H. Dugmore (Acts, 1837), and published by the Wesleyan Mission at Erini, the Xhosa name for Grahamstown (Coldham 1966: 726-28).

On 20 November 1837, the Reverend Francis Owen, of the Church Missionary Society, also recorded in his diary that he was busy with translating Scripture (Cory 1926: 70). He wrote:

Commenced this morning with the aid of my Hebrew lexicon, etc. turning
the 19th Ps. into Zoolu. In the evening commenced the translation from the
Greek Testament of the Gospel of St. Johns [*sic*]—These exercises will I
trust contribute to my improvement in the language, and will accustom me
to the important work of translation: at the same time that they bring me to
a closer acquaintance with the sacred volume itself. I record this humble
commencement of my labours in this branch notwithstanding I am fully
aware that not only every sentence, but perhaps every word of my new
exercise will hereafter bear criticism.

Francis Owen kept in contact with the missionaries of the American Zulu
Mission and often discussed the orthography of Zulu with them (Cory
1926: 89, 106). He was in Mgungundlovu, Dingaan's (*recte* Dingane's)
kraal, reading his Bible, on 6 February 1838, the day that Piet Retief and
his party were massacred, and immediately fled to Port Natal (now known
as Durban), and from there went by ship to Delagoa Bay and eventually to
Algoa Bay (Port Elizabeth). Had he been able to continue his ministry
among the Zulu, he might have been able to play a significant role in
translating the Bible. Instead, he returned to England after a brief ministry
among the Tswana, when the Church Missionary Society decided in
September 1840 to close its work in South Africa (Leverton 1972a: 540).

Gardiner also left Natal after the massacre and sailed with his family for
South America where he ministered in a number of countries before his
death in Terra del Fuego in January 1851 (Kotzé 1972: 259-60).

So, when Bishop Colenso arrived in Durban on 30 January 1854 for
a ten-week tour of his new diocese, the Church of England had no
missionaries ministering to the Zulu population. In this British Colony,
instead of missionaries of the Established English Church, he found
'Dissenters'—American Congregationalists, a Wesleyan Methodist turned
Independent, and German and Norwegian Lutherans.

The Americans had been the first to establish mission work among the
Zulu. At the end of December 1835, during the reign of Dingane, Dr
Newton Adams, the Reverend George Champion and the Reverend Aldin
Grout, missionaries of the American Board of Commissioners for Foreign
Missions, arrived in Port Natal to establish the first mission to the Zulu,
or 'Maritime Zoolahs' as they are called in *Champion's Journal* (Booth
1967; 1968: viii). For the previous four months, they had been on a
London Mission Society station at Bethelsdorp, near Port Elizabeth, which
ministered to the Hottentot (Khoi), and the Xhosa who speak a language
of the same Nguni group as Zulu. Missionaries to the Xhosa had been
reluctant to use the existing words referring to the Supreme Being in that

language, so as to try to avoid any unbiblical connotations which those words, used in local accounts of creation for example, might convey about the God revealed in the Bible. Instead they had begun to use the word *uTixo* (recte *uThixo*), said to have been adopted from the Khoi, to refer to 'God'. This influenced the missionaries who went to the Zulu, particularly as they had first come into contact with an Nguni language in Bethelsdorp, sometimes used Xhosa interpreters, and were given grammars and translations in Xhosa to aid their language study (Booth 1967: xi, 12; Cory 1926: 10).

As Colenso travelled around the country, he sought to discover what concept the Zulu had of God and what word(s) they used to refer to him. In their preaching and publications, the Americans had followed the lead of the Wesleyan Methodists working among the Xhosa and were using the word *uTixo*. It soon became clear to Colenso that this decision had its problems. For example, uNceni, who had been Captain Allen Gardiner's servant for three years told him, 'The Zulus first heard of *uTixo* (recte *uThixo*) from Capt. Gardiner; but before he came, they thought the origin of all things was *umKulunkulu*' (Colenso 1855g: 137). Colenso found that two words, which he gives as *umKulunkulu* (recte *uNkulunkulu*, 'the Great-Great One') and *umVelinqange* (recte *uMvelinqangi*, 'the One Who Appeared First'), were volunteered naturally by the majority of those to whom he spoke. He also found that the Norwegian missionaries had adopted the word *uNkulunkulu* (1855g: 214-16). In addition to their connection with creation myths which differed from the biblical account, the basic objection by others against using either of these words seems to have been that the word *unkulunkulu* was also used to refer to some sort of beetle, and the missionaries did not want to cause confusion by giving the impression that the God whom they were proclaiming was an insect. If the word *unkulunkulu*, perhaps with a different tonal pattern, did have this additional meaning at the time, it is certainly not generally known today, if it is known at all. On the other hand, it was believed that the use of the name *uMvelinqangi* for the God of the Bible would suggest that he was the first of all created beings, whereas in reality he is eternal.

The missionary influence on Colenso's Zulu respondents was no more apparent than at Edendale, where the Reverend James Allison, a former Wesleyan Methodist but at that time an Independent missionary, was stationed. Allison, the son of 1820 British Settlers, was one of a group converted in the remarkable religious revival in the Albany District (Mears 1967: 2; Eveleigh 1920: 116-21). Colenso records that Allison told him that the word *uTixo* had no meaning to the Kaffirs. The proper word for God was *iTongo* (recte *iThongo*), which meant to them 'a Power of Universal Influence'—a being under whom all are placed. How Allison came by this word, let alone to this conclusion, requires more research. Previous to his being obliged to flee to Natal with some Swati refugees from tribal unrest, he had ministered in Swaziland. There he had translated the Methodist Catechism (1846) into Swati, another cognate language to Zulu, and had used the word *iThongo* for God. In an article on this translation, Professor D. Ziervogel (1950: 183) questions the word and I myself was unable to find anyone who knew it while I was Translation Consultant for the Swati Bible (1997) translation during the period 1987 to 1997. In Zulu the word refers to an ancestral spirit (Doke and Vilakazi 1948: 801), while Berglund (1976: 87, 89-90) says that it refers to a shade who reveals himself in dreams during sleep (*ubuthongo*) and appears to be used more in the southern part of the Zulu region. In his *Zulu–English Dictionary* (1905a: 595), Colenso lists the word as meaning 'ancestral spirit; may be used as equivalent to good genius or saviour'. Unfortunately, he does not elaborate on the extended meaning 'good genius or saviour', so it is not clear under which conditions and context such an equivalent meaning would be appropriate. Regarding Allison's followers, however, Colenso comments:

> I cannot account for his people not even naming to me the other two names *umKulunkulu* and *umVeliqange*, which, *in every other instance* were given to me at once by the natives. They might have done so, if I had asked for them; but, at the time of my visit to them, I was not myself alive to the importance of the question. (1855g: 60 [my emphasis])

Why Allison chose this word in favour of *uTixo*, the word used by his erstwhile Wesleyan colleagues among the Xhosa, while it was adopted by the American Congregationalists, remains a mystery.

Daniel Lindley was one of the original band of American Board of Commissioners for Foreign Missions missionaries. After an ill-fated attempt with Henry Venable and Alexander Wilson to minister to the Ndebele, who are referred to as the 'Interior Zoolahs' in Champion's Journal (Booth 1968: viii), he joined his colleagues in Natal. When Colenso visited him, his respondents said that they thought that *umKulunkulu* would be the best word to use for the unconverted heathen and that it was the best word altogether. Colenso records:

> Mr Lindley was quite convinced by their replies, that there was more of truth in their rude conceptions of the Divine Being, than he had imagined;

and regretted with me that the Americans had not—as the Norwegian Missionaries now have done—laid aside altogether the word *uTixo*, and adopted at first *umKulunkulu*, or some other word. He said they had thought of doing so; but, being strangers in the land, they had deferred to the example and judgment of the Wesleyans and others, whom they found in the field before them. (1855g: 239-40)

One can only conjecture as to whether or not these were Lindley's sentiments, for Lindley's daughter was later to write after reading Colenso's book (Smith 1949: 290): 'Papa counted eight fibs in his account of his visit to Inanda. You can't think what a lot of fibs there are in it!'

It did not take Colenso long to become convinced that the American missionaries had erred in using the word *uThixo* in accordance with those who were ministering among the Xhosa. He expressed his conviction as follows:

> It is incalculable what mischief must be done by this barbarous unmeaning, Hottentot name (*uTixo*), for one which is connected in the mind of the Kaffir with such grand associations, as Almightiness and Original Existence—however much they may have lost sight of the full meaning of their own expressive words for the Deity. They are the very ideas contained in the Hebrew words Elohim and Jehovah. (1855g: 115)

So, while the earlier missionaries had feared that the existing vernacular names for God would convey unbiblical connotations about the God of the Bible to the people, Colenso concluded that these Zulu words in fact conveyed the exact meaning of the Hebrew terms! Later, however, after working on translations of Psalm 100 and the Apostle's Creed with Mr (later Sir) Theophilus Shepstone (Gordon 1976: 746-53), the son of a Wesleyan missionary who had been brought up among the Xhosa and who had acquired the language at an early age, he says:

> We have the greatest difficulty in fixing on a proper name for God. I cannot bear the mean and meaningless name *uTixo*, with its disagreeable click, and poverty of sound. *UmKulunkulu* and *umVelinganqe* are both too long for common use; and so would be *uLungileyo*, 'The Good One'. We have thought of adopting *umPezulu*, 'He above, or in Heaven'; and by this Name, in fact, Kaffirs are often sworn in courts of justice. Standing up and lifting the first and second fingers in Dutch fashion, he will repeat the words, *Ngi bona, 'nKos' iPezulu*, 'Behold me, Lord above', or *Ngisize, 'nKos' iPezulu*, 'Help me, Lord above'. But there are objections to this word also. I am not sure that it would not be best to employ the word *uDio*. It is a new word, it is true, like *uTixo*; but it is easy of utterance, is directly connected with the Greek and Latin names for God, and is not very far removed from the word

which it displaces. No one, who has not tried, can conceive how hard, and
almost impossible, it is, to give correct representations in another, and that a
barbarous tongue, of the refined and expressive language of some parts of
the Bible and Prayer Book. (1855g: 159-60)

So, because he found the normal Zulu words 'too long for common use',
and the word used by the American missionaries, not only meaningless,
but to contain a 'disagreeable click and poverty of sound', he proposed
another new, and therefore equally meaningless word of his own invention! It should be noted that the lateral palato-alveolar click, represented
by the letter *x* is one of the phonemes of Zulu, and would not have been at
all disagreeable to them, while two vowels do not occur in juxtaposition in
the Zulu language, as they do in the word *uDio*. In his *Grammar*, Colenso
has a section giving rules for 'obviating, if possible, the hiatus which
would arise when any particle ending in a vowel is prefixed to a word
beginning in a vowel'. The fourth rule is 'In other cases, when *i* or *u* (the
only vowels to which this *can* happen) come before a vowel, they may be
changed to the semi-vowels *y* or *w*' (1855b: 10-11). He does not seem to
have realized that his new word contained the exact type of hiatus which
the *i* changing to a semi-vowel in the examples he gives prevented. Therefore, whereas his new name for God might have been 'easy of utterance'
for Colenso, the Zulu would most naturally pronounce the word with a
semi-vowel between the vowels. This would then result in them pronouncing the word Colenso had coined for the God revealed in the Bible
as an ordinary Zulu word, *udiyo* ('drinking pot'). So, even if Colenso was
unaware of it at the time, the possibility was great that if the Zulu did not
find the word he had coined as foreign to them as *uThixo*, they could very
easily totally misunderstand the meaning it was intended to convey.
Nevertheless, Colenso adopted the word *uDio* in his adaptation of the
American missionaries' 1848 translation of the Gospel of Matthew published in 1855 and continued to use it in his publications for a number of
years. It is therefore interesting to note that in the title of his gospel narrative, published in 1857, *Izindaba Zokupila kuka'Jesu-Kristu indodana
ka'dio unkulunkulu Inkosi yetu* (*Reports of the Life of Jesus Christ the Son
of Dio God Our Lord*) he uses both his own and the traditional word for
God in apposition to one another. Henry Callaway, one of Colenso's early
recruits (Hinchliff 1976: 156-58), and later Anglican Bishop of Kaffraria,
also used *uDio* in his translations. Callaway wrote extensively, both in
books and letters to the newspaper, on what he understood to be the true
meanings of the names for God already mentioned and various other terms

used in Zulu religion and folklore, based on interviews with scores of informants over many years (Callaway 1870). This debate was also recorded by the Reverend W. Wagner of the Catholic Mission at Mariannhill (1923–26). Commenting on Colenso's suggestion to use *uDio*, Wagner says: 'I feel sure that the later Zulu scholar Colenso would not have subscribed to what here the newcomer Colenso says' (1923: 667). It seems that he was right, because in his translation of the New Testament, probably first published in 1876 (Hermanson 1992: 80), Colenso uses *uNkulunkulu* for God, and *YAHWE* in quotations from the Old Testament containing the tetragrammaton (see Mt. 22.37, 44; Mk 11.10). In these verses, the Americans used *uJehova* in 1848 and Colenso used *uYEHOVA* in his 1855 adaptation. Also, the word *uDio* is not listed in the fourth edition of his *Zulu–English Dictionary*, published in 1905.

The American missionaries, however, continued to use *uThixo*, not only in the first New Testament published in 1865, but also in the first complete Bible published in 1883. However, in their extensive revision of the New Testament in 1917 and the complete Bible in 1924, they changed to *uNkulunkulu*. The word *uNkulunkulu* was also used in the translation of the New Testament and Bible published by the Hermannsburg Mission also in 1924.

So, gradually, the term *uNkulunkulu* has been generally accepted for use in Zulu churches and in Bible translations. It is found in the Catholic New Testament (1966) and also in the Bible published by the British and Foreign Bible Society in 1959, and with updated orthography by the Bible Society of South Africa in 1997. This is the Bible in general use in the majority of Zulu churches today. The Bible Society of South Africa, however, also still publishes a facsimile of the 1893 revision of the 1883 Bible which uses the term *uTixo*. This edition continues to be used by a few churches such as the Nazareth Baptist Church founded by Isaiah Shembe, in spite of the fact that it is in an extremely old orthography which has not been used for almost a century.

On 18 February 1835, about a fortnight after arriving in South Africa from America, George Champion recorded in his journal:

> There is an opinion prevalent here among those interested in missions, that those entering new missionary fields should sit down immediately, & in the infant schools teach the children the English Language, in order that in the course of 2 or 3 generations the native language may be extirpated, The English introduced, & thus that all the stores of literature, science & religion that there are in the English tongue may be laid at their feet. Thus you save translations, & you have a language adapted to civilized & Christian

men. The language will not cramp their minds as those minds expand under
the influence of Christianity. This is an experiment probably yet to be tried
in the work of converting the world to Christ. The interest in infant schools
is felt only among the intelligent English in town. (Booth 1968: 5)

Although this opinion was not shared by the American missionaries, one
might not have been surprised if it had been adopted by someone from the
British Establishment with the academic training and as widely read as
Colenso. However, nothing could be further from the truth. Certainly he
established schools and taught English, seeking to give them a good
command of the language. He even taught his pupils to sing 'God Save the
Queen', five verses of which in Zulu are found as hymn 27 at the back of
the Prayer Book (Colenso 1856b: 125). In two essays in Zulu with English
translations by Mankanjane ka Sotyenge and Skelemu ka Magwaza and a
number of drawings by pupils, which accompanied Colenso's letter dated
1 February 1857 to Sir George Grey reporting on the previous year's
progress, both boys mention singing *igama likaViktoria inkosikazi yase-
Ngilande* ('The Anthem of Victoria, Queen of England'), although Mankanjane spells her name *Vikitolia* and it is *Viktolia* in the printed version.
Colenso nevertheless had a deep respect for the Zulu language and culture,
and encouraged the Zulu to continue to do so also. From the very beginning, Colenso realized that if the Zulu were to be reached with the gospel
of Christ, it would have to be through their own language. He immediately
began collecting everything he could find written in and about Zulu and
the related language Xhosa. His aim was to learn as much as possible
about the language himself before his return to Natal to take up his responsibilities as Bishop. In addition, during his sojourn in England, recruiting
clergymen for his mission, he also wanted to prepare material such as a
Zulu grammar and dictionary and to provide them with Scriptures in Zulu.
With these texts they could begin studying the language on the long voyage
out to South Africa and so gain a head start before they even reached the
people to whom they were to minister. This seems an impossible task, but
it is a task he accomplished to the best of his ability in spite of his insufficient experience of the language and the inadequate and often inaccurate
material at his disposal. So, on his return to Natal, he and his recruits
carried with them a Zulu grammar, a Zulu–English dictionary, and an
adaptation of the Gospel of Matthew originally published by the American
Zulu Mission in 1848.

Printed in square brackets across the centre of the cover of the *Gospel*
are the words '[Reprinted, with some alterations, from the Translation
published by the American Missionaries]'. It would be interesting to know

exactly how Colenso decided upon the alterations he made and whether or not some were corrections or improvements requested in the reprint by the Americans themselves. It seems that he must have made the corrections and adaptations he felt necessary, rather inconsistently at first, on a printed copy of the American publication, and submitted that to the printers in England for typesetting. From marked page proofs of part of the *Gospel*, housed in the Grey Collection in the Cape Town branch of the National Library of South Africa, it can be seen that as he read the proofs he not only corrected typographical errors made by the printers, but included many 'author's corrections' in an attempt to make his adaptations consistent. From the published *Gospel*, however, it is evident that he was not entirely successful on either count. A brief overview of some of the main changes he made is presented in what follows.

1. *Orthography*

It is not clear why Colenso made the changes he did to the orthography. In Schreuder's *Zulu Grammar* (1850), written in Danish, which Colenso used as a basis for his *Grammar*, Schreuder had used many different symbols to represent the phonemes of Zulu. The Americans, on the other hand, had used the normal 26 letters of the alphabet. In fact, Colenso says in his *Grammar* (1855b: 4):

> The Zulu–Kafir alphabet contains 26 letters, which are represented by Roman characters. The letters c q x and r are used to represent the three clicks and the guttural, not English, but corresponding in sound to the strong German *ch* (as heard in *auch, noch*).

However, having established a 26-letter alphabet for Zulu, he then goes on to say:

> In addition to the above letters, it will be found convenient to employ Ĵ, ĵ (which may be called the letter *chay*)[1] for the combination of sounds, represented in English by *tsh* or *ch*; and also the Spanish ñ which has the sound of *ni*, as heard in the English word *onion*.

So, Colenso ended up with a 28-letter alphabet, which he uses both in the *Grammar* and the *Gospel*. Notably, he did not use this alphabet when he

---

1.   The characters used by Colenso are *J* and *j* with a horizontal line through them. Due to the non-availability of these characters in modern word processing packages, in the present study the forms *Ĵ* and *ĵ* will be used in place of Colenso's unique characters.

edited Perrin's *Dictionary*, the third book in the trilogy prepared for his new missionary force. In the *Dictionary* it is clearly stated not only that 'The orthography adopted is that which is at present used by the American Missionaries', but also that: '*ty* has generally the sound of soft *ch*, as in "church"' (Perrin 1855a: iii).

So, in the *Grammar* and the *Gospel*, but not the *Dictionary*, words with either a voiced or voiceless prepalatal fricative, previously spelt with *Ty/ty* following the Xhosa orthography, are spelt with *J/j*, usually, but not consistently with a horizontal line through it, for example, *–tyo > –jo* ('say'), *–tyela > –jela* ('tell'), spelt today as *–sho* and *–tshela*. The fact that the horizontal line is sometimes omitted could have caused confusion, particularly as the letter *J/j* is also used for words containing the voiced prepalatal affricative such as *–jabula* ('be happy'). Interestingly, Colenso sometimes uses *sh* in words like *pesheya* ('on the other side'), as did the Americans, which suggests that they could not always clearly distinguish when the Zulu used a voiced and when they used a voiceless palatal fricative. However, Colenso also changed proper names beginning in *iota* in Greek, for which the Americans had used *J* to *Y* as is done in Xhosa, for example, *Ujesu > uYesu* ('Jesus'), *Ujudia > uYudia* ('Judea').

Colenso also substituted the prepalatal nasal *ny* with *ñ* in some words and not in others in the *Grammar* and the *Gospel*, but not the *Dictionary*. It seems that he uses *ñ*, except at the beginning of noun stems. There he uses *Ny* for words which in the singular are in classes with prefixes which do not end with *n*, for example, Class 1a *uNyana* ('son', in Xhosa), *uNyoko* ('his/her mother'); Class 3 *umNyu* ('sourness'), *umNyango* ('doorway'); Class 11/10 *uNyawo* ('foot'), *iziNyawo* ('feet'). All of these words are listed in the *Dictionary* under 'N' (Perrin 1855a: 107), with the exception of *umNyu* which is not listed at all. Instead there is the entry: 'MUNYA (*U or Ubu*) n. Salt, sourness, agony' (p. 97). For words in classes with prefixes ending in *n* he uses *nY*, for example, Class 9/10 *inYama* ('meat, flesh)', *inYoni* ('bird') *izinYoni* ('birds'), *inYoka* ('snake') *izinYoka* ('snakes'). Indeed, all of these words are listed under 'Y' in the *Dictionary* (pp. 161-62). However, the locative form of *iziNyawo* is consistently spelt *ezinYaweni* ('at the feet'), where one would have expected *eziNyaweni*. A possible explanation for the confusion is the fact that the *Dictionary* has two entries, namely, 'YAO n. (*In*) A foot' (p. 161) and 'NYAWO (*I or U*) n. Foot' (p. 107), where not only do the noun prefixes differ, but the one entry is spelt without semi-vowel *w*.

Fortunately Colenso found it 'convenient' to introduce these two extra letters only in his first two publications, and then reverted to the American missionaries' orthography. His system certainly could not have been very convenient for the printers, nor for those who were trying to learn Zulu using his *Grammar* and *Gospel* with his innovations, with the *Dictionary* in the simpler orthography.

It would indeed have been convenient had he found a way to distinguish between the unvoiced and voiced lateral alveolar fricatives. The note in the *Dictionary* reads: '*hl* is used to express two different sounds which, as well as the difference between them, can be accurately expressed only by the living voice' (Perrin 1855a: iii). This, however, was done a few years later, when Colenso (1859c: 2) writes: 'The student must be careful to distinguish between the sounds of *hl* and *dhl*, since there are some words, essentially different in meaning, which only differ in sound by the insertion of the d. Compare in English *thigh* and *thy*.' Although nowhere stated, both the Americans and Colenso used the apostrophe to indicate the elision of a vowel in a word

A problem with translation is that often the grammatical form of the source language and/or that of the non-mother tongue translator, rather than that of the target language is reflected in the translation. It seems that the Americans equated the Zulu verbal infinitive prefix *uku–* with the English infinitive 'to'. They therefore retained the letter *u* in concords and other prefixes before both consonant-commencing and vowel-commencing stems or words, where the prefix usually has an allomorph ending in *w*, or without the *u*. So, for example, they wrote *uku azi* instead of *ukwazi* ('to know', Mt. 13.11); *uku enza* instead of *ukwenza* ('to do', 23.15); and *li ya ku onisa* instead of *liyakonisa* ('it causes you to sin', 5.29). They also retained *u* at the end of nouns before the locative suffix *–ini*, for example, *ezinHluini* ('in the houses', 9.35). Nevertheless they presumably pronounced the *u* before a vowel as *w* wherever it occurred. Colenso was obviously made aware of this, and notes it in his *Grammar*, and so usually changed a *u* before a vowel to *w*, but not at all consistently, for instance, he spells 'in the houses' in three different ways: *eziNhlwini* (4.23); *ezinHlwini* (6.5); *ezinHluini* (9.35).

Colenso, like the Americans, equated the locative prefix *ku–* with the English prepositions 'to' or 'from'. They therefore prefixed the locative prefix *ku–* to nouns and qualificatives without regard to their initial vowel, for example, *ku abahlakanipi* ('from the wise men', Mt. 2.16); *ku enye* ('to one', 6.24); *ku elo 'lizue* ('from that land', 15.22); *ku ilizue lakubo* ('to their country', 2.12); *ku inceko* ('to the servant', 8.9); *ku omunye* ('to another', 8.9). Again, Colenso is inconsistent, but he usually changes *u* to *w*, apparently not having been made aware that in this locative construction in Zulu, the initial vowel of the noun elides, for example, *kubahlakanipi* (from the wise men'); *kulizwe lakubo* ('to their country'); *kunceko* ('to the servant'). Unfortunately, when he deals with this in his *Grammar*, Colenso gives three examples of how *ku* is used 'to express any shade of meaning in reference to place', but in all three he prefixes *ku* to the pronoun *ye* ('him/her'), and so has no examples of what happens when *ku* is prefixed to a noun with this meaning (1855b: 13).

The Americans used the Xhosa form of the demonstrative pronoun *elo* instead of the Zulu *lelo*. Colenso explains that demonstrative pronouns are derived from the Relative by prefixing *l* to imply 'this', prefixing *l* and changing the final vowel to *o* to imply 'that' and prefixing *l* and affixing *ya* to imply 'that further off'. He tabulates the forms and then inexplicably adds: 'NB All the above, except those that are formed from monosyllabic Relatives *a, e, o* frequently drop that *l*' (1855b: 22-23). So in the *Gospel* he changed *ku elo 'lizue* to *kwelo 'liZwe* instead of correcting it to *kulelo 'li-Zwe* ('from that land'). When a demonstrative pronoun comes before a noun in Zulu, the initial vowel of the noun elides, as indicated by the apostrophe. However, Colenso's examples in his *Grammar* do not indicate the elision. Instead he has 'Ex. leli *iliZwe*, lelo *iliZwe*, leliya *iliZwe*'. The Americans always prefixed *ku*– instead of the allomorph *k*- to words beginning in *o*–. Therefore, for example, Colenso changed their *ku omunye* to *kwomuñe* instead of to *komuñe* ('to another').

The Americans also wrote the Class 15 possessive prefix and remote past tense concord as *kua*. Presumably in most, if not all of these cases, they pronounced the *u* as if it were a *w*, for Colenso changes them to *kwa*–.

Colenso seems also to have been influenced by English grammar in the way in which he inserted quotation marks in Mt. 23.18 *Na 'ye o-fungayo gelAti'* ('And he who swears by the altar'). He is inconsistent in some-times having two words *na ye* and sometimes hyphenating *na-ye* ('and he'), the latter indicating the correct connection between the two. This is the second claim made by those the Lord is accusing, the first being in v. 16 *'Yena o-fungayo geTempeli'* ('He who swears by the Temple'). However, Colenso, and probably the original translators, must have un-derstood the morpheme *na* as equivalent to the English conjunction 'and', which would be a separate word. However, *na*, which in Zulu is an associative and not a conjunction, does not join sentences. As it stands, the translation would suggest that what the people said was 'He who swears by the Temple *as well as* he who swears by the altar', in which case it should be punctuated *'Na-ye o-fungayo gelAti'*. It would, however, have been better to use a conjunction like *futhi* ('in addition') and use the same construction as *'Yena o-fungayo geTempeli'* in v. 16, as he did in his translation of the New Testament, so as to read *abati futi 'Yena o-fungayo gelAti'*.

Whereas the Americans used upper case letters at the beginning of sentences and as the first letter of personal and place names, Colenso uses upper case for the first letter of the stem after the nominal prefix in personal and place names. He therefore often starts a sentence with a word beginning in a letter in the lower case, instead of making both the prefix and first letter of the stem upper case as is done today. He also uses many additional upper case letters, apparently to denote the beginning of the stem of the word, possibly to make it easier for a reader to find in the *Dictionary* where 'The root of the word is always placed first. After it the incipient particle or prefix' (1855a: iv), or to distinguish the stem clearly from the surrounding morphemes. Unfortunately, this is not done consistently, so that often a different letter is in upper case in the same word in a different verse. For example, 'on the sea' is rendered as *eLwanhle* in Mt. 2.18 and *elwAnhle* in 21.21 (Perrin's *Dictionary* listing is 'LWANHLE [u] n. The ocean' [1855a: 94]), and 'power; strength' is rendered as *amaNhla* in 3.11 and *amanHla* in 7.29 (the *Dictionary* listing is 'NHLA [Ama] n. Strength, power' [1855a: 102]). It is interesting that Colenso changes *imali*, which may have been derived from the English 'money', or more probably from the Arabic *māl* ('wealth') to *imAli*, whereas the stem is obviously *–mali*. In Zulu this word is in Class 9, which does have *im–* as prefix in certain cases. However, Colenso retains the Class 4 adjectival concord in *imAli emiNingi* ('much money', 28.12) instead of correcting it to Class 9 *eningi*. In the *Dictionary*, this word is listed both as 'ALI (Im) n. Money' and 'MALI (I) n. Money' (1855a: 2, 94), which suggests that Colenso and Perrin were unsure of the derivation of the word.

2. *Vocabulary*

Just after the title page of the 166-page dictionary, *A Kafir–English Dictionary of the Zulu–Kafir Language, as Spoken by the Tribes of the Colony of Natal*, compiled by James Perrin, and printed in England under Colenso's direction, Colenso writes:

> I am indebted to the kindness of Mr Perrin for this Vocabulary of the Zulu–Kafir language, which he has prepared with much care, and after an experience of some years among the natives of the Natal District, and has freely given for the use of our Mission. Through the liberality of the Christian-Knowledge Society, the work has been printed under my superintendence, and will be found, I trust, upon the whole, accurately edited; though, from my limited acquaintance with the language at present, I cannot hope to have escaped error altogether, in deciphering some doubtful words in the manuscript.

> London, January 12, 1855   JWNatal

> The orthography adopted is that which is present used by the American Missionaries.

> If any words of the IsiXosa dialect are inserted in this Lexicon, which do not strictly belong to the Zulu, it is because such are now in frequent use among these tribes.

James Perrin was secretary to Sir Theophilus Shepstone and had worked with the American Missionary Josiah Tyler at Esidumbini. He later joined the Baptist Church (Louw 1972: 554-55). It seems that he too was not idle while Colenso was away, for his 255-page companion volume, *An English–Kafir Dictionary of the Zulu–Kafir Language as Spoken by the Tribes of the Colony of Natal* was published in Pietermaritzburg by the Church of England Missions, soon after the bishop's return. About this, Colenso wrote:

> I am again indebted to Mr Perrin for the contents of this little book, which will be found, I doubt not, a most valuable help for Missionaries and others, in acquiring the language of the Natives. In the compilation of this, and of the Kafir–English Dictionary, Mr Perrin has derived considerable assistance from the Vocabularies prepared by some of the American Missionaries, to which they very kindly gave him free access. I shall be very much obliged to any, who, from their acquaintance with the language, as spoken by the Zulus especially, would suggest to me any corrections or additions to be made in this Vocabulary, or who would point out any words which have been here introduced, but which belong to the AmaXosa tribes, and are not used by the AmaZulu.

> Pietermaritzburg, October 15th, 1855   JWNatal

An understandable vocabulary change in the *Gospel* in the light of the explanation given above concerning the debate about what word to use for God, is the substitution of *uDio* for *uTixo*. This is consistently done, except in Mt. 8.29, where *uTixo* was obviously overlooked in both adaptation and proofreading.

It is interesting to note that in the Zulu–English edition of the *Dictionary*, the word Colenso coined for God, *uDio* is not listed, whereas *udiwo* ('a cracked or broken pot') is. So is *uTixo*, the word used by the Americans, which Colenso had rejected (Perrin 1855a: 33, 143). The *Dictionary* also lists '*Kulunkulu* (*Um*) n. A traditionary being, the Creator, the larva of an insect found in trees' and '*Umvelinqangi* = *Umkulunkulu* A traditionary great Being, the Creator' (pp. 83, 153).

The English–Zulu edition of the *Dictionary* (Perrin 1855b: 108, 60), on the other hand, has the following entries:

GOD UDIO	*uTixo*
God Almighty n.	*uDio, 'nKulunkulu*
	UDio o-namanhla
Godhead	*ubuDio*

and

Creator n.	(Maker) *umenzi* traditional name for *Umkulunkulu*.

So, whereas in the first volume Colenso's neologism is omitted, in the second volume it takes precedence over the word used by the Americans. The *Dictionary* indicates that it may be used on its own, or with the relative *o-namanhla* (recte *onamandla*, 'who has power'), with the meaning 'God Almighty', as may *'nKulunkulu*. Another neologism *ubuDio* 'Godhead' formed by prefixing the abstract Class 14 prefix *ubu–* to the coined nominal stem *–Dio* is also listed. However, all words with the stem *–Dio* are omitted even from the *Isipiki* section, listing what are called 'hybrid words commonly used (1895)', of Colenso's own *Zulu–English Dictionary* (1905a: 721-24). This is clear proof that although he decided to introduce a word of his own invention in adapting the American missionaries' translation of the Gospel of Matthew for use in his diocese and continued to use the word for some years thereafter, he later came to recognize the adequacy of vernacular Zulu terms for deity to refer to the God of the Bible.

The 1848 American publication of the Gospel of Matthew is recorded as having been translated by George Champion, who had returned to Boston in 1839 and died in 1841 (Booth 1968: xi), and revised by Newton Adams. Coldham (1966: 772) says that Bleek records an edition in 1841 and adds in parenthesis '(possibly a misprint?)', as there seems to be no extant copy bearing that date. If the 1848 *Gospel* is Champion's translation, that could explain why it contains Xhosa stems such as *–bini* ('two'), instead of *–bili*, since Champion had been aided by Xhosa material and informants in learning Zulu. However, it is not clear why Adams did not change the spelling to reflect the Zulu form, if he revised the manuscript for printing after having spent at least ten years in the Zulu area, allowing for the period when the missionaries left Natal after the massacre of Piet Retief and his party in 1838. Furthermore, one would have expected that this would have been brought to Colenso's attention as something which needed correcting in a reprint. In the *Zulu–English Dictionary* (1855a: 12) only *–bili* ('two') occurs, whereas in the English–Zulu edition (1855b: 212) both forms are given: '*–bili, –bini* a. two'.

In fact, there are a number of Xhosa words in the American version which Colenso retains in his adaptation, such as: *uNyana* ('son'), *uNyana womuNtu* ('Son of Man'), *ubomi* ('life'). Not only so, but he also introduces Xhosa words where the original Zulu text was correct: *umNyu* instead of *umunyu* ('sourness') in Mt. 5.13, and *ubuKumkani* instead of *umbuso* ('kingdom') in the Lord's Prayer (6.10, 13), although he retains *umbuso* in other places, including 3.2 where the Kingdom of Heaven is *umBuso weZulu*. The word *ubuKumkani* is not listed in the Dictionaries. He also has *umZi* instead of *umuzi* ('town') in 5.14, 35, and *ombi* and *omhle* instead of *omubi* ('bad') and *omuhle* ('good') in 7.17-18. An interesting verbal stem found 16 times in both versions is *–giba* ('take out, cast out'). The Xhosa form of the word *–kupe* (18.9) is also found both in the original and in Colenso's version. The correct stem is *–kipa* (recte *–khipha*), which occurs twice in 7.4-5, where *–giba* also occurs once. The occurrence of *–giba* suggests that the missionaries did not always hear the Zulu phonemes clearly, which also probably accounts for their use of *g* instead of the nasal *ng* and *j* instead of *nj* in many places, such as in the first person singular subjectival concords of the verb, and the instrumental adverb morphemes.

Attempting to determine possible reasons for other changes effected is often made more difficult by the fact that where some words have been corrected, in other places errors have been introduced. Most such errors are probably typographical, the result of an English compositor misreading the text in an unfamiliar language, rather than an error in the text adapted by Colenso itself. For example: *uNyawa* instead of *uNyawo* ('foot', Mt. 4.6); *ku-kona* ('on it') instead of *ku-bona* ('on those', 4.16); *uYESU na-hamba* ('Jesus you pl. went') instead of *uYESU wa hamba* ('Jesus went', 4.23); *na-ti* instead of *wa-ti* ('he said', 9.4); *emTabeni* instead of *enTabeni* ('on the mountain', 5.1); *yi 'nKaniso yeliZwe* instead of *yi 'nKañiso yeliZwe* ('light of the world', 5.14); *na-Yihlo* instead of *no̲-Yihlo* ('and your Father', 6.4); *uka̲vatiswa* instead of *uku̲vatiswa* ('be clothed', 6.29); *gape̲wheya* (8.28) instead of *gape̲sheya* ('on the other side', 14.22); *si-ya-r̲ama* instead of *si-ya-v̲ama* ('we are accustomed', 9.14); *ga-ba-u-sa-hliz̲o̲* instead of *ga-ba-u-sa-hle̲zi* ('it would still be there', 11.23); *emiPefu̲mle̲ni yenu* instead of *emiPefumulwe̲ni yenu* ('in your souls', 11.29); *li-tambe̲le* instead of *li-tambi̲le* ('soft', 11.30); *isi-X̲ukulwana* instead of *isiZ̲ukulwana* ('generation', 12.29); *o-ncili̲leyo* instead of *o-ncoli̲leyo* ('unclean', 12.43); *kwaba̲* instead of *kwabo̲* ('their', 13.58); *wokuG̲ala* instead of *wokuQ̲ala* ('first', 28.1). It is a pity that these errors were not detected and corrected when the page proofs were read.

In places the probable typographical error is not so obvious for one not familiar with the text, as it changes the meaning while still making sense. So, in the Parable of the Sower, some of the seed fell *emaFeni* ('among the inheritances', Mt. 13.5, 20) instead of *emaJeni* ('on stony ground'), which would reflect Colenso's normal change for the word *ematyeni* in the 1848 version. Matthew 6.26 says the birds *a-zi-hlwangeli a-zi-vumi* ('do not sow nor agree') instead of *a-zi-hlwangeli a-zi-vuni* ('do not sow nor reap').

At times, Colenso missed correcting errors which seem so obvious that someone should have seen them in the original American edition and pointed them out to him, even if he did not see them himself. For example, one would have expected him to correct *wa-hla pansi* to *wa-hlala pansi* ('he sat down') in Mt. 13.2, especially as the phrase *wa-hlala pansi* also occurs in the previous verse.

In other cases, however, Colenso did indeed correct typographical errors in the 1848 publication. So, *a yu̲ dabuka* becomes *a ya̲ dabuka* ('they burst', Mt. 9.17). While both forms are used in the American publication, the Xhosa *um̲s̲a* becomes the Zulu *umu̲sa* ('mercy', 9.27), but is retained in seven other verses. The word *umb̲apatiz̲a* is corrected to *umB̲apatizi* ('Baptist', 14.8) in line with other occurrences, *n̲yihlo* is changed to *u̲Yihlo* ('your father', 17.20), and *ku-me̲* to *ku-mi̲* ('to me', 25.45). However, when Colenso changes *um̲tuana* to *umN̲twana* ('child', 2.8, 9, 11, 13, 14, 20, 21; 10.21) and *umT̲wana* (17.18; 18.2, 5; 23.15), there is obvious inconsistency. The Dictionary listings are 'TWANA (Um) n. Child, small person' (Perrin 1855a: 147) and 'Child, n. *umtwana*' (Perrin 1855b: 44). Colenso must have become aware of the fact that the noun stem does begin with a nasal *ntwana* because of the plural *abantwana*. This is also the logical conclusion if the diminutive suffix *–ana* is added to the word *umuntu* ('person')—*umuntu* + *ana* > *umntwana* ('small person'), with the contracted prefix with polysyllabic stems.

Where Colenso changes words, his changes are not always improvements. For example, in the Lord's Prayer in Mt. 6.9-11, the 1848 version had: <u>*Ubaba*</u> *wetu o s'ezuluini:* <u>*ma li dunyisue li be ingcuele*</u> *igama lako:* <u>*Umbuso*</u> *wako ma u ze:* <u>*intando*</u> *yako ma y'enziwe emhlabeni, ku be njenga s'ezuluini. Si pe namhla* <u>*isinkua*</u> *semihla setu* ('Our Father who is in Heaven, may your name be praised and holy; may your kingdom come, may your will be done on earth as in heaven. Give us today our daily bread'). Colenso starts correctly with the vocative, *'*<u>*Baba*</u> *wetu o-se'Zulwini* ('Our Father who is in Heaven'), *Ma-li-hlukaniswe iGama lako* ('May your name be separated as distinct'). He then replaces the Zulu word with the Xhosa word for 'kingdom' twice where it occurs in the prayer, while retaining the Zulu word 35 other times in the Gospel: *Mabu-ze* <u>*ubuKumkani*</u> *bako* ('May your kingdom come'). He also changes the word for *intando* ('will') to *iliZwi* ('word') while retaining *intando* in six other places, including in the Lord's prayer in Gethsemane, for God's will to be done (26.39, 42), *iliZwi lako ma-l'enziwe emHlabeni njenga s'eZulwini*. He changes *isinkua semihla setu* ('daily bread') *to ukuHla kwetu kwemihla* ('daily food'), a change which would find general acceptance in Bible translations today, because in this context what is requested is a daily supply of staple food, rather than 'bread' which would have been a luxury, or at least a foreign food to the Zulu. He nevertheless retains *isinkwa* the 21 times it has specific reference to bread.

It is not clear why he changed *u ya ku hlaulela nga ni umpefumlo wake na?* to *u-ya-ku-kokela nga-ni umPefumlo wake na* ('with what will he pay for his soul') in Mt. 16.26, as both words occur in Zulu with almost the same meaning. The *Dictionary* however does make a distinction, which possibly explains Colenso's thinking in doing so: 'HLAULELA v.n. Pay a penalty, expiate, atone for' and 'KOKELA v.a. Pay for compensate, bribe, remunerate' (Perrin 1855a: 62, 79).

In the *Zulu–English Dictionary* Colenso says: 'Proper names of persons have of course been omitted; but those of the principal and many of the minor rivers are included' (1855a: iv). It might have been good if he had decided on the spelling of proper names in the Gospel of Matthew, for here he changed the American missionaries' spelling of *uPontio Pilati* to *uPontiusi-Pilati* (Mt. 27.2). In the prayer book published a year later in 1856 he has *uPontius-Pilate*, before he finally settled on *uPontio-Pilato* in the New Testament (1876[?]b/1897). In his later translations, Colenso changed the Zulu spelling of many New Testament personal and place names (Hermanson 1995: 204-21).

3. *Grammar*

In his adaptation of the *Gospel*, Colenso drew on what he had learned about the language in the preparation of his first *Grammar*, which he explains as follows (1855b: 39-40):

> In the composition of this Grammar I have derived assistance from those written for the dialect of the Frontier Kafirs, by Messrs Appleyard and Boyce, Wesleyan Missionaries. But I am still more indebted to a Grammar of the Zulu Dialect composed by Mr Schroeder [*sic*], a Norwegian (Lutheran) Missionary, and printed in Danish, but most kindly translated for me into English by Miss Grote of Trumpington, Cambridge. I must also express my thanks to the Rev J Grote, Vicar of Trumpington, and late Fellow of Trinity College, Cambridge, for some valuable suggestions. I cannot hope to have escaped all error in the preparation of this Grammar, after so recent an acquaintance with the language itself; but I believe it will be found correct in all essential particulars. And it was most desirable that the large party of Missionaries who are about to sail with me to Natal, should have the means of studying the Zulu-Kafir language to some extent during the voyage. This they will now be able to do, as they will each be provided with a copy of a Grammar, Dictionary and Translation of St. Matthew, in the Zulu-Kafir tongue.
>
> March 1, 1855
> JWNatal

Nouns in Zulu are categorized into classes according to their distinguishing prefixes. In this first *Grammar* Colenso refers to 'species' of nouns, but to 'classes' in his later publications. Syntactically there is concordial agreement between words based on the prefixes of the nouns in the sentence. Twice, in Mt. 8.1 and 18, Colenso makes the error of mixing concordial agreement between the noun and adjective by changing the noun to the singular and retaining the adjective in the plural: *isiXuku ezikulu*, where the original *iziXuku ezikulu* ('large crowds') is correct. Similarly, in 13.30 the correct possessive concord in *s'esiKatini sokuvuna* ('the time of harvest') has been incorrectly changed to *lokuvuna*.

Whereas some African languages are written disjunctively, Zulu today is written conjunctively, that is, prefixal and suffixal morphemes are joined to nominal stems and verbal radicals to form longer words. Colenso began to do this in his adaptation of the Gospel of Matthew by inserting hyphens between the morphemes which go together, although once again he

unfortunately did not do so consistently. Griesel (1991: 74) says that
Colenso is generally associated with introducing conjunctivism into Zulu.
He quotes J. Stuart as saying in his address to the Natal and Zululand Conference on Zulu Orthography in Durban in 1906 that Colenso's approach,
which had obviously developed greatly since 1855, was 'the best known
representative of the conjunctive method' (Stuart [ed.], 1907: 6). Griesel
comments that although he was a leader in this as far as Zulu is concerned,
it does not mean that Colenso initiated the conjunctive method, for Bennie
and Boyce had used it in Xhosa, and Colenso had used Boyce's *Grammar*
in developing his own for Zulu. It was nevertheless a positive step forward.

There are some places where it appears that Colenso had been made
aware of improvements which could be made. For example, when a noun
is used as a vocative, it is without the initial vowel. This he corrects in Mt.
7.21, 9.28 and 21.30 where a person is addressed and he has *'nKosi*, but
not in 8.2 where the initial vowel of *inKosi* is retained. In 4.7, he corrects
nokuthi ('and that') to *ukuti* ('that'). He also deletes certain unnecessary
words in some cases such as the *kwa* in *wa-muka kwa lapo* ('he went away
from there', 11.1), but in other places deletes words which should have
been retained such as *kuni* (to you) in *ku-ya-ku-piwa kuni* ('it will be given
to you', 10.19). Possibly mislead by the plural *gi-jo kuni* (I say to you) in
5.28 where Jesus is addressing the crowd and the plural is appropriate, he
incorrectly changes the singular *ku we* ('to you') to the plural *ku ni* ('to
you') in v. 26, where the reference is a warning to a single person being
thrown into prison until restitution is made.

A most useful alteration made to the Matthew text was to introduce
quotation marks to indicate direct speech. In what was apparently the
convention at the time, the opening quotation mark, comes not only before
the first word of direct speech, but also at the beginning of each line of the
continuing speech.

4. *Colenso's Translations—Fruits of Controversy?*

Although Colenso began by adapting the American missionaries' translation of *Matthew*, once in South Africa he began to make and publish his
own Scripture translations and other books in Zulu. In a letter dated 1 February 1857 to Sir George Grey, reporting on his previous year's work,
Colenso said that he was planning to publish a gospel narrative, and went
on to say:

I have also in hand a First and Second Reading Book in Kafir, and a new Ed[ition] of the Zulu Grammar which I hope to produce in the course of this year. But in order to do this I have been obliged to send to England for *type* (I have a press) that we may print at the Station ourselves with the help of my boys: as the Printers' hands in Town are so full of work that it is very tedious to have anything to do with them.

I transmit also herewith copies of the Kafir Liturgy [Colenso, 1856b] and a Zulu Tract on the Ten Commandments which we have produced during the past year. These latter have had the benefit of Mr Shepstone's vision—the Gospel narrative not.

It seems that Colenso had to put up with the tedious printers for a little longer, for the gospel narrative was published in Pietermaritzburg by May & Davis in 1857. However, although the complete New Testament, which is undated but probably published in 1876 (Hermanson 1992: 80), bears the name of the publishers P. Davis & Sons, it was printed at Bishopstowe by Magema & Co., his own Zulu printers. Magema was one of the boys whose essays on life at Ekukhanyeni Colenso had sent to Sir George Grey in February 1857, when the boy must have been about twelve years old. A little booklet *Amazwi Abantu* (*Words of People*) in the Grey Collection in Cape Town, bears the following written inscription on the bottom of the front page: 'Composed and Printed by Magema, a Zulu boy of about 14 years, from a rough M.S. (formerly Skelemu)'. The name Skelemu means 'rogue' or 'scallywag'. Under Colenso's tutelage this young scallywag not only took charge of the press and set and printed the New Testament and other books printed at Ekukhanyeni, but he also was one of the first Zulu authors to have a book published. It was called *Abantu Abamnyama, lapa bavela ngakona* (*The Black People and Whence They Came* [Fuze 1922]).

Other books of the Bible Colenso published were First and Second Samuel in 1871, and Exodus in 1882. When Colenso arrived in Natal, the American Board Missionaries had already begun translating the Bible into Zulu. The translation initiative eventually led to the first complete Zulu New Testament in 1865 and Bible in 1883. Doke (1958: 89) is of the opinion that it was really the theological differences around the name of Bishop Colenso that were responsible both for his own translations and for those of his erstwhile colleague, Bishop Henry Callaway. Colenso published a commentary on Romans in 1861 and the first volume of a critical evaluation of the Pentateuch and Joshua in 1862. The opinions he expressed in these publications led to his being put on trial for heresy (Ive 1966: 22-26), so it is not surprising that Callaway was 'troubled with the Bishop's Scripture translations' (Benham 1896: 115). Doke considered

Callaway's translations to be extremely good, and stated that Colenso's translation of the New Testament 'is also a very good translation'. He continues, 'Colenso spoke scathingly of Callaway's translations, an attitude partly due, in all probability, to the bitterness of the controversy: but it is a pity that Colenso, accomplished Zulu scholar, found it difficult to acknowledge another's ability in Zulu' (Doke 1958: 89-90). It is a great pity that these two could not work with one another and that the missionaries of the Congregational, English and Lutheran traditions did not co-operate in the task of Bible translation in Zulu until much later.

5. *Conclusion*

When Colenso arrived in Natal he found that Matthew's Gospel was the only book of the Bible published in Zulu. While the old adage states that a little knowledge is a dangerous thing, nevertheless Colenso can be commended that after only a brief encounter with the Zulu language, he undertook not only to adapt this translation, but also to provide a grammar and dictionary, so that those he recruited to work with him in Natal should have at least some knowledge of the language before they arrived. Colenso's first attempt at Bible translation in Zulu was therefore more of a revision to meet his own needs, but it also included grammatical and lexicographical work as an integral part of the same task. Although he was not able to correct the problem at the time, he was very aware that the *Gospel* and *Dictionary* contained words which were probably not Zulu, but Xhosa. He therefore pleaded that those with such knowledge should point out any inaccuracies they found in the publications he had produced, realizing that although he had done his best with his limited acquaintance with the language, he could not expect to have escaped error completely. The result of his first endeavours was that in spite of the errors he missed and those which were introduced in resetting the text, he made two significant contributions. First, although sometimes inconsistently and inaccurately, he started to identify what constitutes a word in Zulu as different from what constitutes a word in English; then, by joining the morphemes he believed should go together with hyphens, he began the tradition of writing Zulu conjunctively. Second, he introduced quotation marks to identify direct speech, a definite advantage which inexplicably was not used in other translations of the Bible in Zulu until recently. From these first imperfect efforts, Colenso went on to become a most competent Zulu linguist, eventually publishing his own translation of the New Testament.

He also produced his own *Grammar* and *Dictionary* which Griesel (1991: 32) describes as important reference books during the second half of the nineteenth century. After his death on 20 June 1883, his daughter Harriette continued to edit and publish new editions of the *Grammar* to at least 1903, and the New Testament to 1905. The *Zulu–English Dictionary* was still in print in 1940.

Scripture Translations Cited

1837(?)	*Incuadi Yokuqala Yabafundayo* (*First Book for Readers*) (Port Natal: American Zulu Mission Press).
1848	*IVangeli E Li Yingcuele E Li Baliweyo G'uMatu* (*The Holy Gospel Written by Matthew*) (UMkungunhlovu [Pietermaritzburg]: D.D. Buchanan & Co.).
1855	*IVangeli Eli-Yingcwele Eli-baliweyo G'uMatu* (reprinted, with some alterations, from the translation published by the American Missionaries; London: Richard Clay).
1865	*ITestamente Elitya Lenkosi Yetu uJesu Kristu NgokwesiZulu* (*The New Testament of our Lord Jesus Christ in Zulu*) (Esidumbini, Natal: American Zulu Mission).
1897	J.W. Colenso, *Izindab'ezinhle Ezashunyayelwa Ku'bantu ng'uJesu-Kristo Inkosi Yetu Kanye Nezinncwadi Ezalotshwa Ng'abapostole Bake* (*The Good News Preached to People by Jesus Christ Our Lord Together with the Letters Written by His Apostles*) (London: J.M. Dent & Co. [printed and published for Miss H.E. Colenso] [1st edn = 1876?]).[2]
1883	*IBaible Eli Ingcwele NgokwesiZulu* (*The Holy Bible in the Zulu Language*) (New York: American Bible Society).
1917	*ITestamente Elisha eli isivumelwano esishaseNkosi uMsindisi wetu uJesu Kristu li hunyushwe li kitshwa olimini lwesiGreki li hunyushwe ngokusha.1916* (*New Testament Being the New Covenant of Our Lord Saviour Jesus Christ Translated from the Greek and Translated Anew in 1916*) (New York: American Bible Society [printed for the British and Foreign Bible Society])
1924	*IBaibele Eli Ingcwele Eli neTestamente eliDala, neliSha kuhunyushwe isiHeberu nesiGreki izilimi okwa lotshwa kuqala. Li hunyushwe ngokusha* (*The Holy Bible which has the Old and New Testament Translated from the Hebrew and Greek, the Languages in which it was First Written: Translated Anew*) (New York: American Bible Society).

2. The edition I have and used is dated 1897. The first edition, a copy of which is in the Grey collection of the South African Library, is undated. Through my own detective work I have established the date of publication as being 1867, and cover the problem in this article by saying 'However, although the complete New Testament, which is undated but probably published in 1876 (Hermanson 1992: 80), bears the name of the publishers P. Davis & Sons, it was printed at Bishopstowe by Magema & Co., his own Zulu printers' (p. 25, above).

28 The Eye of the Storm

1924   *ITestamente Elitsha Lenkosi Umsindisi Wetu uJesu Kristu Ngolimi LwesiZulu* (*The New Testament of Our Lord Saviour Jesus Christ in the Zulu Language*) (Empangweni: Moorleigh; Natal: Hermannsburg).

1924   *Incwadi Engcwele etiwa IBibele noma ImiBhalo: ITestamente Elidala neTestamente Elitsha Ngolimi LwesiZulu* (*The Holy Book Called the Bible or the Scriptures: The Old Testament and New Testament in the Zulu Language*) (Empangweni: Moorleigh; Natal: Hermannsburg).

1959   *IBhayibhile Elingcwele* (*The Bible in Zulu*) (London: British & Foreign Bible Society).

1966   *Izincwadi Eziyingcwele ZeThestamente Elisha Lenkosi Umsindisi Wethu uJesu Kristo, NgesiZulu, Zahunyushwa, Zachazwa Ngabafundisi BeBandla EliKhatholika.* (*The Holy Books of the New Testament of our Lord and Saviour Jesus Christ, in Zulu, Translated and Explained by Ministers of the Catholic Church*) (Mariannhill: Mariannhill Mission Press, 2nd edn).

1979   *Indaba Enhle kaNkulunkulu* (*Good News According to Mark, Acts, Ephesians, Psalms in Zulu*) (Cape Town: Bible Society of South Africa).

1986   *IThestamente Elisha namaHubo* (*The New Testament and Psalms*) (Cape Town: Bible Society of South Africa).

COLENSO, JOHN 1.1-18
AND THE POLITICS OF INSIDER- AND OUTSIDER-TRANSLATING

Maarman Sam Tshehla

Whenever the translation is approached in a theoretical manner, a type of
perfectly competent translator, who does not exist in reality, is presupposed.
(Whang 1999: 48)

1. *A Pretext for the Present Exercise*

Translations bear the marks of their makers as much as they communicate
something of the source culture.[1] We differentiate between the translator's
culture, the broader milieu of the literature being translated, as well as the
target language's cultural environment. If we accept that something of
each of these factors[2] is captured in the translation, then the translator can
clearly tip the balance this or that way. It is from this perspective that I
believe South Africa must see the emergence of insider-translators[3] of the

---

1.   We remain warned that 'no culture can be reproduced completely in any literary text, just as no source text can be fully reproduced in a translation' (Tymoczko
1999: 23), with stern emphasis on the adverbs 'completely' and 'fully'.
2.   These three aspects are singled out without ignorance of other contributing
factors, such as the period in history when a translation was effected or for instance the
policies of the commissioners/funders.
3.   My use of 'insider' and 'outsider' is not meant in any racist or xenophobic
sense, rather only to distinguish those who were breastfed the language into which a
translation is being made from those who come to that tongue as adult learners. In this
sense I am like Colenso since *isiZulu* is not my mother tongue. In fact, I prefer the
expression 'missionary-translators' to 'outsider-translators' because their goal is to
benefit the target culture through the translated corpus and, chronologically, their
endeavours strictly belong in the so-called missionary era. For 'insider-translator' I
should prefer 'endogenous-translator' since their work (ideally) arises from within
their cultural milieu. Nevertheless, for reasons of convention, I will retain the use of
'insider' and 'outsider'.

Bible on a more convincing scale than is yet the case after some centuries of sustained missionary efforts in the region.

This need is bluntly betrayed by a recent publication, composed of papers read at a symposium I was privileged to attend, entitled *Contemporary Translation Studies and Bible Translation: A South African Perspective* (Naudé and van der Merwe 2002). In the words of the local Bible Society's General Secretary (Kritzinger 2002: v), 'the Bible Society of South Africa has had the privilege of arranging a symposium involving academics and Bible translators from South Africa and the United Bible Societies'. Of the 16 papers presented at the symposium and subsequently published under the above title, only one was by a person of indigenous African descent, the non-South African Regional Coordinator of the Africa Region of the United Bible Societies (UBS). It is no longer sufficient to explain this disparity on the grounds of our apartheid past.[4]

'A vital part of the mission of the Bible Society of South Africa is to provide affordable Bibles in the language of the people. As a first step, this entails the translation of the Biblical source texts into the constantly changing languages indigenous to Southern Africa, a task which requires well-trained and competent translators' (Kritzinger 2002: v). The process of producing competent translators in all indigenous African tongues has begun, I believe. I wish though that all stakeholders could play a more meaningful role instead of delegating the entire responsibility to the various national Bible Societies as such. The African Church will have positively come of age when it can boast renditions of the Bible inspired by and articulated through indigenous perspectives.

Those who in missionary discourse are characteristically called 'informants', in addition to being the actual missionaries in many cases, are also the ones responsible for our missionary-translators or translation consultants' acquaintance with native languages; it is only unfortunate that in its Western wrappings Christian historiography could not escape the tendency to credit individuals for what are in fact products of collective activity. Thus the coming of age of African translators as envisaged by this paper leans more on the inclusive than on the exclusive side.[5] (The

---

4.   See my comments on this saddening South African reality in Tshehla 2002 and 2003.

5.   'Because the Bible functions so pervasively in the black community we black biblical scholars are relieved of the impossible burden of carrying on the task of interpretation alone. It is exciting to think about real collegiality, wherein individuals don't have to be responsible for everything' (Felder 1991: 5)—surely this is equally true of translation!

possibility of an individual taking credit for the conception and articula-
tion of a particular translation of the Bible could arise only in the case of
an insider-translator. This is because an insider-translator, provided s/he is
translating 'biblical source texts' in their original tongues, approximates
what in biblical studies is called 'an exegete'. This explains the abundance
of English versions of the Bible: each English exegete has a duty to benefit
the rest of the English-reading world with insights gleaned from his/her
exertion.[6])

It is thus heartwarming to see that Bishop J.W. Colenso's Zulu translation of the New Testament (1897) is not titled after him. It is simply
called *Izindab'ezinhle ezashunyayelwa ku'bantu ng'uJesuKristo inkosi
yetu kanye nezinncwadi ezalotywa ng'Abapostole bake* (*The Good News
Preached to [the] People by Jesus Christ Our Lord and the Books [or
Letters] that were Written by His Apostles*). The terms '[the] people', 'our
Lord', 'his apostles' all urge a significant degree of community and plurality in the propagation of this Good News. Whereas 'news' bears a singular
sense in English (and Afrikaans), and thus an implicit homogeny, for
isiZulu—*Izindaba*—and the other indigenous South African tongues the
concept is plural and thus multifarious. In Colenso's translation even Jesus
Christ stands in relation to us his modern subjects ('our Lord') and his earliest messengers (*apostoloi*). To what might we ascribe this high sense of
community if not to indigenous Africa?[7] However the publisher's(?) hand
is observable in places. The short title that appears on the spine, *Izindaba
ezinhle* ('Good News'), is no meddling. But the inscription on the front
hard cover, *Izindaba ezinhle zikitshwe ngusobantu* ('Good News released
by Sobantu'), introduces Colenso (a.k.a. Sobantu) as the author or producer
of this 'Good News'. On the one hand, reminding us that Colenso is
responsible for the Zulu and other aspects of this translation is not such a
bad idea. However, these kinds of associations are usually intended to
convey accomplishment and authority rather than liability. Notwithstanding this slight interference, turning to Colenso's translation of the Bible is
an inviting affair from my cultural perspective. More 'good news' is that

6.   Needless to say, I too, as informed by my exegesis, offered my 'translations' of
John's Prologue in Northern and Southern Sotho in the study about which more is said
below.
7.   'What I have done, I have done by hard work—by sitting with my natives
day after day, from early morn to sunset, till they, as well as myself, were fairly exhausted,—conversing with them as well as I could, and listening to them conversing,—
writing down what I could of their talk from their own lips, and, when they were gone,
still turning round again to my desk, to copy out the results of the day' (1864e: 44-45).

neither Colenso nor the London publishers saw it fit to add (sub-)headings to the various supposed sections or chapters as is often observable with many other versions of the Bible.

In the present study I venture to chart out some of the issues that arise on account of the translator's background, and to do this with reference to Colenso's rendition of John's Prologue (Jn 1.1-18). In a nutshell, I am anxious to assess if it makes any difference whether the translator is an 'insider' or 'outsider' to the so-called target language. This inquiry is a development of my earlier attempt to study John's Prologue as found in Northern and Southern Sotho Bibles vis-à-vis the meanings and interpretations intimated by the Greek text (Tshehla 2000).[8] The study in question was inspired and framed around the following declaration:

> We have emphasized that the church must be allowed to indigenize itself, and to 'celebrate, sing and dance' the gospel in its own cultural medium. At the same time, we wish to be alert to the dangers of this process… Thus we should seek with equal care to avoid theological imperialism or theological provincialism. A church's theology should be developed by the community of faith out of the Scripture in interaction with other theologies of the past and present, and with the local culture and its needs. (Committee for World Evangelization 1978: 26-28, also accessible in Stott 1996)

The centrality of 'the Scripture' out of which each community of believers should develop the Church's theology cannot be overstated. Thus, I sought to challenge the 'theological imperialism' of our context by scrutinizing John's Prologue rather rigorously in Sesotho, which currently has no place in South African Biblical Studies. And to avoid 'theological provincialism' I then wrote out the study in 'the one master-language of our post-colonial worlds, English' (Bassnett and Trivedi 1999: 13). I now pithily restate some of the findings. *Lentswe* (and so too *uLizwi*) immediately stood out as personal names in contrast to 'Word' and 'Logos' that are not ordinarily understood in personal terms. Evidence was brought forth that persons have been named *Lentswe* and *uLizwi* both prior to and after the missionary period. The significance also of *Lentswe* as the means whereby the living dead communicate with their earthly relatives was noted, alongside the theological appropriateness therefore of the phrase *Lentswe la Modimo*, 'the Word of God' (Tshehla 2000: 36-40).

---

8.   My parents' mother tongue is Northern Sotho and so this is the language I studied in school and speak at home. But in order to get by in the district of my upbringing I had to be fluent in Southern Sotho from an early age. Consequently, I am just as comfortable with spoken Southern Sotho.

Moreover placing side by side the four current Bible Society of South
Africa versions of the Bible (two Southern and two Northern Sotho)
alerted me to the value of concurrent multicultural exegeses. Different
cultures express various concepts with differing degrees of clarity. I found
no reason why Bible students who each take seriously their own cultural
manifestations and expressions of God's communication cannot then
dialogue as equals across lingo-cultural boundaries. There and then, in the
midst of such discussion, the relativity of each translation or exegesis will
be laid bare and a measure of humility will emerge that can only benefit all
who are involved in the discipline. Besides, I found very liberating the discovery that Sesotho can debate as equals with English. That is why in the
end of the present study I urge collaborations that transcend lingo-cultural
and academic barriers. Basically, I affirm Y.C. Whang's cautionary statement that a 'perfectly competent translator' is an illusion (when presupposed) and a delusion (when self is believed to be one). I do so without
implying that there can be no competent translators, only that such competence has to be qualified since it could never be perfect competence.

In the absence of 'perfectly competent translators' it should follow that
the existence of perfectly competent translations is fiction. This caution is
significant notwithstanding our efforts to render ourselves the best possible
translators and our translations the most useful there could be. 'Many
translations have had the purported aim of producing a text faithful to the
sense or meaning of the original, while at the same time being able to be
understood by its users. It is hard to imagine a translation arguing otherwise' (Porter 1999: 24).

Nevertheless the absence of perfectly competent translators and translations does not simply demand abstention from this important task of rendering the Bible available in as many tongues as are spoken on our planet.
All it does is urge us to continue seeking ways and means whereby the
Bible can be most effectively translated while not deceiving ourselves
about the products of our labour. Does Colenso's translation validate our
view that translators and translations are necessary yet imperfect? What
does it reveal of the strengths and weaknesses of outsider-translators?

2. Missionary-Translating vs. Endogenous-Translating

Eric Hermanson's contribution to this volume makes overt mention of the
influence of English upon Colenso the translator into Zulu. In the section
dealing with Orthography for instance, Hermanson discloses, 'A problem

34 *The Eye of the Storm*

with translation is that often the grammatical form of the source language and/or that of the non-mother tongue translator, rather than that of the target language is reflected in the translation' (p. 15) and 'Colenso seems also to have been influenced by English grammar in the way in which he inserted quotation marks...' (p. 16). These two excerpts already intimate something of the truth that advantages (e.g. the innovative introduction of useful linguistic devices) and disadvantages (e.g. the inability to perceive grammatical forms that are not found in the translator's own language) attend translations by outsiders.

Now I wish to demonstrate these pros and cons by looking intently on Colenso's translation of John's Prologue into *isiZulu*. I cannot overstate the reality that Colenso translated before much was established of what forms the basis of our current views on translation. It is precisely for this reason that my critique of his rendition of Jn 1.1-18 is rather sympathetic. Moreover I am no mother-tongue Zulu speaker myself and so I, like my interlocutor, belong on the outside in significant ways. (I also assume that the publishers did not inadvertently alter the submitted text, thereby un-intentionally misrepresenting Colenso's intentions—although the marking of v. 16 as 61 makes me wonder.[9])

2.1. *Translations are Products of an Age*
We cannot ignore the reality that with Colenso we are investigating a time when *isiZulu* was emerging as a written language and thus an era charac-terized among others by experimentation and misunderstanding between the Zulu and the missionary. Also, as Kritzinger already intimated, we are dealing with 'the constantly changing languages indigenous to Southern Africa' and should thus beware of the temptation to charge Colenso with transgression of concepts that were perfectly acceptable in his day. Several of my learned Zulu friends to whom I presented a copy of Colenso's translation of the New Testament were disheartened by their inability to read and follow the grammar, orthography, and even concepts or terms he used. They found themselves literally spell-reading while vaguely re-membering that *isiminya* (for *alētheias*, 'truth', v. 14) is used when one is prepared to swear on their very life that they are telling the truth.[10] But as

9. See above, pp. 31-32, on the question of editorial intervention in Colenso's publications.
10. In his *Zulu–English Dictionary*, Colenso has two entries for 'truth', namely, *minya* (*Isi-*) and *qiniso* (*I-*). I shall return to *qiniso* (*I-*) shortly. As for *minya*, it could either be a noun or a verb. As a noun it means 'truth' but as a verb it means either

for *emhlalukisileyo*[11] (for *exēgēsato*, 'show forth', v. 18) they were at a complete loss.

Among missionaries themselves there existed no uniform guidelines over, say, the adoption of the name of 'God' in indigenous tongues. Some imported *uTixo* into Xhosa and others extended that name to Zulu Christianity. Others invented *uDio* for obvious European connections. Some endeavoured to understand and represent the names they found their prospective converts using. Others were uncertain about which term to use and frequently changed their usage according to the prevailing opinion. Our assessment of the achievements of nineteenth-century translator missionaries cannot overlook the teething problems of incipient written languages. It is easier to see in retrospect what eludes those immersed in complex processes like the one we are revisiting.

Colenso was a 'man whose views [were] severely limited by the accepted ideas of the time' (Guy 1983: 15),[12] but he was a man also aware of the attendant 'evil consequences of contact with civilization' to which the native was exposed (Colenso 1865[?]e: cclxxvii). However there can be no question that he

> was nonetheless as unaware of his ideological function in the colonial system and the springs of African resistance to missionary endeavour, as the very men he criticized... Colenso certainly questioned some of the methods used, but he never questioned Britain's right to revolutionize the lives of the inhabitants of Southern Africa—indeed he found it a privilege to lead such an endeavour. (Guy 1983: 80)

'to drink to the last drop' or 'to purpose in the heart' (1878[?]a: 297). The first verbal meaning survives to this day, but the second one, though rarely used today, has clear connections with the nominal *minya*.

11. The Dictionary has *hlaluka* meaning 'appear, come to sight, turn up, come to light; turn out to be' and *hlalukisa* meaning 'make to come to light' (1878[?]a: 178-79). It is quite interesting that whereas the American Bible Society's *Ibaibele eli ingcwele eli netestamente lidala, nelisha* (1924) differs from Colenso's in practically every other detail, it too adopts *emhlalukisileyo* in v. 18. Today's preferred terms would be *chaza* and *veza*, both of which appear in Colenso's Dictionary, alluding to what biologists call 'natural selection'.

12. For instance, the sociopolitical circumstances of the day permitted him to conceive of *isiZulu* as 'another, and that a barbarous tongue' (1855g: 160). We too in our generation are guilty of similar prejudices and idiosyncrasies that will embarrass subsequent generations. The bottom line is that such biases find their way into our work, translating not excluded.

2.2. *Translating is Missionary Work*
Colenso perceived himself a missionary among the Zulu prior to his other obligations as Bishop, parent, writer, teacher and thinker. Missionary work, he lamented (1865[?]e: cclxvii),

> is one of the highest, most interesting, most ennobling, that can engage our powers [*sic*]. Yet this great work is left for the most part in the hands of men comparatively ignorant and illiterate, with narrow views and limited education,—earnest in spirit it may be, simple and pure in life, unwearied in industry,—yet greatly deficient in some of the primary qualities, which go to make up the true ideal of a missionary.

Among the primary qualities Colenso was talking about was 'the subject closest to his heart—that area which he believed to be the most important and in which he had already achieved so much—learning the vernacular and the translation of the scriptures' (Guy 1983: 76). In Jeff Guy's estimation, Colenso was adamant that 'there could be no genuine communication between the missionary teacher and the heathen pupil' unless he and the other missionaries proceeded in this manner (Guy 1983: 65). Thus, Colenso's translating is first of all missionary work; just as his desire to learn *isiZulu* was a means to a missionary end. Christ could not be properly preached to a Zulu in English, so the missionary has to take pains to learn *isiZulu* in order to be effective in his/her communication of the gospel.

Thus, as part of his missionary work, Colenso had made it a habit 'to sit down, hour by hour, in closest friendly intercourse with the natives of all classes, and in the spirit of earnest, patient research, with a full command of the native language' and thereby 'sought to enter, as it were, within the heart, and search for the secret characters of light, which may be written by God's own finger there' (1865[?]e: cclxxii).

2.3. *Translations are Theological and Political Enterprises*
Colenso the Bible translator into *isiZulu* was also a man persuaded that 'secret characters of light may be written by God's own finger' in the hearts of his Zulu subjects. Theological debates back home in Britain (or, better still, Europe), his own observations of missionaries and colonists' dealings in Natal, as well as the treatment he got from the Zulu people in the mission field, all profoundly shaped his convictions about certain theological subjects. To pretend that translations are conceived of and carried out in vacuums is counterproductive to the advancement of the discipline:

> Modern biblical translations inevitably arise out of particular political and
> cultural contexts. Translators are themselves products of one or another
> political culture (ideology). The ability to publish and disseminate the result
> of translation is also governed by local publishing conventions. Even the
> textual bases selected in translation and the linguistic medium employed
> rarely are entirely outside the influence of local political and cultural con-
> straints. (Batalden 1992: 68)

And like its translation, the appropriation of the Bible is also a complex
political affair.

But far more than the sociopolitical factors,[13] theological concerns are
poignant, although separating the two is an oversimplification:

> Translation undertaken under conditions of *necessity* or perceived necessity
> is something altogether different than translation undertaken simply as the
> result of a desire to read what has been written in another language... The
> large majority of biblical translators do not undertake their tasks to simply
> allow different language groups to read a nice book called the Bible, but
> rather because they believe that it is, for religious reasons, imperative that
> the content and message be communicated to these different language
> groups. (Pearson 1999: 81)

Colenso's eventual choice of *uNkulunkulu* (as opposed to *uThixo* as the
other missionaries preferred the Zulu name of 'God' to be) as well as his
preference of *ukuthemba* (meaning 'to hope', v. 7 for *pisteusōsin*) instead
of *ukukholwa* (used by the other missionaries and to this day by Zulu
Christians, literally meaning 'to be satisfied or convinced') have been
cause for interesting study.[14] Similarly the motivation to omit the somewhat redundant *oude ek thelēmatos sarkos* in the translation of v. 13 must
also be theological or perhaps arise from a pragmatic desire to evade the
likely confusion with the *sarks* of v. 14 which *uLizwi* ('the Logos') became. (It should be noted however that Nestlé–Aland's *Novum Testamen-
tum Graece* acknowledges that these words are omitted in some part of the
tradition, which raises the difficult question of Colenso's textual bases.)

In keeping with the personal *uLizwi*, Colenso translates v. 3a thus,

---

13. 'What is the social location of the translator? What is the ethical responsibility
of the translator? Is an anti-racist/oppression/colonizing Translation of the bible possible? What are the possible responses to the silence of popular and legitimized
academic Translations on issues of race and class? Where has the heritage of bible
Translations left us? What are the liberatory options in the Translation process?'
(Bailey and Pippin 1996: 1).

14. See J.A. Draper's study on Romans in this volume.

Konke kw'enziwa ng'uye ('everything was made by him') and not *ngaye* ('through him'). *ULizwi* is thus seen not as an instrument during creation but indeed as the creator of all things. This is an interesting point from a christological perspective.

2.4. *Translating is Undertaken by Driven Skilled Persons*

> Few fields draw on as many disciplines as does Bible Translation. Indeed, a good Bible translator, in addition to knowing well the source and target languages, will at some point in the work employ at least the following: text criticism; canon criticism; various tools of exegesis such as form and redaction criticism and studies of the history, culture, and sociological aspects of the peoples of the Bible; communication science; linguistics; semantics; semiotics; sociolinguistics; discourse studies; literary criticism; anthropology. Every one of these helps the translator either to understand the meaning of the text or to find the best way to communicate the meaning in the receptor language, or both. (Stine 1988: vii)

As Colenso (1855g: 160) himself intimates (in, retrospectively, not so politically judicious terms), 'No one, who has not tried, can conceive how hard, and almost impossible, it is, to give correct representations in another, and that a barbarous tongue, of the refined and expressive language of some parts of the Bible and Prayer Book'. It is only the trying that will inform the would-be translator of the difficulties that accompany this task for an outsider-translator. (I have already noted that insider-translating is tantamount to exegesis. Exegesis is the first step to be taken by an outsider-translator but the only one required by the insider-translator.) Yet it is true that not everyone who might have the desire will necessarily also have the ability to engage in translation. Colenso had no illusions about this as he urged that the caliber of people sent out as missionaries be of such a quality that they can meet these demanding responsibilities.

Colenso's skill in handling *isiZulu*, his innovations as a translator-author,[15] as well as his relatively admirable command of Greek and Hebrew reveal just how gifted and highly motivated an aspiring translator ought to be. In v. 7 *martureō* is translated *ukuqinisa* as opposed to the popular *ukufakaza* ('to testify or bear witness').[16] *Iqiniso* ('truth') thus

---

15. 'The translator resolves for that one of the possible solutions which promises a maximum of effect with a minimum of effort' (Bassnett-McGuire 1980: 37).

16. Colenso's Dictionary only gives the noun *fakazi* (*U-*) meaning 'witness for a thing or person' (1878[?]a: 120); this omission of the verb-form must go some distance in explaining his choice of *qinisa*. A number of entries are given the stem *-qina* ('hard'

seems an essential ingredient of bearing witness; the implication is that false witnesses are not witnesses at all. This example shows that Colenso did not always accept at face value what was popularly used.

However, several choices remain hard to elucidate with confidence; these will by and large have to be left to insider-exegetes to decipher. Verse 1c is translated *uLizwi uNkulunkulu* treating this instance of complement as though it were one of apposition. Verse 4 sees *zoē* translated *amandhla* ('power') instead of *ukuphila* as one would expect and as indeed the American Zulu Bible readers do.[17] *Onoma* is variously translated *ibizo* (v. 6) and *igama* (v. 12). These are synonyms and the only question that arises is why use both. In v. 11 both *ta idia* and *hoi idioi* are rendered *kubantu bake* (to his people)—the aim here seems to be to convey the message as unambiguously as possible. Verse 12 sees *exousian* rendered *amandhla*, the same word used to translate *zoē* (v. 4)—this, to me, is simply baffling! Then there is that constant thorn in my outsider's flesh: for as long as I was acquainted with the so-called 'Lord's Prayer', I have never been able to understand why the Zulu Bible translates *doxa* ('glory') as *ubukhosi*.[18] So too does Colenso in v. 14 while the American Zulu Version uses *ubucwazicwazi*.[19]

or 'firm'). *Qinisa* is given the following meanings, 'make strong, firm, steady, &c.; confirm; persevere; speak confidently; speak truly'. *Qiniseka* means 'get made strong, fast, confirmed, &c.'. *Qinisela* approximates 'make strong, fast, firm, &c. for'. Then come *qinisisa* meaning 'confirm thoroughly' and finally the noun *qiniso* (*I-*) meaning 'truth' (1878[?]a: 430). His translation demands that we understand *martureō* to mean 'to speak confidently; to speak truly'. This is a plausible request though it does not explain the neglect of *fakaza* which the American Bible Society version duly picks up.

17. The Dictionary has an entry of the verb *pila* translated 'live; recover from sickness; change colour in any way (except in death), as by anger, &c.' The only nominal form of *pila* (*Im-*) given means 'plant, whose tubers are used in medicine' (1878[?]a: 403). *Amandhla* ('power') on the other hand appears twice, as *andhla* (*Am-*) and *ndhla* (*Ama-*). Their definitions are practically identical, which must only lead one to the explanation that Colenso was unsure how to classify this noun or had forgotten the earlier entry when he made the second. As for the choice of *amandhla*, as well as the absence of *ukuphila* in the Dictionary, I remain at a loss.

18. In what might be a useful feat, Colenso's Dictionary defines *Kosi* (*Ubu-*) as 'chieftainship, royalty, supreme authority; majesty, glory' (1878[?]a: 232). I have not been able to locate *inkazimulo* in Colenso's Dictionary, the only word that would fit perfectly for me.

19. Colenso's Dictionary defines *ubucwazicwazi* as 'brightness, splendour, effulgence, and glitter' (1878[?]a: 79). I am making peace with the possibility that the translation of *doxa* into *isiZulu* will always be beyond my outsider's reach.

It would appear that the temptation to compensate for one's limitations as an outsider, the enduring problem of not fully understanding the intricacies of a language and culture that one was not raised in, as well as the theological and/or ideological battles one is engaged in, and sometimes perhaps the desire to leave behind one's mark, will at times enhance while at other times undermine the missionary-translator's work. But whatever the strengths and drawbacks of outsiders, there is a lot to be said for cross-cultural expeditions when it comes to translating. And during such expeditions people's perspectives and depth of understanding of texts have been known to get enriched:

> At first, it seemed a matter mainly of language; communication of the gospel would be easy once missionaries could speak the languages of Africa and Asia. It was not long before it became plain that language is only the outer skin of the consciousness we now call culture. The gospel had to pass beyond language into the depths of a consciousness that had taken centuries to form and which now shaped the way people thought and acted. The missionary movement introduced a new element into western Christian experience. A very surefooted, confident Christianity with centuries of cultural interaction behind it, had to make its way in other people's terms, terms that, at the time, were only vaguely comprehended, and seemed alien if not repellent. Western Christianity came to Asia and Africa assured about its own tradition of learning, and then found that tradition had huge gaps, vast areas where the western academy, theological or secular, had nothing useful to say (Walls 2001: 45-46; cf. Sanneh 1993: 18-19).

3. A Case for Translation by Equals

It is from this perspective that Bible translation undermines all the socio-political boundaries that we are fond of erecting against our neighbours. It is as we engage the biblical text in its original languages, the wealth of commentary on the biblical text over the centuries, the lessons learnt by those who pioneered the translation of the Bible into thitherto 'barbarous' tongues, as well as the cultural worlds in which we are raised that *uLizwi* will enlighten our path and give grace upon grace.

If, then, we ask the question, 'Did it make any difference that Colenso was an Englishman translating into isizulu?' And it seems that the answer is a confident 'Yes, it did matter'. Then I sought through reference to John's Prologue to see the extent to which it would matter that the translation was made by a missionary and not an insider to the Zulu culture. This investigation was made notwithstanding the reality that Colenso's translation surfaces at a time of much experimentation with the writing down of *isiZulu*. This means that our judgment cannot be the same as we would inflict upon a modern translator or missionary who has ample precedents and a relatively established writing tradition in *isiZulu*.

This study demonstrates, albeit summarily, that there are advantages as well as disadvantages accompanying the outsider-translator—the case of Bishop Colenso ably illustrates this. I have purposefully not said more on the disadvantages that would attend an insider-translator. As our subject is a outsider-translator, I am not eager to even highlight such shortcomings with regard to my work in Sesotho—it is easier for one who is not immersed in a situation to assess it fairly. This study has established nonetheless that the translator is a significant (though certainly not the only) player in the production of translations. But most importantly for me, and something that I believe Colenso's legacy should urge us to correct, my discussion has called us to remember how uneven the translation field is in South Africa, and how urgent the need is for the emergence of insider-translators in the previously marginalized languages of this country. Otherwise, the old business of translation as traffic between languages still goes on in the once-and-still colonized world, reflecting more acutely than ever before the asymmetrical power relationship between the various local "vernaculars" (i.e. the languages of the slaves, etymologically speaking) and the one master-language of our post-colonial worlds, English' (Bassnett and Trivedi 1999: 13).

BISHOP COLENSO AND HIS CRITICS: THE STRANGE EMERGENCE
OF BIBLICAL CRITICISM IN VICTORIAN BRITAIN*

Timothy Larsen

In October 1862, John William Colenso, Bishop of Natal, published a book entitled *The Pentateuch and Book of Joshua Critically Examined*. Although this volume proved to be only the first of seven parts, and the bishop's life was eventful in other ways, the controversy surrounding this volume did more than any other single factor to determine Colenso's enduring reputation. To his critics, the publication of such a book was an outrageous and heretical act. When the book was discussed in the Lower House of Convocation, C.E. Kennaway was convinced that it should be labelled 'Poison!' and Archdeacon Denison declared that 'No book can ever be brought under our consideration of a worse character than this' and that 'if a man asserts such things as are in this book—*anathema esto*— let him be put away' (*Chronicle of Convocation, Lower House* [hereafter *CC, LH*] 11 February 1863: 1041, 1049-50). In the end, both houses of Convocation resolved that 'the main propositions' of the book 'involve errors of the gravest and most dangerous character' (*CC, LH* 19 May 1863: 1180, 1184; *Chronicle of Convocation, Upper House* [hereafter *CC, UH*] 20 May 1863: 1208).

Colenso himself, on the other hand, presented his work as a labour on behalf of 'Truth', as revealed by scientific investigation.[1] He wrote to a friend[2]: 'the "scandal" they complain of is not caused by me, but by those who maintain a state of things in the Church opposed to the plainest results

---

* An earlier version of this article appeared in the *Scottish Journal of Theology* 50.4 (1997). Reprinted here with permission.

1. The second edition replaced the first in less than a month. It contained only minor changes, all of which are listed in the front portion of part 2, for the benefit of those holding first editions of part 1 (Colenso 1862c: viii-ix).

2. Letter to Theophilus Shepstone dated 2 March 1863.

of modern science' (quoted by Cox 1888: 236). He boasted that the 'men of science and literature are almost in a body with me' and there was at least some evidence to support this claim: the eminent geologist, Sir Charles Lyell, became friends with him and he was received into the Athenaeum Club. Colenso even talked of forming a scientific society, similar to those formed for geology or astronomy, for the study of the history of religions (Cox 1888: 235-37, 271). Therefore, while his critics compared him with heretics like Arius, the defenders of his memory evoke the names of scientists such as Galileo—people who discovered great truths that the world ultimately would not be able to suppress.[3]

The term 'biblical criticism' in this context refers to the modern discipline as it has evolved, and not older attempts, whether negative or orthodox. In Continental Europe, most notably in Germany, the modern discipline of biblical criticism had already been well established for decades before Colenso's work. In Britain, there was, of course, a portion of educated people who were reading the European literature and agreeing with some of its methods and conclusions. A few of them had even published writings that reflected this influence. Benjamin Jowett, tutor at Balliol, was one such person and his *Epistles of St Paul*, published in 1835, was one such work; however, it was not a significant contribution to the field of biblical criticism and the controversy that it generated did not focus on this aspect of the work (Hinchliff 1986: 54-56). Samuel Davidson's *The Text of the Old Testament Considered* (1859), deserves special recognition. Although it was far more conservative and less sensational than Colenso's work, Davidson was enough of a new student of the new discipline to provoke a conservative backlash that caused him to be driven out of his professorship at Lancashire Independent College.[4] The controversial *Essays and Reviews* (1861), sought deliberately to force upon British society some of the findings of Continental biblical critics; therefore, this work should be viewed more as containing an appeal on behalf of the discipline rather than an actual embarking upon its work. Moreover, the notion that biblical criticism was a powerful tool that could no longer be ignored was not central to the heated public discussion that the book provoked.[5] From his vantage point at the end of the twentieth century,

---

3. Professor Max Müller listed Colenso with Galileo and Darwin as a defender of truth. Cox (1888: 215) allows his subject to bask in this light in which Müller had placed him as does, in recent years, Ferdinand Deist (1984: 129-30).

4. His story is told in Davidson 1899.

5. A detailed examination of this work can be found in Ellis 1980.

T.K. Cheyne, in his *Founders of Old Testament Criticism*, unequivocally reserved for Colenso the place of 'founder' in Victorian Britain. When he comes to discuss Colenso's book, Cheyne dramatically exclaims, 'At length, in 1862, the hour came, and the man; and strange to say, the champion was a bishop' (Cheyne 1893: 196). Even though Cheyne might have overstated the case, we may nevertheless safely admit that Colenso's book was the first thoroughgoing, indigenous attempt at modern biblical criticism that brought the young discipline to the general attention of British society.

But what a strange book it is upon which to place so much passion and weight! Irrespective of whether one is looking for shocking heresy or seminal science, the actual book can hardly live up to the excitement that it generated. The substance of it is based almost entirely upon mathematical calculations derived from the numbers recorded in the Pentateuch. Before he had been ordained, Colenso had been a mathematician. At Cambridge, he had been second wrangler in the mathematical tripos and then went on to teach mathematics at his college, St John's. During this early period of his adult life, he wrote several highly successful mathematical textbooks. In Part I of his *The Pentateuch*, numbers given in the Pentateuch are examined by the mathematical bishop and are found to prove that the narrative contains internal inconsistencies and implies physical impossibilities. Most of these calculations begin with the statement made in Num. 2.32 and other passages that Israel had around 600,000 warriors. From this number it is estimated that the whole people must have numbered around two million and this, in turn, is found to be an unwieldy number of people to force into various other passages. For example, such a number would imply that the Israelites' camp in the wilderness would have needed to have been approximately twelve miles square, which would have made into a burden to the point of absurdity the command in Deut. 23.12-14 to go outside the camp in order to attend to a call of nature (Colenso 1862c: 39-40).

Patiently, similar problems are unfolded: How could two million people have been told in one day about the need to keep the Passover? How could enough sheep to serve the needs of two million people have been found for the Passover? How could Joshua have read the law in the hearing of two million people? And so it goes on and on. Each problem is usually given an entire chapter in its own right, which is filled with an exhausting trail of assumptions, estimations and calculations. For example, on the question of the number of lambs that would have been needed for the Passover, explanations are given as to different theories concerning the probable number of people sharing a lamb, calculations are made as to the total population of a flock compared to the number of first-born males that it produces, sheep-tending authorities from New Zealand and Australia are cited on the amount of land needed for grazing per sheep, all in order to come to the conclusion that, according to the Pentateuch, the Israelites must have had 'an extent of country considerably larger than the whole county of Hertfordshire'; the probability of this actually having been the case and the other difficulties that this fact would necessarily entail are then explored (Colenso 1862c: 57-60). Although Colenso had read German biblical criticism and had imbibed many of its methods and ideas, for this first and crucial volume he confined his work almost exclusively to these kinds of numerical critique.

A fair number of the problems that Colenso explored were well-known 'difficult passages' that had already been addressed explicitly—however inadequately—in existing works. Colenso, however, found the standard answers unconvincing. Instead, he said that the honest course was to admit frankly that these difficulties were insurmountable. Therefore, upon the evidence of his calculations, despite their relentlessly narrow focus, he was lead to a breath-taking sweeping conclusion: 'very considerable portions of the Mosaic narrative' are 'unhistorical' and the account of the Exodus '*is not historically true*' (Colenso 1862c: xvii, xix [italics in original]). Indeed, in its initial form, which was printed privately in Natal, he had declared that his sums led him to conclude that 'the whole story of the Pentateuch is *fictitious* from beginning to end', but those whom he consulted, such as F.D. Maurice and A.P. Stanley, persuaded him to avoid the word 'fiction' in the version to be published in London for general circulation.[6]

One cannot help but be curious as to the experiences and the process of thought that led him to undertake this study and to follow it through to such a conclusion. Colenso gave his own account of this intellectual journey in the book's Preface. He admitted that he had begun to study the matter only in the early part of the previous year. Doubts about the Pentateuch had been thrust upon him when an 'intelligent native', who was helping him translate the story of the Deluge into Zulu, had innocently asked him, 'Is all that true?' (Colenso 1862c: vii). This story won him the sympathy of many people who had come face to face with honest doubt.

---

6.   A copy of the more unguarded version found its way into the hands of *The Record*, which duly exploited the opportunity to the full (*The Record* 13 October 1862: 2; see also Cox 1888: 195-96; Prothero 1893: 103).

For example, the freethinking journal, *The Westminster Review* (January 1863: 69), said of the book, 'The account given of its origin is the simplest possible, and one which must win for it a candid perusal from all but the bigoted and narrow-minded'.[7] On the other hand, this story also won for Colenso the disdain of his critics, who taunted him as the missionary who was converted by the natives. Therefore the story has been retold endlessly, and uncritically, as the origin of his thinking—whether by his critics, like the Evangelical Anglican newspaper, *The Record*, or his defenders like Cheyne, or sources that particularly strive for neutrality such as the *Encyclopaedia Britannica*.[8] Nevertheless, it might prove instructive if the tale of the questioning Zulu was critically examined.

The most obvious point that needs to be made is that his translator was not troubled by biblical arithmetic. His question concerned the accuracy of the biblical account of the Deluge. Colenso admits that he himself was suspicious of this passage even when he had been ministering to the natives of Norfolk rather than Natal, and he had already decided it was impossible to believe in the literal historical truth of the story before his encounter with his Zulu colleague. Moreover, he admits that, in holding these opinions, he was no different from numerous other clergymen who also treated the early chapters of Genesis in a manner different from the subsequent history (Colenso 1862c: vi-viii, xxi-xxii). In short, Colenso did not need to go to Africa in order to encounter sceptical questions concerning the Deluge.

Second, it is illuminating to realize that this story is similar in kind to other remarks by Colenso—that it fits into a pattern of persuasion of which he was fond. For example, elsewhere in the book Colenso cites Exod. 21.20-21, a passage that rules that a master who beat a slave is not to be punished unless his victim dies immediately, on the grounds that a slave is the equivalent of money. Colenso then writes (1862c: 9):

> I shall never forget the revulsion of feeling, with which a very intelligent Christian native, with whose help I was translating these words into the Zulu tongue, first heard them as words said to be uttered by the same great and gracious Being, whom I was teaching him to trust in and adore.

7. It has been tentatively suggested that Mark Pattison, one of the contributors to *Essays and Reviews*, was the author of this article (Houghton 1979: 643).

8. *The Record* compared Colenso unfavourably with Robinson Crusoe who was not reduced to doubt by the hard theological questions posed to him by his man Friday (*The Record* 19 November 1862: 2; Cheyne 1893: 199-200; *Encyclopaedia Britannica* [15th edn], III: 445).

The heated subject of clerical subscription—the requirement that all clergymen had to swear at the time of their ordination that they believed
unfeignedly certain documents and doctrines—was tackled by Colenso in
a similar way. He argued that his missionary experience highlighted the
need for change. A Zulu ordinand could not possibly give his unfeigned
assent because 'the nice distinctions of the Athanasian Creed for instance,
cannot possibly be translated into his language' (Colenso 1862c: 149). This
argument, however, could only go so far in helping the numerous clergymen whose difficulty with the Athanasian Creed was that they understood
what it said all too well.

In 1861, Colenso published a commentary on the letter to the Romans in
which he attempted to overturn traditional doctrines such as substitutionary atonement and eternal punishment and to advocate a form of universalism. The subtitle of the work claimed that Romans would be 'explained
from a missionary point of view' and the Preface claimed that it was 'the
results of seven years of Missionary experience' (Colenso 1861h: v). Even
an extremely hostile review of this work conceded that developing intimate relationships with so many damned heathens, over a prolonged period
of time, must have been a great psychological pressure on the bishop (*The
Guardian* 9 April 1862: 353). This picture, however, is misleading. The
basis of this book, his non-traditional interpretation of Romans, he had
taught in a series of addresses to his companions on his first voyage to
Africa, before he had began his missionary work (Cox 1888: 135). Peter
Hinchliff has shown that Colenso was airing some of these views such as
universalism as early as the 1840s, at gatherings of the Depwade Clerical
Society (Hinchliff 1964: 41-46). In the case of his book on Romans, he is
raising such issues as eternal punishment, and then it is as if he is encouraging his readers to imagine the whole heathen world asking the question:
'Is all that true?' One final example of this rhetorical habit: his biographer
tells this anecdote of Colenso, 'Looking at one of his own children in the
innocence of her infancy; he asked a friend how anyone looking on a babe
could be a Calvinist' (Cox 1888: 129-30).

This habit is illuminating because Colenso's desire to personalize—his
critics would say sentimentalize—an intellectual issue betrays a Romanticist way of thinking. This, of course, is more profoundly illustrated by his
theological views; his growing revulsion with ideas such as substitutionary
atonement and eternal punishment reveal a theological evolution that is
being guided by the sensibilities of Romanticism. Jeff Guy has shown how
Colenso's encounter in 1842–43 with the writings of S.T. Coleridge and

F.D. Maurice filled him with an excitement almost akin to a conversion experience (Guy 1983: 26-29). This influence was reinforced by his becoming friends with Maurice shortly thereafter. This exposure was the dominating influence upon Colenso's intellectual development, deprived as he was of any formal theological training. During his first year of work in Africa, when he was confronted with the ridiculous charge that he was a Tractarian, he confided in a letter how baffling it was that 'I, a Maurician could be so mislabelled'.[9] Colenso drank deeply from wells dug by Romanticists, and he imbibed their moral and theological instincts in the process. In this light, one could see his commentary on Romans as a kind of last-ditch attempt to show that his Romanticist convictions were reconcilable with the teachings of Scripture.

In short, what was growing inside Colenso was a moral critique of certain passages in the Bible. Despite the narrow focus of his book, this factor comes to the surface in the last biblical difficulty Colenso addressed: the story in Numbers 31 of the war with Midian. He also finds in this passage internal inconsistencies and impossibilities chiefly based on the numbers that it contains. His calculations upon the number of Midianites, however, enticed him to make other points (Colenso 1862c: 144):

> We may fairly reckon that there were…altogether 80,000 females, of whom, according to the story, Moses ordered 48,000 to be killed, besides (say) 20,000 young boys. The tragedy of Cawnpore, where 300 were butchered, would sink into nothing, compared with such a massacre, if, indeed we were required to believe it… How is it possible to quote the Bible as in any way condemning slavery, when we read here, *v.* 40, of 'Jehovah's tribute' of slaves, thirty-two persons?

In other words, the numbers reveal that the narrative is unreliable and prove that it is unhistorical. This realization frees us from having to embrace those passages that offend our sensibilities. Romanticist instincts caused Colenso to wish to be freed from the letter of the Law and, paradoxically, the Enlightenment tool of science became a weapon that allowed him to liberate himself from his bonds in the name of truth.

Therefore, his new convictions regarding the Bible actually brought a great psychological release to the bishop. At times, he seemed intoxicated with the possibilities that he imagined his discoveries heralded. He wrote to a friend, 'The movement, however, is begun which will end, I cannot

---

9. Letter to the Secretary of the Society for the Propagation of the Gospel dated 31 March 1856 (quoted in Rees 1958: 58).

doubt, in a revolution of the English Church'.[10] In his original, unguarded draft of the book, he announced that his conclusions necessitated 'a very considerable modification of Church dogmas and formularies' (*The Record* 31 October 1862: 2). This ulterior reward enticed him to marshal whatever evidence he could find and place it in as damning a light as possible, sometimes with results that seemed comic to many. For example, because the Pentateuch claims that the Israelites lived in tents during their sojourn in the wilderness, Colenso takes a chapter to inquire suspiciously where they obtained them from and to attempt to prove that it would have been physically impossible for them to have carried the required tents out of Egypt. Leviticus 8.3-4 claims that Moses obeyed the Lord's command to gather 'all the congregation together unto the door of the tabernacle'; however, after careful calculations and measurements, Colenso deduced that only nine grown men could actually fit in front of the door, as opposed to the two million that the text required (Colenso 1862c: Chapters 4 and 8). In the minds of his critics, passages like these betrayed a perverse desire to manufacture difficulties. If Colenso came to the point where he wanted to disbelieve the Bible, many of his critics, of course, had the exact opposite disposition. The Bible for them was not a source of bondage to be shed, but a source of security and certainty to which to cling. They, therefore, did not concur with Colenso's assumption that once one had noticed numerical difficulties in the Pentateuch, there was an inevitable momentum of thought, leading to the abandonment of some of the most cherished doctrines of the Church. Moreover, Colenso was not short of critics. The high and low wings of the Established Church, together with the Evangelical Nonconformists, all made common cause against him—that is to say, the vast majority of the religious world.

So the religious world set out to attempt to answer him. It was easy enough for Colenso's critics to pick one of his weaker arguments and give it a good working over in a letter to a religious newspaper or in an article. For example, Colenso had made much of the duty of the priests, as commanded in Lev. 4.11-12 to carry the carcass of a bull whose fat had been used for an offering outside the camp. He argued that, given the size of a camp for two million people, it would have been a long and difficult trek for the beleaguered priests to make, and therefore was an absurdity when compared with their small number and numerous other duties. His

10. Letter to Theophilus Shepstone dated 29 December 1862 (quoted in Cox 1888: 234).

critics, however, were quick to claim that the Hebrew verb in this passage merely meant that the priests were to cause this action to be done rather than necessarily do it themselves. This critique had the added advantage of arousing the suspicion that Colenso was not a credible scholar. Joseph M'Caul, in a letter to *The Record*, claimed smugly, 'His palpable ignorance of the Hebrew idiom is calculated to excite a titter from amongst true critics' (*The Record* 12 November 1862: 4). A letter to the High Church newspaper, *The Guardian*, from the clergyman, J.P. Gell, covered similar ground, except that it confined itself to making a scholarly point (*The Guardian* 10 December 1862: 1170). It is true that Hebrew was not Colenso's strong point. After a worse linguistic blunder was made in the next part of his study, Colenso enlisted his erstwhile critic, Gell, to examine the third part in advance in order to save himself from further embarrassments (Colenso 1863 [1862]d: xii). Other passages in Colenso's book were also attacked quickly on other grounds. The requirement to relieve oneself outside the camp, for example, was declared, when read in context, to refer to encampments of soldiers during military campaigns rather than to the whole congregation. The Congregational magazine, *The Christian Witness*, never reviewed the book, humbly confining itself to attempting to resolve only one of Colenso's difficulties (*The Christian Witness* 20 [1863]: 54-58).

Colenso's critics were also quick to ridicule his tendency toward a 'perverse literalness', such as his legalistic handling of the passages that claim that the people gathered in front of the door and that the whole people heard the law read (*The Guardian* 3 December 1862: 1149). A letter in *The Guardian* (24 December 1862: 1218) provided a spoof critical examination of Colenso's book *Ten Weeks in Natal*, which did a fine job of sending up his literalism; likewise, the Anglican Evangelical journal, *The Christian Observer* (60[300] 1862: 930-31), applied Colenso's methods to the standard history of King Edward I's attempt to assemble an army with which to fight William Wallace, showing that, if valid, these methods would prove that account to be unhistorical as well. Perhaps, however, conservatives should have looked first to the mote in their own eye: in his book, Colenso patiently, and without ridicule, dealt with a conservative scholar's theory that the fact that every tribe's census produced a round figure—Judah, 74,600; Issachar, 54,000 and so on—was proof of a special providence of God in their birth-rates (Colenso 1862c: 43-44). Nevertheless, some of the bishop's points were shown to be particularly vulnerable to a counter-attack. Undoubtedly, it was these passages, along with a bit of confidence-boosting bravado mixed with wishful thinking, which enticed some of his critics to dismiss the whole book as so obviously erroneous that one should hardly waste one's time answering it. The Archbishop of Canterbury himself, Charles Longley, provided one of the foremost comments along these lines, pronouncing Colenso's objections: 'so puerile, that an intelligent youth, who read his Bible with care, could draw the fitting answers from the Bible itself,— so trite, that they have been again and again refuted, two hundred years ago'.[11]

Eventually, some of his critics took a stab at answering every one of his objections, one by one. *The Record* did not actually begin to review the book until over a month after it had begun to denounce it—apologetically claiming that it was delayed due to 'accidental circumstance' (*The Record* 21 November 1862: 4). It then began to review the book in parts. The first two parts simply gave background, context and denunciations. *The Record* then took a week off—pleading insufficient space—before it actually began to answer the arguments that the book contained. Nevertheless, it did eventually attempt to answer every one of Colenso's difficulties. Others did the same; the controversy generated publications with such hopeful titles as *Solutions of Bishop Colenso's Bible Problems* and *The Nineteen Alleged Impossibilities of Part I of Colenso on the Pentateuch Shown to be Possible*.[12] This kind of response might have come close to a tacit admission that Colenso's slippery slope was a valid one—that if one unanswered difficulty remained, then the authority and inspiration of the entire Bible would be undone.

A slightly less absolutist response was the hypothesis of the transcriber's error; a ploy much loved by conservatives faced with a seemingly insurmountable difficulty. A letter to *The Record* suggested the possibility that somewhere along the way a mistake had been made that changed tens of thousands to hundreds of thousands. Thus it was actually 60,000 rather than 600,000 warriors.[13] The scholarly journal of the Evangelical Nonconformists, *The British Quarterly Review*, also cast doubt on the perfect

11. He expressed similar sentiments in more formal language in a letter which was printed in *The Times* on 7 February 1863: 9; see Colenso 1863 [1862]d: xvii.

12. The first was by 'An Unknown Pen' (G.H. Mason) and the second by James G. Murphy. Jeff Guy (1983: 137), who does not cite a single item from the flood of such literature or even one of the numerous lengthy articles published in the religious Press, is simply mistaken when he asserts: 'There were few attempts to answer him [Colenso]'.

13. Letter from 'Clavis' to *The Record* dated 10 November 1862: 4.

transmission of all the numbers, adding: 'an error of this kind once introduced being so liable, not only to be repeated, but to lead to further cor-
ruptions that other figures might be brought into harmony with it'.[14] It was
quick to affirm, however, that it was quite possible to assert that 'these
errors of copyists whether coming as oversights or from design, have left,
not only the moral and religious teaching, but the chain of historical facts
contained in the record, undisturbed' (*The British Quarterly Review* 37[73]
January 1863: 184). However probable or improbable this theory might
be, it did expose the narrowness of the bishop's attack; if these concessions were granted then the vast majority of his catalogue of difficulties
would be swept away in one (false) stroke.

   Even more broadly, some of his critics argued that even if Colenso's
difficulties were real, they were not of sufficient import to justify over-
turning the historicity of the Bible. The High Church journal, *The Christian Remembrancer*, took this line (45[119] January 1863: 245, 248-49):

> Let it be repeated—we are not attempting to explain a difficulty, but place it
> in the strongest light we can to further Dr. Colenso's purposes. We are
> supposing—what is perhaps not to be supposed—that it is insurmountable;
> and we ask, what then?... It is a pregnant fact that such difficulties have
> been seen by everybody, have been commented upon, have exercised the
> ingenuity of expositors with more or less of success or failure, and that the
> Christian world has paid very little attention to the matter. If it is asked
> what is the reason of this, the obvious reply is, Because the authenticity of
> the books of Moses is abundantly proved from external sources of various
> kinds, and because they are unmistakably endorsed by the whole subse-
> quent history of the Jewish nation, and by the writers of the New Testa-
> ment. People have been content to leave difficulties unexplained, for which
> they could see no probable solution, and which, after all, did not affect their
> belief either way, whether explained or unexplained.

Likewise, *The British Quarterly Review* (37[73] January 1863: 156-58)
conceded, 'We do no mean to say that the matters set forth by Dr. Colenso
as difficulties are in no case real difficulties'. Nevertheless, the testimony

---

   14. John Rogerson, whose book also manages to deal with Colenso's critics almost
entirely without citing their writings, claims that 'Colenso's argument did not rest upon
this figure alone [the 600,000 adult males mentioned in Exod. 7], as some of his critics
supposed' and then goes on to list some of the other passages in the Pentateuch in
which this number is either reiterated or implied. Colenso's critics, however, whatever
other deficiencies they might have had, knew their Bibles. The 'harmonization hypothesis' was incorporated into this speculative explanation from the very beginning,
anticipating Rogerson's objection. See Rogerson 1984: 221.

of the New Testament—and of so many righteous witnesses—to the truth of the Old, although it 'would not warrant us in receiving statements as true which we see to be contradictory and false', 'should dispose us to accept of *any* explanation of difficulties in the Hebrew Scriptures that may take with it probability, or even possibility, rather than discard those writings as untruthful'. Indeed: 'Every allowance of the kind indicated is due in sheer justice to writings that have come to us from so remote an age, with a purpose so limited, in a language so ancient, and through processes so perilous to their literal accuracy'.

The Bishop of Natal, however, like a man with no respect for due justice, has run a trial in which the rules are: 'The presumptive evidence in favour of the defendant, however strong, shall be wholly ignored, and the circumstantial evidence tending the other way shall be retained, and urged to the letter' (*The British Quarterly Review* 37[73] January 1863: 156-58). *The Record* complained that many of Colenso's critics had conceded too much ground in the debate, grumbling that it would not do to have a 'half infallible' Bible; nevertheless, some were content to allow some difficulties to rest unanswered (*The Record* 1 December 1862: 4).

The fame of Colenso's book can largely be attributed to the near hysteria that it produced in the Christian camp. But to what can this panic reaction be attributed? Inside the Church of England there was already a great deal of unease. The Church was divided from within into various factions, assaulted from without by Nonconformists and—it had only recently begun to realize—rendered virtually powerless to thwart theological or liturgical mavericks by the courts. The uproar caused by *Essays and Reviews* was still raging; Colenso's book coming so soon on the back of if might well have made loyal Churchmen wonder if the dam had now broken, releasing a torrent of heresies, of which this was but the beginning. Therefore, particularly for High Churchmen, Colenso's status as a bishop was especially alarming. One of the fathers of the Tractarian Movement, Edward Pusey, wrote to Bishop Tait, 'Had he been *Mr.* Colenso still, his book would have been stillborn. Now it is read by tens of thousands because he is a Bishop. It is his office of Bishop which propagates infidelity.'[15]

Concern over Colenso's position as a bishop was often fuelled, as Pusey's comments imply, by a pastoral concern for the effect that the book might have on the public. This concern was shared by the majority of the bishop's religious critics, irrespective of their denomination or the wing of

---

15. Letter dated 17 December 1862 (quoted in Davidson and Benham 1891: 337).

the Church to which they belonged. If the masses hear a rumour that the Bible has been overthrown, would this cause vast numbers of people to lose their faith and morals? One of the most popular adjectives for the bishop's book was 'dangerous'. Chancellor Massingberd, despite the fact that he had opposed the condemnation of *Essays and Reviews* by Convocation, wanted to see the leadership of the Church take a stand against Colenso's work. Alluding to one of the Lord's strongest statements of condemnation, he felt that the book had gone a long way toward 'offending Christ's little ones' (*CC, LH* 11 February 1863: 1036). Colenso himself had helped to provoke this reaction; he had made an appeal to laymen in the Preface of his book and it was clear throughout that he was writing with one eye on influencing those without pretensions to scholarship (Colenso 1862c: xxxv-xxxvi). His critics, likewise, pitched many of their comments with the gallery in mind. A letter to *The Guardian* from a vicar in Wiltshire recommended the book as 'a short and easy answer for simple-minded and hard-working men to the doubts which are now being raised as to the truth of Bible history' (*The Guardian* 19 November 1862: 1098). Many of Colenso's critics wrote books that they would have deemed highly successful if found worthy of such a recommendation.

The pastoral dimension of the controversy is well illustrated by an address given by Canon John Miller, a well-known Evangelical clergyman in Birmingham, which provoked such interest that the aisles were filled with those who could not find a seat and numerous others were not even able to enter the building. Miller sought to strengthen the faith of those who might have been shaken by reaffirming his own faith in the Bible. With disarming frankness, he admitted that it might well be true to say that he was: 'unable to follow all Bishop Colenso's calculations, unable to correct his Hebrew, and unable, in other commentaries to find the difficulties he had raised solved'. He went on to say:

> Understand, then, the existence of difficulties is not denied—difficulties in philology, in chronology, in ethnology, in geology. But, in a world full of difficulties—difficulties in God's works, in God's providence, in God's grace, where to yourself your very self is a mystery, will you, on this ground, reject God's Word, or any, even the least portion of that priceless book? (*The Record* 12 November 1862: 1)

He then went on to advise that those who read Colenso's book also read 'something else' and to recommend some titles, both more substantial works and ones that were more likely to be 'within reach both of your purse and your ability' (*The Record* 12 November 1862: 1). Cheap volumes were wanted in order to secure the place of 'that priceless book' in the hearts and minds of the people. Miller was neither the first nor the last of Colenso's critics to use the simplistic, but forceful, tactic of quoting Christ's words: 'For had ye believed Moses, ye would have believed me: for he wrote of me. But if ye believe not his writings, how shall ye believe my words?' (Jn 5.46-47 AV). Moreover, some of the Bishop of Natal's condemnations of the Pentateuch were so sweeping as to make this response more compelling than it might have been. Colenso and his critics were grabbing crude weapons that they imagined would be effective on the masses and both parties therefore could readily find reasons to charge the other with using unworthy arguments. The scholarly debate was deeply intertwined with the desire to influence the thinking of the general populace.

Although reciting the words of Christ was not an answer to Colenso's criticisms, Evangelical and High Church critics continually trumpeted the argument that the numerous references in the New Testament that attribute quotations from the Pentateuch to Moses and that refer to the events recorded there as if they were historical, did indeed settle these issues for believers. Even the report produced by a special committee in the Lower House of Convocation, which had come from a sober process of carefully winnowing down the charges to those which could be best defended, made much of this point. Colenso had tried to pre-empt the retort that he was accusing the Lord of being mistaken by suggesting the answer that perhaps Christ's comments were merely reflecting the common assumptions of his day, but this concession had the reverse effect—causing many of his critics to suggest that his comments contained the seeds of Christological heresy (*CC, LH* 19 May 1863: 1177-80). Indeed, this was one of the points upon which he was found guilty at his ecclesiastical trial in Cape Town:

> in imputing to our Blessed Lord ignorance and the possibility of error, the Bishop has committed himself to a most subtle heresy, destructive of the reality of the Incarnation, and he has departed from the Catholic faith... (Cox 1888: 326)[16]

Such arguments were difficult to sustain theologically. It was demonstrated by his supporters that Colenso's remarks were consistent with those made

---

16. The trial, which was the work of Bishop Gray of Cape Town, was not recognized as valid under English law and therefore Colenso retained the legal rights of a bishop.

by numerous well-respected divines.[17] These charges were undoubtedly highlighted because they had the polemical advantages of substantially increasing the seriousness of Colenso's crimes and of being far easier for people to understand than the complex trains of thought often involved in biblical criticism. Raising the stakes, however, means that either party might lose more. The short-term gains that such arguments might have made were at the expense of making pronouncements that could not be sustained if the legitimacy of the modern discipline of biblical criticism was to be recognized and an endless battle against its most fundamental assumptions and findings was to be avoided.

At a time when the Church had just begun to struggle with the theories of Charles Darwin, a nerve seemed to be touched when Colenso's critics had the counter-accusation that they were opposing science thrown at them. This appears to be an area where hidden anxieties lurked, anxieties that, perhaps, had to do with the critics' own, internal, fears rather than just fears concerning public perceptions. Criticisms of the book were often coupled with strong denials that there was any desire to suppress valid pursuits of the discipline of biblical criticism. For example, the report condemning the book produced by the Lower House of Convocation denied that its authors had any such intention, claiming that: 'On the contrary, they insist upon the duty and the advantage of bringing all the appliances of sound scholarship, and all the real results of learned and scientific investigation, to bear upon the Books of Holy Scripture' (*CC, LH* 19 May 1863: 1181). The anxieties behind such statements are perhaps more apparent in some wistful comments made by Canon Stowell, when he made reference to the controversy over Colenso's book that was then just beginning:

> The use that is made of science at present in certain quarters is utterly unlike the use that was made of it by Newton, the prince of science…now-a-days the study of many scientific men seems to be to discover discord, and not harmony, and to find in science, not the handmaid of revelation, but the antagonist. (*The Record* 5 November 1862: 4)

Colenso might not have been a terribly frightening opponent, but his new weapon was perhaps an ominous sign of things to come.

Broad Churchmen and liberal-minded clergymen did not rally to the defence of Colenso's book either. Indeed, what is perhaps most striking

17. Colenso published a long letter he had received which documented similar remarks made by respected figures from the Church Fathers to the present day (Colenso 1863 [1862]d: xxxiii-xl).

about their reactions is how much common ground they shared with those of the Evangelicals and the High Churchmen. One might have imagined that if anyone would have defended Colenso it would have been his friend F.D. Maurice. When Maurice had been himself under intense attack for alleged heterodoxy during the previous decade, Colenso had bravely dedicated a book to him. Nevertheless, this new controversy ruined their friendship. Maurice wrote to a friend:

> The pain which Colenso's book has caused me is more than I can tell you. I used nearly your words, 'It is the most purely negative criticism I ever read', in writing to him. Our correspondence has been frequent but perfectly unavailing. He seems to imagine himself a great critic and discoverer...his idea of history is that it is a branch of arithmetic.[18]

Maurice felt so strongly on the matter that he decided to resign his living so that no one would be able to claim that he was not defending Colenso in order to save his own position. In the end, his bishop did not accept his resignation and his alarmed friends dissuaded him from pursuing this course of action any further.[19] The relationship was so strained that Colenso's mother-in-law felt a need to attempt to thwart the plan of the bishop and his wife to take up lodgings in Russell Square, lest this would prove embarrassing for Maurice, whose residence was also there, and Colenso's relationship with Maurice never recovered.[20]

In fact, it is very hard to find anyone, particularly anyone influential in the religious world of Victorian Britain, who was willing to give a hearty defence of Colenso's book. Liberal and Broad Churchmen usually distinguished themselves from the crowd in this controversy by their willingness to defend the bishop himself against persecution. The religiously liberal or secular press was sometimes willing to make strong statements in favour of applying scientific techniques to the Bible and against the prejudices of conservatives, but it is not easy to find a whole-hearted defence of the publication itself. For example, the *Edinburgh Review*, in an article which was officially meant to be a review of the bishop's volume and related works, scarcely discussed the book at all, choosing instead to make general statements about the need for the old view of the Bible to be overthrown. Moreover, it did concede, in a rare allusion to Colenso, that he had 'pressed a narrow line of argument to extreme conclusions, which,

18. Letter to J. Davies dated 23 September 1862 (quoted in Maurice 1884: 423).
19. Letter to J. Davies dated 23 September 1862 (quoted in Maurice 1884: 424-35).
20. Letter from Mrs Colenso to Margaret Bell dated 3 November 1863 (quoted in Rees 1958: 78).

in our opinion, it fails to support' (*Edinburgh Review* 117[240] April 1863: 501).[21] The British men of science who rallied to the bishop's side belong in this same category. There is no apparent evidence that any of them defended the volume's intrinsic worth, and the botanist, Sir Joseph Hooker, the one of their number whose letters contain a lengthy passage on the controversy, admitted at the outset of his remarks that he had not read it. Moreover, after his social interaction with Colenso increased, he confided to Charles Darwin, 'I have seen a good deal of him, and consider him sanguine and unsafe'.[22]

The Broad Church publication, *The Spectator*, repeatedly condemned *The Record* for the way in which it was attacking Colenso (e.g. *The Spectator* 25 October 1862: 1178). Nevertheless, this stance did not translate into a defence of the book itself. Its own review freely conceded that the Pentateuch's 'numerical statements are magnified by the mists of time and the imaginative arithmetic of the Orientals (who habitually use numbers much as we use a varnish of sentiment)'. This might be a problem for some conservatives, but not for *The Spectator*. Nevertheless, it went on:

> This once admitted, what remains on which we differ from the Bishop of Natal?... [T]hat whole undercurrent of thought which seems to imply that when once we have detected bad arithmetic in the Pentateuch, we may entirely change our *attitude* of mind towards the narrative—cease to feel under any divine obligations to its history, and thenceforward, though we pick and choose from its text little bits of spiritual sentiment that we like or fancy better than the rest, as oases in the desert, dismiss all idea of studying the developing purpose of God's revelation in the history as a superstition which only those can afford who are satisfied with every detail in the numeration. (*The Spectator* 8 November 1862: 1250-52)

Dean Stanley, who was far more sympathetic than most, also made many familiar points. He too felt that Colenso had tried to draw too many conclusions, when all he had really called into question was the accuracy of the numbers. He admitted to a friend that 'I regret the book extremely' and, in correspondence with Colenso in response to a copy of the original

---

21. *The Times* never reviewed the book and avoided expressing its own view of the controversy. *The Record* noted with disapproval the favourable review in *The Daily Telegraph*, but was delighted with the negative review, in response to it, which appeared in *The Morning Post* shortly thereafter, after taking Colenso's decision to attempt to answer some of its points in a letter to *The Daily Telegraph* as proof of its force (*The Record* 10 November 1862: 3; 14 November 1862: 2).

22. Letter to B.H. Hodgson dated 6 December 1862; letter to Charles Darwin dated 16 February 1864 (quoted in Huxley 1918: 57-59).

draft that the bishop had sent to him, he told him that 'I regard the whole plan of your book as a mistake'. Moreover, he reaffirmed the essential historical accuracy of the narrative 'from the time of Abraham downwards'. As to the specific points which Colenso had raised, he answered in a way which would have resonated with many Broad Churchmen, 'Whether any answer can be made I know not, nor do I much care'; and perhaps an even wider audience would have identified with a comment he made to another correspondent, 'Of course the arithmetic is entirely beyond me' (Prothero 1893: 99-104). Benjamin Jowett, who was one of the contributors to *Essays and Reviews* and himself an author of biblical criticism, does not seem to have praised the book. On the other hand, he apparently confined his criticism of it, given in a letter to Stanley, to the comment, 'I think the tone is a good deal mistaken'. Neither agreeing nor disagreeing, praising nor denouncing, he simply took the apathetic view that he and Colenso worked in different ways (Abbott and Campbell 1897: 301).

Bishop Tait, who championed Colenso's rights against his persecutors, nevertheless spoke of the Bishop of Natal's 'rash and arrogant speculations' and of his own duty to warn 'the people committed to my care against his errors, and what appears to me the very unbecoming spirit in which they are urged' (Davidson and Benham 1891: 341-42). Connop Thirlwall, Bishop of St David's, was the only member of the Upper House of Convocation who voted against the resolution condemning Colenso's work, arguing that it failed to show how the bishop had violated the doctrines of the Church (*CC, UH* 20 May 1863: 1205-1206, 1208). Thirlwall himself was a student of the new German scholarship; he had translated Schleiermacher's *A Critical Essay on the Gospel of Luke* and published it in 1825 along with his own learned introduction.[23] Nevertheless, he charged Colenso with possessing a 'very rash and wild' scepticism, and his book with

> confounding the accuracy of arithmetical calculations with that of the premises on which they are based. Difficulties are magnified into 'plain impossibilities'; seeming discrepancies into direct contradictions. Whatever is narrated so as to raise such difficulties, is pronounced 'unhistorical'.

Moreover, the Bishop of St David's strongly rebuked Colenso for his pastoral irresponsibility and declared that his arrogant style was particularly

---

23. See the entry in the *Dictionary of National Biography* (Oxford: Oxford University Press), XIX: 618-21.

distasteful.[24] Even the leading Broad Church clergymen and the most sympathetic bishops did not approve of Colenso's book.

Matthew Arnold—who was not a clergyman, and therefore was not prey to the Church's muzzle, and who belonged, at least intellectually, to the liberal and broad wing of the laity—nevertheless disapproved of the book so much that he determined without solicitation to publish an article condemning it (ed. Arnold 1895: 175-76). He purported to judge the book by the standards of literary criticism, and finding in it nothing new to add to educated debate and nothing edifying to make it a useful popular work, he decided that 'the Bishop of Natal's book cannot justify itself for existing'. Arnold ridiculed Colenso's method, claiming that it would have been possible to write the book on 'a single page' because all one would have needed to do would be to offer one calculation which produces a faulty sum per book of the Pentateuch for, according to Colenso's way of thinking, one of these is sufficient to dispose of an entire volume. He contrasts Colenso's work with that of Spinoza, the latter of whom however unorthodox his opinions might have been, had genius enough to stimulate the elite and discretion enough to write in Latin (*Macmillan's Magazine* 7[39] January 1863: 241-56). Arnold's 'not-in-front-of-the-children' approach to biblical criticism naturally enough laid him open to the charge of snobbery. He hit back, however, claiming that he too had a pastoral concern for the masses—that he was not against the dissemination of ideas, but only their careless introduction without a sufficient attempt to help people integrate them into their existing spiritual life.[25] Liberal and Broad Churchmen often agreed with many of the criticisms of Colenso that were made by Evangelicals and High Churchmen.

In a recent study of Colenso, Jeff Guy has made a quixotic effort to defend the bishop's first volume on the Pentateuch. In doing so he is, as he is well aware, defying the considered opinion of the vast majority of weighty figures (let alone the rest) who have taken the time to evaluate the book, from Colenso's contemporary, F.D. Maurice, down to Guy's own contemporary, Owen Chadwick (Chadwick 1970: 91-92). In addition to several secondary lines of reasoning, he offers as his central explanation

24. Thirlwall gave a charge to the clergy of his diocese triennially. These comments are taken from the one that he delivered in October 1863 (Perowne 1877: 62-65, 75).

25. For an example of criticism of Arnold's stance, see *The Westminster Review* (NS 23[2] April 1863: 503-16). Arnold wove his reply to his critics into his next review: *Macmillan's Magazine* (7[40] February 1863: 327-36).

for this alleged critical injustice an argument bordering on a conspiracy theory in which the clergy, and particularly the hierarchy of the Established Church successfully used their wealth and influence in order to place a lasting slur on the book's reputation: 'They had access to the men who ruled the nation...the newspapers and journals in which they could make their views known, and funds to attract and support men in their cause' (Guy 1983: 183, see also pp. 184-88). This argument is unconvincing. The leadership of the Church did not have the ability to suppress unwanted religious opinions, as witnessed by the power of Nonconformists to disseminate effectively views which annoyed the Church; and the entire religious world—Dissenters and Churchmen together—were not capable of burying whatever awkward contributions might emerge, as Charles Darwin's *On the Origin of the Species*, published just two years before Colenso's work, amply proved. In fact, the other Church controversies of the era clearly reveal that Church leaders were often unable to bring their influence to bear upon undesirable views that arose within their own ranks, let alone manipulate the opinions of society as a whole. Colenso's book was not the victim of a clerical conspiracy.

One of Guy's secondary lines of argument is that in the prudish Victorian age readers were offended by the bishop's willingness to address 'the physical aspects of the biblical narrative'. In order to substantiate this argument, he quotes Maurice's comment:

> To have a quantity of criticism about the dung in the Jewish camp...thrown in my face, when I was satisfied that the Jewish history had been the mightiest witness to the people for a living God against the dead dogmas of priests, was more shocking to me than I can describe. (Guy 1983: 180)[26]

The part of the quotation that Guy replaced with an ellipsis was the phrase 'and the division of the hare's foot' (Maurice 1884: 490). Maurice was not shocked by allusions to the necessities of nature, but rather by the fact that someone could imagine that queries regarding such trivial aspects of the story would cause anyone to jettison a narrative with such manifest liberating power. The attempts by both Guy and Rogerson to evaluate Colenso's critics are substantially weakened by their failure even to acknowledge that one of the most fundamental flaws of the bishop's first volume—a flaw which was central to its widespread rejection—was its unconvincing assumption that difficulties in the details of the narrative, the existence of

---

26. The quotation comes from a letter to 'a clergyman in South Africa' dated 21 March 1865.

which had long been known, must inevitably lead people to abandon vital parts of the story of salvation history and fundamental doctrines of the Church (Rogerson 1984: 233-34).[27]

The emergence of biblical criticism in Britain was inevitably going to be difficult. Nevertheless, it certainly was not inevitable that it would have been this strange and emotive. Conservatives could hardly be expected to react well to biblical criticism in the hands of a bishop who had already proven himself—to their satisfaction—to be a heretic. Colenso's work was polluted with some crass and dubious arguments and he dramatically over-played the conclusions that could be drawn from his evidence; therefore, even for friends of biblical criticism, it was an awkward gesture to embrace him as a champion of truth and the herald of a new science, let alone for the defenders of orthodoxy he had already alienated by his commentary on Romans. None of these peculiar facts, however, could justly be used by Colenso's critics to disprove the validity of the entire discipline of biblical criticism or to suppress its emergence in Britain. Unfortunately for those who were wishing for a path of peaceful coexistence, the rhetoric of many of these critics, despite their protests to the contrary, did not position the religious world well for a reconciliation with the findings of this new discipline. The great biblical scholar, J.B. Lightfoot, lamented when the Bishop of Natal's book was first published that 'a more frank and liberal treatment of the difficulties of the Old Testament, if it had been general, would have drawn the sting of Colenso's criticism', but now he feared the effect of the book would be 'to discredit reasonable inquiry' and 'to divide men into two extreme parties, who will wage fierce war against each other and trample the truth under foot between them'.[28] The way in which Colenso's critics handled this controversy did not lend itself to creating an environment in which a more liberal attitude toward biblical criticism could immunize the community against extremist positions; and, for that matter, neither did the actions of Colenso himself. In the end, if they wished to remain credible in the eyes of the wider world of thinking, spiritual men and women, both Colenso and his critics needed to moderate their claims and rhetoric. Both the Bible and biblical criticism were here to

27. Rogerson purports to list the four main lines of approach taken by Colenso's critics, but this crucial response is not one of them. Moreover, his third point—an assumption that Colenso's alleged difficulties were overcome by special miracles—is hardly representative (no references are given).

28. Letter to Bishop Tait dated 19 November 1862 (quoted in Davidson and Benham 1891: 338).

stay—to imply that the stories of the former had no foundation in history, or that the theories of the latter had no foundation in science, was to fight a losing battle. Biblical criticism already existed, and British society was going to be exposed to it whether Colenso's critics wished it or not; but the Bible, despite its great antiquity, and excited rumours to the contrary, was not in danger of being killed off by the young discipline. Indeed, its very age pays tribute to its profound resilience.

COLENSO ON MYTH OR COLENSO *AS* MYTH:
A RESPONSE TO TIMOTHY LARSEN

David Jobling

I happened to come to my second reading of Timothy Larsen's essay, 'Bishop Colenso and His Critics', directly from a reading of the chapter on Colenso in Brookes and de Webb's *History of Natal*. That chapter ends with '[Colenso] has left...a noble and enduring reputation among the Zulus' (1987: 112). Larsen's second sentence reads, 'this volume [Part 1 of *The Pentateuch and Book of Joshua Critically Examined*, published in 1862 (hereafter *The Pentateuch*)] did more than any other single factor to determine Colenso's enduring reputation'. This coincidence, reading the words 'enduring reputation' twice in a few minutes, prompted the question: Where does Colenso's reputation endure, and where should it endure—as part of the history of Euro-American biblical studies, or as part of African history? It is with this question that I am primarily concerned in my response to Larsen. I shall eventually suggest that the choice is a false one, but in order to reach that point I shall argue the necessity of seeing Colenso as part of African, and of colonial, history.

I

In order to give a context to my response, I must spend some time laying out my own approach to Colenso. It is similar to that of R.S. Sugirtharajah, who devotes a chapter to the bishop in his 2001 book, *The Bible and the Third World*. This book consists of a series of exemplary scenes from territories colonized by Europeans (including the periods before and after, as well as during, colonization) in which the Bible plays a role. It is a measure of Colenso's importance in current debate that he should here command a whole chapter, as a prototype—and the outstanding exemplar—of the 'colonizer [whose] perception is...sharpened and interrogated by the experience of the colonized Other' (2001: 110).[1] I agree that Colenso deserves a prominent place on the broad canvas of current biblical studies that is coming to be called 'postcolonial criticism', and by which the field is at last coming to terms with its complicity in the practices of colonialism over many centuries (for anthologies, see Sugirtharajah 1998 and *Semeia* 75).

Sugirtharajah helpfully lays out Colenso's 'three exegetical ambitions' (p. 127), which involved him in some extravagances, but which show the seriousness with which he took—and we must take—his African context. First (pp. 128-30), he wanted to change unfavourable missionary perceptions of Africans. The background here is Colenso's universalistic theology, and his unusual interest in and considerable knowledge of world religions, which went against 'the dominant notion of revelation' in the Christianity of his time (p. 121; see also Guy 1983: 125, with direct reference to Colenso's *The Pentateuch*). The presence of God in African religions before the arrival of missionaries was therefore something that Colenso simply assumed, and it was of a piece with his whole outlook that, in his biblical work, he 'drew on the very Zulu culture and insights which were despised at that time, but came to be seen by him as a vital key in opening up the biblical narratives' (p. 112). He used not only the customs of Africans, but also their philosophical concepts, to explain the Bible (p. 126). His depth of understanding of Zulu culture was based on his pioneering work on the Zulu language (Guy [1983: 65-66] cites tributes to his accomplishment here). Something of Colenso's extravagance can be seen in his speculation that the Zulus were not only *like* the Jews of old, but actually descendants of Abraham (p. 128)!

Second (pp. 130-31), he wanted to speak truth about the Bible, however unpalatable it might be. This was essentially a missiological position; he insisted that converts be able to 'place entire confidence in "our honesty of purpose" and good faith' (p. 130, quoting Colenso *The Pentateuch*, I: xxvi). Sugirtharajah rightly claims that 'being credible to his converts was more vital [to Colenso] than the credibility or accuracy of the Bible' (p. 117). But his overall hermeneutic was one of 'commonsense' (p. 133), and on the whole 'conservative' (p. 134); in everything he did he was trying to make the Bible more practically usable, not to tear it down. He sought 'for the truth which underlies the whole' (p. 118, quoting Colenso 1861h: 261). There was certainly much in the Bible that he rejected; he in effect created

---

1. Unattributed page references in this section are to Sugirtharajah 2001.

a canon within the Canon, including only those parts of the Bible that he saw as suitable for church use (p. 123). Above all, he offered 'the gospel as an invitation and not an admonition' (p. 120). For Sugirtharajah, the ultimate result of Colenso's work was 'to reinforce the Bible's authority' (p. 135).

Third, his was an 'exegesis of practical engagement' (p. 131). Sugirtharajah notes Colenso's involvement in political issues, in which he took the Zulu side. Indeed, Colenso became directly and deeply involved in the colonial affairs of Natal and Zululand. For a full account of his involvement, the reader needs to consult Guy's study. The main *causes célèbres*, those involving the Zulu chief Langalibalele and the Zulu king Cetshwayo, arose in the last decade of Colenso's life (see the whole of Part 3 of Guy's study), and it was during this decade that he most clearly cast his lot with the native Africans whom he believed to have been wronged—eventually forfeiting what remained of his standing with the Natal settlers, increasingly despairing of the colonial administration and, in the end, of British colonial policy as a whole. But this decade was entirely of a piece with his earlier career in Africa; his pro-native stance and his critique of administrative policy and settler attitudes was established as early as his preliminary visit to Natal in 1854 (Guy 1983: 46-51).

What did this political activity have to do with Colenso's biblical scholarship? In answer, it is hardly necessary to look further than his 'Micah sermon' of 1879, in which, with incomparable passion and clarity, he brought the entire record of the settlers and the colonial administration to the bar of the biblical demand, 'What doth the Lord require of thee?' (Mic. 6.8; see Sugirtharajah 2001: 132; Guy 1983: 275-80). Colenso formed his colonial attitudes simply in conformity to what he took to be the biblical mandate. (In addition to Sugirtharajah, see the interesting argument by Guy [1983: 353-57]—from a Marxist rather than a specifically biblical or theological perspective—against those who have tried to separate Colenso the theologian from Colenso the political activist.)

My reply to my opening question, then, whether we should look at Colenso's legacy primarily as part of the development of Euro-American biblical studies or as part of African history, is firmly on the latter side. Even by 1862, Colenso had become in a serious sense an *African* biblical scholar. He would not so put it himself, but from the perspective of postcolonial studies this is how we have to see him.

II

What we are now witnessing in biblical studies—and this is the point at which my question becomes a false one—is the impact of the history of the Bible in Africa, and more generally in all the 'peripheral' regions of the world, on the assumptions and practices of the global 'centre'. The two histories are coming back together, becoming one, in a process which is often conflicting. This process, chronicled and furthered by scholars like Sugirtharajah, is recasting our whole sense of what the single discipline of biblical studies is going to look like. The case of Colenso is important primarily as an early part of a history that is only now beginning to be written, indeed whose existence is only beginning to be acknowledged. It is the history of how, as it has been wittily put, 'the Empire writes back' (see Ashcroft, Griffiths and Tiffin 1989).

Until recently, Europe and North America have been seen as the centre from which true knowledge of the Bible and theology have been delivered to the 'Third World' periphery, without any thought that the periphery might have something of value to send back. Colenso lived in the heyday of this colonialist thinking. But, as the various vignettes in Sugirtharajah (2001) show, there has been a long, mostly hidden, history of ideological activity around the Bible in many areas of the colonized periphery, activity that has tended to subvert both the 'truth' of the standard European approach, and the structures through which this 'truth' is delivered.

Colenso and his converts were creating biblical scholarship, African biblical scholarship. My resistance to Larsen's essay (see below) really began when I read that 'Colenso's book was the first thoroughgoing, *indigenous* attempt at modern biblical criticism' (p. 44 [my emphasis]),[2] 'indigenous' meaning British as opposed to continental European. My instinctive reaction was, 'No! Colenso's work was not indigenous to Britain'. He was, of course, British, very British, and always so thought of himself. But for my analysis he was more importantly African. This is an analysis that neither Colenso nor anyone else in his age (with the possible exception of Marx) could have achieved or imagined. But in the age of postcolonial studies it has become possible and necessary.

The African biblical scholarship that Colenso and his converts were creating was fed back from periphery to centre through Colenso's publications in England, of which the 1862 volume had the most impact.

---

2. Page references to Larsen are to his essay 'Bishop Colenso and His Critics', in this volume.

There were many other reasons (ably presented by Larsen) why the book was controversial, but, in a long historical perspective, I suggest that the most important reason was precisely that his work originated in the colonies. Those (from Disraeli down) who joked of bishops being converted by the natives were expressing a worry whose meaning they could not yet know (on the racism latent in the humorous response to Colenso, see Guy 1983: 187-88). For us now, it is a commonplace that the Church has much more real social power in Africa than in Europe, and there is no longer anything jocular about the idea of African missionaries to England. At the time of this writing I am examining a University of Natal doctoral thesis by a Congolese student that demonstrates how the pathos of God in the book of Hosea is far closer to African conceptions of God than to European ones; this is simply one example that could be endlessly multiplied.

In fact, it is perfectly obvious, as Niels Peter Lemche has remarked (see West 1997: 100-101), that African readers are in a much better position than European readers to interpret the real subject matter of the Bible (for a generalization of this point to other Third World scenes, particularly Asian ones, see Sugirtharajah's chapter [2001: 175-202] on 'vernacular hermeneutics'). The achievements of biblical scholarship in the West over the last centuries, remarkable as they have been, are being seen more and more as limited by their intellectual and political assumptions, and we are entering a period when the most important advances in understanding are likely to come from the developing world.

Our situation is ironic. The West, during the centuries of colonization, has tried in various ways to respond to the ancient and unfamiliar cultures with which it has come into close contact. One of the main tools that it has used to form its attitudes to these cultures is the Bible, on the assumptions that (1) the Bible understands the nature of human culture and (2) the West understands the Bible (see Jobling 1993: 101-105). But now we must come to terms with the discovery that the Bible itself belongs much more to that realm of the ancient and unfamiliar than it does to the West!

The case I am arguing is, of course, threatening to the Western theological industry, which responds to postcolonial biblical studies, as to other biblical discourses emerging out of practices of liberation (feminism, Black reading, etc.), sometimes with outright rejection, more often with neglect and a 'business as usual' attitude. Over these issues there is a new *Kampf um die Bibel*. My response to Timothy Larsen's essay, to which I now turn, comes out of my own location in this struggle.

III

Larsen is to be commended for the useful review he has given us of the main lines of response in Britain to the publication of Colenso's first volume on the Pentateuch in 1862. He rightly regards this controversy as a critical moment in the history of the study of the Bible in England (see his subtitle: 'The Strange Emergence of Biblical Criticism in Victorian Britain', and cf. Rogerson 1984: 220-37), and he has added much to our understanding of how the lines of controversy were drawn.

In addition to chronicling the affair, Larsen in his essay offers two other main things: a good deal of comment on and assessment of Colenso and his book; and a closing assessment of whether the debate over biblical criticism in nineteenth-century Britain needed to unfold as it did. I shall return to these points shortly, but first need to say something about a difficulty I have in responding to his work.

Larsen says nothing about his own location, and little directly about his point of view. He does not even make clear for what pressing reason he wrote his essay. I have tried to discern what he really wants to say about Colenso, and have reached the conclusion that, despite his attempt to seem even-handed, he is very negative towards Colenso and his book at a variety of levels (his theology, his forcing of controversy by insisting on publishing, the ineptness of his work). As one who is highly sympathetic to Colenso at all these levels, I hope my response to Larsen is not unfair. In any case, my interest lies less in disputing his position than in opening up his essay, and the 1862 controversy, to modes of discussion beyond those he has in view.

I suspect that Larsen sometimes hides his own point of view behind general references to Colenso's critics (e.g. 'his critics would say' [p. 47]). But there are certain places where his position, particularly his dislike of Colenso's theology, seems barely disguised. For example, having discussed the bishop's 'Romanticism', he comments 'one could see his [Colenso's] commentary on Romans as a kind of last-ditch attempt to show that his Romanticist convictions were reconcilable with the teachings of Scripture' (p. 48). I find this shift from chronicling the controversy to entering into it disturbing. If Larsen finds certain beliefs incompatible with Scripture, and takes some negative view of things that are incompatible with Scripture, he would help his reader by clearly saying so. Similar rhetoric infects the next page, where he ascribes to Colenso the argument that proving the Bible unhistorical 'frees us from having to embrace those passages that offend our sensibilities' (p. 48). What on earth does 'embrace' mean here?

Another place where Larsen's position seems clear, and where I find him at his most passionate, is in his closing summary (pp. 61-62). He perceives it as a tragedy that orthodoxy and biblical criticism got off to such a bad start with each other in England; his sympathy is with 'those who were wishing for a path of peaceful coexistence' (p. 62). For this bad start, he lays a considerable blame on Colenso (though he does not spare some of Colenso's critics). While admitting that the arrival of biblical criticism in Britain could never have been an easy process, he believes that the debate might well have been more gradual and peaceful had it not been for Colenso's publication of his book. If only, I seem to hear him say, this colonial bishop who was not even a biblical scholar had let well alone.

I am not persuaded that 'a path of peaceful coexistence' was open in the Victorian situation (though I should confess that I am no more constitutionally inclined to seek such a path than was the bishop). Larsen believes (see especially his closing paragraph) that the challenges of criticism to orthodoxy were such as a reasonable measure of good will could have overcome. I believe that the challenges were (and continue to be) much more fundamental, and that most Victorians experienced them as fundamental. A reading of the case that I find more plausible is that Colenso became the catalyst for a struggle that had to happen, between people of widely opposed convictions.

Further, I agree with Colenso's analysis of his situation, and sympathize with the sense of urgency that he felt. What impelled him to act as he did was what he saw as intellectual dishonesty on the part of some clerics and academics who were hiding from the laity disturbing truths that they already knew. For Colenso this was not only outrageous, it was also disastrous, whether in Britain or on the mission field. In Britain, the Church was forfeiting the allegiance of an intelligent laity—see the passionate words in the Preface to Part I of *The Pentateuch* (pp. xxiii-xxiv, discussed by Guy 1983: 184-86). Hence his practice of addressing his theological appeals directly to the laity, for example in the Natal Sermons (appreciatively discussed by both Guy [1983: 163-72] and [Sugirtharajah 2001: 113 and *passim*]). His later publications, and his life and work taken as a whole, make it clear that the bishop gave deep and agonizing thought to the controversy that he helped to foment; and he worked at least as hard as anyone (here I refer to the generous closing paragraph of Rogerson's treatment) at the task of a genuine reconciliation between biblical science and belief.

Larsen believes (pp. 44-45) that the 1862 volume, in its intrinsic quality, simply was not worth the controversy it aroused: 'what a strange book it is upon which to place so much passion and weight!' (p. 44). It consists mostly of arithmetical calculations purporting to show that the number of Israelites in the wilderness claimed by the Pentateuch (Num. 2.32, etc.) cannot be historically correct. Larsen clearly thinks it would have been better if the bishop had confined himself to his 'highly successful mathematical textbooks' (p. 44), rather than turning the Bible into one.

I have to agree that this mathematical line of argument makes embarrassing reading to us now. But here I must fault Larsen for his exclusive concentration on this *first volume* of Colenso's work on the Pentateuch. I realize that the topic of his essay is the controversy over just this volume, but I believe he gives his reader (especially now that the essay is being reprinted in a volume devoted to reassessing Colenso) a quite wrong estimate of the scholarly power of Colenso, who in the later volumes shows himself master of much more sophisticated forms of argument. For a corrective, the reader should turn to the treatment by Rogerson (1984: 220-37), which covers all the volumes. 'Colenso', says Rogerson, 'was far more than a mathematician dabbling with biblical figures and dimensions...he mastered, as probably no English scholar had before him, the technicalities of Old Testament criticism' (p. 236)—this from a biblical scholar of the utmost distinction.

Though there is an excessive amount of numerology in the 1862 volume, it is by no means all that the book contains. As Guy (1983: 178) points out, any 'fair reading of Part 1 would...have revealed that the arithmetical demonstrations were only a means to a sound theological end'. My own sense is that Colenso decided to take what seemed the shortest route (a mathematician's route!) to his initial goal, which was to blow out of the water any idea that the Pentateuch could be accepted as literal history (cf. Rogerson 1984: 221, referring to Colenso's impatience with the apologetics of Hengstenberg and others). In this initial volume he was working at a level where it came down to 'a simple question of facts' (*The Pentateuch*, I: xx; see Guy 1983: 122-23). That he hit his mark, Larsen's own account (esp. p. 51) makes clear: the many in his audience who tried to answer him point by point did not find the *level* of his argument embarrassing or inappropriate.

IV

In relation to my earlier discussion of postcolonial biblical criticism, I have a particular interest in how Larsen deals with Colenso's African location. In a word, he sees it as irrelevant to the controversy that the bishop aroused. He shows an interest in Colenso's pre-African career, but not in the almost 30 years spent in Natal. That the chief figure in the events he discusses had come only briefly to England after almost a decade in the mission field, and would soon return there for the rest of his life, is not seen by Larsen as having anything to do with the intrinsic meaning of the controversy.

The one place where Larsen does refer to Africa only proves my point. He works hard to refute Colenso's own claim that his African location had a decisive effect on his work. According to Colenso's account, 'Doubts about the Pentateuch had been thrust upon him when an "intelligent native", who was helping him translate the story of the Deluge into Zulu, had innocently asked him, "Is all that true?"' (*The Pentateuch*, I: vii, quoted by Larsen on p. 45). Larsen thinks that this story has gained credence merely by being 'retold endlessly' (p. 46), and that it is high time it was 'critically examined' (p. 46).

Larsen's argument (pp. 47-49) is that Colenso's theological views were fully formed before he went to Africa. From Coleridge and F.D. Maurice he had learned the 'Romanticism' and universalism that characterize his theology (a theology which, I have suggested, Larsen dislikes). Colenso's writings during his African period, particularly the Romans commentary, simply reproduce these views. The story of the 'intelligent native' (William Ngidi) enables Larsen to give a neat further turn to his polemical screw—such a story is just another example of the Romantic frame of mind.

Larsen's essay clearly remains within the framework of standard Church history, biblical studies, and theology as pursued in Europe and North America. He shows no knowledge of or interest in recent currents like postcolonial criticism. As a comparison with Sugirtharajah's treatment of Colenso quickly shows, Larsen's approach belongs to what I have called 'business as usual'. But is it fair to go further and see him as actively *resisting* a postcolonial analysis? I have to suspect that he does so. He has read the work of Jeff Guy, which unavoidably highlights the colonial and postcolonial currents in recent thought, and yet his references to Guy steer clear of such issues. And I find it hard to explain the vehemence with which he rejects the idea that Africa shaped Colenso's views. Perhaps he is simply resisting the possibility that Colenso had *any* defensible reason for an action—the publication of his book in England—that Larsen sees (I have argued) as a disaster. But I have to wonder whether—perhaps not altogether consciously—he is defending conventional approaches in theology from invasion by postcolonial criticism; for example, by hinting that it is mere foolish Romanticism to suggest that the opinions of new colonial converts (and perhaps even colonial bishops who are amateur scholars) could ever have an impact on the European bastions of Church and Academy.

Against Larsen, it is universally attested of Colenso that, from the beginning of his time in Africa and throughout his life there, he paid the closest attention to his African converts and let their point of view influence his actions and policy. The astute Sugirtharajah, who, given his location, would certainly pursue any suspicions he might have about Colenso's colonialist attitudes, finds nothing fishy about the bishop's repeated claims that he shaped his study of the Bible according to African social realities, and submitted it to African criticism. The Ngidi story fits so entirely into this general picture that it is hard to see how one could doubt its veracity without casting doubt on the whole picture (which, I suspect, Larsen does want to do). And if the story is merely an instance of Colenso's indulging a 'rhetorical habit' (as Larsen puts it on p. 47), this was an indulgence for which he was willing to pay an extraordinarily high price—of derision in England (p. 46) and ostracism at home! It is for a fundamental truth, surely, that one bears such costs, not for a rhetorical habit.

Larsen's argument that Colenso's views were formed before he went to Africa does not, I believe, get us very far. Of course he took with him the influences that had shaped him. In fact, we might suggest that the influences helped take him to Africa—the Romantic influence is likely to have been a factor in his decision, when he was already in mid-life, to uproot his family and begin such a totally new career. Certainly this influence helped create his astonishing sensitivity in his new setting; after all, one of the positive legacies of Romanticism is that it makes us look at the unfamiliar and exotic with positive, rather than negative, expectations. The views that Colenso took to Africa were, I believe, of a kind that the experience of Africa would tend to confirm and deepen, and I assume that this is what happened. Of course the Romantic attitude can also be taken to bad extremes in such a setting, as in the idea of the Noble Savage. But I don't believe that Colenso espoused this idea; his sense of the superior nobility of the typical African to the typical European settler was based on empirical observation rather than a fixed idea (Sugirtharajah 2001: 127, referring to Colenso's account [1855g: 88-89] of his first experiences in Natal)!

Larsen's position is vulnerable in other ways to postcolonial critique: for example, what he has to say about Colenso and eternal punishment. Colenso, of course, rejected and detested this doctrine. Larsen uses this (p. 47) as another instance of Colenso's theology being formed in his pre-African period, thereby discounting once again the bishop's own testimony that his Romans commentary (where he most fully combated the doctrine) was written from a specifically 'missionary point of view' (as claimed in the very title of Colenso 1861h). A postcolonial critique can sharpen the issues. It is not at all hard to see eternal punishment as a doctrine hand in glove with colonialism. If one is convinced that people are going to suffer eternally unless one can reach them and change their beliefs and behaviour, one is going to use any means, including taking advantage of imperial power, to move into their society and acquire the social authority to promote one's message. The rejection of a doctrine might thus entail a wholesale reconception of the missionary enterprise. This again is an analysis that no one in Colenso's day could have accomplished; but in our day, his missionary practice is revealed as being in remarkable agreement with such an analysis.

V

It is impossible and absurd to try to lift Colenso out of the colonialist project to which he belonged and make him an anticolonialist hero (Guy, Sugirtharajah and others make this clear in different ways). For example, his (fortunately short-lived) plan in the late 1850s, to give up the bishopric of Natal and move to Zululand as bishop (Guy 1983: 84-86), was related to Theophilus Shepstone's dream of a Zulu society separated from white settlers but ruled by a white chief (Shepstone himself!). We can now clearly see this as an example of a widespread colonialist fantasy (fictionalized by, for example, H. Rider Haggard in *Allan Quatermain* and Kipling in *The Man Who Would be King*). If Colenso had possessed the critical resources available to us, he could not have been tempted by such a scheme. Sugirtharajah, for all his positive appreciation of Colenso, ascribes to him an ambiguous place in colonial discourse (2001: 136), as one who to the end was still trying to operate entirely within a Victorian Christian value system (p. 137). Sugirtharajah's summary, ascribing to Colenso 'an imaginative hermeneutical and political enterprise, modified and controlled by a colonial mode of thinking' (p. 111), seems fair.

Nevertheless, if one is clear about what one is doing, one may propound a productive *myth* of Bishop Colenso. It is a myth of how the meeting between the European churches and Africa (the Americas, Asia, the Pacific, and so on) might all have been done differently. (So, like Larsen [pp. 61-62], I close with a nostalgic wish that a historical process had unfolded differently!) A myth of how it could have been a meeting for mutual enrichment, a laying of theological questions on the table to be discussed respectfully by people of good will; of how the missionary churches could have stood steadfastly against becoming identified with the forces of empire, and used all their influence to prevent abuses. Colenso is far from embodying this myth—if he or anyone else had done so, it would be no longer a myth. But he powerfully evokes it.

When one promotes a myth, one had better believe it oneself. I first read Colenso and the literature about him before my first visit to South Africa in 1996. During that visit, I spent a long weekend driving alone around Kwazulu, inspecting historical sites (often, sadly, battlefields), running an informal taxi service in my rented car for people lacking other transportation. On that trip, I felt quite secure, much more than I have felt in other parts of South Africa, and the name I gave to my sense of security was John William Colenso. Despite the enormous forces ranged against him, despite his own many limitations as a man of his age, my influential predecessor among these people (who happens also to have been my predecessor not only as a biblical scholar but also as a Cambridge mathematician) had done an extraordinary job in his relations with them, and I felt I was somehow the beneficiary of that.

Whatever doubts I may have about Colenso's biblical scholarship in detail, with the basic impulse inherent in it—and in his whole career—I am at one, and it is from this position that I view the controversy discussed by Larsen.

COLENSO AS SEEN BY KUENEN, AND AS KNOWN FROM COLENSO'S LETTERS TO KUENEN*

Cornelis Houtman

1. *Introduction*

My dear Dr Kuenen

We are very grateful for hearing your testimony to the value of my dear
Husband's critical work.

With these words the letter opens which Mrs Sarah Frances Colenso
(1816–93) wrote on 3 October 1884 to the Leiden professor Abraham
Kuenen (1828–91), one of the most eminent biblical scholars of his times,
known especially for his theory on the origin of the Pentateuch, the first
five books of the Old Testament (Houtman 1998: 270-74). The reason for
this letter was that Mrs Colenso had a tract she had read, written by
Kuenen on the life and work of her husband, John William Colenso. Mrs
Colenso mentions the pamphlet in question in a letter to Mrs Katherine
Lyell (Rees 1958: 391):

> I had a letter from Prof. Kuenen... He always spoke in terms of affectionate
> friendship of my dear Husband, and he was one who could appreciate his
> work. I hope you saw his pamphlet on the subject which I had had trans-
> lated from the Dutch. It appeared in a little Dutch periodical... (27 January
> 1885)

It is not clear which periodical is meant. When Mrs Colenso wrote these
letters, an extensive biographical notice written by Kuenen had been published in the series *Mannen van beteekenis in onze dagen*.[1] Mrs Colenso

---

*   This article was translated from Dutch by the Reverend Jacob Faber (Kampen,
the Netherlands).
    1.   This work on *Men of Note in Our Days* bears the sub-title *Levensschetsen en
portretten (Biographical Sketches and Portraits)*, assembled by Dr E.D. Pijzel (Haarlem, 1884). Kuenen's article (quoted below as Kuenen 1884) is found on pp. 1-28.

was probably alluding to that.[2] In the series Colenso's name appears alongside giants such as Moses Montefiore, Alphonse Daudet, Hermann Schlegel, Ivan Turgenev, Matthew Arnold and others. The biographical notice appeared in 1884. This means that in less than a year after his death, a Dutch tribute was paid to him as a man who had made himself heard in the ecclesiastical and political history of England, the country of his birth, and of South Africa, where he was a bishop, and whose name bore ill omen with many people.

The 1884 article was not the first treatise in which Kuenen acquainted the Dutch intellectual community with Colenso and his work. As early as 1865, in an article in *De Gids* called 'De kerkelijke beweging in Engeland', Kuenen had paid minute attention to the place and the role of Colenso in the then raging English 'church struggle' (Kuenen 1865). Both articles are based primarily on information furnished by Colenso himself. Colenso and Kuenen met in 1863 and 1864, and corresponded for years.[3] The special

2. In the periodical *De Hervorming* of 30 June 1883, Kuenen published a short biographical sketch. On account of the characterization 'pamphlet', it is unlikely that Mrs Colenso has that article in mind.

3. Colenso's letters to Kuenen (29 letters and a scrawl) are part of the Kuenen Collection in Leiden University Library (Dousa Department BPL 3028; they are quoted by their date). They cover, with exception of the scrawl, the period June 1863 to March 1878. Fourteen letters come from the period 1863–65, when Colenso lived in London (23 Sussex Place, Kensington). One was written 6 December 1874, during Colenso's second stay in London (37 Phillimore Gardens, Kensington). The others were written at his home in Bishopstowe (Natal). The first letter opens with 'My dear Sir', the next one with 'My dear Prof. Kuenen'; from the seventh letter dated 11 June 1863, it is 'My dear Friend'. All are signed 'J.W. Natal'. They fill 152 pages of approx. 12.5 × 20 cm. It is uncertain whether all letters to Kuenen have been preserved. It was Colenso who took the initiative for this contact. He had sent volumes I and II of his *The Pentateuch and Joshua* to Kuenen who reacted in a letter dated 23 June 1863 (see below). Colenso in turn requested a meeting, 'though my knowledge of your language is much like yours of mine. Indeed, I learned Dutch *in order* to read your book, *in the reading*' (25 June 1863). According to Cox (1888, I: 221), at the beginning of 1862 the Reverend Henry Rawlings had drawn Colenso's attention to the first part of Kuenen's *Historisch-kritisch Onderzoek* (Leiden, 1861), 'a work of rare merit' (as Colenso noted in the Preface of Part I of *The Pentateuch and Joshua*); he also had advised him to visit Kuenen in Holland. Colenso met Kuenen in Leiden in September 1863 (see the letters dated 25 June 1863; 17 and 26 August 1863) and in London in July 1864 (see the letters of 9 February, 11 June, 2 September 1864). Cf. Colenso's letter to T. Shepstone (3 July 1864): 'I have now Professor Kuenen staying with me for a week, and of course we are discussing the Pentateuch at every available moment...' (see Cox 1888, I: 250). Despite Colenso's wish for another meeting with Kuenen (see the letters dated

attention paid by Kuenen to the life and work of Colenso for Dutch readers proves his appreciation and admiration. This article will analyze these sentiments further. Fragments from Colenso's letters to Kuenen will allow us to hear the bishop's voice so that a portrait of him will emerge.

To Kuenen, Colenso was a man of 'nobel frankness, practical mind, a strong sense of justice, accuracy', of 'love for the truth, sincerity, resolution' (1865: 187, 190), 'a man of great strength and iron perseverance' (1884: 2). He gave proof of these qualities through his concern for the fate of the South African Zulus, his role in the Church struggle about the authority of the Scriptures, and his activities as a biblical scholar (see, for instance, Cox 1888; Hinchliff 1964; Guy 1983; Rees 1984; Deist 1984, 1999; Mitchell 1997). On the last two aspects, which are closely connected, Kuenen had a clear opinion. We give an impression of both, preceded by a description of Colenso's situation when he and Kuenen met and a life-long friendship began.

2. *Under Fire on a Charge of Heterodoxy*

In May 1862, Colenso, after a stay of seven years in Natal, arrived in England with his family. The report that he was a heterodox theologian had preceded him. In 1861 his *Commentary on St Paul's Epistle to the Romans: Newly Translated, and Explained from a Missionary Point of View* had been published (see Cox 1888: 128-70; Hinchliff 1964: 79-84; Guy 1983: 69-73). In it he had criticized the doctrine of the atonement and opposed the idea of eternal retribution for the unrepentant. Also, the rumour that a most critical study on the Pentateuch was ready to be published had sped on ahead. Colenso arrived in the land of his birth at the very moment that the Church of England was in an uproar about *Essays and Reviews*, a book published in 1860 to inform the British public of recent developments in contemporary thought and scholarship in various fields of study. Two of the seven essayists had been arraigned for expressing views which were at variance with the formularies of the Church. The ecclesiastical

20 January 1870 and 6 December 1874 [from London]), it appears that it never came about. His letters show that Colenso provided Kuenen with detailed documentation on everything that befell him. The Colensiana also include the letter of Mrs Colenso (see above). Kuenen's letters to Colenso were probably lost as a result of the fire, also described by Mrs Colenso in her letter to Kuenen, which destroyed Colenso's house at Bishopstowe in September 1884. A letter of Kuenen's (certainly the first), dated 23 June 1863, is printed in Colenso's *The Pentateuch and Joshua* (IV: xxiv-xxv). Cf. the letter dated 17 November 1863.

lawsuit, brought in December 1861, concerned Rowland Williams, who had written an article on the German biblical scholar C.J.J. Bunsen (Williams 1860: 50-83; see Rogerson 1984: 212-124), and Henry Briston Wilson, a friend and kindred spirit of Colenso's (see the letters of 13 April and 14 August 1865 in Rees 1958: 82, 360), who in his contribution (Wilson 1860) appealed for greater freedom in the handling of such questions as the inspiration of the Bible by the clergy of the National Church. The charges led, after a preliminary verdict on 25 June 1862 in which but a small portion was considered relevant, to a conviction by the Court of Arches on 15 December 1862. When Colenso published Part I of his *The Pentateuch and Joshua* in October 1862, the first of seven volumes to be published under the title *The Pentateuch and book of Joshua Critically Examined* (1862-79), the issue was still so controversial that the book raised a storm of protest (see Cox 1888: 481-96; Hinchliff 1964: 85-114; Thompson 1970: 43-44, 54-56; Guy 1983: 95-122, 174-89; Rogerson 1984: 220-37; Le Roux 1993: 91-107). The reaction was little short of hysteria. Especially the fact that he, a *bishop*, had been guilty of higher criticism without any restraint, and had undermined the Church and the faith from within, was held against him. When Part II was published in January 1863, even the vast majority of his colleagues, the English bishops, urged him to resign. Well aware that the issue of the essayist-case[4] would have consequences, Colenso followed it avidly, as he did their appeal to the Queen against the ecclesiastical sentence—a matter she had entrusted to the Judicial Committee of the Privy Council.

During the appeal he became involved in an ecclesiastical lawsuit himself, not in England but in South Africa where he had consecrated a bishop. Accusations of heterodoxy, based on his commentary on Romans and on the first two volumes of *The Pentateuch and Joshua*, induced the Bishop of Cape Town, Robert Gray, who was the metropolitan of South Africa, to bring a lawsuit against Colenso. Held in November and December 1863, it led to his conviction (16 December) and deposal (16 April 1864). Colenso, then in London, had a representative in Cape Town. At roughly the same time, the verdict was passed in the case of Williams and Wilson (8 February 1864)—both were acquitted. That result made Colenso hopeful about his own case. The right of a bishop to think as he did had been legitimized:[5]

4. See the letters to T. Shepstone dated 4 September 1862 and 1 May 1863 (quoted in Cox 1888: 232-33, 238).
5. Cf. also the letter to T. Shepstone dated 29 March 1864 (quoted in Cox 1888: 248-49, 361).

That decision [the judgement of the Privy Council in the case of *Essays and Reviews*] was given yesterday, & I am glad to say that, under all the circumstances of the case, it may be regarded as a complete & decisive triumph on the side of liberty & truth. I send you a copy of it… They [the judges] have reversed altogether the professions of the 'Court of Arches', & therefore, in *all* the points of accusation the Prosecutors have been defeated… It will be obvious to you that several of the points, here decided, completely cover me in my controversy with Capetown. The Bp. of Capetown, in short, is now directly at issue with the High English Courts on several questions. (9 February 1864)

The lawfulness of the Cape Town process had been challenged by Colenso in an appeal to the Queen. The times were tense, the future was uncertain:

But I think it is possible that the *first* hearing of my case before the Privy Council may come on while you are here—which will probably be only a formal affair of a few minutes. (11 June 1864)

…so that we may now hope to have the case heard in November. And I shall probably have to go out—*for a time* at all events—soon after Christmas. (1 October 1864)

we are still kept in suspense by the deliberate movements of the Law…but all the future lies in darkness at present before me. I literally know not what a week may bring forth. The 'case' was heard at full length—two eminent lawyers on both sides speaking…in the early part of *December*… You shall hear when I know the result—by which my own future…must be guided. I may go out to Natal in a few weeks. I may challenge Bp. Gray to bring me now lawfully before the Queen. I may resign, & have to begin life anew—all will depend on the *tenor* of their judgement—& on the form it takes, even if (as all seem to expect) it should be *generally* in my favour. (3 February 1865)

While his case was before the Judicial Committee of the Privy Council, Colenso, unable to return to South Africa, defended himself in various ways in reply to his opponents:

I delayed my reply, wishing to be able to send you a pamphlet which I have had in hand, in reply to Bishop Gray's last proceedings. This work, however, has expanded to a greater length than I intended, & has taken up a great deal of my time—since, you know, every word of mine requires to be carefully weighed at this particular crisis. The pamphlet[6] is now complete,

---

6.   *Remarks Upon the Recent Proceedings and Charge of Robert Lord Bishop of Capetown and Metropolitan* (London, 1864). A second pamphlet, not mentioned in the letters to Kuenen, but known to him, is *A Letter to the Laity of the Diocese of Natal* (London, 1864).

& will be published, I hope, next week—when copies will be sent to you & other friends in Leyden—& from this you will be able to gather better than from anything else how matters stand just now in England & at the Cape. Of course, my case is patiently waiting for the sitting of the Privy Council in November; but things are moving forward. And, if I do not mistake the signs of the times, we are rapidly tending toward a rupture between the High Church Party & the State. Very probably, my affair, will help to precipitate this. But Dr Pusey[7] has just published a violent attack upon the late judgment of the Privy Council, which shows how uneasy that party feels under present circumstances. Should the Privy Council decide in my favour, they will be driven to fury. (2 September 1864)

You received, I hope…the copies of my 'Remarks'. They are producing, I think, considerable effect. (1 October 1864)

In passing he commented on the offensive launched by his antagonists: upon the advice of the Speaker of the House of Commons they had taken the initiative to prepare a running commentary on the Old and the New Testament (*The Speaker's Commentary*).[8] Colenso had earlier described this initiative to counterbalance heterodox ideas as follows:

the *conservative* party have been compelled to *show fight* as we say—that is, the Archbishops of Canterbury & York, upon the advice of no less a personage than the Speaker of the House of Commons, a *very* great layman in this country, as you may know—have formed a committee, & superintend a *critical* commentary of the whole Bible—the first which the English Church has ever been favoured with. The Pentateuch is assigned to Prof. Harold Browne of Cambridge[9]—the *best* man whom they could find—but they were greatly at a loss for Hebrew scholars—the difficulty having been to find men, who are at once, clergymen—good Hebrew scholars—well-read in continental theology—& *strict orthodox*. But Prof. Browne is about the best they could have found, being an *honest* man. I fully believe though, of course thoroughly imbued with the traditional views, & as I believe, knowing at present very little indeed about the subject which he has undertaken. (17 November 1863)

7.   E.B. Pusey was the organizer of a petition signed by about 10,000 clergymen. Cf. Cox 1888: 249. On Pusey see Hinchliff 1964: 11-14, 19, 48, 108, 149-50, 154-59.

8.   The commentary bore the official title *The Holy Bible, According to the Authorised Version, With an Explanatory and Critical Commentary—by Bishops and Other Clergy of the Anglican Church.*

9.   Browne, who became Bishop of Ely, was a friend of Colenso's. The Preface to Part I of *The Pentateuch and Joshua* contains a letter by Colenso, written to him, but not forwarded. Browne revealed himself as one of the most prominent critics of Colenso's work. On Browne see Hinchliff 1964: 87, 109-14, 164.

A year later he returned to the subject:

> The grand 'Commentary' is promised to appear *next year*... To any one
> who knows about the subject, it is perfectly ludicrous that a work of this
> nature—purposing to give full information on all the points of difficulty
> throughout the *whole Bible* can be completed in 18 months—by men who
> two or three years ago were in almost total ignorance upon the whole
> question of Biblical Criticism as regards the O.T. However, we shall hail
> the appearance of these volumes with great satisfaction—& I doubt not,
> shall be able to give a good account of them. (1 October 1864)

He continued his studies on the Old Testament with a view to reinforce his
position. Successively, Parts III and IV of his *The Pentateuch and Joshua*
were made ready for publication (1863):

> I believe that the good cause is now in a fair way to a complete victory. My
> Part IV is nearly ready, and you should have a copy forwarded to Leiden.
> (17 November 1863)

> The fact is that, by my last volume [Part IV] especially, the ground appears
> to have been so effectively opened in England, that it seems desirable to
> leave things to settle down a little for the time—so that men's minds may
> come to be habituated to the very considerable modifications of the tradi-
> tionary views, which have been already forced upon them. And the con-
> clusions of my work, if known to be the product of five years careful study,
> would come with more decisive effect upon the English mind. (9 February
> 1864)

One of Kuenen's major studies was translated from the Dutch in the hope
that acquaintance with it would support his case:

> I now wish to ask your leave for me to translate & publish that part of your
> Hist. Krit. Onderzoek,[10] which pertains to the Pentateuch & Book of Joshua.
> Indeed, I have translated the greater part of it already—&, if I get your
> permission, I shall send it to the press in two or three weeks from thus—as I
> should like to bring it out before I leave England—which I *may* have to do
> soon after Christmas—& leave it as my parting present to the community. I
> cannot complete my own book [Part V]: in fact, under present circum-
> stances, it would be wisest for me not to publish any more of my own for a
> little while[11]—& I would also rather wish to take more time for the delib-
> erate completion of the whole work before I publish Part V. But your views
> approximate on the whole sufficiently to my own—your criticism is so

10. *Historisch-kritisch onderzoek naar het ontstaan en de verzameling van de
boeken des Ouden Verbonds* (1861).

11. Cf. Guy 1983: 146-47.

accurate & comprehensive—that I think it would greatly further my own
cause to show to English people a good continental work, which goes over
pretty much the same ground. (2 September 1864)[12]

Ultimately, Colenso did choose to leave Part V as a 'parting present':

I hope to bring out another Part of my own work. (3 February 1865)

I have gone to press with Part V. (13 April 1865)

I have long been waiting to write to you, wishing to be able to say that my
Part V was out of my hands. I hope now that you will receive it from
Messrs. Longman in about a week's time—& with it several other copies
[to distribute among the countrymen of Kuenen]... Of course, in writing, I
have had my own course..., & in judging of this book, will be *merciful*, I
hope, to the infirmities of English Criticism. When I am wrong, at any rate,
I have opened ground for further discussion... (16 July 1865)

The translation of a minor work by Henricus Oort (1865) came into the
bargain:

But I have also sent to the Press another little work—wishing to see it
through the Printer's hands before I leave England, which I expect to do
about Aug. 15! This is a translation of Dr Oort's Treatise on the Baalim,[13]
largely annotated[14]... My view, in fact, lies midway between Dozy's[15] &

12. The translation, published under the title *The Pentateuch and Book of Joshua
Critically Examined by Professor A. Kuenen of Leyden* (1865), is also mentioned in
subsequent letters. Among other things, Kuenen's remuneration is mentioned. In the
end, the translations never came about because the work proved commercially unat-
tractive ('But it is, as you know, a book only for *scholars*—& I am afraid that we have
hardly enough "scholarship" in England to welcome it heartily' [3 February 1865]).
The edition was limited to 500 copies ('the circulation will be apparently so limited,
that the expenses of publication may not be covered'; 'nor, to say the truth, do I expect
that they will sell speedily' [13 April 1865]). Nevertheless, Colenso was able to write:
'but I am very well satisfied with the *effect* it has produced...as the fruit of my labour'
(16 July 1865).
13. *De dienst der Baälim in Israël. Naar aanleiding van het geschrift van Dr
R. Dozy 'de Israëlieten te Mekka'* (1864). Dozy's study had been published in 1864 in
Haarlem.
14. Published under the title *The Worship of Baalim in Israel: Based Upon the
Work of Dr R. Dozy, 'The Israelites at Mecca', by Dr H. Oort* (1865). The original fills
55 pages; the translation, enlarged with notes and appendices, 94 pages.
15. In an earlier letter Colenso had qualified 'Dozy' as 'extremely interesting'; 'but
I must read him again, before I can express a judgment about him' (3 February 1865).
Cf. also Cox 1888: 223-26. Dozy's thesis that the ancient religion of Arabia owes its
origin to the religion of Israel in the times of King David, provided a strong impulse to

Oort's—I may help to reconcile... I have not written to ask, Dr Oort's leave
to publish it. (16 July 1865)[16]

Colenso won his case on 20 March 1865:

> The decision was given yesterday. I copy the last words which contain the
> substance of it. 'Their Lordships therefore will humbly report to Her Maj-
> esty their judgement & opinion that the proceedings taken by the Bishop of
> Capetown and the judgement or sentence pronounced by him against the
> Bishop of Natal, are *null & void in law*'. (21 March 1865)

On August 15, after a legal battle ('another *fight*' [13 April 1865]) on his
income (cf. Guy 1983: 150), Colenso returned to his diocese. The complicated situation in the Natal Church resulted in two competing Episcopal
sees, that of the Bishop of Maritzburg[17] as Bishop of the Church of South
Africa, and that of Colenso, Bishop of Natal, 'Queen's Bishop' of the
Church of England. After Colenso's death his seat was no longer filled.

3. *Kuenen's Judgment on Colenso's Role in the Church Quarrel*

Kuenen greatly admired the stand Colenso took in the Church. Looking
back on Colenso's life he praised him for the open manner in which he
had expressed his critical view of the Scriptures against the prevailing
opinions. In his unyielding love of the truth he merited comparison with
Luther at the Diet of Worms, who was so deeply convinced of his duty to
speak that he could neither be silent nor couch his conviction in unoffen-
sive cloak.[18] To Kuenen, Colenso was a real 'Reformer' and a true-blue

---

the interest of critical scholars in the history of religions. Colenso devoted an Appendix
to the question in Part V of his *The Pentateuch and Joshua* (1865: 265-78).

16. In the letter, Colenso asks Kuenen's advice on the translation of a number of
passages. Oort's name is mentioned elsewhere in the letters as well. Oort sent a number
of his publications to Colenso. He was a rather radical student of Kuenen's (Houtman
1998: 350-53).

17. Bishop W.K. Macrorie, characterized by Colenso as 'the gallant clergyman
who is willing to encounter the Goliath of Natal' (9 January 1869), and as the one who
'heads "the faithful"' (20 January 1870).

18. Kuenen 1884: 11-12. Cf. Kuenen 1865: 208. Also Cox (1888, I: 481-82) com-
pares Colenso with Luther. Rees (1958: 91) notes: 'Bishop Colenso believed himself
to be fighting, all over again, the battle of sixteenth-century Protestantism against
priestcraft. The two most honoured portraits at Bishopstowe were of Luther and
Melanchton' (cf. Guy 1983: 144-45). In a letter dated 6 December 1874, Colenso
remarks: '& people will, I fear, begin to think that I love fighting for fighting's sake.
They could not make a greater mistake.' Colenso's radical attitude was, without doubt,

Protestant. He argued his case in the article in *De Gids* which consists of two parts: (1) a description of the chapter by H.B. Wilson in *Essays and Reviews*, a description of Wilson's defence against the lawsuit brought against him,[19] as well as Kuenen's evaluation of both pieces; and (2) a description of the events in which Colenso had become entangled with his publications, together with Kuenen's evaluation of those. The first part determines the interpretation of the second.

Kuenen concurs with Wilson in his opinion that orthodoxy, when appealing to the creed of the Church, has in fact made a criterion of her own opinions and view of Scripture, identifying those with the doctrine of the Church, without considering that the Church's confession originated in a concrete historical situation, and unaware of the extent to which the position of orthodoxy has been influenced by contemporary philosophical and theological views that must be brought under the denominator of 'supranaturalism'. As far as the expression of faith is concerned, orthodoxy stands closer to the Reformers than does the modernist party, but the latter acts much more in their spirit and after their example, 'when it tries to express its religious convictions in the language and according to the needs of the present times'. The Reformers were men who had the courage to break with tradition. In short, not the orthodox but the modernists are the true heirs of the Reformation. The struggle in the English Church was one 'between authority and freedom; between the Protestant principle of free investigation and the Roman *Index*'.[20] Colenso has fought an exemplary fight to preserve the heritage of Protestantism. He is 'the great champion of the principle of *free trade*, i.e. of free debate and criticism'. He belongs to 'the valiant men [of the party of progress] who have borne the brunt of the battle'.[21]

Kuenen ends his article of 1865 with the conclusion that 'the party of progress' in the fight for its right to exist has gained the victory. Looking back in 1884 he remarks that with respect to 'the Church's capacity for

one of the reasons why even friends of biblical criticism in Britain were not ready to embrace him as a champion of truth and the herald of a new science (cf. Larsen 1997: 433-58).

19. Characterized by Colenso in a letter to T. Shepstone as 'a most masterly document' (26 August 1863). See Cox 1888: 242.

20. Kuenen 1865: 24-28; cf. also 197, 205-206 (quotations on pp. 24, 28).

21. Kuenen 1865: 196, 216. Facing Colenso on the stage as a true Protestant, Kuenen ironically positions Bishop R. Gray as a typical Roman Catholic: 'Fortunate Church of South Africa! If you leave Dr Gray to it, you preserve true doctrine and get the Pope into the bargain!' (Kuenen 1865: 213).

reform according to the demands of the times', Colenso was mistaken (1884: 12). Initially, Colenso had been quite optimistic about that:

> I share entirely in the confident hope expressed by yourself that it [the truth] will ultimately prevail, & obtain a triumphant victory even over such long-established & deeply-rooted prejudices, as still (I am sorry to say) abound in England. (25 June 1863)

> The storm is lulled just now in England: but I expect it will break out in a *final* gust of fury upon the publication of this Part [Part IV of the *The Pentateuch and Joshua*] which touches the vital questions of Calvinistic teaching the Fall, the Evil Spirit, & I hope that it may be the last burst of a gale which will bring us into *port*. (14 October 1863)

Later, that optimism lessened considerably. To Colenso's disappointment the triumph of Modernism never came:

> My books, however, find access, where those of a non-conformist (as Dr [S.] Davidson) & of a Jew (as Dr [M.M.] Kalisch) do not—& slowly, slowly. Yet I hope certainly—the good work is progressing in England. (20 January 1870)

> May your five children & ours breathe a freer air than we did in our youth, & help the good work forward when we are gone. (24 December 1871)

After informing Kuenen about his sons, who are studying in England, Colenso explains why they could not choose, much to his regret, theology as their discipline:

> Alas for the state of theology in the English Church at present! Nothing would have gratified us more than if they could conscientiously have devoted themselves to the clerical office, and we could have conscientiously wished them to do so. But the miserable state of theological feeling in England is sufficiently evidenced by the Bible Commentary put forth under the patronage of the Archbishops and Bishops, as well as by the determination *not* to get rid of the Athanasian Creed as one of our standards, and a number of other exhibitions of strict orthodoxy, which make one almost despair of the future of the Church of England—at least during my own lifetime. (25 July 1873)

That does not alter the fact that Kuenen in retrospect is able to conclude that in the English Church much has changed in 20 years (1884: 20):

> Criticism has now been accorded the freedom of the city where once it was excluded as the scion of the Evil One. It is the results of that criticism one still wrestles with… But there is no denial that the once dominant view of Scripture stands in need of amendment, and that the Church must take account of the progress of scholarship.

For Kuenen that change is largely the result of Colenso's writings, in particular of the influence of his *The Pentateuch and Joshua*. In that connection he praises the tone of Colenso's writings (p. 20): 'Always earnest and dignified; never bitter, not even towards those who had reviled him; resolute and fearless, and yet, where it was called for, kindly and devout'. Kuenen opened his remarks on the dignity with which Colenso defended his ideas with the phrase: 'Apart from his contributions to the solution of questions pending...' This reservation brings us to Kuenen's judgment on Colenso as a scholar. That is less complimentary.

4. *Kuenen's Judgment on Colenso's Biblical Criticism*

In 1884 Kuenen writes that strict scholarship calls for criticism of Colenso's *The Pentateuch and Joshua*: 'There is no unity in the work. At times he is excessively sceptical, going much too far in his denials; at others he is ultra-conservative. Now and then one meets with arbitrary theses, or stands in wonder at the ease with which the author allows others to take him in tow' (1884: 10).

Colenso returned to the supposed scepticism in one of his letters:

> You called me once 'a great sceptic' because I would not believe in the historic reality of Joshua. I am afraid that you will think me a greater one when I say that I see no ground whatever for believing in the historical existence of Moses. But so it is. (25 July 1873)[22]

In Kuenen's eyes (1884: 19-20), Colenso's review of *The Speaker's Commentary*[23] was useful insofar as it demonstrated that the 'adversary' was powerless, but clearly the work never charmed him: 'It may be doubted whether there were many who perused it from the first page to the last. It was, and could not be anything but a fatiguing discussion'. On Colenso's commentary on the Epistle to the Romans, Kuenen remarks: 'At times it is more than questionable whether that book gives a true account of the apostle Paul's views'. There is no doubt of Colenso's good intentions: 'But it is evident, always and everywhere, that the author shows pity for the heathen, and is dominated, in his thinking and in all his doings, by the

---

22. Kuenen disliked bold hypotheses. See Houtman 1993.
23. See below. The commentary was also reviewed by Kuenen for the *Theologisch Tijdschrift* 6 (1872): 96-100; 7 (1873): 378-86, 544-48; 8 (1874): 457-61; 9 (1875): 567-76; 10 (1876): 498-506. His review of the first volumes was translated by J. Muir and published in England: *Three Notices of 'The Speaker's Commentary'* (1873).

sincere desire to understand them and to raise them from the ignorance
and the vice in which they have sunk' (p. 8). To Kuenen's mind the commentary failed to meet the strict demands of scholarship. This critical
judgment he had already expressed more fully in 1865 (pp. 188-189, 206).
To Kuenen's judgment Colenso objected:

> I don't admit that I have mistaken St. Paul's views. I do not mean that
> he drew out the consequences of his *principles*, as I have tried to do:
> but I think that they are the genuine consequences of those principles.
> (14 August 1865)

Kuenen's judgment on Colenso's scholarship was less generous in 1884
than it had been 20 years earlier. This may well have to do with the fact
that in 1865 Colenso's *The Pentateuch and Joshua* had only been published in part. Kuenen then had been particularly impressed by Part I
(1862), in which Colenso had not yet thetically expressed himself on the
origin of the Pentateuch, but had only with a very detailed and exhaustive
argumentation demonstrated the unhistorical nature of the Pentateuch as
well as the immoral character of certain sections, for instance, the precepts
concerning slaves (Exod. 21.20, 21).[24] Judging by the Preface of Part I, the
work originated on the missionfield. Colenso explains that he came to
these investigations through the critical questions of a Zulu convert who
assisted him with his Zulu Bible translation. It was a love for the truth that
had led him to list all exaggerations and contradictions in the text. A
thorough dismantling of the popular view concerning the literal inspiration
of the Bible was the result.

Also in 1884, Kuenen praises Part I,[25] resuming his comments of 1865
(1865: 190-94). He defends it against the suggestion that Colenso had
brought nothing new[26] by insisting that the data Colenso brought up in
1862 had been all but forgotten and neglected by the leading Bible
scholars of his day (1884: 10). In so saying, Kuenen must have thought of
himself in particular. Speaking of Part I in 1865, he remarks (1865: 194):
'As for me, I recognize gladly that it was he who made me aware of the
difficulties which before that I had discounted, or not fully appreciated'. In
1870 he argues how Colenso's Part I has been a major influence on his

---

24. Examples in Rogerson 1985: 221-23 and Le Roux 1993: 96-98.
25. Cf. also Kuenen's letter to Colenso dated 23 June 1863. See n. 3 above.
26. Kuenen mentions no names, but must have had in mind Heinrich Georg August
Ewald, who, in a critical review of Part I, had argued that Colenso was in fact repeating
the criticism of the English Deists and Hermann Samuel Reimarus. Cf. Rogerson 1985:
8, 223, and see further Houtman 1994: 70-71, 76-78.

framing a theory on the origin of the Pentateuch.[27] The unhistorical character of the narrative sections of the so-called *Grundschrift*, as proved by Colenso, led Kuenen to conclude that they were later additions. Accepting the late date of the priestly-ritual precepts in the Pentateuch as argued by Karl Heinrich Graf,[28] Kuenen went on to defend the thesis that the *Grundschrift* (later designated P, the Priestly Codex) was the youngest document of the Pentateuch (Houtman 1994: 101-102).

In 1884, Kuenen makes no express mention of Colenso's influence on his views. There are remarks, however, which may be read as an explanation of why Colenso was not won over to Kuenen's position. Kuenen observes that as a critical Bible scholar Colenso was a self-taught man, and as such vulnerable to errors that a good school would have instructed him to shun. Besides, at the start he had been over-hasty. Prior to the publication of Part I many results of his research, which would not be published until later in subsequent volumes, had already been put on paper. Kuenen remarks: 'On those points, then, he had already made up his mind. Later he was unable to abandon this opinion, even though it could not hold up against criticism and detracted from the unity and the scholarly value of his work' (1884: 11).

All of this makes it clear that, in terms of scholarship, Kuenen is convinced that his own theory, which later became dominant with Julius Wellhausen's help, is superior.[29] It must be kept in mind, however, that in the period 1865–84 the question of the origin of the Pentateuch and

27. For an English translation of the pages on Colenso, see P.H. Wicksteed's translation of Part I/1 of the second edition of Kuenen's *Historisch-critisch onderzoek* (Amsterdam, 1885) under the title *An Historico-Critical Inquiry into the Origin and Composition of the Hexateuch* (London, 1886): xiv-xvii. Colenso's own translation in *The Pentateuch and Joshua* (VI: xxx), followed by among others Guy (1983: 175) and Deist (1984: 110-11), is not correct. Cf. Rogerson 1985: 233.

28. Kuenen had drawn Colenso's attention to Graf's *Die geschichtlichen Bücher des Alten Testaments* (Leipzig, 1866). See the letters of 27 November 1866, 9 January 1869 and 20 January 1870. Colenso suggests that Kuenen should send a copy of his Part VI to 'any representative of Graf' (who had died in 1869) 'as a token of my respectful admiration of his critical works' (14 September 1871).

29. T.K. Cheyne's judgment (1893: 196-204) is much like Kuenen's. Cheyne's sketch of the life and work of Colenso shows he was familiar with Kuenen's description. Among other things he writes: 'he was not qualified to do thoroughly sound constructive work either in historical criticism or in theoretic theology' (p. 203); 'He is a genuine but not an eminent critic, and misses the truth on that very important point, on which Graf himself finally gave way—the unity of the laws and narratives of the *Grundschrift*' (pp. 202-203).

particularly the question of the age of the materials later designated by the siglum 'P' were still a matter of open debate (Houtman 1994: 106). In Colenso's correspondence with Kuenen from 1866 onward the question is frequently mentioned:

> I may as well enclose a copy of my work [a provisional version of Part VI], which will show how entirely I agree with your views in the above article [in *Theologisch Tijdschrift* of 1870; see n. 27] as to much of the history as well as to the laws belonging to the L.L. (*Later* or *Levitical* Legislation) having been written after the Captivity. As you feel, this is *absolute certainty* now to be attained as to the general question of the manner in which the whole Pentateuch has been formed. My only remaining doubt of any importance is as to the 'Elohistic' matter in *Genesis*—I fully admit—& to a greater extent than Graf does—the resemblance in *phraseology* between this matter & the L.L.: but yet there are many phrases of the latter, if I mistake not..., which do *not* occur in the former, & might support the conclusion that the later writer was only imitating the style of the *oldest* writer in the work that lay before him... (20 October 1870)

> I feel compelled at present to maintain that the Elohistic matter in Genesis does not belong to the L.L., & is the oldest portion of the whole story of the Exodus. You will see that I have given fully my reasons for this conclusion...[in Part VI]. (14 September 1871)

> Another argument in support of the greater antiquity of the Elohistic narrative Genesis has occurred to me, & that is the existence of passages using *only* or *chiefly* Elohim in other parts of Genesis, which I regard as possibly due to the same writer at an earlier stage of his literary activity, but which you will at any rate (I suppose) admit to be more ancient than the more decidedly *Jehovistic* passages. As far as I can see, there is no difference whatever in point of style between these pseudo-Elohistic & the Jehovistic passages—though *fancy* might suggest that they had perhaps a more antiquated air, & were not so fluent. But, however this may be, I assume that they *are* more ancient than the more thoroughly Jehovistic passage, & if so, how can we account for the use of Elohim? If they existed only in Genesis, I might say from *my* point of view that some disciple of Samuel was merely following the lead of his master, & suppressing Yahveh until the revelation of the name in E. vi. But then such passages occur in Exodus also after the revelation of the name. Thus I make no doubt that you will agree with me that E. xix 14-19; xx 18-21 were consecutive passages of the Original Story. But why have we here Elohim five times & Yahveh once— if the use of Yahveh was as *familiar* to the writer as that of Elohim? (1 April 1872)

> As another indication of the Elohistic document being the *oldest*, I would refer to the *gradation* in the commands about abstaining from blood noticed

by me in (VI.425). It is of such importance to come to the right decision on this point that you will not mind my troubling you with another note upon the subject. (22 April 1872; see also below)

It is even the subject of Colenso's last written communication to Kuenen in the year 1883:

To Prof. Kuenen
My Dear Friend

I am quite satisfied that the Elohistic Narrative is *the earliest layer of the Priestly Document*; but I see reason to think that it may yet be earlier than D or even J,[30] though I doubt if I can print any more critical matters.

Very truly Yours,
JW Natal

The message has not been written on normal stationary paper but on a page torn from the notebook of a Dutchman (or at least a man of Dutch origins) who was an acquaintance of Colenso's.[31] Stopping over one Sunday in Pietermaritzburg on a trip to Europe, he 'heard the Bishop whom I deeply venerate preach'. After the service Colenso visited him in his hotel and asked him to bring his greetings to Kuenen together with a message on his changed opinions about Old Testament matters. At the suggestion of his host, Colenso then wrote the words printed above on the scrap of paper. For various reasons, those words, written on Sunday 11 February 1883, did not reach Kuenen until 1886—and that thanks to Miss Harriette Colenso[32] who had inquired of the bearer how Kuenen had reacted to this message. She wrote:

I was very sorry not to see you last time you returned from Europe through Natal for I wanted to hear from you of your visit to Professor Kuenen, what he said to the Bishop's little message to him written in your pocket-book:

30. The tenor of the remark is that Colenso has changed his view and has abandoned the Supplementary Hypothesis. Nevertheless, there are still serious differences with Kuenen's view on the age of the priestly narratives, notwithstanding the fact that also according to Kuenen the Priestly work contains old elements. In his view it has had a history of growth in five phases (cf. Houtman 1994: 103-106).

31. The information that follows is derived from a letter written in Pretoria on 18 April 1886, now found among the Colensiana in Leiden University Library. From the signature, the name of the sender, who in the letter calls himself 'a victim of political complications', cannot be reconstructed.

32. Harriette Emily Colenso (1847–1932), Colenso's eldest daughter, had inherited her father's social conscience. She assisted him with his political activities since 1875 and continued his political work after his death. See, e.g., Rees 1958: 311, 315-16, 319-20, 323, 348, 350-51, 353, 358-59, 374, 378-79, 401, 418.

and indeed anything which he or any of the Bishop's friends in Holland said about my dear father. I write now to ask what became of your pocket-book, because I should very much like to possess a copy of it, (it was the last bit of biblical criticism that he did) and to ask you if you will kindly lend me any of the Bishop's letters to you which you may possess, because we hope to bring out in the course of this year some account of his life, taken as far as possible from his own letters.

5. *The Image of Colenso as a Biblical Critic as it Emerges from his Letters to Kuenen*

Those who take note of Colenso's position at the beginning of the twenty-first century—a time when the old dogmas on the genesis of the Penta-teuch are, if not abandoned, at least controversial—will be less inclined than Kuenen was to detract from its scholarly quality. They will be im-pressed by the steadfastness and independence with which Colenso pursued his study of the Scriptures.[33] Throughout, Colenso showed great respect for Kuenen's work. After having received the first volume of Kuenen's *Religion of Israel*, in Dutch (Kuenen 1869) Colenso wrote:

> & I need hardly say that I sat down at once to read it with intense inter-est…& finding myself wakeful at night, I lit my candle & read for some hours, till in short I had actually finished the whole book. Then came the explanation of my wakefulness in a severe attack of rheumatic fever, which prostrated me for more than 3 months… (20 January 1870)[34]

After having received Kuenen's article in *Theologisch Tijdschrift* of 1870, Colenso wrote: 'I read with the greatest satisfaction your article' (20 October 1870).

That did not, however, alter the fact that Colenso attached great impor-tance to an independent judgment:

33. Cf. also the positive judgment of Rogerson (1984: 220, 226, 232, 236).
34. Cf. Guy 1983: 158-59. Colenso appears to have had the book in his possession already for a considerable amount of time. He begins his letter with excusing his late reaction. The book is also mentioned in other letters. Mrs Colenso, in a letter to Lady Lyell dated 16 April 1869, says: 'This mail has brought my Husband a book from his friend Kuenen of Leyden…which has delighted him very much. He finds Kuenen's views far nearer his own than they were when they met in Europe' (see Rees 1958: 200-201). Colenso himself wrote to W.H. Domville (17 April 1869): 'I am delighted to receive…from Professor Kuenen the first volume of his *Religion of Israel*, a very im-portant book…and to find that he has entirely abandoned the ground which he took in his *Historico-Critical Inquiry*…and is now on the most important points substantially at one with myself…' (see Cox 1888b: 216).

I have read the papers of Land & Oort on N. xvi, xvii, & I confess that my own view in Part VI seems more simple & satisfactory. But I am disposed to adopt Oort's view on Joel. (22 April 1872)[35]

I have been reading with much interest your article on 'De Stam Levi' in the Theol. Tijdschr. for November, 1872,[36] which has just reached me. With your general conclusions in that paper I entirely agree. But there are one or two statements made in the course of your argument with which (from my own point of view) I venture at present to differ... But, as far as I can see, there is not a shadow of ground for supposing that Aaron was recognized anywhere in the O.S. as a priest...

And later in the same letter Colenso remarks:

I wish very much that I could have approximated more closely to your views & Dr Oort's on some points, e.g. it seems to me, with the evidence before me & I have produced in Part VI, impossible to maintain that Moses gave the Israelites the Ten Commandments in a shorter form, as Ewald holds, and as I gather from Part III of 'Bible for Young Persons'[37] you also hold, or at least Dr Oort does. There is absolutely no room for the Decalogue in the Original Story. (24 February 1873)

I need not say that I always read with the greatest interest whatever you write in the Theol. Tijdschr.; and in the Theol. Review. I have carefully perused your article on the name Yahveh.[38] But I am not convinced by it, that the Israelites did not adopt the name from the Canaanites, while to my mind it is *clear* that the idea of *Moses* having introduced it in the supposed shorter form after the 1st Commandment is contradicted by the fact that there is no room for the Ten Commandments in any form in the narration of Exodus, the original story going on without interruption from Ex. xix 19 to Ex. xx.18. I have never met with any reply from you to this point, or to some others which I have advanced in my Parts V & VI, & which still appear to me of importance, e.g. the fact that the *Second Elohist* uses only Elohim, & yet preceded the Jehovist in writing, as (I suppose) is universally admitted. *I wish I could bring myself over to your view on this point*: I have tried my best to, but I cannot with a clear conscience give up the arguments I have advanced without seeing them disproved. (26 December 1876)

And I need hardly say that I shall very much desire to see how you are able to make room for the Ten Commandments in any form in Exodus. To me, at present, it seems impossible that the Original Story can have contained them. (30 March 1877)

35. See Land 1866; Oort 1866a; 1866b.
36. See Kuenen 1872.
37. Referring to *De Bijbel voor Jongelieden, door Dr H. Oort en Dr I. Hooykaas, met medewerking van Dr A. Kuenen*, III (Harlingen, 1872).
38. See Kuenen 1876.

Colenso showed this judgment also when he translated the work of others;
often such translations were attended with extensive comments.[39] In this
way he not only brought foreign scholarship to the attention of the British
public, but also his own ideas:

> I send you by this mail another copy of my treatise on Wellhausen[40]...
> which I have amended considerably after a careful study of the essays by
> [A.] Klostermann, Hollenberg, and [A.] Kayser, which last I have trans-
> lated, and compared throughout in notes with my own results... In the
> corrections in this pamphlet I have assumed some conclusions for which I
> could not here give the full proof—but I give it in my translation of
> Kayser.[41] In this pamphlet the most important amendments are on p. 60,
> 61, 62, & p. 74, 75, 76, 77, 78, which I commend to your consideration.
> (21 March 1878)

Under adverse circumstances, preoccupied with pastoral duties, in conflict
first with the ecclesiastical, then with the political establishment, with no
access to a good library or to the possibility of discussing his views with
other scholars, Colenso conducted his inquiries with seriousness and dedication:

> The truth is that I have never been so hardworked in my life, I think, as
> since I returned to Natal—not in criticism, for I have only very lately given
> a few odd movements to that kind of work—but you will easily understand
> that in the internecine war which I am waging, almost single-handed, with
> all the might of clergy-dom in England & here, I have had abundant em-
> ployment of all my faculties. (14 May 1866)

> Of course, I have very little time for criticism, having two sermons to write
> for the Cathedral every week. I send you a few that you will see what sort
> of work I am about... (2 November 1866)[42]

---

39. On the translation of works of Kuenen and Oort see above.

40. *Wellhausen on the Composition of the Hexateuch Critically Examined* (London, 1878), a translation of Julius Wellhausen's *Die Composition des Hexateuchs und
der historischen Bücher des Alten Testaments* (1876–77).

41. Perhaps a translation of *Das vorexilische Buch der Urgeschichte Israels*
(Strassbourg, 1874). Evidently the translation had not been published. It appears that
Colenso had started the translation of other works. In a letter of 14 May 1866 he speaks
about his intention to translate ('as Hupfeld once suggested') W.M.L. De Wette's
treatise on Chronicles (*Kritischer Versuch über die Glaubwürdigkeit der Bücher der
Chronik* [Halle, 1806]).

42. The sermons were published under the title *Natal Sermons. First Series* (London, 1867). A Second Series has also been published (London, 1968). On the sermons
see Guy 1983: 163-71.

I am terribly preoccupied with work here, like Nehemia having had all along to fight with one hand, while building with the other—nay, I have needed the hands of an Indian Deity—for, besides trying to build *up* my flock with sermons, I have had to do my best to pull *down* old superstitions, & to pursue at the same time my own critical investigations... (20 January 1870)

[I am] not only harassed by perpetual warfare & the necessity for going from home on visitation tours, perhaps for weeks together, without writing a line—but also deprived of the benefit of studying such books as have appeared since I left England except the few which you yourself have so kindly sent or recommended, as well as for the benefit of discussing critical questions, mouth to mouth, with friends who know something about them—Then not having a single individual here, who is in the least degree acquainted with modern Criticism, except one of the clergy in opposition, living 120 miles away, & as selfconceited and opinionated, as he is ignorant... (14 September 1871)

How much I wish that I could run over to Leiden & have a talk with you & Dr Oort on some points on which my views still differ materially from yours as I gather them from Part III of the 'Bible for young persons'... (24 February 1873)

I need hardly say that Criticism has had very little of my attention during the last twelve months. But I should like to discuss with you the question about the age of the Elohistic matter in Genesis. (6 December 1874)[43]

...for I have very little time at my disposal for such work ['preparing my final Vol. Part VII for the Press'], & I don't feel as strong for my work of any kind as in former days, I am beginning (at 63) to look for rest. (26 December 1876)

My Part VII, completing my work on the Pentateuch, is in the Press, & will be published, I hope, during this year. I dare say that other articles or books have been published in Europe, which I ought to have read... But there is no Library here, and it is only through some friend like yourself, or else by mere accident, that I hear of such publications. (21 March 1878)

From 1866 onwards, Colenso's research was concerned primarily with the preparation of Parts VI (1872) and VII (1879) of *The Pentateuch and Joshua*. Initially Part VI was meant to be the concluding volume, but the expanding materials made a seventh volume necessary:

43. The letter was written in London, where Colenso resided, in connection with the so-called Langalibalele affair, through which Colenso became deeply involved in local politics of Natal (see Cox 1888b: 340-448; Rees 1958: 258-324; Guy 1983: Index).

I have, however, completed to my satisfaction the Analysis of *Joshua*, in the same way as I have treated Genesis—& I believe that I have separated clearly the Deut. from the older matter, which appears to me to be entirely Jehovistic—at least none of it Elohistic. (27 November 1866)

I am *printing* (for private purposes) my *last* volume on the Pentateuch, previously to sending it to the press in England. The results of my enquiry— spurred on to it by Graf's book, you recommended me to read, though I glimpsed at the conclusions to which I have now come before I received it—are to my mind most satisfactory—I have no doubt that large parts of the three middle books & Joshua are due to the Later or Levitical Legis- lation *after* the Captivity—& I think that I shall be able to give the 'Original Story' almost in its complete form as it lay before the Deuteronomist. (9 January 1869)

At every spare moment, I have been employed upon my 6th and final volume of the Pentateuch…& I have now nearly completed my work for publication. (20 January 1870)

The fact is that I am just on the point of sending my 6th volume to England for the printer… This is too large for one volume, & I have decided to print half of it first… In the 7th and final volume all the other books. (20 October 1870)

Part VI is published, and about 250 pages of my Part VII, which completes my work, have also been printed in England, having formed part originally of Part VI. In those pages I have come through Judges–2 Kings comparing them with my previous research… (24 December 1871)

I am now (very slowly) preparing my final Vol. Part VII for the Press… (26 December 1876)

My Part VII…is in the Press, & will be published, I hope, during this year. (21 March 1878)

Besides, Colenso was hard at work on a review of the comments on the Pentateuch in *The Speaker's Commentary*.[44] He requested his publisher, Longman & Co, to forward to Kuenen two copies of

a reply which I have written to the long-expected 'Bishops' Commentary on the Pentateuch, which in this pamphlet I have handled so far as regards Bp. Browne's work upon Genesis. I have also completed a similar exami- nation of the Commentary on *Exodus*, which I hope to send to England by the next monthly mail. And by keeping up a dropping fire in this way, at

---

44. *The New Bible Commentary by Bishops and Other Clergy of the Anglican Church Critically Examined*, I-VI (London, 1871–74). Cf. Cox 1888: 266-312; see also Rees 1958: 234, 236, 243-44.

interval of about three months, I am inclined to hope that a good deal may be done to keep alive the attention of the English public to these questions. The Commentary, however, & its friends & opponents, will not be likely to interest much a foreign reader—as it is utterly beneath the attention of any well-informed Biblical Scholar, being merely a feeble repetition of [E.W.] Hengstenberg and [C.F.] Keil,[45] with such information on matters of geography, etc. as may be drawn from any good 'Dictionary of the Bible'. (14 September 1871)

This is the first evening that I have really had a leisure hour in many months past, having been hard at work in demolishing the Speaker's Commentary. I have now finished my work upon it, & sent most of it to England for publication—& Deuteronomy is in a friend's hands for revision... I consider its publication under the circumstances of the time a positive disgrace to the Church of England. I am afraid from what you said in your letter to me that you will speak too greatly of their performances. The best of them are mostly copied, I believe, from Smith's Dictionary of the Bible, which is really a work of some value... But the Commentary...is merely *Keil* done into English... There are, to be sure, Canon [F.C.] Cook's Egyptological researches, which *look* very learned: but I know the writer well...& I have not the least confidence in any of his criticisms. (24 December 1871).

Although Colenso was willing to recognize the imperfection of his labours, he was convinced nonetheless of making an important contribution to the scholarly discussion. Obviously he yearned for recognition in the world of biblical research. He felt like an exile whose work scarcely gained notice, certainly not the notice it deserved:

[A]t any rate, they [my own critical investigations] are not *behind* the march of critical science in the *Church of England*, however much they fall short of the results obtained by the great Dutch & German critics...

After having told that Dr Frederic S. Temple, one of the authors of *Essays and Reviews*, has become Bishop of Exeter, Colenso continues,

But there is no room as yet for *me* in England. I must bide my time, if life lasts...[Colenso does not expect a change in his position] though I should be glad of some quiet nook for old age, where I might pursue my critical studies. (20 January 1870)

In connection with a request to distribute twelve copies of Part VI of the work on the Pentateuch among scholars in Holland and Germany, Colenso remarks:

45. Conservative German Old Testament scholars.

> Of course, they will be already acquainted with the main results maintained in this volume—especially those who have adopted your views as to the late origin of the Levitical Legislation. Still I think it possible that they may find one or two suggestions worthy of consideration, & at any rate the Appendices, which have cost me a good deal of labour, will I hope be of use to spare the same toil to others… (14 September 1871)

Further down in the letter he writes: 'Now I must ask you, in looking at my book…not be appalled & offended by its *size*'. The volume in question having over 800 pages, the remark is followed by an apology with diverse arguments: 'I am obliged to put everything before my readers…' Noting that the book had been edited in England by 'friends, who have done their best, but have left much which might have been omitted, so as to condense & reduce the book in size, if I had been on the spot',[46] Colenso then continues: 'However, having said all this, I still hope that it may be of use to smooth the path for others.'

Colenso mentions the names of several 'foreign professors' before remarking, 'please add such others as you know to be the names of men really interested in these studies—& perhaps your Leiden Bookseller would kindly forward them' (14 September 1871).

Colenso suggests that Kuenen should also distribute the books to other scholars suggesting that it is better that it come to the notice of 'persons who will really appreciate whatever is good or ill in them, than that they would lie idle upon my publisher's shelves. I shall have to pay for them all the same…' Colenso considers it to be 'a chance of being read by worthy readers' (1 April 1872).[47] In a later letter, Colenso continues the lament of a lack of readers:

> Unfortunately, there are few in England who take sufficient interest in these studies to care to read a book of laborious criticism, much less to review it with sufficient care & previous knowledge of the subject. My excellent friend, the Rev G.W. Cox, reviewed Part VI in the Theological Review with the best intentions: but it was quite superficial, & did nothing whatever to point out the real merits or defects of the work… Dr [S.] Davidson also has written two most kindly meant reviews in the Athenaeum and Westminster, in both of which his well known style can easily be detected. But even he deals in generalities—comments or conventions of equal positiveness, but

46. In the letter dated 20 January 1870, Colenso writes: 'I hardly know how I can print it, without coming to England: & if I do so, I shall certainly hope to see you, & renew my acquaintance with my friends at Leyden'.

47. Mrs Colenso, writing to Mrs Lyell on 19 April 1872, states: 'Volume VI will, I fear, be a pecuniary loss'. See Rees 1958: 244; cf. Guy 1983: 160.

without giving any other than subjective reasons for his assertion that the notion of the post-Captivity of the L.L. is not likely to be accepted—& altogether disappoints one's hope for a searching examination of the contents of the book. (24 February 1873)

For a moment Colenso had the idea he would be able to play a significant role in the world of biblical scholarship as the central figure in efforts to write an international scholarly commentary on the Bible. On the very day he returned to Natal he wrote:

> We sail, please God, tomorrow—so that I have very little time to write to you. But an important proposition has just been made to me at the 11th hour, about which I must write to you... A wealthy English gentleman, who has all along stood by my side...has now proposed to bear the whole expense of bringing out a first-rate Edition of the Bible with new translation & Notes and Excursus, bringing up the matter to the level of our present knowledge. He wishes me to return to England as soon as my case is decided—that is, next summer—& take the post of Chief Editor... I need hardly say that the work in question is exactly what I should desire on all accounts—& it seems to me that nothing would so admirably forward the liberal movement both at home & abroad as the carrying out of this measure. Our translation—if we get the just men of Holland, Germany, France, & England to engage in it,[48] might be *the* translation for all Europe & the world... (14 August 1865)

The plan did not prove viable (Rees 1958: 89). During the turbulence in the Church the first year after his return Colenso writes: 'I may perhaps return to Europe. This is what *at present* I see before me' (14 May 1866). In the same letter, and with regard to the commentary project, he remarks 'that it, I suppose, will fall to the ground—at any rate, it must stand over till I return (if ever so) to England'.

After that, the theme of Colenso's returning to England for good is broached only when political reasons make his position untenable—during the Langalibalele affair he writes from London:

> I have completely succeeded, thank God, in the object for which I came to England. But I hardly know what reception I shall be likely to meet with on my return to the Colony, & it is even possible that it may be such as to compel my return to England,—for there is no doubt that I had when I left, and shall probably still have, almost the whole colony against me. (6 December 1874)

---

48. As 'continental labourers' he suggests A. Kuenen, J.H. Scholten, H. Oort, F. Hitzig. As English contributors he mentions, among others, H.B. Wilson.

Clearly, he was convinced that his Old Testament studies in the fields of literary criticism and history of religions had significance for the reformation of theology and of the Church. The terms he used show how he considered these studies as weapons for the battle:

> But as they [Colenso's opponents] *will* keep me longer in England, I shall be able to *fire another barrel of my revolver*—i.e. I have gone to press with Part V. (13 April 1865)

The effect of the proposed commentary (see above) will be

> a death-blow to the old orthodoxy. (14 August 1865)

> I hope to startle them [= those 'who are doing all in their power to assimilate the Church of England to the Church of Rome'] by another discharge from my 'revolver' [= Part VI of *The Pentateuch and Joshua*] before long; but I wish to make good my ground very carefully before publishing. (9 January 1869)

> To return, however, to Part VI, which I may hope may come as a bombshell upon our sleek English dignitaries, who suppose that they have silenced & in fact crushed me... (20 October 1870)

With regard to the publication of the review of *The Speaker's Commentary*, Colenso remarks:

> [it] enables me to load *another revolver* of five barrels, or rather five *mitrailleurs*,—for each of my Parts (upon this Commentary) discharges a whole volley of destructive muscles against the foe... (24 December 1871)

The effectiveness of those weapons, to Colenso's mind, made unanimity of conviction among critical scholars imperative. With regard to the proposed (but ultimately ill-fated commentary), he remarks: '& the consensus of so many authorities would have an overwhelming weight' (14 August 1865). The same sentiment is conveyed in the following:

> & it is, I assure you, a real source of regret to me that I cannot at present wholly adopt your view, not only because I do not like to differ from you, but...for the triumphant sneers of our adversaries at our want of agreement. (14 September 1871)

> And, as it is desirable that at a time, when with many eminent critics of this day the fact of the post-Captivity origin of the Levitical Legislation of the Pentateuch has attained the rank of a positive certainty, there should be as little difference as possible in respect of the details of that Legislation, I should wish to lay before you the points in question & request your consideration of them... (24 February 1873)

I have just published in *Zulu* Genesis with a *Commentary* (after modern ideas) which I imagine will give other missionaries some trouble. But the time is past when ignorant natives should be examined with falsehoods, now known to be such. I have also prepared in manuscript a similar edition of Exodus with Commentary. Of course, I am obliged to adopt for these my own present views as to the authorship of different portions: but I have said that difference of opinion may exist still on these points, but not on the *great* questions, as to the non-Mosaic origin and composite character of the whole Pentateuch, & the Post-Captivity Date of the L.L. (30 March 1877)

6. Concluding Remarks

The contact with Kuenen has been of great importance to Colenso. In the Colenso home his name was mentioned with deep respect (Rees 1958: 200-201, 391). He was one of the few scholars of name[49] to pay serious attention to the bishop's scholarly work.[50] In Leiden he introduced Colenso in 1863 in a circle of like-minded spirits, where a most cordial reception made him feel instantly at home.[51] All his life Colenso would remember it. Many years ago he spoke of it again:

49. H. Hupfeld (1796–1866), too, showed friendship towards Colenso. A letter of his to Colenso is printed in the People's Edition of *The Pentateuch and Joshua* (London, 1871: 283). Colenso made an effort to meet him also: 'I was sorry not to find Prof. Hupfeld at home at Halle: he was out upon his summer tour as I suppose' (14 October 1863). Beside Kuenen, Hupfeld is the only continental scholar mentioned in the letters of Mrs Colenso. After having told that Colenso was informed of the death of Hupfeld 'in a very friendly letter by Prof. Bohmer, Hupfeld's coadjutor', she continues: 'How different is the tone of these great German scholars in speaking of my Husband's work, from that which is affected by some people in England...' (6 September 1866) (see Rees 1958: 120). Colenso also seems to have been in contact with F. Hitzig. On the continent Colenso's work was known to, among others, A. Kayser (see Külling 1964: 62-63), A. Merx (see Thompson 1970: 44), E. Reuss (see Vincent 1990: 261), and J. Wellhausen (see Smend 1991: 168). Colenso is mentioned by Wellhausen in his *Prolegomena zur Geschichte Israels* (1927: 346). The number of scholars in Britain who paid serious attention to Colenso's work also was very small. Mrs Colenso only mentions M.M. Kalisch, characterizing him as 'an enthusiastic admirer of my dear Husband' (January 1885) (see Rees 1958: 389). In his letters to Kuenen, Colenso himself mentions, besides Kalisch (20 January 1870; 6 December 1874), also S. Davidson (20 January 1870; 24 February 1873).
50. Colenso is a frequently cited and discussed author in Part I/1 of the second edition of Kuenen's *Historisch-critisch onderzoek* (Amsterdam, 1885).
51. His letters usually conclude with remarks like 'Please remember me very kindly to my friends at Leiden' (3 February 1865). Very frequent mention is made of the Leiden professors J.H. Scholten and W.A. van Hengel. A few times mention is

Please tell me what has become of that charming young lady, your sister-in-law, who talked English so nicely, & whom I have not by any means forgotten—as indeed I never shall forget the pleasant days—only too short—which I passed under your roof. Is she married & a happy mother? Please remember me very kindly to her... (24 December 1871)

How I should like to look in upon you & yours for an hour of two!... Pray remember me most kindly to Prof. Scholten, and any who may still remember me in Leiden. (26 December 1876)

Kuenen saw to it that Colenso was invited to become a member of the *Maatschappij der Nederlandsche Letterkunde* in Leiden.[52] He opened the window to the world of scholarship for him by sending him publications, or calling attention to them, and by helping him not only with relevant literature, but also with other matters.[53]

To return, in closing, to the beginning of this article. Was it sheer admiration and appreciation which moved Kuenen, when in 1865 he published an elaborate treatment of Colenso's role in the Church of England's struggle? It would appear that Kuenen with his article in *De Gids* had a wider aim than informing the Dutch intellectual community of a small part of contemporary English Church history.[54] Evidently he wanted to make

made of Professor L.W.E. Rauwenhoff. Other Dutchmen he refers to by name are F.C. Donders, R. Dozy, M.J. de Goeje, I. Hooykaas, J.P.N. Land, H. Oort, A. Pierson and A. Réville.

52. See the letters dated 9 January 1869, 20 January 1870 and 14 September 1871.

53. After being fleeced of a large sum of money by a Dutch immigrant, Colenso tries to get back the money by asking Kuenen to approach the immigrant's father at Leiden (26 December 1876; 30 March 1877). To the Colensiana in the Leiden University Library also belong three letters of Miss Harriette Colenso (see above, n. 32), dated 7 and 16 November 1886, and 15 February 1887. She informs Kuenen about the political situation in Natal and asks him to draw the attention of the Dutch public to the real situation and the injustice which is done. The letters are accompanied by a number of relevant annexes such as 'Statement of Melakanya made to Miss Colenso, 13 January 1885' (with regard to the death of Cetshwayo), and 'The Zulu Message to the Queen', dated 11 November 1886. On Colenso's relationship with Zulu king Cetshwayo, see Rees 1958: 325-75; Guy 1983: Index.

54. Church affairs in England had Kuenen's lasting attention. He had a close relationship with several representatives of Modernism. In the column 'Foreign Countries' of *De Hervorming: Orgaan van den Nederlandschen Protestantenbond*, Kuenen reported on events in England and Schotland for many years. On these countries he published 84 contributions in the period 1876 to 1885. In 14 of these Colenso is mentioned: seven times in 1879 (22 February, 22 March, 19 April, 24 May, 20 September, 22 November, 25 December), three times in 1880 (24 January, 21 Feb-

clear to his compatriots, through that exposition, that it was not orthodoxy (as the orthodox claimed) but Modernism that was the true heir of the Reformation. 'And still there are those who refuse to admit that the orthodoxy of today is different from that of yesterday and the day before!', he complains (Kuenen 1865: 27). Without a doubt he was thinking of his fellow Dutchmen here. To make a long story short, the 1865 article was a weapon in the struggle of Dutch schools of thought. The story of Colenso's conduct was more than a sketch of the deportment of a brave man: it was to serve as an example. In bringing to light Colenso's passion to reveal the truth, Kuenen revealed what he himself pursued. For him Colenso was a comrade in arms.

ruary, 27 March), twice in 1881 (30 July, 26 November), twice in 1883 (30 June, 28 July).

COLENSO'S *COMMENTARY ON ROMANS*: AN EXEGETICAL ASSESSMENT[*]

Jonathan A. Draper

1. *Theoretical Presuppositions*

The nineteenth-century Christian missionaries, who took their gospel to the world newly opened up by colonial conquest, left home with a social universe that appeared self-evident, secure and superior to the indigenous cultures and beliefs of the colonized peoples. Inevitably, however, their role as agents of the dominant culture, situated at its boundaries, also placed this taken-for-granted social universe side by side with rival social universes of meaning that destabilized and challenged their own. Berger and Luckmann (1966: 109) rightly observe that 'The historical outcome of each clash of gods was determined by those who wielded the better weapons rather than those who had the better arguments'. The missionaries used to their own advantage both the opportunities provided by colonial administration, indeed they often aided and abetted and legitimated the process of colonization, and also the desire of African people for trade in European goods. Yet the African people were not mere passive victims of European aggression, but purposive participants in events. Their relationship with both the missionaries and the colonialists consisted from the first of both resistance and negotiation. Because the outcome of such a confrontation of competing social universes is not known at the outset, the African people saw not only threats but also opportunities in their contacts with the white missionaries. The missionaries were only ever partially in

---

[*]   This paper brings together work on Colenso undertaken over a number of years. The first section of the paper is taken in part and modified from my article, 'The Bishop and the Bricoleur: Bishop John William Colenso's *Commentary on Romans* and Magema Kamagwa Fuze's *The Black People and Whence they Came*', in G.O. West and M. Dube (eds.), *The Bible in Africa* (Leiden: E.J. Brill, 2000), pp. 415-54. The second part of the paper draws heavily on my Introduction to the reprinted edition of Colenso's *Commentary on Romans* (2002). A draft form of the whole paper was published in the *SBL 2000 Seminar Papers*.

control of the process of evangelization, whatever they themselves imagined.

In other words, the history of the missions and of the reception of the Bible must be seen as a dialectical process, an unequal one in many respects to be sure, but nevertheless a more intricate, contested and mutual process than has usually been recognized. This has been aptly characterized by Jean and John Comaroff in their study of the mission among the Tswana people as a 'long conversation' in which 'many of the signifiers of the colonizing culture became unfixed', so that:

> They were seized by the Africans and, sometimes refashioned, put to symbolic and practical ends previously unforeseen, certainly unintended. Conversely, some of the ways of the Africans interpolated themselves, again detached and transformed, into the habitus of the missionaries. Here, then, was a process in which signifiers were set afloat, fought over, and recaptured on both sides of the colonial encounter. (Comaroff and Comaroff 1991: 17-18)

European military power and technology certainly ensured that the missionaries could insert their agenda into the conversation and be heard. However, from the very beginning, their converts talked back and did not always agree. They experimented with the numinous sources of power they imagined (rightly or wrongly) to lie behind European might, in the attempt to control and use them for their own purposes. They did not always understand what they were doing, nor, for that matter, did the missionaries, but the path of the missions was not the smooth and triumphal one so often portrayed in the missionary reports home. Since, however, the records were written by the conquerors, with apologetic intent, they often have to be 'read backwards' to hear the other side of the 'conversation'.

Of course, the ability to hold a conversation depends in part on the ability to speak a common language. Berger and Luckmann (1966: 39) have pointed to language as the vehicle of the 'objectification' of social universe: language is the medium through which my experiences become 'both objectively and subjectively real'. In the confrontation of the European and African social universes, language played an especially intricate and central role. Many missionaries spoke and listened only through interpreters, so that they were not really engaged in a conversation in any deeply meaningful sense. Nevertheless, they still wrestled with the language of symbols, names, words and gestures and, inasmuch as they were fully dependent on the interpreters, they were also more easily manipulated by these cultural intermediaries for their own purposes. Knowledge of the

language of the conquerors not only subverted the culture of the indigenous Africans but also enabled them to begin subverting the work of the
missionaries in the interests of cultural survival (whether they were conscious of doing so or not). On the other hand, those missionaries who did
undertake the arduous task of learning another language faced a more
massive challenge to their own reality, since one cannot learn a language
without learning a culture. Fluency in another language and culture rela-
tivizes and destabilizes one's own, but also enables one's thinking to be
intimately understood by one's interlocutors. This was especially true for
those like Bishop Colenso, in situations where there were no dictionaries,
grammars or translations of the Bible, and even what the name God should
be called was a matter of grave dispute.

Jean and John Comaroff (1991: 24) develop a particularly helpful model
of the relationship between hegemony as the power of the taken-for-
granted worldview which is shared by particular communities and controls
human behavior unseen, and ideology as the conscious and contested
'effort to control the cultural terms in which the world is ordered and,
within it, power legitimized'. The relationship between hegemony and
ideology is fluid, unstable and constantly shifting:

> Hegemony, we suggest, exists in reciprocal interdependence with ideology:
> it is that part of a dominant world view which has been naturalized and,
> having hidden itself in orthodoxy, no more appears as ideology at all. In-
> versely, the ideologies of the subordinate may give expression to discordant
> but hitherto voiceless experience of contradictions that a prevailing hegem-
> ony can no longer conceal. (p. 25)

Most significantly, for our purposes, the Comaroffs argue that there is
always a gap between hegemony and ideology, a liminal space, out of
which forms of resistance and new consciousness may emerge:

> Between the conscious and the unconscious lies the most critical domain of
> all for historical anthropology and especially for the analysis of colonialism
> and resistance. It is the realm of partial recognition, of inchoate awareness,
> of ambiguous perception, and, sometimes, of creative tension: that liminal
> space of human experience in which people discern acts and facts but
> cannot or do not order them into narrative descriptions or even into articu-
> late conceptions of the world; in which signs and events are observed, but
> in a hazy, translucent light; in which individuals or groups know that some-
> thing is happening to them but find it difficult to put their fingers on quite
> what it is. It is from this realm, we suggest, that silent signifiers and un-
> marked practices may rise to the level of explicit consciousness, of ideo-

logical assertion, and become the subject of overt political and social contestation or from which they may recede into the hegemonic, to languish there unremarked for the time being. As we shall see, it is also the realm from which emanate the poetics of history, the innovative impulses of the *bricoleur* and the organic intellectual, the novel imagery called upon to bear the content of symbolic struggles. (1991: 29)

Colonial conquest plunged the African social universe into crisis, since neither 'therapy' nor 'nihilation' (Berger and Luckmann 1966: 105-16) could hold it together in the face of European power and the growing number of 'deviants' from the African social system (the converts to Christianity). But the crisis was not one-sided, since the missionaries themselves also came from an England in acute intellectual and social crisis, arising out of the related phenomena of the Enlightenment and industrial capitalism, so that the (contested) area of ideology was proportionately large in comparison with the (silent and uncontested) area of hegemony. The Comaroffs argue (1991: 77-78), indeed, that the missionary enterprise was in some respects an attempt to resolve cognitive dissonance in Nonconformist Britain by the creation of a new world in their image in the 'blank spaces' of Africa. The collision of their European culture with African culture thus provided a rich liminal space for potential exploration (1991: 49-85). It was both social universes which were destabilized by the colonial encounter, and not just the African one, and this study of Colenso's work bears out their contention that 'the missionary encounter must be regarded as a two-sided historical process; as a dialectic that takes into account the social and cultural endowments of, and the consequences for, all the actors: missionaries no less than Africans' (1991: 54).

In this contestation, both parties became *bricoleurs*, in their own ways, sorting through the debris of the two collapsing social universes for usable odds and ends of culture. Of course it is more obvious in the case of the African converts, since their predicament was the more severe, but it was true also for the missionaries as well, since they constantly found that things did not work as they should and their received ideas were challenged. Both parties engaged in the work of cultural *bricolage*, as this has been aptly defined (and positively evaluated) by Marilyn Legge (1997: 6) in her attempt to address the crisis of the Christian faith in the post-modern era as 'the art of using what is at hand, odd materials for purposes other than intended, to create something useful and distinct to meet a yearning or need. This is an accessible practice often found where people aim to survive against the odds.'

For Colenso, crucial areas of British hegemony (what is 'self-evidently true') were breaking down under the impact of the African experience, and this in the situation where important gaps in the ideology of post-Enlightenment, industrial Britain were emerging among the educated elite he represented. His *St. Paul's Epistle to the Romans: Newly Translated and Explained from a Missionary Point of View* (hereafter called, peri-phrastically, *Commentary on Romans*), published in 1861, is a valuable source of insight into the hermeneutical and cultural issues that came into play in this meeting of Africa and Europe, particularly since the nature and authority of the Bible was one of the focal points of conflict. The Comaroffs suggest that both the missionaries and the colonized Africans should be understood as actors in a two-sided drama, and that the context of both parties should be explored before any attempt is made to delineate their interaction. This is the procedure we shall follow here, albeit briefly.

The Nonconformist missionaries of the Comaroffs' study were largely drawn from upwardly mobile men from the newly industrialized areas, as well as poorly educated and socially marginalized: 'persons caught between the rich and the poor, either indeterminate in their class affiliation or struggling hard to make their way over the invisible boundary into the bourgeoisie' (1991: 85). They enacted their marginalization in the mission field by moving beyond the boundaries of colonial administration. They were subsequently caught between and manipulated by both the colonial authorities and the African authorities. Their response to the Tswana people was pragmatic, reactive and unreflective, assuming that simply proclaiming the Word found in the Bible and teaching cleanliness and industry would evangelize the natives. Their assumption was that African languages were simple 'folk languages' not difficult for advanced (Euro-pean) people to grasp and utilize, so that their translations were 'a hybrid creation born of the colonial encounter itself' (1991: 218). Colenso pre-sents a profile with marked differences.

2. Bishop John William Colenso (1814–83)

In 1853 John William Colenso was consecrated as the first missionary Bishop of Natal, the raw, insecure and unsettled British colony in Africa carved out by traders and adventurers from the newly emerged Zulu King-dom and the Dutch trekkers who had moved up from the Cape seeking land. Born a lower middle class Nonconformist, he had converted to the established Church of England and worked his way through St John's

College, Cambridge as Clerical Sizar. A brilliant mathematician, he became a fellow of the college before he met and married Francis Sarah Bunyon in 1842, a step which changed the direction of his life. Francis and her family were part of a circle of freethinking Broad Church people, centred around F.D. Maurice (1805–72). She herself had initiated the contact with Maurice because of her admiration for the philosophy of Samuel Taylor Coleridge (1772–1834), writing to him to thank him for his defence of Coleridge since 'young ladies talking about philosophy…would not be listened to' (Rees 1958: 27). The Romantic poet, political radical and philosopher, Coleridge, late in his life, adopted Christianity and sought a renewal of the life of the Church of England centred on religious experience and ethics. He argued for the existence of a universal harmony underlying all particulars, rooted in a God apprehended by all humankind experientially through natural phenomena, 'who from all eternity doth teach Himself in all, and all things in Himself' ('Frost at Midnight' in *Lyrical Ballads*). Francis's letters (collected in Rees 1958) show that she was a powerful presence in Colenso's life, thinking and work. She introduced him to a group of Anglicans deeply concerned over the future of a Church that had not even begun to face the challenge of the revolutionary Enlightenment sweeping Continental Europe.

Colenso was deeply influenced by Maurice's Christian universalism and rejection of eternal damnation, and also by his brand of Christian socialism, although, when the storm burst over Colenso's *Commentary on Romans*, Maurice disowned him and called on him to retract the book. Colenso was also convinced of the truth and importance of the evolutionism of Charles Darwin and Sir Charles Lyell, and, indeed, translated and taught their theories to his converts in the mission school at Ekukhanyeni ('Place of Enlightenment') in his *First Lessons in Science* (1861), at the same time as he translated and taught the Bible. The *Commentary on Romans* was also published in 1861 at Ekukhanyeni, seven years after his arrival in Natal. It resulted in his excommunication in 1863 for heresy by the Metropolitan of the Anglican Church in Southern Africa, Bishop Gray of Cape Town, which set off a storm of legal and theological controversy that rocked the entire Church of England establishment (for a good account, see Guy 1983). Few of the accounts of these events have taken the *Commentary on Romans* itself seriously as a work of exegesis.

Timothy Larsen (forthcoming) has argued recently that Colenso should be understood primarily within the context of the Broad Church party in England. The African context falls away altogether. Yet it is, in my opinion, precisely the tension inherent in his role as an intelligent and sensitive European conversation partner with Zulu people that drives Colenso to break ranks with the 'civilized caution' usually maintained by English liberal churchmen. Bishop Colenso's *Commentary on Romans* begins with an extraordinary, but concealed contradiction between his role as missionary (who identified himself with his Zulu community) and his role as bishop (a peer and an official of empire), which was not clear to him or others at the time, though it was to become painfully so later.

2.1. *The Missionary*
Thus, on the one hand, Colenso subtitled the work, *Newly Translated and Explained from a Missionary Point of View* and stated in his Preface that

> The teaching of the great Apostle to the Gentiles is here applied to some questions, which daily arise, in Missionary labours among the heathen more directly than usual with those commentators, who have not been engaged personally in such work, but have written from a very different point of view, in the midst of a state of advanced civilization and settled Christianity. Hence they have usually passed by altogether, or only touched very lightly upon, many points, which are of great importance to missionaries, but which seemed to be of no immediate practical interest for themselves or their readers.

Colenso spent the first seven years of his episcopate learning Zulu through endless conversations with the young men at his school, who were his first converts, and busied himself with producing and publishing on his mission press a Zulu *Grammar*, *Dictionary* and *Translation* of the Bible. On 4 July 1959, two years before the publication of the *Commentary on Romans*, Colenso wrote to Reverend Hose, Rector of Dunstable:

> My rule is to visit the white population, once a year. But my time is principally occupied with work for the heathen. This is at present, I fancy, the only diocese where the work of preparing grammars, dictionaries, and translations must necessarily fall upon the Bishop. Our work began here with the foundation of the See; and though other Christian bodies, as usual, preceded us into the field, they had done very little indeed towards laying down the language for other teachers, or preparing books for the use of the natives. (Cox 1888: 119)

Colenso positioned himself alongside Zulu people in his daily life at the Mission Station, which began when he arrived and continued for the seven years prior to the publication of the work (and subsequently, of course). Remarkably, following the model of 'conversation' I am proposing here,

Colenso also 'gives voice' to his converts in print. When he went on a pioneering visit beyond the borders of the colony to meet the Zulu King Mpande and his heir Cetshwayo, Colenso required his three Zulu companions to keep diaries of their experience and he published these, in the first indigenous literature in Zulu—*Three Native Accounts of the Visit of the Bishop of Natal in September and October, 1859, to Umpande, King of the Zulus; with Explanatory Notes and a Literal Translation, and a Glossary of All the Zulu Words Employed in the Same: Designed for the Use of Students of the Zulu Language*—in 1860. One of the three, Magema KwaMagwaza Fuze subsequently wrote the first book by a Zulu person in the Zulu tongue, *Abantu Abamnyama, Lapa Bavela Ngakona* (*The Black People and Whence They Came*), which he only succeeded in getting published in 1922 as a very old man.

Colenso spent extensive periods talking, in Zulu, to these young men. 'You probably know by this time the sort of questions which natives, such as these, if they are only allowed to think about religion, and to inquire about the matters which the missionary sets before them, are likely to ask their teacher' (Colenso 1865[?]d, reprinted in 1982: 227). When Colenso defended the principle of missionary work against the evolutionism of the anthropologists in a speech to the Marylebone Literary Institution in 1865, he spoke poignantly of his conversations with William Ngidi, who called for more sympathetic and open talk between missionaries and Zulu people, commenting: 'I am afraid William meant to include in this talk hearing and answering their questions also' (p. 228). In the same talk, he cited a sermon preached by Jonathan Ngidi, who emphasized, as Colenso did, the importance of conscience and natural religion. Colenso refused to conceal the problems with the Bible which he brought with him from his Broad Church circle in England, arguing: 'How is it possible to teach the Zulus to cast off their superstitious belief in witchcraft, if they are required to believe that all the stories of sorcery and demonology which they find in the Bible...are infallibly and divinely true... I, for one, cannot do this' (p. 232). In other words, the Zulu people at Ekukhanyeni were Colenso's primary dialogue partners and reference points.

2.2. *The Official of Empire*
On the other hand, Colenso dedicated the work to Theophilus Shepstone, the Secretary for Native Affairs in the Colony of Natal, and talked of the great work to which he felt God was calling Shepstone (that of extending British rule into the independent Zulu kingdom). Shepstone was at the

centre of an aggressive expansionist colonial policy in Natal, and something of a wheeler-dealer in the drama being played out between the Dutch trekkers, the Zulu kingdom and the Colony of Natal. Colenso was indebted to Shepstone for his first information and advice on his mission, and trusted him. For Colenso, as colonial missionary bishop to the Zulu people, it was a natural alliance between social equals. Shepstone became godfather to his daughter. Yet Shepstone's devious dealings with the Zulu people led to a bitter feud between him and Colenso, when the bishop discovered what was going on from his converts. Shepstone's comment on the affair was that 'he did not think the Bishop would have thrown over his old friends for the sake of a *dirty* Kafir' (Rees 1958: 371). Most of Colenso's life in Natal, after the publication of his Romans commentary, was spent in active resistance to colonialist aggression against the Zulu people, both in the Natal law courts and in the British parliament. In the end, this defence of the Zulu people completely overtook 'conventional missionary work', but opened up a more profound missionary 'conversation' that bore fruit in political struggle continued by his wife and family even after his death.

It seems that in 1861, when Colenso published *Commentary on Romans*, there was an inherent social ambiguity in his position and thinking. He was both the agent of empire and the Christian missionary and philanthropist. He did not yet see the contradictions inherent in the two positions. Ironically, it was precisely his exegesis and interpretation of Paul in the Romans commentary that plunged him into a crisis that resolved the ambiguity at one level, but opened it up at another level. It led to his isolation from his own class and an ever-increasing identification with Zulu resistance to colonial domination, but forced him to adopt an Erastian position, asserting the supremacy of the state over the Church in law, in order to retain his bishopric over against a Church which declared him a heretic.

The fact that Colenso was working on the translation of the Bible into Zulu at the same time as he was working on his *Commentary on Romans* was significant. While he provided a translation into English from the Greek, I will examine his translation into Zulu from the Greek alongside it, since it is, in many ways, more interesting and rich in significance. The need to find dynamic equivalents to Greek words, where none were fixed by tradition (as in English), destabilized the text, and opened up new semantic possibilities and questions.

3. *The Colonial Context*

Colenso is best known as an Old Testament scholar, in which field he dialogued with Dutch scholars, translated their works and was influential in the evolution of Pentateuchal studies. Why then was his first biblical work a *Commentary on Romans*? It seems clear that it was partly a result of questions raised by the thinking of Maurice, long before he set sail for Natal, since he described it as 'the results of seven years of Missionary experience, as well as of previous close study of this Epistle' ([1861i: i] 2003: xliii).[1] He also considered his *Commentary on Romans* and his *Commentary on the Pentateuch* to be a contribution to the rethinking the church in England would have to do, when the impact of the Enlightenment was brought home: 'I fully believe that a terrible crisis is at hand for the Church of England and have tried to do my part to help some to stand firmly, when many props upon which they have been hitherto relying shall be felt to give way under them' (a letter to Mr Allnutt, 2 August 1861, enclosing a copy of the *Commentary on Romans*; Cox 1888: 126).

On the other hand, a commentary on Romans became urgent for Colenso because of the conditions he found in Natal, where the existing missions were emphasizing fear of hell as a motive for conversion and were pushing the penal theory of the atonement as the basis for their Christology. He wrote to Reverend Ferguson on 9 August 1859, saying:

> The great drawback here is that the country is already saturated with a corruption of Christianity, and the natives have acquired such a view of the character of God and of the Gospel as keeps them back from desiring to have a much closer acquaintance with it. This they have obtained partly from the example they have constantly before them in the lives of the unfaithful Christians, partly from the mistaken teaching of the missionaries. 'God said, Let them be destroyed: the Son rose up and said, Let them be saved, let me die in their place'. (Cox 1888: 119-20)

Such a viewpoint was 'little short of blasphemy', 'utterly contrary to the whole spirit of the Gospel' and 'operating with most injurious and deadening effect, both on those who teach, and on those who are taught' for Colenso ([*p. 198*] pp. 201-202):

---

1. Because of its controversial nature, Colenso's *Commentary on Romans* went out of print almost as soon as it was published in 1861. In 2003, I edited and republished Colenso's work in an edition that includes the original page numbering in italics within square brackets. In this paper I will follow the same convention, while including the page references for the new edition after these bracketed references.

Such questions as these have been brought again and again before my mind in the intimate converse which I have had, as a Missionary, with Christian converts and Heathens. To teach the truths of our holy religion to intelligent adult natives, who have the simplicity of children, but withal the earnestness and thoughtfulness of men, to whom these things are new and startling, whose minds are not prepared by long familiarity to acquiesce in, if not to receive, them, is a sifting process for the opinions of any teacher, who feels the deep moral obligation of answering truly, and faithfully, and unreservedly, his fellow-man, looking up to him for light and guidance, and asking, 'Are you sure of this?' 'Do you believe this?' 'Do you really believe that?' The state of everlasting torment after death, of all impenitent sinners and unbelievers, including the whole heathen world, as many teach, is naturally so amazing and overwhelming an object of contemplation to them, and one so prominently put forward in the case of those, who have been under certain Missionary training, that it quite shuts out the cardinal doctrines of the Gospel, the Fatherly relation to us of the Faithful Creator.

Central to the problem, in Colenso's mind, was the particular, exclusivist interpretation and emphasis given to *sola fide* by Protestant missionaries in Natal. Central to their understanding was a view of all human beings as fallen sinners and God's wrath waiting to punish all sin with death. Christ came, then, to die in our stead and take the punishment which rightly belongs to us. The only way for a human being to avoid damnation and eternal hellfire was to make an act of faith and be baptized into Christ's death. The rest of humanity was a *massa damnata*. The Christian mission was understood by them in terms of individual faith, conversion and baptism, which must separate the Zulu converts from their community, their culture and their ancestors. The arbitrariness and injustice of such a conception outraged Colenso ([*p. 190*] p. 194):

This dogma makes no distinction between the profligate sensualist and the ill-trained child. And it is often so stated as to involve the multitudes of ignorant, untaught, heathen, the great mass of humankind, in the same horrible doom of never-ending despair, making this beautiful and blessed world the very shambles, as it were, of Almighty Vengeance.

For Colenso, who spent his time talking with his Zulu people, this posed a massive problem. Zulu culture emphasized the continuity of the living and the dead in unbroken community. The ancestors were honoured and constantly made present to the living, and provided the cultural coherence and ethical underpinning of the Zulu social universe. If the broad mass of unbaptized Zulu people, living and dead, were consigned to hellfire by the Christian religion for failing to make a public act of faith, how could a

Zulu person conscientiously accept Christianity? Against this Colenso asserted his own understanding of the *sola fide* as simple, joyful acceptance of what God has already done in Christ, which does not require any act on the part of human beings to be efficacious, and he argued that this is the correct understanding of Paul's teaching in Romans.

In addition, Colenso noted that the colonists found in their Christian faith and baptism a ground, namely their 'election' as Christians, for feelings of superiority over the Zulu people. Their interpretation of the Bible provided them with legitimation for their seizure of the land from the Zulu, whom they believed to be depraved, primitive and childlike. Doctrines of evolution and election went hand in hand in the popular mythology of colonialism.

It is for these reasons that Colenso undertook to write a commentary on Romans, which had provided the traditional Scriptural underpinning for the *sola fide* in Protestant thinking since Luther. He was convinced that a proper study of the text would show that Paul taught no such thing, but rather supported his own universalist theological position.

4. *Colenso's Reading of Romans*

Colenso's interpretation hinged, to some extent, on his view of the letter as written to Jews and not to Christians. He argued at length that there was no Christian Church in Rome at the time Paul was writing, but only Jews and proselytes still attached to the synagogue, who had come to some elementary form of belief in Jesus as Messiah, perhaps from having heard the disciples preach in Jerusalem at the first Pentecost. This is why Paul felt free to go to Rome, since he was not 'building on anyone else's foundation'. These Jewish incipient believers ('a "sect" of the Jews') were characterized by what Colenso ([*p. 9*] p. 29) termed 'the three great prepossessing errors of the Jewish mind': namely, that they thought they had a special status before God; consequently, that they had a special claim on the Messiah over against the Gentiles; and thus, that those Gentiles who believed must keep the law if they were to be regarded as equal to Jews. Paul knew the situation from his discussions with Priscilla and Aquila in Ephesus, who had now returned to Rome with Paul's teaching concerning salvation for all humankind without works of law. Paul was concerned to share the gospel with them clearly before he came himself to Rome on his way to Spain. In reply to the Jewish reliance on election and pride of race, Paul was determined to show in his letter that salvation is pure gift of God, that it was meant for both Jews and Gentiles 'without any special favour or distinction' ([*p. 9*] p. 29), and that it was received by faith alone without law and ceremony.

At this point, with our post-holocaust sensitivity, we would rightly detect here an essentialism with regard to the Jewish people on Colenso's part. Yet his purpose was the opposite of anti-Semitism in his own context. He wished to show that the English Christian settlers had no grounds of racial pride over against the Zulu, and made the same point vis-à-vis modern Jews, namely that Christians have no basis for racial pride over against the Jews. On the contrary, their cruelty and bigotry towards the Jews has made it impossible for Jews to believe in the Christian religion:

> But, as for the Jews of the present day, we cannot presume to say that they too have been 'given over to a reprobate mind', or that their eyes are darkened as a penal consequence of their continuing in unbelief. It may be so in certain individual cases, where light has reached the inner man, and been rejected. But, probably, in our days, amidst the great body of the Jewish people, such cases are very rare. It is far more likely that the acts of abominable cruelty, injustice, and contemptuous bigotry, with which, in Christian lands and by Christian people—too often, alas! by Christian ministers—they have been so frequently, and are even now, treated, have gone far to fix them in holy and righteous horror of a religion, which taught that such outrages were right. All, surely, that an humble-minded Christian can allow himself to say of the present state of the Jews generally is that they are not actually incurring great moral *guilt* (he cannot judge of that,) but suffering great moral and spiritual loss from the acts of their forefathers. ([*p. 33*] p. 29)

Colenso's point was that no human being can base feelings of racial superiority against another on the basis of their Christian faith. On the contrary, the gospel meant that all human beings now stand equal before God in 'Christ their Head'. He was about to argue that the English colonialists were 'the Jews' of his day, while the Zulu and the modern Jews were in the position of 'the Gentiles' in Paul's argument. Everything Paul said about 'the Jewish' reliance on their race and culture as giving them a privileged position before God, applied in the context of colonial Natal to the colonialists. This was a radical and powerful exegetical move in the colonial context. In our context, we would, of course, question the inherently negative symbolic content given to the notion of 'the Jew', even with Colenso's liberatory intention, as tending to confirm negative essentialist categories. Nevertheless, the rhetorical force of Colenso's interpretation remains an effective corrective to ethnocentrisms of every kind.

Like many interpreters of Romans, Colenso believed that the essence of Paul's argument was introduced in 1.16-17, but that he held back from drawing the full implications of his teaching at this point, delaying until 3.21-22. Colenso argued that 1.18–3.20 is rhetorical in nature, intended to lull the Jewish reader into agreement and prepare her/him to accept the proposition that God's righteousness is sheer gift to all without distinction of race. Hence, Colenso read the two passages together. We will come back to this later.

He translated 1.16-17 as follows, 'For I am not ashamed of the Gospel of Christ; for the power of God it is unto salvation to everyone that believeth, both to the Jew first and Greek. For the righteousness of God is being revealed in it, (a righteousness) from faith unto faith, as it is written, "The righteous shall live out of faith"'.

The first point to note is that Colenso interpreted 'the righteousness of God' to refer not to the nature of God, nor to any act by which human beings make themselves righteous before God, not even the act of faith, but to the gift of righteousness which God gives to humans in his Son:

> Let this be distinctly noted that, throughout this Epistle, the righteousness of God, or God's righteousness, means God's gift of righteousness, not God's own personal inherent righteousness or justice, not *God's way of justifying sinners*, of making them righteous, of giving them righteousness, (which is by giving it to them in His Son), but the very righteousness itself which God gives to men, so that by his free gift they stand before Him accepted and beloved, God's righteousness, in short, opposed to *Man's* righteousness, to that which a man may fancy he can claim or work out for himself. ([*p. 12*] pp. 32-33)

In his Zulu translation of Romans, Colenso was able to capture this understanding with the passive verbal form, *ukulungiswa okungoNkulunkulu* ('the being made right which is from God'). God had simply provided a righteousness to the whole human race in Christ, whether they knew it and accepted it by an act of faith on their part or not ([*p. 14*] p. 34). All of us, Christians, Jews, heathen, were dealt with by Creator God as righteous creatures, not only now, but 'from all eternity'. This was the reason for the universality of human religious experience, which impels people to live moral lives:

> The tokens of God's favour have been shed abroad on the human race from the first. He 'gave them rain from heaven, and fruitful seasons, filling their hearts with food and gladness'. He wrought by His Spirit on theirs, teaching men everywhere to 'feel after Him, if haply they may find Him, in whom

they lived and moved and had their being, who was not far from any one of
them'. But now in the Gospel is being revealed the secret of all this. (*[p. 14]*
p. 34)

This understanding underlay Colenso's translation of the Greek present
passive as a continuous tense: 'is being revealed', which in his Zulu
translation became *kuhlalukiswa* ('is being made to come to light'). This
was an ongoing process of enlightenment at work in every human heart
through the conscience, since 'the tokens of God's favour have been shed
abroad on the human race from the first' in nature (*[p. 14]* p. 34). This was
an important component of his understanding of Romans. Just as salvation
is being revealed from day to day in the life of every human being, so
judgment or 'wrath' *is being revealed* every day in the life of every human
being: 'It is being daily, hourly, constantly, revealed, by the dealings of
God with men; and especially by the secret witnessings of our own hearts.
All men everywhere know in themselves that there is a Divine displeasure
threatening those, who *do what they know to be wrong*, who "keep back",
hold down, restrain, suppress, "the truth through or in iniquity"' (*[p. 21]*
p. 40). However, it was God's salvation which had the last word:

> Thanks be unto God! one Love embraces all. Already side by side with this
> revelation of God's wrath for wilful sin in the heart of man, there is a
> revelation of His Mercy—a secret sense that there is forgiveness with our
> Father in Heaven, in some way or other, possible or actual. (*[p. 21]* p. 40)

In their religious experience and practice, all humankind had always
experienced the presence of God dimly through nature. All human beings
were conscious of sin and guilt but also had a sense that forgiveness was
possible and felt innately that they were children of a merciful God. For
the Christian, wrote Colenso, we find the 'secret' of this universal human
experience of God in the gospel:

> For therein is revealed, the righteousness which God gives us, which He
> gives to all, the evil and the good, the just and the unjust alike, that we may
> be regarded as children before Him, undutiful and disobedient children,
> it may be, self-willed and prodigal, but children still, and to be dealt with
> as children, even when He visits us with His displeasure, children who
> have been called to inherit a blessing, and are not lying under a curse.
> (*[pp. 21-22]* p. 41)

Colenso did not allow the interpretation of 'from faith to faith' to mean
the sanctification of the elect in 1.17, but drew a convoluted parallel with
3.21-22:

But now, apart from law, [of which he had been speaking in the digression] the righteousness of God has been manifested, (though being witnessed of by the law and the prophets,) but *the righteousness of God through faith in Jesus Christ*, (= from faith), *unto all* and upon all *them that believe* (= unto faith).

His Zulu translation made Colenso's underlying understanding clear, particularly his choice of the word to express *pistis*, namely, *temba* (in modern Zulu orthography, *themba*), which expressed confidence, hope, trust, while he explicitly rejected the alternative favored by the American Board Mission, *kolwa* (in modern Zulu orthography *kholwa*), whose root meaning was 'to be satisfied, have enough of a thing, to be satisfied with the evidence of a thing', commenting in his *Dictionary* (p. 234), 'N.B. The word *kolwa* only expresses *belief* in the sense of *assent*, not of *trust* or *affiance*, for which *temba* must be employed. Hence it is a very improper word to be used generally, for the faith of a Christian.' In confirmation of his observation, that *kholwa* retains its root meaning of being satisfied, I can point to a Zulu saying still current, despite the 'holy' use of the term *amakholwa*—namely, *sibhema sekholwa*, which is said in appreciation at the end of a good party and which means, literally, 'we have smoked and we are satisfied!' The word *kholwa*, however, won out and is the commonly used word for a believer in Zulu today, as in the Bible Society version of the Bible. Colenso was undoubtedly right in his observations, and the use of *ukukholwa* ironically undermined the *sola fide* understanding of its missionary proponents. Colenso was concerned to maximize the nature of justification as objective, universal gift and human response as a simple trusting reliance on the Creator God.

This understanding of 'faith' as simple trusting hope, rather than as an act of conversion, was important, since it connected with the universalist position Colenso went on to adopt. It was inherently possible for heathens to have this kind of faith, to trust in a God experienced through nature and served by obedience to the promptings of conscience, since there was 'a faith in the Living Word, which spoke within them' and 'a living obedience to the law of truth and love, which they found written upon their hearts by the finger of God' (pp. 63-64).

'The righteous shall live out of faith' is cited from Habakkuk as a prelude to the rhetorical exercise that follows, to reassure the Jewish listeners and to arouse 'the sense of *their* needing (as well as the "sinners of the Gentiles") the "righteousness of God" which is "revealed in the Gospel"' ([*p. 17*] p. 36). The implications were drawn only in 3.21-26, where the righteousness of God (understood as God's gift of putting us right freely given) was extended 'unto all and upon all that believe' apart from the law and prophets. In other words, there was no special status before God for the Jew over the Gentile and by extension for the colonial Christians over the heathen Zulu people. This gift of righteousness in Christ was *being made* real in every human being all the time from the beginning, 'the Greek Present, implying their continuing state of righteousness' ([*p. 62*] p. 78). As we have already seen, Colenso understood 'belief' in a broad sense of the positive response of any human being, Christian, Jew or heathen, to the spiritual promptings of God as they knew and experienced God's love. Thus, 3.21-26 already, in his opinion, extended justification to the whole human race, though he conceded that Paul *might* in this case be referring to believers only ([*p. 63*] p. 78). After all, he argued, while Paul might be ambiguous about how far the 'all' extends in 3.23, in 5.15-19 Paul *must* refer to all humankind, 'So then, just as through one fault, *it* [death] *passed* unto all men, unto condemnation, so also, through one righteous act, *it* [the gift of righteousness] *passed* unto all men, unto justification of life' (Colenso's translation, [*p. 99*] p. 111). 'Let the words of this verse be well noted', wrote Colenso, 'By Christ's one act of loving obedience, the free gift of God has come upon *all* men, unto justification of life, that is, unto a justification which brings with it the gift of life' ([*p. 103*] p. 115). 'For "the many" who died in Adam, were, of course, the whole race; and therefore also, blessed be God! "the many", to whom "the grace of God abounded, and the free gift by grace of the one man Jesus Christ", the gift of righteousness, must be the whole race, the whole family of man' ([*p. 102*] p. 114).

While 5.19 used the future tense, 'the many shall be made righteous', this was because of the continuous nature of God's redeeming work in:

> 'the multiplied declarations of righteousness, which shall be made in this life to the individual members of the great human family. Whenever the 'unrighteousness' of any Jew, Christian, or heathen, 'is forgiven, and his sin covered',—whenever he feels any measure of the peace of God's children, in the faithful discharge of any duty, or in forsaking any path of evil,— whenever there is brought home to his heart in any way the message of God's Fatherly Love by means of any one of Earth's ten thousand voices,— then he hears, as it were, a fresh declaration of righteousness, he may know that he is recognized again as a child of God's House'. ([*p. 103*] p. 115)

This was indeed the essence of the good news, that the whole human race was righteous before God in Jesus Christ, 'their Head', and every human being already experienced the redeeming work of the Spirit of God which Christians expressly experienced through their baptism:

He Himself, the Father of Spirits, is everywhere enlightening and quickening the spirits of men. Every good thought, which has ever stirred within a heathen's mind, is a token of that work which God's good Spirit is working within him, as one of the great Human Family, redeemed by the Love of God in Christ Jesus, and related all to the Second Adam by a second spiritual birth, (of which Baptism is the express sign and seal to the Christian,) as they are by their natural birth to the first Adam. ([*p. 107*] pp. 118-19)

Paul went on to work out the implications of this in chs. 6–8, in terms of the sacraments, human nature and natural religion.

5. *Theological Implications of Colenso's Exegesis of the* Sola Fide

5.1. Anakephalaiosis

In rejecting the penal theory of the atonement ('He did not bear the weight of the curse; He did not suffer the accumulated weight of woe, due, as a punishment, to the sins of the world. St. Paul says not a word of this', [*p. 112*] p. 123), Colenso gave maximum weight to Paul's use of the formulation 'as in Adam all die, so in Christ shall all be made alive', to see Christ as the head of humanity, encapsulating and restoring humanity in his own person on the Cross ('What He, our Head, did, that we, the members of His Body, share in, we, the whole brotherhood of Man, we, the whole race, whose nature He took upon Him' [*p. 113*] p. 124). Although the concept of the headship of Christ did not appear in Romans, but mainly in the deutero-Pauline epistles (Eph. 1.22; 4.15; 5.23; Col. 1.18; 2.10, 19; but cf. 1 Cor. 11.3), Colenso interpreted Paul's first and second Adam typology in this way (Christ as head occurs no less than 49 times) to refer to the work of Christ in the *Commentary on Romans*. Christ's work was effective in gathering up the whole of humankind since creation and up to the final resurrection into one in himself and restoring it to what God all along intended it to be. So people were no longer accursed creatures but children, whether or not they came to conscious Christian faith.

Colenso's thinking at this point was reminiscent of the *recapulatio* Christology of Irenaeus, though there is no evidence that he was conscious of it. The summary Aloys Grillmeier (1975: 102) gives of Irenaeus's theology provides resonates with Colenso's exegesis of Romans:

Just as in the invisible world the Logos is already the head of all being created in him, so now in the incarnation he becomes head of the visible and corporeal world, and above all the head of the Church, so drawing everything to himself. This represents at the same time a recapitulation of

creation and above all of fallen Adam, i.e. a renewing and saving permea-
tion of the whole history of the world and of mankind by 'Christ the Head',
from its beginning to its end.

For Colenso, this Adam Christology, which stresses the Fatherhood of
God and the solidarity of all human beings as bothers and sisters in Christ,
is what ought to provide the motivation for Christian mission, and not fear
of damnation or selfish hope of individual privilege which leaves the rest
of humankind to perish:

> We are to go forth in the confidence that all men everywhere are sharing
> these blessings, though as yet they may not be privileged to know it—
> honouring our brother-men, whoever they may be, as members of the Great
> Human Family, whom God hath redeemed for Himself in His own dear
> Son,—and longing and labouring to tell them, in life and act, in our own
> persons, if we may, or by helping others in our name to tell them, of One
> Love, of which all earthly loves are telling, of which all precious thought
> are whispering in the very centre of their being, which embraces us all.
> (*[p. 119]* pp. 129-30)

When the missionary met those who have not heard the gospel, s/he had to
recognize that the Spirit of Life was already in them: 'All men, then, have
this spirit, this spiritual life, though all men may not realize it to themselves nor exhibit it to others' by virtue of their relationship to Christ as
head (*[p. 147]* p. 155).

5.2. *Purgatory and the Ultimate Salvation of all Humankind*
The second theological implication of Colenso's understanding of Paul
was that it problematized the concept of eternal damnation. After all, if
there was this human solidarity in redemption, whether a person made an
act of faith or not, and if the penal theory of the atonement was set aside,
then how could one talk of punishment at all, except as a corrective
measure for deliberate and obstinate sin. But if punishment was corrective,
then it could not be eternal. Interpreting 8.21, Colenso insisted that the
words 'that the creature also itself shall be set free from the bondage of
corruption, into the freedom of the glory of the children of God' referred
to the whole of the created order and had to mean that there was hope
for the whole race, including the unrighteous in the end (*[pp. 175-76]*
pp. 179-80). So, in one of the most sustained pieces of argumentation in
the whole commentary, he argued for the doctrine of Purgatory as repre-
senting the majority Christian viewpoint through the ages and even in his
own. There had to, in God's good time, be the hope of redemption even

here. So, while there would be judgment for all now and at the hour of death, according to the light given each person, and all people would experience the 'worm' of guilt and the 'fire' of God's anger against sin, at the last all people would be brought into the light of God's glory and presence.

5.3. *Sacraments as Signs to the World*

Third, if all were already redeemed by the work of Christ as head of humanity recapitulating the race from creation, then what role could the sacraments play? Certainly, the sacraments did not effect redemption (*ex opera operandi*), but they showed it forth. Baptism, like circumcision for the Jew, was an outward sign of God's blessing already given, but a sign that did not guarantee any special privilege for the Christian. Colenso paraphrased Paul in 2.25 as follows:

> The baptism of a Christian has a meaning and use, if he walks faithfully; otherwise his baptism becomes a mere nullity. If, then, an unbaptised heathen does that which is good and right and true, shall not his unbaptised state be reckoned for baptism? and they, which are heathens by nature, and walking according to the light vouchsafed to them, judge those, who, baptised Christians as they are, yet knowingly transgress the law of their Lord? For he is not a Christian, who is so merely in name and profession, nor is that true baptism, which is only outwardly with water. But the Christian in God's sight is he who is one inwardly; and the baptism, which is of value before Him, is that of the heart, in the spirit, not in the outward form… It might be asked, 'If you say the heathen may be saved without the knowledge of the Gospel, what advantage then, hath the Christian, or what profit is there in Christian Baptism?' And a similar answer might be given: Much, in every way: in the very first place, because to them are entrusted the Holy Scriptures, the books of the New Testament as well as the Old. And to this we might go on to add, 'To them are given the means of grace, and the hope of glory'. (*[pp. 51, 53]* pp. 68, 69-70)

The blessing was already given before baptism to all humankind, and served to ratify that gift long ago given (*[p. 75]* p. 90) for the individual 'receiving each for himself, personally, in baptism a formal outward sign of ratification of that adoption, which they have shared already, independently of the sign, with the whole race' (*[p. 200]* p. 203). Central to Colenso's thinking was the insistence on humankind as one. He used the phrase 'the whole race' 16 times, to emphasize human solidarity in the Christ event.

The same could be said about the Eucharist. It likewise represented a gift already given objectively to all in their daily experience of life, but signified outwardly in the sacrament:

> The Body and Blood of Christ are represented to us by the Elements, whether we come to feed by faith upon them at that particular time or not. These things, *out of ourselves*, are set forth to us in that Holy Sacrament, as the source of all Life of every kind to us all, of all the blessings which we enjoy in our daily life, personal, family, social, or national, as the great provision of our Father's Love for us, of which we are partaking, day by day, at every moment, as redeemed creatures, though we may not know it or may not heed it, of which every man everywhere is partaking, though he may not know what the Word made Flesh has done at His Father's bidding for the children of men. ([*p. 115*] p. 126)

This conclusion that the 'Body and Blood of Christ' were given 'to all the human race, not only in the Sacrament, but at all times, and of which, in fact, all men were everywhere partaking, through God's mercy, and so receiving all the life they have' ([*p. 116*] p. 126) was one of the conclusions which most outraged the Anglo-Catholic orthodoxy of Bishop Gray and his supporters in the heresy trial.

5.4. *Natural Religion and the Conscience*
Finally, the consequence of this Christian universalism that Colenso drew from his interpretation of Romans, was a new emphasis on natural religion and conscience. All human beings experience the Fatherhood of God, had access to the gift of salvation given in Christ and were called by the creator Spirit to an ethical life by the conscience given to every human being. The Christian had the advantage of knowing and experiencing this good news and the responsibility of sharing it with the rest of the human family. The Christian, however, had no ground for pride or for a sense of superiority. For Colenso, the Epistle was specifically written by Paul to counter feelings of racial privilege and pride. He specifically drew the implications of this for colonial society in the *Commentary on Romans*. This would inevitably set him on a collision course with the colonial government and the settler community.

6. *The Consequences*
Colenso's *Commentary on Romans* was printed only at his mission station and received brief attention, largely as source material for his heresy trial.

As an examination of the charges shows, it was on the basis of his exegesis of Romans that he was excommunicated, and not, as is sometimes asserted, his challenge to Scriptural inerrancy in his *Commentary on the Pentateuch*. Yet his exegesis was hardly taken seriously as an interpretation *of Paul's letter*. No attempt was made to refute Colenso's exegesis by his accusers. Colenso's work at Ekukhanyeni did not succeed in making conventional converts. As I have argued elsewhere in examining the relationship between Colenso and Magema Fuze (Draper 1998a, 1999, 2000; cf. Mokoena 2003), Colenso's theology, propounded in his interpretation of Romans, undermined the logic of conventional mission work. If all were already saved, whether they accept the Christian gospel or not, then what they stood to benefit from by baptism was enlightenment, knowledge of what they already possessed. Colenso's emphasis on the value and importance of natural religion, of the universal operation of conscience, and of the equality of all races and cultures, made for a 'cool conversion' in the terms of Berger and Luckmann. There was no need for an absolute break with their former way of life for his converts, no severance of family and kinship ties. Instead, his teaching encouraged the emergence of a Zulu national identity and cultural revival. However, if Colenso's *Commentary on Romans* is measured as part of the 'long conversation' between European Christianity and Africa, then it was profoundly successful.

The mission station itself was abandoned after the traumatic events of Colenso's excommunication and legal battles in the Privy Council. Colenso abandoned his early visions of an alliance with imperial authorities to put a Christian king on the Zulu throne and came to be a fierce defender of Zulu independence and legal rights against the colonialists: first Langalibalele, then Cetshwayo, and then, posthumously through his family, Dinizulu. He excerpted decisions and reports of the Natal colonial government and sent them to a network of activists in England. He lobbied in the imperial Parliament and fought in the courts. His converts and scholars from Ekukhanyeni were among the vanguard of a new Zulu consciousness and resistance to colonialism, known early on as 'the Bishopstowe Faction', after his house at Ekukhanyeni. This is certainly not the kind of outcome which missionary societies expected or welcomed at the time, but one of which, with hindsight, the Church can be proud. Exegesis can have unexpected consequences.

Part II

THEOLOGY

COLENSO IN THE WORLD
OF NINETEENTH-CENTURY INTELLECTUAL FERMENT

John W. Rogerson

In a cartoon of the 1870s preserved in the archives of the Imperial College
of Science, Technology and Medicine in London (it is reproduced in
Rogerson 2001: 224) there is portrayed 'The Battle Field of Science and
the Churches'. A crowned female figure of divine appearance and repre-
senting Reason and Truth presides over the Battle Field, whose forces
face each other. On the left, backed by London University and the Mech-
anics' Institute, are representatives of the British Association and the
Social Science Association. Prominent individuals include Charles Darwin,
T.H. Huxley and John Tyndall. The disciplines of Geology, Astronomy
and Biology are also featured. On the right-hand side, opposite London
University is the 'National Religion', that is, the Church of England,
which is designated as the Tower of Babel on account of its deep divisions
between High Church, Low Church and Broad Church. The Archbishop of
Canterbury (A.C. Tait) is seated backwards on Balaam's ass facing away
from the battle lines, presumably an indication of his unwillingness to
back his inclinations in favour of science. No such equivocation is attributed to the Roman Catholic Church, whose leader, Cardinal Manning, is
shown to be saying 'doubt and be burnt up'. Similarly, the Baptist representative, C.H. Spurgeon, offers the alternative of 'faith or damnation'.
Arranged together with the churches are representations of biblical
incidents that contradict the findings of science: the sun standing still at
Joshua's command, the talking serpent in Genesis 3, the whale that swallowed Jonah, Balaam's talking ass, and Noah's ark. Two biblical scholars
stand with the forces of science. They are the German Jewish émigré
Moses Kalisch, whose commentaries on the Pentateuch contained pioneering critical insights (Rogerson 1984: 242-44), and Bishop J.W. Colenso.
What were Colenso's views on matters of science, and how did he come to
be placed on the side of science against the churches, in the view of the
author of the cartoon?

Colenso's connections with leading scientists of his day are well known. He was invited to dine with the exclusive X Club founded in November 1864 and consisting of eight members, including Huxley, Herbert Spencer and Tyndall (Huxley 1900, I: 256-58). He became a close friend of the geologist, Sir Charles Lyell, and through him established himself in the literary and scientific circles of London (Hinchliff 1964: 140). The list of those who subscribed to a fund to support his appeal to the Crown following his 'deposition' by Bishop Robert Gray included Lyell, Darwin and Huxley, as well as the botanist and member of the X Club Sir Joseph Hooker (Hinchliff 1964: 140-41). His own views on science were set out in a lecture read to the Marylebone Literary Institution in May 1865 and entitled 'On Missions to the Zulus in Natal and Zululand' (Colenso 1982: 205-33).

The lecture was a defence of Christian missions against the view derived from, but not sanctioned by, Darwin that natural selection was responsible for some races being 'higher' than others, that 'lower' races would consequently disappear, and that missions were a vain attempt to interfere with this natural process. This anthropological theory was a secularized version of the explanation that had been developed by theologians in the eighteenth and nineteenth centuries to explain the existence of so-called primitive peoples in the modern world. Granted belief in the literal truth of Genesis 1–4, where the descendants of Adam are presented as metal-workers and founders of cities, the existence in the modern world of peoples at a much lower level of culture than that imputed to Adam's descendants was explained by the theory of spiritual and cultural degeneration. Where races had rejected the knowledge of God they had sunk into savagery (Rogerson 1978: 22-23). Colenso's case was, basically, that the human race has always been rising from lower to higher states, that so-called savage peoples (as illustrated by the Zulus) are capable of moral and spiritual awareness, and that both these situations (cultural progress and spiritual awareness) can be attributed to the work of God in the world.

In defending this position Colenso argued as follows. The opening chapters of Genesis were at variance with modern science. No intelligent person could accept that the world was created 6000 years ago, and that the first man spoke Hebrew in the Garden of Eden. There had been no 'fall' that precipitated the human race, if not from the status of angels, at any rate from a higher culture of Adam, to the status of the savages that the first tribes of the human race undoubtedly were. The good news was that the history of the human race was that of progress. To quote Colenso (1982: 208):

It is joyous and refreshing to know that we are not laboriously toiling to recover some of that almost infinite extent of ground which Adam lost for us by his one act of sin; it is hopeful to be assured, by the plainest evidences of scientific research, that all our present advances in art and science are the just result of the proper development of the great human family, as part of the great Creator's scheme from the first, and to know that every fresh fact, brought to light by a course of honest and persevering inquiry, is a fresh blessing bestowed upon the race from the Father of Lights.

The question of why some present-day peoples seem still to be at a stage of savagery was partly answered by an acknowledgement that humans might indulge, against their inner moral and spiritual laws, in sin and vice, and in so doing might sink to the level of savage or even beast. But Colenso passed quickly over this to consider the possibility that the first humans developed from a lower, that is, animal, race. His acceptance of the Darwinian theory was not complete, because Colenso was inclined to accept that the human race had had a plural origin, rather than being descended from a single pair or race, and he did not see how the Darwinian theory could explain this plural origin. At the same time, he left open the possibility that subsequent scientific research would demonstrate that the human race or races were descended from a lower race of animal life. His concern was to reconcile this possibility with his belief in the Divine Education of the human race.

Colenso's argument drew attention to the existence of members of the human race, especially those suffering from idiocy, who had the physical *form* of humans but who lacked any intellectual or moral capacity. They exhibited a distortion or disturbance of the mechanism that enabled the divine Spirit to enlighten and guide them. As applied to the development of the human race from lower animals, the emergence of humans would mean that, by natural selection, the barrier was passed that had prevented the growth of moral and spiritual faculties. The possibility would be opened up for the development that had reached its highest point in modern civilization. Yet this progress was not inevitable, and the loss of spiritual and moral progress was possible.

Colenso (1982: 213) was not, therefore, alarmed by the possibility that science would one day prove that humans had developed from animals, neither had he any problems with the likely view that the human race had a plural rather than a single origin:

Suppose that we find our fellow man fashioned in all points like ourselves, with reason, intellect, conscience, speech, and all the affections and attrib-utes of our nature—differing, in fact, only from us in this, that he has not

sprung originally from the same pair of parents as ourselves,—shall we not
be ready at once to recognize a common brotherhood with him higher than
that of mere blood,—and feel that we are one in the truest sense of the
word, in having one common Father, whose creatures we are...?

Colenso had thus completed the first part of his argument, that dealing
with the origins and progress of the human race. He now turned to the
second part, whose aim was to show that contemporary 'savage' peoples
did, in fact, possess the capacity for moral and spiritual growth, which was
why Christian missions were necessary. Colenso was not starry-eyed
about contemporary 'savages', and acknowledged the existence of various
forms of cannibalism. Nonetheless, the great majority, even of 'savage'
races, displayed signs of human feeling and affection as well as of a belief
in another life. The main burden of the demonstration of this was a moving account of Colenso's own experiences among the Zulu, including a
visit to King Umpande, who had been devastated by a civil war between
two of his sons in December 1856. In the battle, thousands of the king's
subjects had died, his favourite son and chief heir Umbulazi had been
killed, and his favourite wife Monase and her only surviving son Umkungo had gone into exile, eventually being entrusted to Colenso's care.
Colenso's visit took place some three years after this incident, and he took
with him a letter from Umkungo to his father and a photograph of the
young man, who was now about 16. The king could not believe that his
son had written a letter and gazed at the photograph for a long time. He
exhibited deep emotions of love and grief, as both husband and father.

This encounter had clearly had a great effect of Colenso. He recalled the
incident in 2 Samuel 18 in which David lamented over Absalom and then
boldly asserted (1982: 220-21 [the quotations in the last sentence are from
1 Thess. 1.3]):

I thank God that I *am* commissioned by the Queen of England...to be 'a
preacher and a teacher' to these heathens, as well as to others, of God's
eternal truth and love. And if I am asked, 'Have we any ground of hope on
which to pursue our labours?' I point at once to such instances as these of
true, human affections...and I say that where in Zululand or in England, in
the hut of the savage or in the dens of vice and misery at home, there burns
yet unquenched one spark of true human love, *there* still is the sign of life,
there still is ground for steadily pursuing the 'work of faith, and labour of
love, and patience of hope', on behalf of our fellow-man, 'in the sight of
God our Father'.

Before giving other examples of what could be achieved in missionary
work, Colenso returned briefly to the charge that had occasioned the

lecture, namely, that natural selection decreed that 'lower' races would become extinct and the missions to them were therefore ill conceived. Colenso doubted whether future history would see the complete demise of the Chinese, or the Hindus of India, or the inhabitants of Central and Southern Africa, but he was willing to consider the implications of this possibility, and to admit that contact with the white races might expose such peoples to new vices and new diseases. Granted these things, was there not a responsibility laid upon the white races to extend to these people, while they still existed, the benefits and blessings of civilization as well as its evils? And should not such activity include care for the soul as well as for the body, by teaching these peoples the eternal truths of religion and morality?

Colenso gently brought his argument back to the achievements of missionary work among the Zulus by asserting that even if such work could not raise the whole Zulu nation, this did not diminish the importance of a ministry to individuals such as King Umpande. They needed to hear words of hope, and to be helped to trust in 'the Living God as their Father and Friend' (Colenso 1982: 223). But there was also another point. Given that Christianity had been affected, in its development, by contact with the philosophy of Persia, Alexandria and Rome, who could say whether contact with Africa was also part of the divine plan; that the thinkers of Zululand might have a part to play in perfecting 'the common stock of human thought'?

This was left as a rhetorical question, and Colenso resumed the theme of the achievements of missionary work. These included quotations from letters written to him in English by a Zulu lad who, in Colenso's absence in England, was continuing the work of Colenso's printing press, as well as the outline of a sermon preached by one of the Zulu catechists at Colenso's mission station at Bishopstowe. The evidence thus provided of what could be achieved, led to a ringing conclusion to the lecture in which Colenso linked the savagery of the objects of missionary work with the superstitions contained in the Bible. How, he asked, could savage tribes be raised to higher levels of religious and moral understanding if they were expected to accept literally the superstitions and the questionable morality contained in the Bible, not to mention those aspects of it that were shown by modern science to be false? Colenso made much of the Old Testament command that witches should be put to death (Exod. 22.18) and how so-called Christian nations had pursued this aim up to recent times. Savagery was not confined to the backward races when it came to believing the Bible. If such savagery was to be overcome in all societies this would involve an abandonment of that view of the Bible that required belief in the date of creation (i.e. 4004 BCE), that woman was created from the rib of man, that there had been a fall and a universal flood, that an ass had spoken and the sun had stood still. Did this mean an abandonment of the Bible altogether? Certainly not. Faith was not in a book, but in the Living Word which spoke in the book, and which had continued to speak down the ages, including in the most recent discoveries of science. The Bible contained the earliest record of the Divine Teaching

> which has led men more and more out of darkness into light, out of slavish fears and superstitions into the liberty of God's children, out of confusion and ignorance into the clearer knowledge of the Living God. (Colenso 1982: 233)

Looking back over this lecture it is difficult not to be impressed by its mastery of the subject matter and its generosity of argument. There is no trace of the kind of point-scoring refutation type of argument to which Colenso's own work was being subjected by opponents who knew far less than him about the issues in question (Rogerson 1984: 233-34). Instead, we find a willingness to concede that views with which Colenso did not agree might turn out to be correct, and a readiness to work out the implications of these views should they be established. Where Colenso is firm and positive in his conviction there is a sincerity and dignity about his language.

Where does this lecture place Colenso within the intellectual ferment of his times? Although opinions were sharply divided over belief in God, belief in the Bible and acceptance of the findings of science, these agreements took place within a broad stream of common ground among the opponents. John Durant (1985: 9-39) has argued that natural theology in the forms developed around the beginning of the nineteenth century by Thomas Malthus and William Paley provided a coherent worldview that was able to integrate a wide range of knowledge and values. Paley was concerned to show that items in the natural world were marvellously designed, and that this proved the existence of a Designer. Paley, of course, believed in the fixity of species. Darwin's attempt to show that species had developed out of other species did not necessarily undermine Paley's general position. For liberal believers in God, natural selection could be seen as the method by which God had created the human race, and by which he was continuing to lead it to higher moral and spiritual attainment. The design, in other words, was a process. For non-believers, Darwin's theory was a secularized version of this view, with a kind of personified nature guiding the human race. There were two main causes of unbelief: the existence of natural evil and the impossibility of reconciling the Bible with scientific and moral progress (see, generally, Cockshut 1964). The existence of natural evil has always been a powerful objection to belief in design, as well as a belief in the argument for God's existence from design, and the shattering effect upon Charles Darwin's faith of the death of his daughter Annie at the age of ten in 1851 is well known (Desmond and Moore 1992: 375-87). At the same time, it was belief in moral and spiritual, as well as natural, development that enabled liberal thinkers who were believers in God to account for moral and some physical evil. If there had been a divine education of the human race (Temple 1861: 1-49) the parts of the Bible that offended nineteenth-century moral standards could be seen as instances of the necessary stages through which the human race had passed on its way to enlightenment. To use a later expression, the Bible was a record of a revelation rather than the revelation itself, although the record it contained was sufficient to sustain belief in a purposeful and benevolent creator. Even 'nature red in tooth and claw' (Tennyson, 'In Memoriam' canto lvi) could be partly accommodated to the scheme of natural selection. Among liberal-minded thinkers, then, there was a certain amount of common ground, even if they were sharply divided over belief in God. Before Colenso is placed within that matrix, it will be instructive to consider the position of a learned churchman, whose *Notes and Introduction to the Holy Bible* were being written about the same time that Colenso was preparing his lecture for the Marylebone Literary Institution.

Christopher Wordsworth, who was later to become Bishop of Lincoln (1869–85) published the first volume of his *Notes*, in fact a very thorough commentary, dealing with Genesis and Exodus in 1865 (the Preface is dated September 1864) and a second edition appeared the following year (Wordsworth 1866). A learned and scholarly work and one that paid attention to Colenso, Darwin and German biblical criticism, it nonetheless displayed none of Colenso's generosity of argument, and was essentially a defensive and apologetic piece, but noteworthy as the product of a highly intelligent man who was committed to defending Christian orthodoxy as he understood it. He is an interesting representative of that part of the intellectual ferment of those times that condemned Colenso, and when one reads his work it is not hard to understand why Colenso found the company of the X Club more congenial than that of the theological establishment in England.

A fundamental principle of Wordsworth's use of the Bible was the decisive authority of the New Testament, and in particular of the teaching of Jesus, in matters of criticism. The story of Jonah in the whale's belly was confirmed by Jesus, who also used the incident as a type of his own death, burial and resurrection (Wordsworth 1866: xxxii). Old Testament incidents, indeed, were repeatedly authenticated by being types prefiguring the New Testament. The history of the flood, for example, was a pre-figuring of the sacrament of Baptism and was therefore a miracle that was 'not to be scanned by natural Reason' nor 'to be reduced to the standard of ordinary events' (Wordsworth 1866: xxx). The truth of the story of Balaam's ass was guaranteed by the reference to it in 2 Pet. 2.16 on the authority of 'the divinely-inspired Apostle St. Peter' (Wordsworth 1866: xxxii).

Granted such an approach, it is no wonder that Wordsworth had little sympathy for views such as those of Darwin and his followers. 'This notion…is altogether erroneous, that we existed first in a savage state. Barbarism, Cannibalism, etc., are *not natural*, but *contrary* to nature' (Wordsworth 1866). The Bible similarly settled the question of whether the human race had a single or a plural origin unanswerably in favour of the former. 'The doctrines that all men are from *one pair*…is taught in this passage' (i.e. Gen. 1.21; Wordsworth 1866: 18). Wordsworth also referred to 'physical researches' that confirmed this view. But more was at issue than the accuracy of biblical assertions. It was necessary to believe that man was created in the image of God, otherwise the theology of the loss of the image in the fall and its restoration in Christ was undermined. Simi-larly, the single pair Adam and Eve was a prefigurement of the pair Christ and his Church.

In one respect, Wordsworth was prepared to take into account the discoveries of science, and that was the evidence that the world was much older than the 6000 years attributed to it by James Ussher's biblical-based chronology. 'The discoveries of Geology bear testimony to the great antiquity of the Earth, and show that it was inhabited by many species of animals and was clothed with great variety of vegetation' (Wordsworth 1866: 3). This, according to Wordsworth, was *before* the six days work of creation described in Genesis. The justification for this was the verse in Genesis describing the earth as 'without form, and void'. Somehow, an agency hostile to God had intervened, with divine permission, to distort an original creation. The six-day account in Genesis is therefore of a re-creation; the geological and other findings pertain to this earlier creation.

A consideration of Wordsworth puts Colenso in context, and makes it easy to see why the cartoon with which I began placed him on the side of science. Within the broad stream of the liberal and scientific thought of his day he opted for an interpretation in terms of the loving purposes of God because he had felt the need for, and seen the results of, such belief in his missionary work. Belief, especially in the moral and spiritual development of the human race from savagery to Christianity relieved him of the need to accept the superstitions and immoral parts of the Bible. They were the record of the work of the Divine Spirit in the past, a Divine Spirit whose teaching was 'still going on by all the new revelations in science' (Colenso 1982: 233) and which was leading to the completion 'of the History of Man'.

In a letter to Sir Charles Lyell written by Henry Milman, Dean of St Paul's, in June 1867, the Dean took exception to some of Colenso's views on biblical criticism. But he was surely right to state that Colenso was 'a bold, honest, single-minded man, with a deep and sincere love of truth. He is a man, too, of remarkably acute intellect and indefatigable industry.' Milman (1899: 284-85) concluded:

> I have read some and intend to read more of his sermons. None of his adversaries, of course, read them. If they did, it might put them to shame, especially as contrasted with their cold, dry dogmatism.

They could similarly have benefited from studying Colenso's lecture to the Marylebone Literary Institution, a piece that has stood the test of time remarkably well.

THE PENTATEUCH IN PERSPECTIVE: BISHOP COLENSO'S BIBLICAL
CRITICISM IN ITS COLONIAL CONTEXT

Gwilym Colenso

On 29 June 1866, in a speech to the Lower House of Convocation, Dean
Stanley had responded to a resolution supporting a rival bishop to Bishop
Colenso following his 'deposition'. Dean Stanley pointed out that, if they
were to condemn Bishop Colenso for his criticisms of the Pentateuch, they
should also condemn others who shared his views and these others included not only some of the early Church Fathers but also Stanley himself. 'But', Stanley added, 'in that same goodly company I shall find the
despised and rejected Bishop of Natal. At least deal out the same measure
to me that you deal to him' (Cox 1888, I: 369; Cockshut 1959: 110). It
appears that the bishops in Convocation were not impressed by the logic
of Stanley's argument, compelling though it might seem.

It has been argued that it was thought time for the Church to be seen to
assert its authority by making an example (Cockshut 1959: 113). But, if
so, once Stanley had revealed that he, and therefore presumably others of
his persuasion within the Church, shared the same views, why was Bishop
Colenso singled out for this purpose?

In 1868, F.W. Farrar, a liberal Church of England theologian, referred
with a mixture of sadness and despair to the strength of feeling within the
Church against 'the hated name of the Bishop of Natal' (Farrar 1868: 440).

Some years later, Stanley again spoke in defence of Bishop Colenso. In
1880 he told a meeting of the Society for the Propagation of the Gospel
that Bishop Colenso had been 'assailed by scurrilous and unscrupulous
invective unexampled in the controversy of this country, and almost in the
history, miserable as it is, of religious controversy itself...' (Cox 1888, I:
370).

The language used by the opponents of Bishop Colenso against him was
described by Frances Colenso, Bishop Colenso's wife, as 'violent abuse'
(Rees 1958: 256) and sometimes sought to associate him with the forces of

darkness. Denunciations included references to him as 'an instrument of Satan' (*The Pentateuch and book of Joshua Critically Examined = The Pentateuch*, III: xv); the 'wicked Bishop', as 'doing actively the Devil's work' (cited in Neil 1963: 282) and (from Bishop Gray) as 'being led captive by the Evil one' (Cox 1888, I: 30, cited in Guy 1983: 156). In a review of the Preface of Part IV of *The Pentateuch*, there is an unsympathetic reference to those considered to support him being 'tinged with that blackness which, in its more pronounced degree, has been called Colensoism' (*The Reader* 26 December 1863).

What is the explanation for the strength of feeling against Bishop Colenso?

One possible answer is that it was felt that Bishop Colenso's rank within the Church made his criticism of the Bible all the more deplorable. '[His book] is read by tens of thousands because he is a Bishop. It is his office of Bishop which propagates infidelity' (a letter from Pusey to Tait cited in Guy 1983: 130; Rees 1958: 74). However, other high-ranking members of the Church had supported him or had expressed views in sympathy with his. Moreover, as Dean Stanley also pointed out, disagreement with the formularies of the Church of England as expressed in the Book of Common Prayer was common to all ranks within the Church of England up to the Archbishop of Canterbury. Yet this had been one of the charges of heresy levelled against Bishop Colenso (Cox 1888, I: 368). Furthermore, on other 'errors' that he was charged with, Bishop Colenso was able to cite in support of his views 'the consentient opinion of very many of the greatest divines both ancient and modern' (*The Pentateuch*, III: xlvi).

Another possible answer is that Bishop Colenso's scholarship was inadequate or that he argued his case ineffectively. However, Jeff Guy suggests that Bishop Colenso's *The Pentateuch* was attacked not because 'it was *incompetent* but because it was *effective*' (Guy 1983: 188). The question arises, if it was effective, why did this not result in a change in the view of the Church?

A further possibility is that Bishop Colenso may have committed what William Irvine describes as 'that last Victorian enormity, the worst of virtuous errors…a mistake in tone' (Irvine 1956: 31). He was counselled by sympathizers to 'soften his tone' and he did make some concessions in this direction, but possibly not sufficient to avoid causing offence (Guy 1983: 117-18, 177-82).

Gerald Parsons has suggested that, as most history is written by the winners, those on the losing side, as Bishop Colenso was, tend to have their defeats explained in terms of their alleged personal failings, rather than in terms of the historical context (Parsons 1997: 141-42). We will therefore look at the broader context, beginning with the background to Bishop Colenso's criticism of the Pentateuch.

In 1862, Bishop Colenso travelled with his family to England from Natal, seven years after his consecration as bishop of the newly created colonial see. Between his arrival in England in May 1862 and his departure in August 1865 to return to Natal, he published the first five parts of his seven-part study, *The Pentateuch and Book of Joshua Critically Examined.* In this work, he set out detailed arguments to support his view that the Pentateuch was not a historical document and that its author was not Moses, but rather that it was a composite work derived from a number of sources all of which were composed much later than the age of Moses.

In the Prefaces to the various volumes of *The Pentateuch*, Bishop Colenso gives examples of the statements illustrating the viewpoint that he is questioning—the doctrine of Scriptural infallibility.

One example given is the following: 'The Bible is none other than *the Voice of Him that siteth upon the Throne!* Every book of it—every chapter of it—every verse of it—every word of it—every syllable of it—(where are we to stop?) every *letter* of it—is the direct utterance of the Most High! The Bible is none other than the Word of God—not some part of it more, some part of it less, but all alike, the utterance of Him who siteth upon the Throne—absolute—faultless—unerring—supreme' (*The Pentateuch*, I: 6). This address was made by Dr Burgon, the future Dean of Chichester, from the pulpit of the university church in Oxford (Neil 1963: 283). Another example is provided by Canon George Rawlinson. In his Bampton lectures in 1859, Rawlinson said 'we possess in the Pentateuch not only the most authentic account of ancient times that has come down to us, but a history absolutely and in every respect true' (Neil 1963: 259).

The results of Bishop Colenso's investigation were clearly at odds with the doctrine of Scriptural infallibility, but his central criticisms of the Pentateuch were not original. For some time, biblical criticism had been present as an intellectual current in Great Britain, but one which by the middle of the nineteenth century had become suppressed by a religious orthodoxy that maintained the literal truth of the Bible as the verbal inspiration of God. By this time, biblical criticism was associated with centres of learning on the Continent, particularly in Germany, where biblical scholarship was much more advanced than in England. In the early decades of the nineteenth century, Old Testament studies in Germany had a degree of professionalism matched only by the sciences in England and America (Moore 1986: 332). However, the influence of German scholarship in England was referred to by orthodox Churchmen (derogatorily) as 'Germanization' and it was identified with unbelief (Moore 1986: 333; Rogerson 1984: 249-50).

How hostile this climate had become before the publication of Bishop Colenso's *The Pentateuch* can be seen by the reaction to other works suggesting the unhistorical character and non-Mosaic, composite authorship of the Pentateuch. Authors of such works faced denunciation and deposition from their academic positions.

Despite this hostility from the Church establishment in the middle of the century, biblical criticism continued to find expression in the Church of England among those associated with what was known as the 'Broad Church Party'. Among these were the authors of *Essays and Reviews*, published in 1860 as a collection of essays by seven different authors, six of whom were clergymen, two of whom were prosecuted for denying the inspiration of Scripture. The sentence of the Court of Arches to suspend the writers from their benefices for one year was reversed on appeal to the Judicial Committee of the Privy Council of the House of Lords. Nevertheless, the book was condemned synodically in Convocation (Vidler 1961: 128).

The Broad Churchmen, as they were known, took a liberal view of Church doctrine and sought to ameliorate some of its harsher aspects such as the doctrine of eternal damnation. They also took a liberal view of the interpretation of biblical history. Rather than a literal historical narrative, they preferred to see it as a progressive revelation of God's message and therefore as a text that should not be considered equally true in all ages. Indeed, Benjamin Jowett, in his contribution to *Essays and Reviews* included the dictum that scholars should 'interpret the Scripture like any other book' (Moore 1986: 335).

In theory, Bishop Colenso's investigation of the Pentateuch was situated within this tradition. However, while in agreement with the liberal views of the Broad Church Party, he may have had more in common with the scientists in terms of his uncompromising attitude towards the pursuit of truth.

Within science, confident challenges were being mounted against religious orthodoxy. The traditional Christian view of the natural world based on the Genesis narrative of the Creation and the Deluge was being called into question.

In geology, there was increasing support for the view that the history of the world was immeasurably longer than the timescale envisaged in the biblical chronology and that presence of humankind on earth had been relatively recent in comparison with the original act of creation and in comparison with the presence of other living creatures. Notable among the geologists who criticized the traditional view was Charles Lyell whose *Principles of Geology* was published in 1830–33. Lyell poured scorn on those later known as 'scriptural geologists' who asserted the right to interpret earth history from the book of Genesis alone (Moore 1986: 329). In contrast, Lyell advocated that 'The physical part of the geological enquiry ought to be conducted as if the Scriptures were not in existence' (Moore 1986: 337). In 1859, Darwin's *The Origin of Species* challenged the traditional assumption that species were separately created and were immutable.

While in London between 1862 and 1865, Bishop Colenso met, corresponded and dined with key figures in the scientific world and particularly those associated with Charles Darwin. These included T.H. Huxley, Charles Lyell and Joseph Dalton Hooker. He shared with them a commitment to free inquiry and a distaste for dogma.

In November 1864, the 'X Club' was launched by T.H. Huxley and his associates largely in opposition to the defenders of religious orthodoxy within science. One of the founders of the club described its members as united by a bond of 'devotion to science pure and free untrammelled by religious dogma' (Jensen 1972: 539). In similar vein, Bishop Colenso expressed a wish to be 'yet still a Bp. of the *National Church* whose principle is *enquiry & truth*, not dogma & tradition' (letter from Colenso to Bleek dated 5 April 1864 [held in the Killie Campbell Colenso collection, quoted by Guy 1983: 148).

Bishop Colenso and T.H. Huxley both saw themselves as playing a leading role in a reformation that was to be of considerable significance. Huxley thought, 'we are in the midst of a gigantic movement greater than that which preceded and produced the Reformation' (Irvine 1956: 217). For Bishop Colenso in January 1863, 'The Reformation now begun will be of the deepest and most extreme character' (Cox 1888, I: 235).

Bishop Colenso and the Darwinists shared some of the same opponents. Not least among these was the Bishop of Oxford, Samuel Wilberforce, who, as a figurehead for orthodoxy among the bishops of the Church of England, had publicly opposed Darwin's evolutionary theory as 'absolutely incompatible with the word of God' (Vidler 1961: 117; Neil 1963: 260) and, at a meeting of the British Association in Oxford in 1860, had engaged in the debate which included his famous exchange with T.H. Huxley (Irvine 1956: 3-5; Chadwick 1970: 9-11). Bishop Wilberforce and others were responsible for 'a concerted scheme' to turn 'public opinion' against Bishop Colenso and to undermine his position within the Church. In conjunction with the Bishop of Cape Town, Bishop Wilberforce coordinated the measures which led to the 'trial', deposition and 'greater excommunication' of Bishop Colenso (Cox 1888, I: 239, 175 n. 1).

Publications defending the traditional view against the attacks from both the Darwinian evolutionists and from Bishop Colenso's biblical criticism lumped them together, as for example in the volume entitled *Modern Scepticism, Viewed in Relation to Modern Science; More Especially in Reference to the Doctrines of Colenso, Huxley, Lyell and Darwin* (Young 1865). A leading article in *The Reader* facetiously speculated on the kind of State Church that Bishop Colenso would prefer and suggested that it might be one 'in which Darwin, and Huxley, and Sir Charles Lyell might, if they chose be ministers...' (*The Reader* 30 January 1864: 127).

The X Club is described by a recent biographer of T.H. Huxley as a 'robust group, all of a mind on Darwinism and Colensoism' (Desmond 1998: 327). It appears that the supporters of 'Darwinism' and 'Colensoism' were looked on by their friends as well as by their enemies as being in the same camp.

Perhaps the opposition to Colenso from within the Church could have been aroused by this close and public, albeit brief, association between Colenso and a group of scientists openly committed in their opposition to religious orthodoxy.

However, there was also much common ground and a close association between, on the one hand, the X Club members and other scientists and, on the other hand, liberal clergymen and Broad Churchmen such as the essayists Benjamin Jowett, H.B. Wilson and Baden Powell. In articles and lectures, Dean Stanley and other liberal Churchmen, such as F.W. Farrar, commended the efforts of the scientists and defended them against the condemnation of the orthodox bishops (Farrar 1868). Stanley was unofficially '*the* Dean' to the X Club. He officiated at Charles Lyell's funeral at Westminster Abbey and Farrar, his successor as Dean of Westminster, officiated at the funeral of Charles Darwin (Desmond 1998: 329, 520-21; Moore 1986: 343).

The network of connections between the Broad Churchmen and the scientists has been described as 'the progressive center of English thought' in the mid-nineteenth century (Moore 1986: 333). In intellectual terms we could see Bishop Colenso as situated at the heart of this movement.

The Broad Churchmen did not think that the discoveries of science should be rejected on the grounds that they conflicted with the Old Testament narrative. They tended to share with scientists a view of knowledge as something that results from investigation and which therefore can evolve and change. This contrasts with the view of knowledge as passively received, which tended to be the view held by those accepting the doctrine of Scriptural infallibility. The following quotations illustrate the contrast between the two views. The first quotation is from Baden Powell's contribution to *Essays and Reviews*:

> Any appeal to *argument* must imply perfect freedom of conviction. It is a palpable absurdity to put *reasons* before a man, and yet wish to *compel* him to adopt them, or to anathematise him if he find them unconvincing; to repudiate him as an unbeliever, because he is careful to find satisfactory grounds for his belief; or to denounce him as a sceptic, because he is scrupulous to discriminate the truth; to assert that his honest doubts evince a moral obliquity; in a word, that he is no judge of his own mind; while it is obviously implied that his instructor is so—or, in other words, is omniscient and infallible. (Powell 1860: 96)

The opposing view is put by Archdeacon Denison, who said 'those who accept the Bible do not investigate truth, they receive it' (Chadwick 1970: 25). This comment was specifically criticized by F.W. Farrar and rejected (1868: 440).

The Infallibility of Doctrine

In 1863, a Committee of the Convocation of the Province of Canterbury investigated Parts I and II of Bishop Colenso's *The Pentateuch*. Their findings were that his books involved 'errors of the gravest and most dangerous character' (Cox 1888, I: 308). But what were these errors?

Bishop Thirlwall, to devastating effect, showed how the Committee of the Convocation had judged Bishop Colenso's statements not against the doctrines of the Church of England as they ought to have, but against the Scriptures, prevalent belief, or their own opinions. He pointed out that, far from being 'contrary to the faith of the universal Church'—as the Committee solemnly declared—none of the views expressed by Bishop Colenso contradicted any of the articles or formularies of the Church of England, nor did they contradict Scripture (Cox 1888, I: 305).

'The Committee...have omitted to refer to any doctrine of the Church that the author has contradicted', Bishop Thirlwall commented (Cox 1888, I: 308). Neither the Bible nor the formularies of the Church could be shown to say that Moses wrote the Pentateuch. Despite this, the Committee maintained that Bishop Colenso was in grave error for denying this 'truth'.

Likewise, the Committee failed to demonstrate that Bishop Colenso had contradicted any doctrine of the Church in claiming the Pentateuch to be unhistorical. On this point, F.W. Farrar (1868: 442) later declared his opinion that the 'disastrous doctrine of Scriptural infallibility...is a doctrine in no sense required by a single document of the Church of England... It is a doctrine wholly unsupported by the claims of the Scriptural writers themselves'.

Nevertheless, in a letter to him in December 1865, Bishop Gray still insisted that Bishop Colenso's view contradicted the 'true faith' of the Church.

But what is this 'true faith'? Bishop Gray supplies his answer to this in his letter. It is:

> What the Catholic Church while yet one, during the first thousand years of her history, under the Spirit's guidance in her great Councils, declared to be, or received as, the true faith, that *is* the true faith, and that we receive as such.

Bishop Colenso countered this by pointing out that Article 21 states that:

> the same 'great Councils'...'when they be gathered together...they may err, and sometimes have erred, even in things pertaining to God'. (Cox 1888, I: 384)

In any event, it may be doubted whether Bishop Gray's 'true faith' can be found even in the decisions of the 'great Councils'. Indeed, as Bishop Thirlwall pointed out, the attempts by the Committee to substantiate any Scriptural or doctrinal basis for the Mosaic authorship, historicity or verbal inspiration of the Pentateuch had foundered.

A further charge that the Committee brought against Bishop Colenso was that he questioned the divine knowledge of Christ. The grounds for this charge were that, whereas, in the view of the Committee, Christ guaranteed the genuineness and authenticity of the Pentateuch, Bishop Colenso questioned it and, in so doing, imputed ignorance to Christ. His view was that there was no inconsistency between Christ's divinity and his ignorance as a man. Just as, in his human nature, 'He hungered and thirsted, was weary, weak, and faint, suffered and died as man', so also would he lack perfect knowledge (Cox 1888, I: 382-83). As Stanley and others pointed out, many of the early Fathers of the Church had been in agreement with Bishop Colenso's view on this point, and the efforts of the Committee to demonstrate, as doctrine, their contrary view of the perfection of the humanity of Christ came dangerously close, in Bishop Thirlwall's view, to an attempt to 'promulgate a new dogma' (*The Pentateuch*, III: xxxiii-xl; Cox 1888, I: 308-309; Cockshut 1959: 109).

But if Bishop Gray's 'true faith' cannot be found in the doctrines of the Church of England, or in the decisions of the great Councils, or in the sayings of the early Fathers of the Church, where does it come from? The answer, it appears, is that *it is an invention*—a projection, back in time and forwards to the Day of Judgment, of a doctrine that may never have existed. Or, if it had ever existed, it was not at that time a doctrine of the Church of England and, if it were, in Bishop Colenso's view, it would be

> a dead body of dogmas…[which] shall be bound as a yoke upon all future ages as Infallible, Divine, Eternal Truth. (Cox 1888, I: 385, 391)

In contrast, Bishop Colenso's own vision of the Church was one with a constitution which

> from time to time, as knowledge advances, her system shall be modified… to meet the demands of the age… (Cox 1888, I: 391)

For Bishop Colenso, therefore, truth is not fixed or eternal but must evolve. It is historically relative.

For Bishop Gray, on the other hand, the 'true faith' is based on an idea of truth that is infallible and certain. It is wedded to the position of a single interpretation of doctrine or Scripture as the instruments of truth. It denies exactly what Bishop Colenso was arguing the case for: alternative interpretations across history and between cultures. For Bishop Gray, truth is fixed in a text or a declaration of faith which, it is supposed, is able to transcend differences of history and culture, or rather, ignore them because it exists outside history, or at least so far back in history (when the Church was 'while yet one') that it can appear to be eternal. Doctrine and Scripture become transcendental signifiers, signs that fix the meaning of an eternal transcendent truth (Eagleton 1992: 131). In this view, truth is trapped in a single authoritative language that claims to convey eternal truths literally and directly to man, rather than recognising itself as one of a number of possible languages, each conveying its own interpretation of the truth, conditioned by the differences and diversity of history and culture (Ridge 1994: 23).

This view of the certainty and infallibility of Scripture and doctrine relates back to a view of knowledge that I considered earlier. That is, knowledge as passively received rather than actively acquired by investigation. It embodies a conception of Scripture, doctrine and their interpretation that is timeless and this is closely associated with a belief in the desirability of a stable and unchanging social order.

Bishop Thirlwall comments that the resolution of the Convocation of Canterbury condemning Bishop Colenso's criticism of the Pentateuch 'assumes a paternal authority which...presupposes a childlike docility and obedience, in those over whom it is exercised' (Cox 1888, I: 304). The image is indicative a particular attitude towards authority and subordination and one that would be consistent with a conviction that knowledge is passively received. It might therefore not be an inappropriate for the time, since a passive view of knowledge could be considered to reflect the interests of the landed classes and the landed interests of the hierarchy of the Church of England.

In contrast, an active view of knowledge is associated with a conception of society which is dynamic and therefore subject to change. Such a conception of society would support a view of truth as historically relative. It would also connect with the ideals of improvement and progress that are associated with the emerging commercial and professional social classes in the mid-nineteenth century.

As we have already observed, the 'faith' that was being affirmed by Bishop Gray, rather than deriving from any current doctrine of the Church of England or from the 'great Councils' of the Church in the distant past, had in fact, at least to some extent, been invented. If, therefore, the 'faith' that Bishop Colenso was accused of contradicting was, in reality, an invented doctrine which, as Bishop Thirlwall had shown so cogently, had no part in the doctrine of the Church of England, how could there be any grounds to persist in the opinion that his views were erroneous? However, it turned out that this question was soon to be rendered irrelevant by subsequent developments which seemed to suggest that the consideration on which it was based was to be of little consequence. For, as events unfolded following the publication of the early parts of *The Pentateuch*, it was to become clear that the overriding issue was less to do with the truth of a doctrine, the correctness of its interpretation, its conformity to the doctrines of the Church of England, or even what the doctrine said. It had more to do with who had the authority to assert it, and to depose those who denied it, and how this authority was legitimated.

How did the orthodox bishops consider their authority to be legitimated? In the view of Bishop Colenso, Bishop Gray's regard for himself as one of 'the guardians of the Church's faith' (Cox 1888, I: 179) presupposed

> the existence of a spiritual caste to whom the Supreme King has delegated his power... (Cox 1888, I: 391)

and a man

> claiming for himself, and for his 'Church' Divine Authority and infalli- bility... (Cox 1888, I: 379)

But in secular terms, at any rate, the authority supposed by Bishop Gray for those who saw themselves as the orthodox bishops of the Church was apparently dealt a blow in March 1865 by the decision of the Judicial Committee of the Privy Council which declared 'null and void in law' Bishop Gray's proceedings, judgments and sentence of deposition against Bishop Colenso (Cox 1888, I: 260). Nevertheless, while Bishop Colenso's view of the need for freedom from the 'dead body of dogmas' gained sup- port from, and appeared to be vindicated by, the highest court in the land, it was Bishop Gray's view of doctrine and authority within the Church that, in practice, eventually prevailed.

The Privy Council's judgment denied the authority of the bishops to depose Bishop Colenso. But in defiance of this judgment, the bishops went ahead with the consecration of a rival bishop, which the Crown was unable to prevent. Thus, the bishops comprising the Church establishment had successfully defied the State, and equilibrium was established on the basis that

> the State decides, and then leaders of the Church...do not question the right of the State to decide but simply refuse to obey. The State ignores this disobedience. The absolute power of the State [therefore]...was overthrown without a revolution, without a change of written principles... (Cockshut 1959: 49)

Though the results of a series of decisions in the courts had made it clear that historical criticism of the Scriptures 'like any other book' was a perfectly legitimate activity within the Church and was not inconsistent with its articles and formularies, it was, nevertheless, suppressed by the Church.

Moreover, it became apparent that not only were the bishops able to defy the Crown and its courts with impunity, they were also able to exert a large measure of control over Churchmen whom they considered to be recalcitrant or rebellious.

The intimidating effect of what Benjamin Jowett referred to as 'terrorism' cannot be underestimated. In 1858, Jowett wrote to A.P. Stanley, before he became Dean of Westminister, inviting him to contribute to *Essays and Reviews*. In the letter Jowett said:

> names shall be given…we are determined not to submit to this abominable system of terrorism, which prevents the statement of the plainest facts…
> (Parsons 1988b: 195)

Although the legal action subsequently taken against two of the essayists of *Essays and Reviews* failed, it appears that Jowett was so affected by it that he never again produced a major theological work (Parsons 1988a: 45).

In the Preface to Part II of the *The Pentateuch*, Bishop Colenso illustrates the pressures that can be placed on clergymen not to express views that are contrary to the orthodox position (*The Pentateuch* II: xxviii-xxxi). A short story entitled *The Clergyman Who Subscribes for Colenso* by Anthony Trollope evokes an atmosphere of McCarthyism in the lives of clergymen who are known to have signed their names to the Bishop Colenso support fund (Trollope 1974: 119-30).

The 'Acceptance' of Biblical Criticism

There is another point of significance in this struggle over doctrine and one that also has a bearing on the questions that I originally set out to answer. When Bishop Colenso's criticisms of the Pentateuch apparently became acceptable to the Church of England's establishment, there was a disinclination to recognize the fact that these views, now accepted, were the same as those for which Bishop Colenso had been condemned with such ferocity.

When, in 1873, Frances Colenso, Bishop Colenso's wife, was given to understand (whether correctly or not) from a news report that a majority of the bishops of the Church of England now agreed with her husband's views on the composition of the Pentateuch, her reaction was as follows:

> Yet they don't come forward as they ought, and say—you were right and we were wrong and we retract all our hard words against you!… Just think of all the violent abuse that has been poured out upon him for making it plain to the common people that Moses did not write the P[entateuch]… And now not a word of just or generous apology, or confession, but they go on talking about Colensoism as if it were the equivalent of Atheism…
> (Rees 1958: 256)

In this connection, I now turn to consider whether Bishop Colenso's criticisms of the Pentateuch were eventually accepted by the Church and, if so, in what way.

Bishop Colenso put forward his view of the unhistorical and composite character of the Pentateuch in Part I of *The Pentateuch* in 1862 and in Parts II, III and IV in 1863. His arguments were met with a flat rejection by the defenders of orthodoxy within the Church, and the defence of the orthodox position against them continued to be maintained until long after the defence of religious orthodoxy within science, against evolutionary theory, had collapsed. When, in 1865, Bishop Colenso left England to return to Natal after the publication of the fifth part of his study, although exonerated by the secular courts, he remained under ecclesiastical condemnation as a heretic and there was no sign of any relaxation on the part of the Church establishment in their unequivocal opposition to his views.

The turning point seems to have been during the late 1880s and early 1890s.

Lux Mundi, published in 1889, was a collection of essays by High Churchmen from Oxford and was considered to be 'the high church counterpart of *Essays and Reviews*' (Neil 1963: 286). It questioned the historical truth of the Old Testament and aroused a storm of controversy. However, it did not receive the corporate condemnation that *Essays and Reviews* had suffered. In 1891, publications by S.R. Driver, Regius Professor of Hebrew at Oxford, and by A.F. Kirkpatrick, Regius Professor of Hebrew at Cambridge, indicated an acceptance of the unhistorical character of the Pentateuch (Rogerson 1984: 275, 285).

By 1903, the author of a history of the study of the Bible in the nineteenth century was able to say that

> The fact that critical views resembling those reached by Dr. Colenso have long been taught with undisputed authenticity in the universities and theological colleges of Great Britain, makes it difficult for this generation to realise the terror and wrath excited by the episcopal application of arithmetical tests to the narratives of the books of Exodus and Numbers. (Carpenter 1903: 34)

It therefore appears as though, after almost 30 years, Bishop Colenso's view of the unhistorical character of the Pentateuch had finally replaced the doctrine of Scriptural infallibility in the Church of England. However, if we look into the situation a little more closely, it is not quite so straightforward as it appears.

The 'acceptance' by the Church of biblical criticism in the 1880s and 1890s was not an acceptance of it in the form practised by the German scholars or by Bishop Colenso in his study of the Pentateuch. It was rather the

> development of a cautious, conservative criticism, a critical orthodoxy, a biblical criticism in which a moderate application of critical methods was wedded to a reassuringly orthodox doctrinal stance. (Parsons 1988b: 252; Rogerson 1984: 234, 287-88)

In 1914, the Bishops in Convocation asserted the truth of the historical facts stated in the creeds, with the exception that it recognized the need to 'face the new problems raised by historical criticism', and therefore

> the need for considerateness in dealing with that which is *tentative* and *provisional* in the thought and work of *earnest* and *reverent* scholars. (quoted in Livingstone 1974: 53 [my emphasis])

Key terms in the lexicon of this new moderate biblical criticism, or 'critical orthodoxy', were 'caution', 'restraint', 'reserve', 'moderation' and sometimes a combination of two of these (as in 'cautious reserve'). Also important were the terms 'reverent' and 'devout'. *Lux Mundi*'s 'reverent tone' may have been one factor that saved it from corporate condemnation. However, as Parsons has pointed out, this was a reverence for *orthodoxy* rather than for the *truth* (Parsons 1988b: 252).

Such words abound in the works of biblical scholars working within the 'critical orthodoxy' in Britain at this time. Not only do they use these terms to define their own approach towards biblical scholarship, they are also careful to apply them to other scholars in the field. To take the examples of two biblical scholars of this period, T.K. Cheyne refers to Driver's 'free but devout critical views' (Cheyne 1893: 314). In turn, Driver in his *Introduction to the Literature of the Old Testament*, mentioned above, refers to three other scholars as 'all men of cautious and well balanced judgement' (Driver 1897: xvi). There are also terms that signify an attitude which devout and reverent biblical scholars would want to dissociate themselves from. Such terms as 'immoderate', 'excess', 'extreme' and even 'fanatical' are used to describe the undesirable traits of a biblical scholar. One has the impression of an attempt to continually re-assure the reader that they are on safe ground albeit in close proximity to potentially hazardous terrain.

In the Preface to his *Introduction*, Driver refers to the 'critical position' (biblical criticism) as consistent with the principle of 'progressive revelation'. He also affirms the 'entire compatibility of the critical position with…the fullest loyalty to the Christian creed' (Driver 1897: xvi-ii). Hence, while assenting to the principle of the historically conditioned character of knowledge, biblical criticism had come to accept a subordinate position in a corporate reaffirmation of orthodoxy (albeit in a critically revised form) in which it had achieved official endorsement but only on condition that it restricted itself to the confines of scholarship.

Thus, the biblical criticism of Bishop Colenso had not, in fact, gained acceptance. The spirit of 'free inquiry' had not been allowed into the study of biblical texts except within the limited circles of those who adopted the appropriate attitude. Biblical criticism, 'untrammelled by religious dogma', as it were, could only be conducted in private, it seemed. 'The Reformation', in the form that Bishop Colenso had conceived it, had not yet arrived.

It is clear then, that the level of caution, restraint and reserve which was expected of biblical scholars, even in the 1890s, was far greater than Bishop Colenso had exercised 30 years earlier when the early parts of *The Pentateuch* were published. This was therefore an accommodation between biblical criticism and the Church from which Bishop Colenso was excluded.[1]

The exclusion of Bishop Colenso from the critical orthodoxy can be seen in operation, even after his death, by considering the position attributed to him within the historical development of biblical scholarship in Britain.

Again we refer to Driver's *Introduction*, which is recognized as one of the works signalling the acceptance of biblical criticism in Britain (Rogerson 1984: 275). In it, Driver sets out several reasons to justify the argument that the book of Deuteronomy was not written by Moses (Driver 1897: 82-87). However, these reasons include a number of points that are identical to those put forward by Bishop Colenso almost 30 years previously in support of exactly the same position, which at the time had been condemned as erroneous. Yet no reference is made to Bishop Colenso in

---

1.   At the same time, a corresponding accommodation between science and the Church was achieved by the reassertion of the Baconian compromise: the acceptance by both sides of the separate study of 'the two books' of Nature and Scripture (Moore 1986: 344). Since, as a result of this compromise, the study of Scripture was once again to come within the province of the Church, it was something that science need no longer concern itself with. Hence, the energy and resources of the increasingly professionalized enterprise of science and the full power of its guiding principle of free inquiry were diverted away from the critical investigation of the Scriptures.

Driver's book in this connection. Furthermore, among the vast amount of literature cited in connection with criticism of the historicity of the Pentateuch, no references to works by Bishop Colenso can be found. Driver explains that 'The older literature which has been superseded by more recent works is of necessity omitted altogether' (Driver 1897: 1). Where Driver does make reference to Bishop Colenso, it is only in order to disagree with his view that the author of the book of Deuteronomy could be Jeremiah (*The Pentateuch*, III: 618). However, if Bishop Colenso's work had been superseded, one may wonder why there was a need to take issue with him concerning the authorship of Deuteronomy, particularly he made it clear that to establish the actual authorship of the books of the Pentateuch was an aim which was secondary to his 'great main point', which was the demonstration of the unhistorical, non-Mosaic and composite character of the Pentateuch (*The Pentateuch*, IV: xxx).

Driver disagrees with Bishop Colenso's view of the authorship of Deuteronomy on the grounds of style, but he also places the composition of the work before the time of Jeremiah (Driver 1897: 87). T.K. Cheyne's review of biblical scholarship, published in 1993, is in the main complimentary about Driver's *Introduction*. However, in connection with the authorship of Deuteronomy, Cheyne says: 'Dr Driver does not quite accurately state the prevailing tendency of recent investigations', namely, 'the ruling critical opinion that Deuteronomy was composed in the time of Jeremiah' (Cheyne 1893: 266-67). This opinion is therefore consistent with Bishop Colenso's chronology.

Among the reasons cited by Driver in support of the case for the non-Mosaic authorship of Deuteronomy are contradictions or inconsistencies between the book of Deuteronomy and the earlier books of the Pentateuch. These include references to the priests as exclusively members of the tribe of Levi; the impoverished and insecure condition of the priests and the minimal provision made for their sustenance; and the commandment to sacrifice in one place only. The description in Deuteronomy of all these aspects of the Israelite religious system differs markedly from the corresponding accounts in the books of Leviticus and Numbers. Driver also cites certain phrases used in Deuteronomy such as 'unto this day' that imply a time gap between the date of composition and the events described which is inconsistent with its composition in the age of Moses. Similarly, the reference in Deuteronomy to Eastern Palestine as 'beyond Jordan' implies the residence of the author in Western Palestine. This would therefore have been at a time when the Israelites had settled in Canaan *after* the conquest rather than when they were in the desert prior to the conquest during the time of Moses. (Driver 1897: 82-85).

However, in Parts II and III of *The Pentateuch*, Bishop Colenso identifies all of these points, in much more detail and many others besides, in order to establish the non-Mosaic authorship of the Pentateuch (*The Pentateuch*, II: 209-12; III: 395, 457-58, 473-74). Rather than being superseded, Bishop Colenso's conclusions appear to be reiterated, but in a way that is not so well substantiated as in their original formulation. Thus, it appears that the biblical criticism of 'critical orthodoxy' may withhold recognition from its antecedents while reproducing the results of their scholarship.

If we now return to address the question of why Bishop Colenso was singled out for condemnation and vilification, we can see that an important consideration is to do with his approach to biblical criticism.

First, in his critical examination of the Pentateuch, he did not exercise voluntary restraint, caution or reserve, nor did he limit the range of his inquiries, in the way that seems to have been expected, even after the 'acceptance' of biblical criticism.

Second, he did not restrict the results of his investigations to scholarly circles. On the contrary, he directed these results to the 'general reader' 'in a form intelligible to the most unlearned layman' (Colenso 1864b: 5; *The Pentateuch*, II: vi; I: xxxiii).

Throughout the history of the confrontation between new ideas and religious orthodoxy, hostility on the part of the defenders of orthodoxy has tended to be directed not so much at the person who *originates* a challenging theory as at the person who *promulgates it*.

As we have seen, other Churchmen, and not only those who had been condemned, persecuted, or suspended from their posts, had also questioned the literal truth of the Bible. However, for many, if they expressed these views at all, they did so in a conservative manner that showed reverence and reserve. Others who had expressed such views more forcefully, often refrained from continuing to do so after being subjected to condemnation. The authors of *Essays and Reviews* did, of course, express their views openly in their essays. However, though these views were critical of the historicity of the Bible, they were couched in a conservative manner (Rogerson 1984: 218, 219) and, although those essayists who were prosecuted were legally acquitted, the ecclesiastical condemnation appears to have had a subduing effect on the authors in regard to the production of further works of historical criticism (Parsons 1988a: 45-46).

A.P. Stanley declined Benjamin Jowett's invitation to contribute to *Essays and Reviews* on the grounds that he did not consider that the time was right for such a venture. Alternatively, a calculated lack of clarity seems to have served the same purpose. An example of this is Stanley's *Lectures on the History of the Jewish Church*. In considering this work, John Rogerson comments that his biographers 'complained, not unfairly, that it was often very hard to discover what Stanley thought had taken place' (Rogerson 1984: 238).

In contrast, regardless of the degree of ecclesiastical condemnation that he was subjected to, Bishop Colenso *persisted* in setting out *openly before the public* his criticisms of the Pentateuch. Following the condemnation of Part I of *The Pentateuch*, he immediately proceeded to publish three further parts in the following year and would have released a fifth volume had he not been persuaded by his supporters to delay its publication.

Like Galileo, Bishop Colenso's real crime was not so much the origination of an idea or viewpoint which challenged the orthodox position, but *the fact that he publicized and promoted it.*

As Klaus Scholder points out, 'Whereas Copernicus, as he expressly states in the dedication to Pope Paul, intended his work for specialists, a notion also cherished by Kepler, Galileo spoke to everyone' (Scholder 1990: 54). Galileo's famous trial before the Inquisition in 1633 took place not because he had originated the idea that the Earth went round the Sun but because he made this idea widely available in the form of a readable dialogue which had sold out by the time it was prohibited a few months after publication. The issue for the Church at the time was not so much how true the theory was, as how public it was to become. Copernicus and Kepler produced their scholarly works in Latin consciously keeping their theoretical breakthroughs for the exclusive benefit of a scientific elite. Kepler, in a letter to a fellow scientist in 1598, suggested, 'let us communicate candidly our view to anyone who approaches us privately. In public let us keep silent' (Scholder 1990: 157 n. 36). In contrast, as one of his inquisitors complained, 'Galileo teaches the Earth's motion in writing…and he writes in Italian, certainly not to extend the hand to foreigners or other learned men, but rather to entice to that view common people in whom errors very easily take root' (Sobel 1999: 268).

Use of the vernacular is a key point here. Bishop Colenso refers to a work by an English Divine, Dr Thomas Burnet published in 1692, which showed 'the impossibility of holding the traditionary view, in the case of the Deluge, as well as in that of the Creation and the Fall'. This work was published in Latin and Bishop Colenso comments 'if the views of this able Divine had been published in the English tongue, so as to be "understood of the people", it is probable that we should not now, a century and a half afterwards, be still discussing the historical reality of these ancient narratives' (*The Pentateuch*, IV: xvi).

Ironically, it was seriously suggested, as reported in a speech by Charles Lyell to the Geological Society, that the whole controversy could have been avoided if Bishop Colenso's findings had been published 'in the Latin Language, so as to be confined to a circle which could be safely entrusted with such novelties, without there being any danger of unsettling the creed of the multitude' (*The Pentateuch*, V: xliii). This would have been consistent with one of the principles of critical orthodoxy that I have considered above. However, it is, of course, entirely contrary to Bishop Colenso's main objective, which is precisely to make the knowledge available to 'the multitude', rather than keep it from them (p. xliii).

Bishop Colenso is clearly in a long and honourable tradition of those accused of heresy who have drawn down opprobrium upon themselves by making public their points of disagreement with the orthodoxy of the time.

The Challenge from the Colonized

There is a further factor to take into consideration in accounting for the strength of feeling against Bishop Colenso. It is his emphasis on the fact that the original inspiration for his critical investigation of the Pentateuch was the direct result of questions asked by a Zulu. This point, which others have drawn attention to, is one which distinguishes Bishop Colenso's biblical criticism from that of other biblical scholars in mid-Victorian Britain (Guy 1991: 189; Parsons 1997: 142).

William Ngidi, a Zulu assisting Bishop Colenso in the translation of the books of Genesis and Exodus into Zulu, asked, 'Is all that true? Do you really believe…that all the beasts, and birds, and creeping things upon the earth, large and small, from hot countries and cold, came thus by pairs, and entered into the ark with Noah? And did Noah gather food for them *all*, for the beasts and the birds of prey as well as the rest?' In response to these questions, Bishop Colenso tells us, 'My heart answered in the words of the Prophet, "Shall a man speak lies in the name of the Lord?" Zech xiii.3. I dared not do so' (*The Pentateuch*, I: vii).

Unlike the majority of white settlers and missionaries in Natal and Zulu-land in the middle of the nineteenth century, Bishop Colenso recognized the inherent value of Zulu custom and belief. He defended polygamy and used Zulu words for God rather than importing a non-Zulu word as other missionaries had done in the belief that the Zulu people had no concept of God or even any religion of their own. He identified Zulu words that he equated with the Hebrew words 'Elohim' and 'Jehovah', the names for God revealed to the Hebrew people according to the books of the Pentateuch. Hence, not only did he acknowledge the validity of Zulu religion, in effect, he also suggested that, before any Christian missionaries had ever set foot in their land, the Zulu people, through their concepts of God, had access to the very heart of the Old Testament basis for Christian belief (Colenso 1855g: 115; Mosothoane 1991: 233). More importantly, however, he recognized the validity of their scepticism concerning traditional Christian belief in the Genesis narrative and, in so doing, gave equal weighting to both the critical thinking of a black culture and the traditions and beliefs of a dominant white culture which was the subject of that scepticism. Referring to the Zulu who aided him in his translation of the Bible, Bishop Colenso tells us: 'I have acquired sufficient knowledge of the language, to be able...not only to avail myself freely of their criticisms, but to appreciate fully their objections and difficulties' (*The Pentateuch*, I: vi).

In the third quarter of the nineteenth century, Great Britain enjoyed unchallenged supremacy on a worldwide scale, economically, politically and culturally. This privileged position and capability for worldwide domination fitted comfortably within a religious tradition that accorded a special place in history to a chosen people. This historic national achievement within the Judeo-Christian tradition lent itself to the view of a favoured race and a favoured nation and to the related assumptions of the superiority of the white race and, more particularly, of the British nation. Further support for this viewpoint was provided by evolutionary theory based on the concept of the survival of the fittest.

In mid-Victorian Britain, the dominant view within the establishment of the Church of England was that, along with divisions of social class at home, this social order of empire abroad, was validated by divine authority (Hart 1977: 123-27). This view, which, by definition, excluded all others, was therefore the viewpoint of a dominant race and nation. But there was the potential for it to be undermined by an encounter with the culture of a people who occupied a subordinate position in that empire but who questioned the beliefs upon which the superiority of its rulers was founded.

The connection between Bishop Colenso's biblical criticism and his recognition of the validity of Zulu culture and belief can be explored further by moving to Natal.

Biblical criticism was not the only area in which Bishop Colenso challenged a dominant view claiming absolute authority. From the mid-1870s, he devoted himself to defending the African people of Natal and Zululand from unfair treatment by colonial and imperial authorities. This has been referred to as the 'second important undertaking' in his life and, in this, his role was to be as controversial as it had been in his 'first important undertaking', the critical examination of the Pentateuch (Jarrett-Kerr 1989: 151).

A comparison of Bishop Colenso's involvement in these two controversies reveals similarities between them in regard to the patterns of discourse within each controversy and the changes in these patterns over time.

Stanley Ridge identifies four discourses at play in the context of Bishop Colenso's defence of Africans in Natal. The four discourses were: the colonial discourse; the imperial discourse; the liberal discourse and the muted discourse of the Zulus. Ridge characterizes each of these as follows. The colonial discourse is associated with magisterial power and, in the events in Natal of the 1870s, is characterized by the fear of rebellion and the use of terror, if all else fails, to control the African majority. The discourse of empire stands for superior moral authority first and then the power to impose it. Firmness, fairness, justice and magnanimity are key values and often serve, or are intended to serve, as a restraining influence on the colonial attitudes towards, and treatment of, colonized peoples. The liberal discourse values thoroughness, honesty and detachment and was the discourse in which Bishop Colenso was initially situated. The Zulu discourse was subject to distortion and misrepresentation by those claiming to know the 'native mind' and might not have been heard at all at the time had it not been for Bishop Colenso's attention to it (Ridge 1994: 27-29).

These four discourses confronted one another in a particular social and political context in Natal and I refer to such a context as a 'domain'. They are mirrored, I suggest, by four discourses, which were at play in the separate, but related, domain of the controversy concerning the authorship and historicity of the Pentateuch. If we overlay the set of discourses in the former domain with the set of discourses in the latter, we can see a degree of congruence between the two domains. This becomes apparent in terms of the similarities that can be identified, not only between the corresponding discourses in each domain, but also between the interrelationships among the discourses within each domain. Further similarities can be identified between the processes in operation over time in each domain.

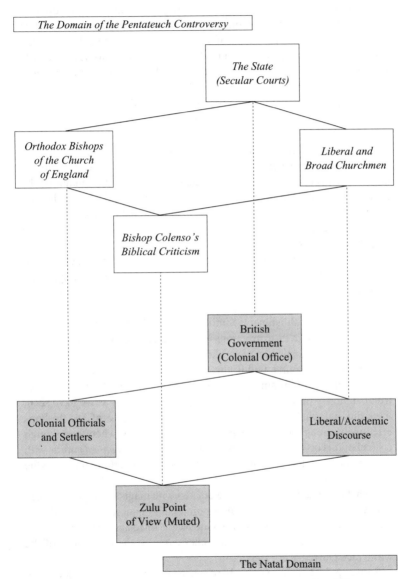

The Domain of the Pentateuch Controversy

The State
(Secular Courts)

Orthodox Bishops
of the Church
of England

Liberal and
Broad Churchmen

Bishop Colenso's
Biblical Criticism

British
Government
(Colonial Office)

Colonial Officials
and Settlers

Liberal/Academic
Discourse

Zulu Point
of View (Muted)

The Natal Domain

Figure 1. *Discourses of the Two Controversies Involving Bishop Colenso*

In the context of the controversy concerning the Pentateuch, the four discourses at play are: the discourse of those who considered themselves orthodox bishops, or 'guardians of the faith' of the Church of England; the discourse of the State as represented by the decisions of its secular courts in Church affairs; the discourse of the liberal or Broad Churchmen and scientists; and finally, the discourse of Bishop Colenso's biblical criticism. Each of these discourses can be seen to correspond to a discourse at play in Natal as set out in Fig. 1 (previous page).

In the domain of the Pentateuch controversy, the discourse of the bishops displays certain features comparable to the colonial discourse in Natal. Both these discourses are characterized by their direct assertion of dogmatic and absolute authority, the fear of challenge to that authority, the need to control those in subordinate positions to it and, if need be, the resort to the use of terror as a defence against actual or perceived rebellion. These two discourses were the dominant ones in their respective domains.

The discourse of the State in connection with the Pentateuch controversy valued justice in its detachment from doctrinal controversy, while seeking to ensure the fair treatment of accused parties. In its judgments, it sought to exercise a restraining influence on the persecution of dissidents by the Church establishment. Similarly, the imperial discourse in Natal had sought, through its instructions in dispatches, to enforce fair treatment from colonial officials in action taken against 'rebellious' Africans.

The liberal discourse within the Pentateuch controversy included the liberal or Broad Churchmen. This group did not accept the absolute doctrinal authority of the bishops of the Church. However, as we have seen, they did not challenge the dominant orthodox view of the bishops effectively enough to call into question their authority. Therefore, though critical of this orthodoxy, their position was *voluntarily muted* and, as with the liberal discourse in Natal, did not represent a serious threat to the dominant discourse.

Both dominant discourses are associated with magisterial power, which believes its authority is based on absolute and unquestionable truths. In one case, on the divine authority of God as evidenced in the Scriptures and doctrine of the Church and, in the other case, on the superiority of the white race (Jarrett-Kerr 1989: 146).

Further points of comparison between the two dominant discourses may be highlighted by considering additional features common to both discourses. These include: the single point of view and the importance of obedience to authority. We have seen all of these features present in the attitude of the orthodox bishops of the Church of England. They were also reflected in the attitudes of colonial officials and white settlers in Natal in the context of the controversy surrounding the Langalibalele 'rebellion'.

The colonists' belief in their own superiority presupposed a single point of view, any dissent from which was seen as 'rebellion' and responded to harshly. Colonists killed in a military manoeuvre intended to 'put down' the Hlubi 'rebellion', had been 'basely murdered'; whereas Africans killed in retaliation were only 'punished', as Bishop Colenso observed (Cox 1888, II: 328 cited in Guy 1983: 204-205).

The belief in infallibility was reflected in the colonists' adamant adherence to their own account of events, as opposed to the account of the African people. The colonists' view of the 'rebelliousness' of the Hlubi people, the 'guilt' of their chief, Langalibalele, the proper conduct and fairness of the trial, the veracity of the evidence presented and the leniency of the sentence, was maintained despite evidence to the contrary gathered by Bishop Colenso from African sources. When this evidence was presented to the Colonial Office and subsequently to Parliament it was received in disbelief. The Lord Chancellor concluded his report to the House of Lords with the rhetorical question: 'Was there ever anything that darkened the annals of British Justice like that?' (Rees 1958: 265).

Ultimately, the colonial account of events, when contradicted by numerous accounts from African witnesses under cross-examination, justified itself on the grounds that the oral tradition of the Africans created an incorrect version of events that 'soon crystallizes into an accepted form' (Guy 1983: 245).

As with Bishop Colenso's questioning of the literal truth of the Scriptures, the questioning by Africans of colonial infallibility was met with bullying, intimidation and humiliation (Guy 1983: 210).

The belief by the colonists in their own account of events was so strong that Bishop Colenso was said to have 'quite lost his head' simply because he sought to question it. The fact that this observation was made with some satisfaction by the bishop who had been appointed as a rival to Bishop Colenso in Natal, points to a link between the two domains in regard to this attitude. The link is further reinforced by a statement by missionaries and clergy of the colony claiming that the proceedings against Langalibalele 'were humane, lenient, just, and urgently necessary', and declaring that 'Those that are against the Natal Government in this case, are actually against almighty God'. The Governor of the Colony, eventually recalled for his role in the affair, claimed that he had taken action 'under God's providence' (Guy 1983: 216-17).

The importance to the colonists of obedience to authority is reflected, for example: in the expectation that African chiefs should follow instructions from magistrates 'cheerfully', rather than 'sullenly' (Guy 1983: 198); by the 'public tongue-lashing' delivered to Zulu leaders by the Governor of Natal (Guy 2001a: 194-95); in the floggings routinely delivered by a magistrate in Zululand (p. 202); by the view of the Secretary for Native Affairs that the Natal Africans should 'submit to the rule of civilization' (Guy 1983: 255); by the characterization of their attitude as 'a spirit of insolent independence' (Kline 1988: 18); and by the expressed desire of the Special Administrator in Natal for a master–servant relationship between colonists and Africans in Natal (Kline 1988: 123).

Another point of correspondence between the colonists and the orthodox bishops of the Church of England is the landed interest. In Natal, the settler farmers found it difficult to make their land profitable due to a labour 'shortage'—contrary to what the immigrant white settlers had been led to believe (Bundy 1988: 168). From this point of view, the real 'rebellion' by the Africans was to retain their own economic independence by successfully preserving their subsistence economy and, in some cases, by becoming successful independent traders, thus depriving the white settlers of a source of cheap labour and even becoming their competitors (Guy 1983: 195; Bundy 1988: 171; Kline 1988: 17). This brought down on them the resentment of the white setters and, along with their resistance to conversion to Christianity and rejection of other forms of cultural domination, can be taken as part of a pattern of resistance by Africans to the dominant point of view in Natal.

As Karl Marx pointed out, in capitalist societies of the nineteenth century, capitalism relied on wage labour being made available by virtue of the fact that the worker is under economic compulsion to sell his labour power having been deprived of any other means of subsistence and of the ownership of the means of production. Where economic conditions do not provide such compulsion, this may have to be created by juridical or political means: by the imposition of taxes, rents, fines, and so on, or by the destruction of the workers' independent means of subsistence. Much in the attitude of the white settlers towards the Africans can be explained by the build-up to, and the justification of, such compulsion being exercised (Marx 1976: 48, 931-40).

In both domains, the dominant discourses responded with defiance to the instructions or judgments of the State, and successfully resisted the attempts to restrain them from exercising their authority to arbitrarily silence dissent. As we have seen, in the Pentateuch controversy, the bishops effectively defied the authority of the State by ignoring the rulings of its courts. In Natal, the colonial officials defied the instructions of the Colonial Office, for example, to release Langalibalele, to rehabilitate the Hlubi and to compensate the Ngwe people for the losses they had suffered (Guy 1983: 228-31). A similar defiance can be seen in the moves leading up to the invasion of Zululand in 1879, precipitating the Anglo-Zulu War, despite instructions from the Colonial Office 'to avoid the outbreak of any such war' (Guy 1983: 258).

In both domains, the dominant discourses were met by challenges from below: from Bishop Colenso, outside the community of biblical scholar-ship, questioning the basis of orthodox Christian belief from one of the remote regions of the empire, and from the African people, particularly from the Zulu kingdom in the assertion of the right of its people to continue to enjoy an independent existence in a self-sustaining economy outside the imperialist capitalist system.

However, the dominant discourses successfully asserted their authority against these challenges. They did so by wielding effective power to silence them, by taking punitive action against those voicing them, or by distorting the content of their message. Although Bishop Colenso's dis-course on the Pentateuch was itself by no means muted, concerted attempts were made by the orthodox bishops and by the Church hierarchy to silence him by means of inhibitions, ridicule and condemnations and by refusing to respond to the content of his criticisms. Similarly, attempts were made by the colonial authorities in Natal to ensure that the Zulu voice would not be heard, to distort their statements through mistranslation (Ridge 1994: 30-32), to discredit their supporters and representatives or (more often) physically to deny them access to any means of communica-tion with the colonial authorities. It was in his efforts to make the Zulu voice heard that Bishop Colenso aligned himself with the Zulu discourse.

Both challenges from the subordinate discourses were ultimately de-feated by assimilation. The destruction of the Hlubi and the Zulu kingdom was followed by the annexation of Zululand and the incorporation of its people into the capitalist economic system and into the political system of the British Empire. As we have seen, eventually, the project of biblical criticism within the Church of England was assimilated into a 'critical orthodoxy' which confined it to the limited circle of biblical scholarship and which therefore rendered it harmless or severely limited its impact on orthodox doctrine or belief.

The Zulu Point of View

Individuals moved between discourses over time. Bishop Colenso's change of viewpoint caused, or contributed towards, the dynamic of opposition and tension between the dominant and subordinate discourses in each domain.

In both domains, the Liberal discourses were the ones that, initially, Bishop Colenso was most naturally associated with. But in both cases, over time, he distanced himself from these viewpoints and aligned himself with the subordinate discourses. From these new positions he became actively engaged in developing a critique of the dominant discourses.

In the Natal domain, Bishop Colenso moved from the relative intellectual detachment of the liberal point of view to align himself with the Zulu position (Guy 1983: 242). This shift of viewpoint was a traumatic experience following his discovery of irregularities in the trial of Langalibalele. It involved a break in his friendship of 20 years with the Secretary for Native Affairs, Theophilus Shepstone. During the trial and its aftermath, and subsequently in the events leading up to and following the Anglo-Zulu War, he sought to put forward 'the Zulu point of view', a campaign which was continued after his death by other members of his family, particularly his daughter, Harriette Colenso (Guy 2001a: 127-28).

In the Pentateuch domain, Bishop Colenso became distanced from the Broad Church Party by not exercising voluntary restraint, caution or reserve in his critical investigations, by not softening his tone, and by publicizing his results and pursuing his challenge to the orthodoxy of the Church openly, publicly and persistently. However, we may now note another point of divergence. We have seen that a key area of agreement between Bishop Colenso and the Broad Churchmen was with regard to the historical relativity of truth. But, Bishop Colenso went beyond this by insisting on the inherent validity of Zulu culture and belief, and on their right to question the fundamentals of Christian belief. In effect, therefore, he was asserting that truth was culturally, as well as historically, relative.

A historically relative view of truth could be incorporated within the Judeo-Christian tradition without undermining the assumption of cultural and racial superiority of Western civilization. However, this assumption cannot be maintained so plausibly within a perspective of cultural relativity and, indeed, is vulnerable to subversion by it.

Although Bishop Colenso did not spell out the implications of this explicitly, they are hinted at by him in a lecture to the Marylebone Literary Institute in May 1865. Peter Hinchliff notes Bishop Colenso's comment in this lecture that 'we cannot presume to assert that the human family will never be benefited by light reflected even from the thinkers of Zululand' and suggests the implication is that the question to be asked is not 'whether the Zulu nation could benefit from European civilization and the Christian religion, but whether Europe and Christianity might benefit from what the Zulus had to give them' (Hinchliff 1986: 109-10).

This highlights a key unifying theme common to both Bishop Colenso's 'important undertakings'. This is 'the Zulu point of view'—which, when it could be heard or made known, questioned otherwise unquestionable assumptions and presented an alternative perspective to the dominant viewpoint which assumed moral superiority and infallibility in both domains: in one, on the part of the religiously orthodox in the Church and in the other, on the part of the colonial officials and settlers in the colonies.

We can now begin to see the importance of the role of the Zulu in the debate concerning the Pentateuch. In mid-Victorian Britain, criticisms of the historicity of the Bible had, in the main, taken place within the perspective of Christian culture. In *Essays and Reviews*, for example, mention of 'the heathen' is hastily passed over (Cockshut 1959: 65). In contrast, the biblical criticism of Bishop Colenso contains a cultural critique and it is the Zulu dimension which provides this.

The Zulu provide concrete expression of the other point of view. They are a symbol of diversity and of the failure of the single viewpoint of scriptural infallibility to come to terms with the changing world that empire was launching it into.

In the challenges to religious orthodoxy from the liberal and Broad Churchmen and from science and its allies within the Church, we can see the expression of a struggle *within* the ruling class in mid-Victorian Britain as traditional power rooted in its landed interests, sought to defend itself from the power of the emerging professional and commercial interests. In Bishop Colenso's challenge to orthodoxy, however, something very different is happening. Here the Zulu are attacking from *below*. It is a radical challenge to the principle of the unquestioned right to the dominance of the viewpoint of one race, one culture, one religion.

Recognition of the symbolic power of the Zulu to mount a critical challenge to orthodoxy may be reflected in a suggestion made by Bishop Colenso to members of the X Club. Before their club had found a name, he suggested that they should call it the 'Zulu Club'. In doing so, he may have sought to explore the potential for this potent symbol of dissent to establish an association between biblical criticism of the radical form favoured by him, and the principle of free enquiry as practised by the progressive scientists of the day. The fact that his suggestion was not accepted points to the possibility that the failure to form such an alliance against orthodoxy was due to reluctance on the part of the scientists (see the letter from Joseph Dalton Hooker to Charles Darwin, April 1865, held in the Darwin Archives, Cambridge University Library [DAR 102: 15-16]).

During the Pentateuch controversy, the degree of interest that there was in the Zulu origin of Bishop Colenso's biblical criticism is notable. Reactions, ranging from ridicule to contempt to anger, indicate that this aspect of the controversy touched a nerve of anxiety.

There were already grounds for associating the Zulu people with a point of view critical of Christianity. The Zulu had been resistant to conversion to Christianity and this appears to be, at least in part, due to the perceptive recognition by them that conversion to Christianity would involve converting not just to a belief system, but also to a way of life and that this would therefore mean the destruction of their own traditions. Missionary accounts of the conversion of Africans reveal the insistence by missionaries that African converts adopt not only the religion, but also the way of life, of the European. This was symbolized well, perhaps, by the very great importance attached by missionaries to converts living in square houses arranged in straight lines rather than in round dwellings as was traditional for the Zulu. This neither accorded with the traditional living pattern of the Zulu nor with the symbolic importance of the circle in Zulu culture (Bundy 1988: 37; Draper 1998: 17 n. 6).

However, the Zulu people had shown themselves adept, not only at resisting conversion to Christianity, but also at challenging the validity of Christian belief. The famous questioning from William Ngidi, which led Bishop Colenso to embark on his studies of the Pentateuch, was not the first example of Zulu scepticism towards Christian belief. Roman Catholic missionaries reported in 1856 that an obstacle to conversion of the Zulu was that 'they raised astute philosophical difficulties on which neither the Bishop nor Father Gerard satisfied them' (Jarrett-Kerr 1989: 149). The association of the Zulu people with scepticism towards traditional Christian doctrine found its way into English literature in the writings of Anthony Trollope in a story entitled *The Zulu in London* (Trollope 1974: <51-62>).

The interrelationships between discourses in each domain changed over time and we can compare the processes of change between the two domains.

In Britain, in the face of defiance by the bishops, the State's inaction had led to its collusion in the restoration of the bishops' control over Church affairs and doctrine. The failure of the challenge by the Broad Churchmen further ensured that the bishops prevailed in matters to do with the Church. Nor was the position changed by the acceptance of biblical criticism since, as we have seen, this amounted to an accommodation which imposed limits and conditions on its practice. The acceptance of these restrictions implied an acknowledgment by the liberal Churchmen of their subordinate position within an accommodation which recognized the authority of the bishops while excluding the discourse of the radical historical criticism of Bishop Colenso. As indicated earlier, the component of the liberal discourse represented by science also found its place in this accommodation in a way which ensured that its powerful analytical tool of free inquiry was directed away from biblical criticism and allowed to go its own way in the study of nature without fear of further harm being done to orthodox Christian belief.

This process of accommodation had its counterpart in Natal. There, the initial defiance of the British Government by the colonial authorities was followed by a conflation of the colonial and imperial discourses within a new unified perspective which provided the justification for the consolidation of colonial and imperial interests to address the supposed 'black threat' (Ridge 1994: 30, 32). This consolidation was one element of a transformation of attitude at the centre of empire in response to changing social, economic and political conditions at the beginning of the last quarter of the nineteenth century. In Natal and Zululand, this new attitude, later to be characterized as the 'new imperialism', found its expression, initially, in the move towards confederation in South Africa and, subsequently, in the invasion of Zululand and the destruction of the Zulu kingdom.

In the Natal domain, the liberal discourse also reached an accommodation with the dominant discourse in which it accepted a subordinate role. By the time of the outbreak of the Anglo-Zulu War in 1879, it appears that most missionaries whose viewpoint had been within the liberal discourse, had deserted this point of view and aligned themselves with the colonial viewpoint. This included many missionaries who had withdrawn from Zululand and who were adding to the chorus of spurious scare stories about the supposed warlike intentions of the Zulu king and the threat of an invasion of Natal from Zululand.

Thus, in Natal, these three discourses arrived at an accommodation around the consolidation of imperial and colonial interests which excluded the discourse of colonized people and those who spoke on their behalf.

The convergence or conflation of discourses in both domains canbe accounted for, in part, by reference to social and political changes that took place during the last half of the nineteenth century in Great Britain and its empire and which resulted in a closing of ranks between the two dominant sections of the ruling class in the home country.

One aspect of this process was a hardening of attitudes towards class and race. From the 1860s, Douglas Lorimer traces a shift in attitude, on the party of the bourgeoisie and landed aristocracy and gentry, from 'ethnocentric paternalism' towards a view of the permanent inferiority of the British working class and the 'black races' (Lorimer 1978: 16, 208). Neither the scientists, nor the liberal or Broad Churchmen in 'the progressive center of English thought' were immune from this hardening of attitude. F.W. Farrar said that it was wrong to assume that black and white could be treated as equals (Lorimer 1978: 193) and in 1866 he spoke of 'savages' as 'depraved and wretched…as little perfectible as the dogs which they domesticate' (Mosothoane 1991: 223-24). Many of the scientists who had associated with Bishop Colenso while he was in London expressed similar views. Joseph Dalton Hooker said, 'I consider the Negro to be *far* below the level of the Englishman' (Lorimer 1978: 194). He also referred to the Zulu as 'not worth a thought' (Huxley 1918, II: 58). T.H. Huxley argued that blacks were inferior to whites and that intermarriage would result in a deterioration of the (white) species (*The Reader* 5 March 1864: 287-88).

At the time of his address in 1865 to the Marylebone Literary Institute, Bishop Colenso's attitude may have been one of 'ethnocentric paternalism'. Subsequently, however, following his work in defence of Langalibalele and the Hlubi people, his attitude seems to have moved in the opposite direction to the general trend described by Lorimer. If, at the beginning of his missionary work in Natal, he started out believing that the Zulu would benefit from assimilation into the British colonial system, he ended up working hard to defend them from it.

In 1879, while he was still being vilified for his biblical criticism in Great Britain, Bishop Colenso preached a sermon in Natal denouncing the invasion of Zululand by British and colonial forces. In this sermon he affirmed his view that if the war were pursued against the Zulu, it would have the effect of 'bringing us Christians below the level of the heathen with whom we fight' (Greaves 1999: 50). As we know, the war *was* pursued.

There is a further aspect of the relationship between the dominant and subordinate discourses that can bear comparison between the two domains. This is the possibility of viewing the interaction between discourses as a long 'conversation', as the encounter between missionaries and Africans in a 'two-sided drama' (Draper 1999: 14-16). Having adopted the attitude of magisterial power of the colonial discourse in their conversation with the Zulu, we would expect the missionaries in Natal and Zululand to make as little headway along the road to the conversion of the Zulu to Christianity, as did the bishops of the Church of England in their attempts to (re)convert Bishop Colenso to an acceptance of Scriptural infallibility and to a recognition of the 'errors' he had made in his criticism of the historicity of the Pentateuch. Bishop Colenso was as critical of, and as resistant to, such conversion as were the Zulus. Rather, his programme for conversion was in the opposite direction.

Conclusion

Bishop Colenso's work in defence of the Hlubi and Zulu people and his criticisms of the Pentateuch were not unrelated missions. They were connected by the fact that in both these undertakings he represented a voice of an alternative and largely unheard point of view, a voice questioning the legitimacy of an absolute authority that recognized no other viewpoint than its own. For him, it was the 'guardians' of the 'dead body of dogma' that were the real 'heathens'. The conversion that he sought to bring to them was one which recognized the value of other cultures, other histories, other points of view.

Ultimately, his criticisms of the Pentateuch were criticisms not only of the Church but also of British society and empire. He found his point of intellectual departure for these criticisms as a missionary to the Zulu in Africa. Later, when he returned to England to publish his criticisms on the Pentateuch, he became a missionary to his own people. But, he brought a message to them that was unwelcome because it threatened to expose as groundless the justification for one race and one nation to dominate others.

In some ways, Bishop Colenso was like a twentieth-century social anthropologist. By immersing himself in the viewpoint of another culture radically different from his own he had gained new perspectives and new insights into his own culture. The fact that he was unable to find a receptive audience for these in his own country is something this paper attempts to account for.

OTHER TIMES AND OTHER CUSTOMS:
A STORM IN A VICTORIAN TEACUP?

Ronald B. Nicolson

Others in this volume will provide a detailed exegesis and critique of
Colenso's theological views. In this paper I intend, in a 'broad brush' sort
of way, to take themes from Colenso as a starting point for a meditation on
where South African, and especially South African Anglican theology
ought to be going today. The emphasis on Anglicanism can perhaps be
forgiven since what has become known as 'the Colenso controversy' was
one that primarily affected the Anglican Church, in South Africa and in
the Anglican communion of the Victorian era.

In these global times, should there even be such a thing as a South
African theology? Yes and No! No theology can or should exist in isolation from global theological concerns, and no theology can or should exist
without being rooted in its own local context. It would be anachronistic, of
course, to talk of a South African theology with regard to Colenso, but
there is no doubt that his theology became increasingly one which was
strongly rooted in the context of the small colony where he ministered. He
sought to marry what he saw as the 'cutting edge' biblical and scientific
scholarship of Europe with the outlook and the needs of his colonial and
missionary diocese. Reading now through his *Natal Sermons* (Colenso
1867d) one wonders what the congregations in St Paul's (Durban) and St
Peter's (Pietermaritzburg) almost 150 years ago made of sermons on the
need to take seriously the insights of Darwin or of the higher biblical
critics in Germany. In one of these sermons Colenso said:

> If the light of Modern Science comes from God—and surely we must
> believe it does—it must be as great a *sin* to despise it or to disregard it, as to
> despise and disregard the Bible. (Colenso 1867d: 9)

Personal knowledge of both congregations in the present day suggests that
much of the sermon would pass over their heads, with mutterings about
the length. Yet, as we know, it was not only the insights of modern science

that Colenso begged his hearers to take into account. He wanted them all, English and Zulu, to learn from their own experience in Natal. More especially, he wanted his white congregations to take seriously the insights to be gained from their Zulu brothers and sisters. He quotes from prayers of the Galla people of North East Africa, and prayers from Hinduism, to show that

> There were multitudes who lived the life of God in earth before there was a Bible; there are multitudes now who, I doubt not, walk with God, even in heathen lands, though they have no Bible. (Colenso 1967: 68)

And therefore, by corollary, the colonists could learn from the colonized just as the colonized could learn from the colonists. All of us learn from our daily experience of God in the world and in other people. Colenso points out that before the missionaries came, Zulus knew God:

> They spoke of him repeatedly to me, and quite of their own accord, as the maker of all things and all men. (Colenso 1967: 2)

Unlike the eastern Cape missionaries, he opted to take the existing Zulu name *Unkulunkulu* as the Zulu name within the Church for God (Colenso 1855g: 59).

Jeff Guy reminds us of the famous story of Colenso being challenged by his interpreter, William Ngidi, on the literal credibility of the Genesis story of Noah's ark, and how Colenso believed that his eyes to truth were opened by Ngidi's question and 'thus I was driven—against my will at first, I may truly say—to search more deeply into these questions' (Guy 1983: 91). In all these ways, Colenso came to realize that there was much to be learned from Zulu culture and from early Zulu converts, and this respect would grow throughout his life.

In each place and context a theology must be born which seeks to bring together the various strands of revelation. Global theology must affect regional theology—but the particular voices, challenges and insights of the regional must not be lost in the global. Even 150 years ago, this was in essence what Colenso was perhaps seeking to embody in his sermons—the academic and the mundane; the global and the local; the 'Christian' and the 'non-Christian'. All of these need to interweave in our conceptions of God and of God's will for us.

This should not alarm us as much as it did his more conservative hearers of the day. As safe and Anglican an authority as John Macquarrie set it out for us in his *Principles of Christian Theology*. The sources of theology—that is, the contexts in which we may hear God communicating with us—

are experience, revelation, scripture, tradition and reason. Macquarrie vigorously defends the concept of natural theology upon which Colenso implicitly builds his approach to faith (Macquarrie 1996: 39-52).

Macquarrie no longer holds the authority he may once have done. I am not suggesting—and Colenso was not suggesting—that these sources of theology are equal. However sympathetic to Zulu culture, Colenso was far too much a man of his time to think that the experience of God in traditional Zulu religion was to be in any way equated with Christian revelation. The Zulus may have been noble savages, but they were, in his view, still primitive and unformed:

> Let us lift up a meek petition also to the throne of grace for the poor dark
> tribes of Africa and for those who shall minister the message of our God
> among them. (Colenso 1982: 40)

The sources of theology were not necessarily equal in status for Colenso, and certainly in his earlier days what Colenso took to be reason or science, alongside the Scriptures, were the fundamental bases for his theology, with F.D. Maurice as his guide and mentor. However, the experience of the Zulus among whom he worked came to take on increasing significance.

In this new era when scholarly evangelicals have perhaps taken the lead, Alister McGrath comments that 'experience' is a slippery word, and he challenges the view that experience provides a foundational resource for Christian theology. Rather, Christian theology provides a framework by which human experience may be interpreted (McGrath 1993: 81). Nevertheless, McGrath also concedes that experience, and especially the particular experience of particular people, is a vital point of contact for Christian apologetics in a post modern world (p. 85); and, as the divisions between Colenso and the colonial Natal government grew, this became for him just that—a vital point of contact between the gospel and the world.

Colenso, then, tried to make theological sense out of conflicting and apparently incompatible contexts:

1. the scientific worldview of his day, especially Darwinism;
2. the contemporary technical insights and challenges posed by biblical scholarship;
3. a situation of conflict between colonist and colonized, between modern and pre-modern;
4. the need to challenge the assumptions of the colonists and to encourage the aspirations of the colonized;

5.   the African worldview of the Zulu people, their culture, their family life, their religion;

6.   the desire to present the gospel to the Zulus in a manner that was appropriate and constructive.

There is something admirable about these aims. On the face of it, he would have done better to restrict his scope. Had he not outraged his conservative fellow bishops by his espousal of Darwin, and more particularly his espousal of the scepticism raised by the biblical scholarship of his day concerning the literal truth of the pentateuchal stories (items 1 and 2 above), those same bishops might have supported him when he needed their aid in confronting the Natal and British governments over the treatment of the Zulus. Had he not outraged the colonists by siding with Langalibalele and Cetshwayo against the colonial government, they might have been more willing to listen to him as he sought to make them more aware of the riches in Zulu culture. Had he not offended Shepstone by criticizing his political manipulation of the Zulu kingdom, he would have found a willing listener among the more educated colonists for his liberal humanist views. By offending on so many sides at once, he lost all support except that of the Zulu people—who almost certainly cared not a fig for his advanced theological views on science and creation.

Yet these strands in Colenso are inextricable. Guy correctly makes the point that Colenso the social reformer cannot be divorced from Colenso the controversial theologian. His liberal theology is informed by, and arises out of his social concerns:

> It fragments Colenso's life in order to have the political activist without the controversial theologian: it conflates South African history by approaching all protest against racial injustice as if it had the same roots...it ignores the fact that devout religious views can also be an expression of social forces in the continuing struggle for power and domination. (Guy 1983: 353)

Academic theology in South Africa has on the whole by the twenty-first century enthusiastically taken on board the need for theology to engage with issues of oppression. Liberation theology, black theology, feminist theology, womanist theology, are all in vogue, as indeed they should be. Rather less has happened in South Africa in academic theology as far as engaging with African traditional religion and culture, though on the ground, in Churches both 'mainline' and independent, a great deal of cross-reference occurs. The delay in seeking to build bridges with African tradition seems to me to have to do with the apartheid ideology and the fear, on the part of progressive black theologians of the 1970s, that the government of the day was seeking to push them back into 'tribalism' and a separate identity. Thus for a while there was a tension between those who supported a 'black theology' of resistance and those who supported an 'African theology' of assimilation with Africa (see Buthelezi 1972: 7). But those days are over, and there is growing interest in exploring the links between Christianity and African 'traditional religion'.

This has, however, raised some new tensions. The aftermath of the charismatic movement which profoundly affected most of the white and Indian members of mainline churches—and indeed most Indian Christians are members of Pentecostal Churches—has left a pronounced conservatism, particularly with regard to fears concerning syncretism. Among African Christians, while the progressive young theologians may be beginning to yearn to re-emphasize African roots (and while many congregants are 'Zionist by night'), many older clergy are still wary of compromising the concept of salvation through Jesus and Jesus alone. The issue of polygamy, in which Colenso unsuccessfully tried to persuade the Church to baptize polygamist husbands, remains unresolved. The issue of offerings to the ancestors and relationships with the ancestors is a highly contested area.

With regard to biblical scholarship, while at an academic level the issue of biblical criticism which seemed so shocking to Colenso's opponents has long been resolved, and while at a grassroots level work done by, for example, the Institute for the Study of the Bible at the University of Natal has shown that readers make their own interpretations of the Bible on the basis of their own experience, the aftermath of charismatism means that Anglican clergy and preachers are often near-fundamentalist in their views, and, no doubt, were Colenso to revive and state as bluntly again his views about the 'Fallibility of the Scriptures' (Colenso 1867d: 36) in the modern congregations of St Paul's in Durban or St Peter's in Pietermaritzburg, there would still be a ruffling in the dovecotes.

However, the major similarity between the Colenso controversy and our own times lies in the first of the points above. South African theology takes little account of liberal trends in international theology. The agonies of much European and American theology in coming to terms with a postmodern worldview and the abandonment of 'grand narratives' have largely passed South Africa by. Don Cupitt, Lloyd Geering, John Spong, as the more outspoken spokespersons for postmodernism in the Church, are unknown names. This is not really surprising. 'Liberal' Christians do not usually make very good evangelists. Most Anglican evangelism in Africa has been done by either evangelical or anglo-catholic missionary societies who have left their stamp behind. The remnant of Colenso's own church, the so-called 'Church of England in South Africa', has become so strongly conservative as to have almost lost touch with the evangelical wing of the Anglican communion.

Peter Hinchliff (1963: 93) provides us with a summary of the nine charges of heresy brought against Colenso. These were:

[1.] That he denied that our Lord died in man's stead, or to bear the punishment or penalty for our sins, and that God is reconciled to us by the death of his Son.

[2.] That he taught that justification is a *consciousness* of being counted righteous, and that all men, even without such a consciousness, are treated by God as righteous, and that all men are already dead unto sin and risen again unto righteousness.

[3.] That he taught that all men are born into righteousness when born into the world; that all men are at all times partaking of the body and blood of Christ; denying that the holy sacraments are generally necessary to salvation, and that they convey any special grace, and that faith is the means whereby the body and blood of Christ are received.

[4.] That he denied the endlessness of future punishments.

[5.] That he maintained that the Bible contained but was not the word of God.

[6.] That he treated the Scriptures as a merely human book, only inspired as any other book might be inspired.

[7.] That he denied the authenticity, genuineness and truth of certain books of the Bible.

[8.] That, by imputing errors in knowledge to our Lord, he denied that He is God and Man in one person.

[9.] That he brought parts of the Book of Common Prayer into disrepute (e.g. the Athanasian Creed and the vow at the ordination of deacons which spoke of 'unfeigned belief' in the Scriptures).

Hinchliff discounts charges 5-9 on the basis that both Colenso and his accusers were partly right and partly wrong. My own view is that this is too weak an assessment, and that in some cases his accusers were simply wrong and Colenso was simply right. What is set out in charge 5 is exactly what most Christians today would think to be true. While Muslims believe that the Qur'an is in itself the literal word of God, Christians believe by contrast that while the written Bible provides us with access to the word of God and to Jesus the living Word, it is not in itself the word of God; hence the significant change of response in the new South African *Anglican Prayer Book* after the recitation of the gospel in the Eucharist from the previous 'This is the word of the Lord', as in the Church of England *Alternative Service Book*, to the revised response, 'Hear the word of the Lord' (*Anglican Prayer Book* 1989: 107; *Alternative Service Book* 1980: 181). In the Bible we may hear the word of God; it is not in itself the literal word of God:

> we should carefully notice that it is only in a secondary or derivative sense that the Bible is the word of God. God's word in the primary and biblical sense is Christ himself; the Bible may be spoken of as God's word only because it is the means by which the knowledge of God in Christ has been transmitted to us. (Richardson 1969: 309)

It is not clear that Colenso did regard the Bible as a purely human book like any other book, as alleged in charge 6. He does say that the Bible 'becomes to us a human book' (Colenso 1867d: 63), but he means by that that the Bible opens up for us the human thoughts of our predecessors in the faith as they sought to identify the hand of God in their experience. He also says the Bible provides a 'special source of comfort' (p. 69). There is no evidence that Colenso believed or taught that the Bible was no different in status from any other book of spiritual wisdom. Certainly he believed that it needed to be critiqued and interpreted by the same means that we use for any other book, and no biblical scholar today would say differently. Nevertheless the Scriptures are still for him the major source of revelation about God.

Words like 'authenticity, genuineness and truth' in charge 7 can mean different things. Colenso certainly believed that the Genesis myths were not authentic history, and that the imprecatory verses in the psalms did not reflect truly God's will. Standing at a greater distance now from the original shock to believers who discovered that scholars did not think Balaam's ass had spoken, or that Jonah was literally swallowed by a whale, most modern believers have easily come to accept (along with many first-millennium Patristic scholars) that many stories in the Old Testament are allegorical and poetic rather than literal history. Now we would say that the scriptures do provide an authentic, genuine and true window to the beliefs of the persons who wrote and who edited them; but we have come to see that the view of history enshrined even in the New Testament was never a literal, journalistic view but always highly interpretative.

As far as charge 8 goes, we must say bluntly with Colenso that the human Jesus in his human knowledge was indeed limited to the insights of his day. To ascribe to the human Jesus the insights of modern biblical critics about the authorship of the Pentateuch, or of modern palaeontologists about the origins of the physical world, would be ridiculous. Indeed, it would be to commit the Apollinarian heresy of denying the true humanity of Jesus. Colenso was not 'partly wrong'—he was wholly right, and modern Christology needs to accept this and the implications. If Jesus was truly human, his conscious human scientific knowledge was limited to the science of his day.

With regard to charge 9, I cannot remember when last I heard the Athanasian creed recited; and the ordination vows now require that the deacon believes only that the Scriptures 'uniquely' reveal the word of God (*Anglican Prayer Book* 1989: 584)—a sentiment with which Colenso would have warmly agreed. The fact is that we need to state bluntly with Colenso that we no longer believe that unless a person believes in the Trinity as described in the Athanasian Creed, then 'without doubt he shall perish everlastingly', and that to even make such a statement would be to deny the fundamental ethical goodness of God. To go further still, for the Church today to propagate a message that those who do not formally ascribe to the Chalcedonian definition of the relationship between the members of the Trinity are destined to eternal punishment would be do evil and harm.

If we are honest, Anglican theologians in South Africa need to say that Colenso was *wholly right* in his views that brought about charges 5-9, and with the hindsight of history we can see that his opponents were wholly wrong. They feared that making concessions to biblical criticism would mean abandoning the authority of the Bible altogether, and with that the essential Christian belief in Jesus as the Son of God. A century and a half later, hardly anyone would still hold that the Bible is providing a literal historical account, were a literal historical account even possible, or that the four gospels plainly show us the historical Jesus.

To return to the comments of Jeff Guy: 'devout religious views can also be an expression of social forces in the continuing struggle for power and domination' (Guy 1983: 353). We are more aware than perhaps earlier generations were of the political power struggles that underlay the Council of Chalcedon and the centuries following. We have seen the harm done in our modern world—in conflicts between Orthodox Serb and Muslim in Bosnia, in conflicts between Muslims and Christians in the Sudan—when the value of a person's life is measured by whether he or her belongs to the 'right' religion and when religion is used as a cloak and justification for repression of human rights.

That brings us to charges 1-4. Hinchliff (1963: 93) says, 'On charges 1 and 4 he was in revolt against certain contemporary errors and one sympathizes with him'. I am not sure what Hinchliff means by 'contemporary errors'. Hinchliff implies that these views were erroneous but common in the mid-nineteenth century but not held currently. While perhaps not predominant in academic theology, a very great part of the Church in South Africa still believes the doctrine of vicarious satisfaction, that Jesus died in order to atone for our sins, to 'pay the price of sin' (Hymn 214 in *Hymns Ancient and Modern Revised*) and that those who are not justified in Christ are damned to eternal punishment because they die in Original Sin. This is still the basis of much evangelistic activity in South Africa.

Hinchliff (1963: 93) says that 'on charges 2 and 3 he did teach what he was accused of teaching, and his teaching was wrong'. It seems to me, however, that charges 1 to 4 are all of a piece. Though it apparently took him some time to accept fully the implications of his beliefs, Colenso found it difficult to reconcile the idea of damnation for the heathen with belief in a loving God. As early as his first visit to Natal he was faced with this dilemma. He describes a conversation with some Zulus:

> 'The profession of Christianity had been much hindered', they said, 'by persons saying that the world will be burnt up...and they will be destroyed. They are frightened, and would rather not hear about it if that is the case'. 'Tell them', I said, 'that I am come to speak to them of their father in heaven who loves them'. (Colenso 1855g: 90)

Clearly, in his later years he firmly rejected the doctrine of vicarious satisfaction and the idea that Original Sin has deprived the human race of righteousness, so that only those justified in Christ can be saved, and that those outside of the body of those thus justified are doomed to eternal punishment (Guy 1983: 72). Colenso explicitly says that

> Once for all let it be stated distinctly, there is not a single passage in the whole New Testament, which supports the dogma of modern theology, that our Lord died for our sins, in the sense of dying instead of us, dying in our place, or dying so as to bear the punishment or penalty of our sins. (Colenso quoted Guy 1983: 72)

Hinchliff (1963: 93-94) says of this

> insofar as his teaching was universalist it was both wrong and dangerous... Colenso was the church's chief missionary. He was first in prestige... If such a man, with so responsible a missionary office, taught an unsound and perverted version of the gospel he could not be left untouched.

Colenso was making an honest attempt to bring together in his theology what he believed were the findings of the science of his day and the experience of his times. To that were added his personal experience of goodness and wisdom in some aspects of Zulu culture, and his perception of wickedness and falseness in parts of Western European Christian culture. For instance, he reminds his readers that not long ago witches and members of rival Christian denominations were being burned at the stake (Colenso 1867d: 351). Given those convictions and his commitment to Zulu people and Zulu social upliftment it is hard to see how he could have come to a different conclusion.

In 1990 I published an attempt to look at traditional models of atonement and Christology out of the context of the struggle and pain in KwaZulu-Natal at the time (Nicolson 1999). It was not long after the furore in Britain about the publication of *The Myth of God Incarnate* (Hick 1977) and all the counter publications. Again, few theologians in South Africa paid any attention to that furore. The twists and turns of what many per-ceived to be 'shallow' Western liberal theology seemed of little relevance to South Africa where the Church was engaged in a full-on struggle against evil and the forces of darkness, and needed the full-on belief in an incarnate Christ to counter the evil. Real evil needs a real God!

The basic and unoriginal theme of my *A Black Future? Jesus and Salva-tion in South Africa* was that the traditional formulations of christological belief in Christ as God and man arose out of different ways of concep-tualizing how Jesus saves us. The book examined what I took to be the traditional models of soteriology—vicarious atonement, victory, as well as more current models in liberation and black theology, and sought to ask what the effect of these various models might be on people involved in the tragic and bloody conflict in KwaZulu-Natal at that time. The conclusion that I reached was that, in the end, far from being irrelevant and wishy-washy, a somewhat agnostic view of the divinity of Jesus and an exem-plarist view of the atonement probably were precisely the models that might speak most powerfully into that conflict.

It so happened that the book was sent by the journal *Theology* to Peter Hinchliff for review—no doubt because of Hinchliff's South African connections. The review was mildly dismissive, and suggested that the book failed to provide a convincing demonstration that theology needed to move in the direction of liberal Christology.

In my heart, at the time part of me agreed with Hinchliff. It was my first book and tried to cover too wide a field in too polemic a fashion. Who was I to throw aside cherished views of great Christian thinkers over many

centuries? I would wish now to be less polemic. But I come back to the
point made by Jeff Guy. We cannot separate Colenso the social reformer
and Colenso the liberal and controversial theologian. Colenso poses some
real challenges that to this day have not been adequately faced and
answered by the Churches in South Africa. It is quite clear that nineteenth-
and twentieth-century belief that the 'heathen' were unsaved and outside
of God's grace was a very major factor in providing an underpinning for
apartheid. Here is what Buis (1975: 11) describes as a summary of South
African Dutch Reformed Calvinist theology about sin and salvation:

> All Adam's descendants having fallen into sin by the sin of their parents
> have the mercy and justice of God revealed to them. God is merciful and
> just because he saves from total destruction all those whom out of goodness
> and mercy and in accordance with his plan he has chosen... God is just in
> leaving others in the sin and ruin in which they have involved themselves.

In other words, all humans deserve total destruction because of Original
Sin. God predestines those who shall be saved by turning to Christ, and
who shall be left in destruction. This is, of course, an unusually strong version of Calvinism that few Anglicans and probably few Dutch Reformed
persons would espouse now. But these views were commonly held. It
would be going too far to say that a strong view of the vicarious atonement
theory was a cause of apartheid, which had its roots in social and economic
factors rather than theological. But there is no doubt that religious views of
this kind made it easy to provide a theological and moral justification for
apartheid (MacCrone 1937: 113). The chilling words of Dr Daniel Malan
in his acceptance speech as he became the first in a long line of Nationalist
Prime Ministers in South Africa from 1948–94, a speech in which step by
step the formal strictures of apartheid were put into place, bear this out:

> The difference in colour is merely the physical manifestation of the contract
> between two ways of life: between barbarism and civilization; between
> heathenism and Christianity. (Malan quoted by van der Merwe 1975: 27)

Formal apartheid may be over. But as long as Christians in South Africa
persist in believing that only Christians are justified in God's eyes, it
makes nation building, in a nation where the majority are Christian but
where there are significant numbers of Hindus, Muslims and adherents of
traditional African religion, very difficult. As long as Christians refuse to
engage seriously with where God is to be found in other religions and
among those who profess no religion, they are refusing to recognize the
truths and lessons that we can learn from those who hold different beliefs
from our own.

Rosemary Radford Ruether (1974) made much the same comments about links between Christology, soteriology and the acceptance of the 'holocaust solution' in Nazi Germany. As I said in my 1990 book about the various versions of belief that Jesus died to pay the price of our sins and that those who are not 'in Christ' are not saved,

> In view of the very great harm that apartheid has done to Sipho and his people, Christians need to be very sure that they need these theories which have proved so easy to use or misuse in this way. The theories carry much potential danger. They have been of no help to Sipho. (Nicolson 1990: 135)

Colenso was outraged by the notion that all humans are wicked and unjust before God until and unless they are justified by faith in Christ, not simply because this disdain was the fashion of modern thought at the time. He was horrified because of the ethical and social and political implications of the belief. And so we should be still!

It is not clear to me exactly what Colenso did think about how Jesus saves, or in what sense Jesus is God and human, and indeed, at least in his public statements, he does not pursue the implications of his beliefs to the logical end. These debates would come later in the Anglican Church, with Rashdall's exemplarist views of the atonement, with the writers in *The Myth of God Incarnate* questioning that Jesus was literally or ontologically divine, and ultimately with Cupitt and Spong problematizing belief in a 'real' or ontological God. The implication of Colenso's sermons is that he sees Jesus primarily as an example of the love of God, as a teacher, and not as vicarious saviour:

> We know...that [Christ] has shown us of the Father, that he has led us to the Father... We know that we show ourselves true Christians, true believers in Christ, true children of God, when we receive that divine teaching. (Colenso 1867d: 197)

However, his theological convictions are not merely the consequence of wishing to conform to progressive and fashionable philosophies, but of his deep social concerns for the people whom he sought to serve:

> The work of a missionary, when regarded in a true light as that of endeavouring not to save a few souls from everlasting burnings, but to raise a whole race to the true dignity of man, as a child of God, a being endowed with intellectual, moral and spiritual faculties, is one of the highest, most interesting, most ennobling, that can engage our powers. (Colenso quoted Guy 1983: 77)

It is this concern that I suggest should still occupy us.

Yet Colenso did divide the Church of his day, and the Diocese of Natal never really recovered from the setback to its missionary work. The Anglican Church notoriously seeks to accommodate a wide, some would say incompatible variety of divergent views. Colenso was no doubt at times arrogant in his views concerning his opponents. And we would be arrogant now if we sought to impose liberal Christian views as the whole truth. Having been duly chastened by Hinchliff, I am not wishing to silence those who hold conservative soteriological and christological views. Alister McGrath suggests that the renewal of Anglicanism will require us to build bridges between what could crudely be called 'liberals' and 'fundamentalists'. He correctly points out that modern Anglican evangelicals are not fundamentalist in the usual modern sense of that word, but that there is a strong movement in the Anglican Church away from the assumptions of the Enlightenment, and that evangelicals and Anglo-Catholics find themselves on common ground here. Indeed, this suspicion of Enlightenment is part and parcel of the postmodern suspicion of the modern. He correctly points out that 'liberalism' has had a bad press but that at its best it stands for 'an inalienable respect for and openness to the views of others' (Guy 1983: 353), and he feels that some of the present 'liberals' within Anglicanism are less than respectful towards opposing views. McGrath himself is more comfortable with an evangelical than a liberal emphasis, but he echoes Hans Kung when he says that 'the Church must find a way between modernism without foundations and fundamentalism without modernity' (McGrath 1993: 129-30).

Evangelicalism is in danger of losing touch with the world. Liberalism is in danger of losing any distinctiveness from the world. The Anglican *Via Media* could provide

> a natural and organic synthesis, grounded in a long history of engagement with the Christian tradition on the one hand and contemporary culture on the other, which affords the means of addressing this vital issue. (McGrath 1993: 129)

My simple contention is that the theological issues that Colenso raised, brushed aside by most Anglican commentators as heretical and unworthy of further consideration, remain issues that still challenge us. To what extent does belief in salvation exclusively through explicit Christian faith in the incarnate Christ make the church in South Africa a hindrance to building a community of justice and peace? To what extent does traditional Christian orthodoxy have harmful social consequences? At the very least, the Church in South Africa needs to consider answers to these questions posed by Colenso as it seeks to make its contribution to what Desmond Tutu famously called the 'rainbow nation'. Do the colours in the rainbow include traditional Zulus? Or Hindus? Or unbelievers? Or can they only take their place in the beautiful spectrum by taking upon themselves Christian orthodoxy?

COLENSO THE SACRAMENTALIST

Ian Darby

Throughout his life John William Colenso was deeply involved in the Church's worship. This commenced for the child and adolescent in the Independent Chapel at St Austell, Cornwall. As tutor, undergraduate, don and schoolmaster, church or chapel was the centre of his life. The parish church of Forncett St Mary, the Mission chapel of Ekukhanyeni and St Peter's Cathedral, Pietermaritzburg, saw Colenso leading worship Sunday by Sunday. The great wealth of Colenso's published writings, including sermons, liturgies and hymnals, provides evidence of how worship was offered, in season and out, and of how the sacraments were celebrated faithfully and regularly.

Colenso did of course live during a time when the Church of England was enjoying considerable religious ferment. His Nonconformist origins gave him the piety of John Bunyan (he later translated *Pilgrim's Progress* into Zulu in 1868 [Colenso 1901]!) and Thomas Boston. The Church of England, to which he switched with some drama at the youthful age of 17, was still bearing the fruits of the Evangelical revival of the previous century, and the Tractarian movement would emerge in just a matter of years.

The Evangelical movement in the Church of England can be traced to the early eighteenth century. Leaders such as John Newton, William Wilberforce and Charles Simeon formed the Clapham Sect for executing their drive for evangelism and philanthropy. The formation of the Church Missionary Society and the emancipation of slaves were their two main achievements, but an enrichment in personal and family piety, the faithful celebration of the sacraments and the introduction of hymn singing were some of the results of the movement.

The Tractarian movement was founded on a quest for the true authority of the Church. On 14 July 1833, with Colenso having completed his first year at Cambridge, John Keble preached the Assize Sermon before the University of Oxford. He preached against the proposed suppression of ten

Irish bishoprics. Thereafter he co-operated with John Newman in the issue of the *Tracts of the Times*. They promoted the belief that the Church was a divine organization, catholic and apostolic, with a high value placed on faith and tradition and its sacramental and liturgical life. The outcome of the Tractarian movement shows how it was an heir to the Evangelical movement with its emphasis upon preaching, evangelism, the sacraments and the loyalty to the Prayer Book.

When Colenso first embarked on his journey to his distant colonial diocese, he was riding the crest of the wave of Anglican missionary outreach. The Church of England missionary societies had done tentative work in North America, and more determined efforts had been made in West Africa and in India. It was only now that Anglican missionaries were moving into other areas of the globe. Once there, as it happened for Colenso, the worship of the Church of England had to be translated into very different languages, cultures, idioms and music.

There is a consistent interest throughout Colenso's ministry in the sacraments of Baptism and Holy Communion. True to the teaching of the Church of England, only these two sacraments have been instituted by our Lord and are generally necessary for salvation. Of the five lesser sacraments, Colenso makes only a brief reference to Ordination.

Baptism

If Colenso's early thinking on baptism was showing influences that come from outside his own Church's formularies, there were three possible sources of such ideas. His own early religious development came from a background of English Calvinism. He nevertheless moved away from that, and towards the time of his Norfolk rectorship he was greatly impressed by the writing of F.D. Maurice. Also at this time there was the current controversy over George Gorham's baptismal theology and his successful appeal to the Privy Council. Each of these left a mark on Colenso's thinking.

Colenso's early ideas are evident in letters he wrote at the age of 16. He refers to the writings of both John Bunyan and Thomas Boston as well as his own conversion experience, a sense captured by the favourite hymn, 'I once was blind, but now I see' (see the letter from the young Colenso to an aunt, Mrs Perry, in the Killie Campbell Archives [Gl.13.12.1830]). Many other indications suggest an Evangelical background. He makes no reference however to his recent baptism at the parish church or to any idea of covenant. While Boston and Bunyan were of the Reformed and Puritan tradition, they do not appear to have set the teenager Colenso in this train of thought.

At the time Colenso was clearly interested in the Gorham affair. In 1847, the bishop of Exeter refused to institute the Reverend G.C. Gorham because he considered him unsound on the doctrine of baptismal regeneration. The judicial committee of the Privy Council upheld Gorham's right to believe in his particular interpretation. While never denying that grace was imparted at baptism, he taught that the Holy Spirit imparted a new nature either *before* Baptism, *in* Baptism, or *after* Baptism, 'as He listeth' (Nias 1951: 173). While unable to accept that the sacrament automatically effected regeneration, he saw it as conditional upon individual justification.

Gorham was of the Evangelical school, which at this period enshrined a moderate Calvinism. John Calvin allowed for the possibility of children being born again in water and the Spirit. In commenting on Mt. 19.13-15, he wrote that the regeneration of infants by the power of God is wonderful and incomprehensible to us, but possible and easy for him (*Institutes* 4.17.8). Calvin could countenance the baptism of infants only of believers. Several Reformed confessions support him, the second Helvetic, declaring that baptism assures us that we are regenerated, purified and received by God though the Holy Spirit. The Westminster *Confession of Faith* says that the sign and seal of baptism is of 'the covenant of grace, of his ingrafting into Christ, of regeneration, of remission of sins...' On regeneration it would appear that the Reformed tradition is closer to the straightforward statements of the Anglican baptismal services and 39 articles than to Gorham's qualified interpretation.

Colenso declared that he did not agree with Gorham's views but he respected his stand and considered him unfairly treated by his opponents. In all this he attempted to steer a course that avoided the partisan loyalties of so many of his contemporaries. Much later, in the 1860s, Colenso would be publishing for the first time his very decided views on regeneration. The Gorham controversy left its mark in this respect.

The writings of F.D. Maurice were undoubtedly the greater influence upon Colenso's thinking. In his *Kingdom of Christ* (Maurice 1840, I: 280) he described baptism as an affirmation of a relationship to Christ, which already existed, it assumed 'Christ to be the Lord of Men; it assumes that men are created in Him; That this is the constitution of our race...'

Of baptismal grace he wrote: 'in the strength of this covenant you must claim it; otherwise your life will be a lie' (1840, I: 262). Ten years later at Lincoln's Inn, Maurice preached that the new covenant prophesied by Jeremiah is the covenant into which we are born by our baptism (Maurice 1879: 441).

Colenso first read Maurice's *Kingdom of Christ* in the early 1840s. Writing the Preface to *Village Sermons* (1854c), Colenso makes it clear that Maurice had taught him many ideas, including some on baptism.

> It is from you that we have learned to treat as living realities, instead of mere empty formulae, the declarations of God's word, that: 'God was in CHRIST, reconciling *the world* unto Himself not imputing their trespasses unto them'—that 'He is the Propitiation, not for our sins only, but also for the Sins of the *Whole world*'.

Thus Colenso pinpoints the central doctrine of universal reconciliation learnt from Maurice:

> And baptism affirms that we are not merely, what we are by nature, fallen, miserable, guilty creatures, 'children of wrath', but raised again in CHRIST from our first parents' terrible Fall, of which Mercy the sign and seal is given to us in our Baptism, wherein we are adopted as the sons of God and made the children of His Grace. (1854c: vii)

Colenso's theology was now destined to take on a distinctive pattern based on the redemption and reconciliation of the whole world by the incarnation of Jesus Christ. The place of baptism would be subsidiary to this idea but nevertheless prominent in his writings.

Colenso was consecrated bishop of the new missionary diocese of Natal in November 1853. Understandably, his writings would not be extensive during his early episcopate. Nevertheless, his Maurician theology was frequently evident. His published works include few references to baptism, but among them we find the controversy of 1854 over the baptism of polygamous converts. While supporting the policy of not expecting second or further wives to be dismissed before baptism, he does not invoke any Maurician ideas, but argues for this approach on the grounds of compassion and reason. In the same year, at the ordination of Henry Callaway at Norwich Cathedral, he preached that baptism provided a promise and pledge of the help and teaching of God's own Holy Spirit. That very work of the Spirit brings about the ongoing growth of the person who is brought 'into conformity with God's own most Blessed Will, yea, into the very likeness of the Lord' (1854a: 9). So Colenso alludes to the continuing effect of baptism upon which he would be expanding some years later.

In 1858, Colenso preached that, while baptism admitted us into God's inner family of the Church, the sacrament was also a witness that Christ had redeemed not only Christians, 'but *all mankind*' (1858c: 13). This universal application of baptism would now figure consistently in Colenso's subsequent publications. Yet when he wrote his commentary on Paul's Letter to the Romans in the early 1860s, he detached regeneration completely from the sacrament and equated it with the universal redemption of humankind, brought about by the incarnation. All people were born again at their physical birth hour when they were redeemed from the curse of the fall of Adam. He wrote in the introduction to the commentary (1861h: ix):

> Nicodemus, in point of fact, was already thus born again, thus born from above; he had already received that second spiritual birth, though he did not know it.

Now all that was needed for Nicodemus was the sacrament of water for his regeneration to be complete. Nevertheless for baptism to have value the recipient must live up to its meaning (p. 51). Colenso thus introduces a condition, but unlike for Gorham, regeneration appears at least at this stage as unconditional as physical birth.

In commenting on Romans ch. 6, Colenso first of all points to the sacrament as the sign of unity that we have in Christ's death.

> And we are reckoned so completely one with Him, and declared to be so in our Baptism, that His Death is regarded as ours. We have paid this debt to sin, the tyrant, because He, our Chief and Head, has paid it. (p. 110)

He adds that Baptism is also

> The assurance and pledge, the sign and seal, of all our Father's loving Kindness to us, the outward token of that other mightier sign and seal, the inward pledge of God's Love, which every living man has, namely, the secret work of His own good Spirit in the heart. (p. 113)

Colenso restates that not only regeneration but also the dying to sin and the rising to righteousness takes place in our very birth-hour.

It is noticeable that any ideas of covenant at this time are absent from Colenso's baptismal thinking. Its universal application appears to have supplanted most other ideas. While Paul's language in Romans can support a universal justification, there appears to be no such support for universal regeneration, either in Romans or in John 3 or Titus 3.5. Colenso is certainly poles apart from Gorham as he would also appear to be from Calvin. The link between regeneration and election, however, is likely to show how Calvin and Colenso reach their respective conclusions. Calvin undoubtedly believed that all the elect are born again. So did Colenso, and the elect for him was the whole human family. Maurice undoubtedly influenced him in this direction by describing Jesus as the regenerator of humanity (Maurice 1975: 166). Colenso applies this concept to any individual, but that may not be the conclusion desired by Maurice.

Nevertheless Colenso's thinking was still to develop. His *Natal Sermons* of 1866 were published in four volumes. Initially we find him reiterating all his universal ideas of baptism, and Nicodemus figures again as the example of one who had been born again spiritually at his hour of birth. Regeneration, however, is present not as a once for all experience but as something which is renewed daily. Colenso also admits this ongoing dimension for redemption, being subject to daily repentance for sin, so our conformity to God's will and perfection consists of a work of constant renewal, redemption, regeneration. By this process God calls back the transgressor to hope, to life, to divine love and penitent gratitude (Colenso 1866d, III: 155).

In this way Colenso's regeneration is undoubtedly more meaningful. It is not simply a rubber stamp that goes with the registration of physical birth. One may ask however whether there is any scriptural support for it and also whether in the end it is credible. It would seem that in Jesus' discourse with Nicodemus he was showing the radical contrast between entering into a faith on the grounds of physical race and of being accepted on a spiritual basis. Nicodemus had been born physically into Judaism and Jesus was showing that that was insufficient. A second birth was required, from above, in water and the spirit. It is clear that Jesus is seeing it as the initiation into the faith and that it is directly related to baptism. Titus 3.5 confirms this interpretation. While it is legitimate to say that the value of regeneration is conditional upon one's accepting and appropriating saving grace, to say that it is repeated does an injustice both to the image of birth as well as to the scriptural support.

Eucharist

Six of Colenso's extant published sermons deal fully with the Eucharist. A major clash in 1858 between himself and his Dean, James Green, surrounded *Two Sermons on Spiritual Eating in the Holy Eucharist*, and made them the most famous (for Green's side of the controversy, see Wirgman 1909). They and three further sermons of the 1866 series embody the main aspects of the bishop's eucharistic theology. In addition to fairly standard Prayer Book teaching on the sacraments which may be found in all the sermons, these in particular provide a eucharistic interpretation of Colenso's general soteriological thinking. What is more prominent, however, at the time causing the controversy, was his presentation of the doctrine of the real presence. In this regard he provides copious references to the writings of Anglican divines and early Church Fathers in order to support his ideas. The aftermath of the 1858 controversy provides evidence of where the bishop could receive support or otherwise.

In exploring the place of Colenso's eucharistic theology one must look back to these earlier traditions. But naturally it is to today that one also must go, over a century later, in order to discover whether there is now a place for the bishop's thinking.

Colenso in his *Two Sermons* of 1858 argued that there was no difference in and between the presence of Christ in the sacrament and in other acts of devotion. Preaching from the text, Jn 6.51, Colenso argued that in referring to the living bread following the feeding of the 5000, Jesus was not speaking expressly of the holy Eucharist. Eating the living bread which Jesus gives means 'every act of true faith which we exercise upon the Life and Death of our Risen Lord...' (p. 16). Yet the true meaning of the Eucharist may be found in these words of Jesus, Colenso added.

Colenso gave two reasons why Jesus was not expressly referring to the Eucharist. He had not yet instituted the sacrament, and his very specific words about the facts of those not eating and drinking the flesh and the blood of Christ would exclude too many faithful people who had no access to the sacrament. Modern commentators find a greater eucharistic significance in the words of John 6 than does Colenso. They have been more ready to see the words of Jesus reflecting the thinking of the early Church and yet not applying exclusively to the Eucharist. Colenso, writing prior to the development of form critical studies, would be out of place in modern New Testament scholarship.

It is noticeable that in all Colenso's eucharistic sermons, he takes care to present the teaching found in the catechism and Communion services of the Anglican Prayer Book. The sacrament is 'a means of grace and spiritual strength to all who worthily receive it...' (1858c: 6). To his parishioners in Norfolk he said that the Eucharist was

> The Bread of Life, which His Love has provided for us—to partake of that spiritual food, which He Himself vouchsafes to give us, for the strengthening and refreshing of our souls—even His own most Precious Body and Blood, 'which are verily and indeed taken and received by the faithful in the Lord's Supper'. (1854c: 86)

He also taught that the sacraments were '*generally* necessary for salvation', with the exception that when deprived for some sound reason from receiving the sacrament, a person would still receive the body and blood of Christ 'by devout meditation and prayer, by acts of repentance, faith, and thanksgiving...' (1858c: 11).

To support this exception, Colenso cited not only Jesus' words in John 6, but also the third rubric at the end of the Prayer Book order for 'The Communion of the Sick'. A sick person unable to receive the sacramental elements may under these conditions still receive the same benefits. Colenso of course went further. He stated that with 'every act of true faith' people consciously or unconsciously, whether believers or not, receive the bread of life. It was this language that provoked the controversy in 1858, but he attempted to show in his subsequent sermons that there were many exponents who supported him.

In the second of the *Two Sermons* of 1858 the bishop argued that he had the support of the eighteenth-century English theologian Daniel Waterland and the Reformation leaders, Cranmer, Ridley and Latimer. The early Church Fathers, Cyprian and Athanasius, were also cited. In *Natal Sermons* he quoted from Origen, Tertullian, Clement of Alexandria and Eusebius of Caesaris. It would seem that, in his quotations from Waterland, Colenso was following very closely this Anglican divine's interpretation of John 6 as applied to the Eucharist. Waterland writes (1737: 138):

> For it is not true that all, who receive the Communion, have life, unless we put in the restriction of worthy, and *so far*. Much less can it be true that all, who have never received, or never shall receive, have not life; unless we make several more restrictions, confirming the proposition to person *capable*, and not destitute of opportunity; making exceptions for good men of *old*, and for *infants*...

It has already been mentioned that two members of his cathedral chapter walked out on the first of the sermons preached in 1858. They were present for the second preached a week later, but proceeded to present their bishop to the Metropolitan on a charge of heresy. A copy of the published sermons was sent to Bishop Robert Gray who consulted with Bishop Wilberforce of Oxford. Gray's final response was that Colenso's views, while being unguarded, did have the support of both the Prayer Book and the Council of Trent. About Colenso, Gray wrote that 'he is strong in the maintenance of a real Spiritual presence of our Lord'. About both Colenso and Green he wrote:

I venture to think then that neither of you have been as guarded in your expressions as might have been desired. First, as to your [Green's] views. You have I think defined too closely and refined too much as to the different modes of our Lord's presence. We are not entitled I think to say that the communication of our Lord's manhood to us, can only take place through the Sacraments; or to define in what way He is present in the Ordinary assemblies. The language which you have used goes beyond that of the Church. She has no where expressed herself as you have done. I do not know that the matter has ever been fully treated of by the Catholic Church, or our own particular branch of it. But the principle involved has been weighted by the Council of Trent; and its language upon a point which bears upon this question is in favour of the Bishop's view.

Gray then proceeded to quote from the catechism of Trent, adding that

> It is at least doubtful whether all the benefits conferred through the Sacrament, may not be conveyed through an act of living faith. The opinion is therefore allowable that it can be so, even in the view of the church of Rome. I will add that the rubric of our church quoted by the Bishop commits our church to the same view. (Letter from Bishop Gray to Bishop Colenso and Dean Green dated 4 June 1858)

Gray on other matters regretted that Colenso had employed such a public attack upon Green and in turn considered that Green and Jenkins were very wrong in abstaining from Communion. In view of the apparent historical support that may be found for Colenso, it is surprising that Gray claimed that the matter had not really been dealt with either in the wider Catholic Church or in the Church of England. Significantly, in 1863 at the heresy trial, the judgment went against Colenso. He, of course, had used more extreme language in his commentary on Romans and had applied similar principles to baptism, saying that those deprived of the sacrament may in a similar manner benefit from the special grace available from it. It would seem that the balance of Colenso's interpretation of the sacrament was deemed sufficient for the trial to rule against him. As has been mentioned, however, Colenso provides enough evidence to show that he was keeping within the bounds of Prayer Book teaching.

There is now a further area to be explored in order to assess the place of Colenso's eucharistic thinking. It has been amply stated that much of his distinctive thinking was derived from friend and contemporary theologian, F.D. Maurice. The same may be said for eucharistic theology, as is shown in a sermon preached by Maurice at Lincoln's Inn on 28 January 1855. Colenso provided an edition of this sermon in a small devotional book containing Maurice's writings and the text of the Prayer Book Communion service.

In affirming the doctrine of the real presence in the Eucharist, Maurice indicated that such an exclusive application could not be made. Referring to the disciples who were commanded to observe the Lord's Supper, in the collection of his writings made by Colenso himself in 1855 as a tribute to Maurice, he writes:

> They would recollect Him more, when they ate the unleavened bread, and drank the wine, than all which the Feast seemed directly to commemorate... They were taught, that wicked works, not distance, had separated them from God, and that now, by the blood of Christ, they were made nigh; that the veil was torn asunder; that in the Mediator, they were once more brought into the presence of the Holy One. They had need to recollect this. They required that He, in whom only they had life, should be brought continually to their minds, which were continually prone to forget Him, and to live as if He were away from them. But, whatever served this purpose, whatever put them in mind of him, must assure them of His real Presence, could not by possibility signify that He was habitually absent, and only reappeared in those elements, or when they strove to bring His image before them. (Maurice 1855: 132)

This same point was made more strongly by Maurice putting the following words into the mouth of Jesus (Maurice 1855: 143):

> Therefore, I give you this token to recollect Me by, to recollect that I am with you always,—on week-days, as well as on Sundays,—when vanity, and anger and bitterness, are tempting you most strongly,—in the public assembly,—in the home circle,—just as much as when you are kneeling at my altar.

The similarity in the style and language at this point between Maurice and Colenso is obvious. Although one notices the unguarded manner of Colenso, his making the point of the distinction in kind shows the differences in temperament and context between the two men. However, as the following quotation indicates, there are sufficient similarities to show that Colenso was three years later keeping to Maurice's tradition:

> It is the result of man's theorising, and not derived from God's Revelation, to attempt to make a distinction *in kind* between our Lord's Presence in the Holy Eucharist, and that which He vouchsafes to us, when we kneel in our own retirement, or meet in our ordinary assemblies for the Common Worship of Prayer and Praise. (Colenso 1858c: 6)

When Maurice preached his sermon in 1855, the Church of England was still embroiled in the controversy over Archdeacon G.A. Denison whose advanced teaching of the real present was being dealt with by the English civil courts.

Maurice was attempting to show that there need not be such bitterness and animosity over such a doctrine, and his tone was generally conciliatory and eirenical. Colenso was of course in the opposite of moods and this makes for the great difference between the two.

Later, in 1858, Maurice expressed his disagreement with Colenso over the teaching of the *Two Sermons*. Preaching again at Lincoln's Inn on 18 July 1858, Maurice opens his sermon with the question:

> 'Can we say', it has been asked, 'that the presence of our Lord, which is promised in the Eucharist, is a presence of a different kind from that which a faithful Christian may expect in ordinary prayer?'

The answer given is in the affirmative, the reason being that the Eucharist provides the standard to which other forms of worship must reach if the presence of Christ is to be realized there as well. Maurice ends by saying (1891, IV: 126):

> Carry the meaning of the Eucharist into your public worship, regard the Eucharist as the centre of it, and worship becomes a reality... Carry the meaning of the Sacrament into private worship, and private worship, becomes indeed an act of communion with a present Lord. But try this communion by the standard of our public or private worship, and it is in danger of sinking, as they so easily and naturally sin, into mere utterances of our own wishes, or mere repetitions of words that we have received from tradition.

The difference that Maurice is pointing to appears to be one of degree more than of essence. The Eucharist is the centre and standard that the rest of worship must reach. Colenso claimed that the two were in agreement on this point, and he had in the first of the *Two Sermons* said (1858c: 6):

> So must we hold that the highest and holiest Form of Worship, in which we can 'eat the Flesh and drink the Blood of the Son of Man', is when we partake together of the One Bread and the One Cup, as members of One Body in Him.

The identification of the Eucharistic presence of Jesus Christ with 'every act of true faith' is a remarkable application of sacramental understanding to life in the world. In this way Colenso is able to anticipate much contemporary thought with regard to sacramental acts that go way beyond the confines of the institutional Church. In his *Sacrament and Struggle*, Kenith David (1994: 122) shows how 'people in struggle have—additional to the Church's sacraments—rediscovered other sacraments which sustain and renew them. The sacraments of life, land, name, identity, community and the vision of "the dawn of a new age" are being celebrated *now* in their lives.'

Conclusion

It was necessary in 1990 for Desmond Tutu to walk onto a beach, where by law he was prohibited because of racial discrimination. Thirty years earlier Albert Luthuli led a group of people in burning their passbooks, the hated instruments of injustice. Earlier still, Mahatma Ghandi led a much greater number of people onto a beach in India, where he collected a handful of salt, so defying a British law that local Indians should not manufacture salt.

A hundred years previously Colenso would not have had such specific acts in mind as signifying the real presence of Jesus, yet he has opened our eyes to look beyond a narrow ecclesiastical interpretation of the eucharistic words of Jesus in John 6.

Colenso's interpretation of baptism as pointing to a daily regeneration is not so helpful, given that we are only born once physically, and that there is plenty of contemporary loose talk about 'born-again Christians'. Perhaps more significant for today is Colenso's emphasis on incorporation in baptism into Christ as 'Head', which recurs frequently in his *Commentary on Romans* (Darby 1989: 65). Incorporation into Christ as 'Head' implies a solidarity with all humankind and not just with our own cultural and religious grouping. Baptism as 'walking in newness of life' has a specific reference to living out truth and justice in concrete terms. The idea lends itself to the pilgrimage of life. The struggle against injustice as well as against any other form of sin and evil is a continuous walk, in which daily the pilgrim must experience the deadly results of those evils. The pilgrim moves on, knowing that the new life with Christ is always present sacramentally, following the resurrection from that time of death.

Thinking and writing about similar ideas at Forncett St Mary and Bishopstowe, the prophetic Colenso saw that the sacraments of the Church were immeasurably more valuable than had hitherto been allowed. The consequences of his thinking in his own struggle and in the development of the Anglican Church in Southern Africa are still being discovered and evaluated today.

Part III

EKUKHANYENI

SUCCESS AND FAILURE OF 'SOKULULEKA':
BISHOP COLENSO AND AFRICAN EDUCATION*

Patrick Kearney

Before he arrived in Natal in 1853 to take office as the first Anglican
Bishop of the colony, Colenso had established a reputation as an educationist on the basis of his school arithmetic text, which was regarded as 'a
classic of its day' (Hinchliff 1962: 204). For part of 1831 he had been
assistant master in a small private school in Dartmouth, prior to commenc-
ing studies at St John's College, Cambridge. Seven years later, on completion of those studies, he went to Harrow as a mathematics tutor. The
school, at that time under Dr Christopher Wordsworth, had fallen into
disrepute and, because the number of students had dropped, Colenso had
to return to St John's to act as tutor. There he took private pupils while
completing his *Arithmetic Designed for the Use of Schools* (Colenso
1855a). A decade later, in 1849, he very nearly accepted the headmaster-
ship of King Edward VI School, Norwich, but decided against it because
no house was provided with the job. From this time his attention was
increasingly focused on the activities of the Society for the Propagation of
the Gospel (SPG), an enthusiasm that led ultimately to his appointment as
Bishop of Natal in 1853.

Colenso set out for this new mission with the highest hopes, describing
the task that lay ahead in these words:

> There is, I trust, a great missionary work to be set on foot there, with decided
> support from Government, and I do not hesitate to say, it is the noblest field
> ever yet opened to the missionary labours of the Church in any part of the
> world. (Colenso quoted in Cox 1888: 47)

* I am grateful to Professor Jonathan Draper for supplying me with typed trans-
criptions of letters of Walter Baugh and Charles Septemius Grubbe from the archives
of the USPG at Rhodes House in Oxford concerning the school at Ekukhanyeni.

An Educational Mission

In a letter to Bishop Robert Gray of Cape Town, in 1856, Colenso made clear that he saw his task as primarily educational:

> I am desirous of establishing, without delay, two institutions for the improvement of the natives, viz. 1st. An Industrial School. 2nd. A Central or Diocesan College. 1st. I have selected the Amaganya tribe, under the chief Ngoza, for our first Industrial School... Ungoza, I am persuaded, will welcome the establishment of an institution such as this, and give every assistance that can be reasonably expected from him, towards making our efforts effectual for the improvement of the condition of his people. My intention is to fix one school in the very midst of his kraals, and endeavour to bring the natives under regular instruction, without drawing them away from their familiar and ordinary occupations... I have a confident hope that, under God, the result of a few months' labour here, will warrant me in requesting...the means of setting on foot other similar institutions in different parts of the country. 2nd. Besides these Industrial Schools I am anxious to found a Central or Diocesan College, which will be planted on a hill about four and a half miles from Maritzburg... To this institution would be removed the most promising youth of both sexes from all the different Industrial Schools, in order to receive closer attention, which may enable them to become, in their turn, the teachers of others. Here also will be a College where young men, the sons of European parents, may complete their studies, especially those intended for the ministry. (*Natal Witness* 15 February 1856: 175)

It is rather sad to read these plans because only the idea of the Central or Diocesan College came to some fruition and that for a matter of a few years and on a limited scale. This is what Colenso called his 'Kafir Harrow' and it commenced with the enthusiastic support of Sir Theophilus Shepstone, Secretary for Native Affairs, who instructed all chiefs to send 'all their children that were losing their first teeth' to the Bishop's school at Ekukhanyeni (Bishopstowe). The first reaction of the chiefs was to fear that their sons would be sent overseas or forced to become Christians, so they refused to comply. One of those who was subsequently to be a pupil of Colenso's, Magema Fuze, described this reaction many years later in the first book written and published by a Zulu:

> On finding that the people had refused to send their children to be educated in accordance with the request of Sobantu,[1] he [Shepstone] assembled his

---

1.   Sobantu, that is, 'the father of his people'—a name given to Colenso by Shepstone, which remains the favourite Zulu name for him.

head men and elders under him—Chief Ngoza Ka Ludaba of the Majozi tribe and Zatshuke ka Mbheswa of the Ngubane, along with the important elders under them—to inform them that all elders were to send their older children to school at Ekukanyeni where they could be taught and thus enabled to assume control of their homes when their fathers were no longer living there. (Fuze 1979: 2-3)

His First Pupils

This time the request was successful, as Colenso was able to report proudly in a letter of 5 February 1856 to G.W. Allnutt (Killie Campell Library [= KC], Colenso Papers, VI, Letter 48896):

Our great experiment is actually in progress. Last Thursday I received at the Station 19 little Kafir boys all the sons of principal men, and 13 more are promised—and it is just impossible to say what the end may be. Perhaps all may speedily come to nothing... However we hope for the best: and up to this time, they are as happy as possible and several can already read all their letters.

While recognizing at the time that the boys were 'but few', Colenso said that 'the eyes of the people are fixed upon these few; and if it goes well with them, this place will be inundated with children' (Colenso 1856[?]a: 175).

Colenso was aware of the parents' apprehension about leaving their sons at his mission and so he assured them: 'We shall always be glad to see the parents, and anything they can suggest for the children's welfare we shall carefully consider. It must be a very great trial, indeed, for the mothers to part with their children' (Colenso 1856[?]a: 175).

But the mothers were not easily convinced:

The hour having at last arrived when the women should have taken their leave, they begged to be allowed to see the children once more in their sleeping-room; and then nothing would content them but to be allowed to sleep outside, under the veranda, that they might see them again, after they had passed the night, the first thing in the morning. (Colenso 1856[?]a: 176)

Eventually the mothers left the next day. They had been rebuked by some Zulu men for hanging around outside the children's room!

Six days passed and Colenso was happy at how well things were going: 'The children, so far from being rude and quarrelsome little savages, are as gentle, good and dutiful, as can be' (Colenso 1856[?]a: 177). In fact, he thought they would be a reproach to many a similar group of English children.

Colenso was delighted by their playfulness:

> They entered at once with spirit into the amusement of blindman's-bluff,
> leap-frog, whipping-top, skipping-rope, and bat and ball; but we were
> miserably supplied in this colony for toys. Nevertheless, he thought they
> would 'make excellent cricketers'. (Colenso 1856[?]a: 177)

Colenso was eloquent about the great significance of these first 19 pupils,
though he clearly knew that success was not guaranteed:

> the sight of those nineteen little ones so trustfully committed to our care by
> their parents' free choice, and those parents heathens—a thing before
> unheard of in the whole history of our dealings with the Kafir race, is one of
> the most pleasing and comforting—a sight never to be forgotten by those
> who have witnessed it. (Colenso 1856[?]a: 178)

Not long after, the most important of Colenso's pupils arrived. This was
Mkungu, son of Mpande the Zulu King and a possible claimant to the
succession. The majority of the boys were six or seven years old, while
Mkungu was twelve and described as 'a pleasant, and at present, very
docile and seemingly intelligent but very fat boy' (letter to G.W. Allnutt
dated 7 July 1857 [KC, Colenso Papers]). The arrival of Mkungu was
clearly regarded as an event of significance as the boy was handed over
into the Bishop's care by the Lieutenant-Governor of Natal and the Secretary for Native Affairs. At the time of Mkungu's arrival, the numbers in
the school had risen to 36. Colenso was prepared to take 50 boys and
looked forward to a time when there would be 500 (Burnett 1947: 30).
Colenso had successfully persuaded Zulu people to entrust their children
to him for schooling whereas other Presbyterian missionaries had struggled for years to attract Zulu children to their schools (letter from Walter
Baugh, Ekukhanyeni, dated 1 July 1856 [C/AFS/6]).

Curriculum at Ekukhanyeni

Not much detail survives about what was taught at Ekukhanyeni. In addition to worship and religious instruction there were four hours of schooling every day, from 10.00–12.00 and from 14.00–16.00. Every evening
there was an 'Evening School' for adults who had been working during
the day 'were attended by an attentive and striving number of pupils'
(letter from Walter Baugh to the SPG, dated 1 April 1858 [C/AFS 6]).

Time was devoted to literacy, and Colenso claimed with considerable
satisfaction that with the twelve-year-olds this could be achieved within a
year (Hooker 1953: 54). Colenso himself taught the mathematics of Euclid

to a particularly promising child, Undiane, and Mkungu had piano lessons with the Colenso children. All had lessons in drawing, some of them showing 'remarkable taste' for art and 'a passion for it' (Baugh 1 April 1858 [C/AFS 6]). A visitor to Ekukhanyeni, Miss Alice Mackenzie (1859: 17), stressed the similarity to an English school: 'the boys of the school under their own master, such a troop of orderly merry fellows—40 of them quite like an English school... the way they march in and out of Chapel reminds me of Rugby'.

Colenso had the highest ambitions for these pupils. In a letter dated 6 August 1857 (KC, Colenso Papers) he writes of some 'very *valuable* men who will be landing just now at the Cape on their way to join us here'. One of these was Dr Robert James Mann (later to be first Superintendent of Education in Natal), who was described as 'very intelligent as a scientific man and *practical astronomer*. He is coming to this Station, where we hope to have some of our Kafir boys brought up as medical men under his care' (letter to G.W. Allnutt dated 12 November 1855 [KC, Colenso Papers]). He was also considering training some as architects.

Mann turned out to be a disappointment to Colenso chiefly because, like Lieutenant-Governor John Scott, he criticized the sort of education Colenso was giving as being unpractical. The criticism by the Governor and Mann led to a response from Colenso which helps us to know more of what was happening at Ekukhanyeni at this time: Colenso requested Mr Walter Baugh, a candidate for the Anglican ministry who was in charge of the industrial training, to write a detailed account of the practical work that was being done. This gives the only detailed record of the school's educational activities.

Baugh pointed out first that Colenso was enthusiastic about industrial training (Baugh 1 April 1858 [C/AFS 6]) and that Africans had been involved from the start in the construction of the mission buildings: 'and as a substantial proof of *their* handiwork we have now a strong stone building on the Mission ground which was walled entirely by natives'. From the time of the boys' arrival they had been engaged in gardening— 'weeding, digging, planting, harvesting. etc.' When this work was completed, six of the older boys were given instruction in carpentry for a few hours each afternoon and during this time prepared the materials that were to be used by skilled craftsmen in the construction of the Bishop's residence. Another six boys were engaged in simple tailoring—'making trousers, bags, etc. A work which they very much like, and rejoice to engage in'.

But the only significant industrial training given at Ekukhanyeni was in printing. Four of the more intelligent boys were trained by Mr Purcell, the master-printer, 'and it is pleasing to report that they have taken the liveliest interest in their new, and to them strange employment'. These boys were to render valuable services to Colenso by printing several of the many books he published at the mission. One of these pupils, Magema Fuze, was, as noted above, to become the author of the first book by a Zulu. Colenso was also keen to establish a girls school and Baugh (1 April 1858 [C/AFS 6]) reports that there were four young women and four little girls boarding and receiving lessons in much the same way as the boys; they were being instructed by the young ladies in the bishop's household, and supervised by Mrs Colenso. The lessons, however, appear to have been very limited: the girls were trained in household work and everything needed to make them good house servants or Christian wives. The young women, in fact, engaged for some hours daily in washing, which provided great service to the mission.

Staffing and Other Difficulties

Baugh (1 April 1858 [C/AFS 6]), though full of praise for what had been achieved, stressed that numerous difficulties had slowed progress. The training of adults had been impeded 'by the ever restless nature of the young men. They remain steadily at work from 1 to 12 months and acquire a fair knowledge of useful labour, and then suddenly they persist in leaving their work and returning to their kraals.' The skills they had learnt were thus soon forgotten. Then there were the ever-present difficulties for the teacher 'having to do with a people in an unknown tongue—having to study their language, their mode of thought, and their peculiar habits and weaknesses'. Such difficulties, he concluded, should have caused observers, especially those recently arrived from England, to be slower to criticize the work of missionaries.

With some bitterness Colenso recorded that what Lieutenant-Governor Scott seemed to find lacking was the growing of cotton and other out-of-door occupations—which 'may make a Native a better *machine* for the purposes of his European Masters, but not a better or a nobler *Man*' (letter to G.W. Allnutt dated 3 July 1858 [KC, Colenso Papers]). The fundamental reason for Colenso's clash with the white settlers in Natal becomes clear from this statement—a clash which was to climax in his support for Langalibalel's rebellion, and which lost him most of his few remaining white defenders, but sealed a close bond with the Zulu people.

Lieutenant-Governor Scott's criticism of Colenso's methods was to cost the latter dearly, since it meant that the financial help (£5000) which had been promised by the Government and was desperately needed for the continuation and expansion of the work went instead to an abortive attempt by Scott himself to set up a number of training institutions all over Natal. Financial difficulties were eventually to restrict severely, if not altogether cripple Colenso's work: after he had been declared a heretic, the SPG refused to provide the mission with any further financial support.

Colenso's problems with Mann are just one example of his numerous difficulties in finding and keeping the services of suitable people. Winckler notes that 'He formed quick first opinions of people, many of which he later revised, or which collapsed at the first serious challenge' (Winckler 1964: 5), while Hooker (1953: 50), describing Colenso's 'bad judgment of character', states: 'There are innumerable later instances where his initial assessment of a person was too charitable'. One of those disappointments was when Charles Grubbe, who succeeded Baugh as Principal of the school, indulged in frequent flogging of the boys. This led to arguments between Colenso and Grubbe, and, ultimately, the latter's removal from the school. Corporal punishment was much used in the English schools at the time, but Colenso wanted none of it in his school (see the letter from Grubbe to the SPG about a quarrel with Colenso over management of the school and justifying his resignation, dated 6 February 1860 [C/AFS/6 (14)]).

Colenso's work was also hampered by an early form of 'job reserva-tion'. It was not long before Mr Purcell, the master-printer, was refusing to pass on his skills to Africans. 'He has thoroughly imbibed the spirit of the town in this respect', wrote Colenso (quoted in Winckler 1964: 82). Three catechists who had been brought out for comparable duties—a tailor, a pastry-cook and a joiner—all likewise failed Colenso, perhaps for the same reason as Purcell.

However, what Colenso especially seemed to lack was a close friend in overall agreement with him, both theologically and in his practical plans for the diocese and mission. He had wished to involve the Reverend T.P. Ferguson, a contemporary of his at Cambridge, in the educational work at Ekukhanyeni. After a year in Natal, Colenso wrote to Ferguson (on 7 July 1857 [KC, Colenso Papers File 16: 49323]): 'O how I long for some congenial spirit, who really will enter with me…into this noble work, and have the intellectual power requisite for bringing knowledge down to the level of these poor barbarians'. G.W. Allnutt was the friend whom he relied upon in England to find the right sort of personnel, and in a letter to him of 7 July 1857 he described his reasons for wanting the assistance of Ferguson:

> I might be able to go away and visit other parts of the country which I cannot without great difficulty now, and the boys are so advanced that they want a *superior Teacher* as I hope to train these up for future *Schoolmasters* among their people. And many books of Education require to be written— and I cannot do everything and I want a *friend* like Mr. Ferguson—loving order in the Church, but loving the Gospel and the souls of men more than mere ritualism. (F.E. Colenso 1885)

But Ferguson did not come to Natal, and this may have been a serious obstacle to the school at Ekukhanyeni ever enjoying any great success, or even continuing in existence. It remained tied to Colenso's supervision, and his energies were increasingly directed to the work of authorship and translation and later to biblical and theological scholarship and controversy, and his political defence of the Zulu people against British imperialism.

A Unique Way of Translating the Bible

Colenso's work of authorship and translation says much about him as an educator. He had realized from the time of his appointment that he would have to learn Zulu as rapidly as possible to write grammars, dictionaries and translations of the Bible which were to be the basis of his missionary work. His son, Francis, writing of his father's efforts at learning Zulu, said:

> his mastery of the Zulu tongue was the reward of stubborn work, of sitting with natives who could not speak a word of English, day after day, from early morn till sunset, till they as well as [himself] were fairly exhausted... and when they were gone still turning round again to [his] desk to copy out the results of the day. (F.E. Colenso 1885)

Colenso translated the Bible in an extraordinarily interesting way. Assisted by William Ngidi (who had been educated by American Missionaries), he would sit for long hours—'a close prisoner at his desk' (Cox 1888: 84)— in a little open-air shelter he had had erected outside his house at Bishopstowe, poring over the Scriptures with dedication equal to that he had devoted to learning Zulu:

> Taking the Greek Testament, for instance, he would first represent in Zulu as accurately as he could the meaning of a clause in the original, and would

then ask the native to repeat the same in his own phraseology. Being trained gradually to understand the Bishop's purpose, the native would introduce those nicer idioms which must distinguish the work of a native from that of a European. (Winckler 1964: 9)

Ngidi's influence extended beyond questions of phraseology, however, into the realm of scriptural interpretation itself. He frankly explained that he found it difficult to accept the literal accuracy of certain biblical accounts, and this led Colenso to examine these more thoroughly. Thus Winckler notes that when translating the Genesis account of the deluge, 'William... had questioned its physical feasibility. To Colenso this was the final sign that it had now become his duty to apply his energy chiefly to probing the scripture' (Winckler 1964: 9). Colenso's humble acceptance of the intellectual insights of his assistant was to make him the butt of some mockery as expressed in a crude popular jingle of the time (Rees 1958: 76):

A Bishop there was of Natal,
Who took a Zulu for a pal,
Said the Kafir, 'Look 'ere,
Ain't the Pentateuch queer?'
And converted the Lord of Natal.

Political Significance of Education

Another source of controversy for Colenso was his appreciation of the political significance of the education he was offering. In this respect, as in so many others, he seems to have been at least a century ahead of his time, for only in the last few decades have the political implications of literacy been given their rightful stress, chiefly by the Brazilian educator Paulo Freire in his 1972 book *Pedagogy of the Oppressed*. Freire argues that literacy training is a profoundly political act whose method determines whether it brings genuine freedom to the learner or further domination by the ruling class. Freire advocates a method in which adult peasants learn how to alter their social situation, in which they have previously been prevented from reaching their full potential precisely because of their illiteracy.

In the Preface to his *First Lessons in Science Designed for the Use of Children and Adult Natives* (1860a), Colenso notes: 'It seemed desirable that they should be gaining some information, as they read, about the state of things around them, instead of wasting their energies upon the child's story of "Dick Bell" and his doings'.

More directly political is his comment on the Zulu Reading Book he published in 1858: 'I have almost completed in M.S. [*sic*] my Zulu–Kafir Reading Book—a pretty castigation, I expect, I shall get from all sides when it is published. I have taken care to let the people know all about the Legislative Council, and their own right to vote for Members when properly qualified, and I hope to have a good many voters before long upon this Station' (Colenso 1885a quoted in Cox 1888: 127).

Colenso wrote numerous other books which, though not of lasting value, provided essential tools for the foundations of African education. With exceptional tenacity he managed to complete in seven years: a grammar of the Zulu language and a summary for beginners; a Zulu–English dictionary of 552 pages; selections and reading books in Zulu; manuals of instruction in English, history and astronomy; and the translation of the books of Genesis, Exodus, Samuel and the entire New Testament.

In addition to his own writings, Colenso encouraged Zulus to write, a crucial step in their liberation. Thus we have in Zulu an account of a visit to King Mpande by Colenso, written by three Zulus, one of whom was Magema Fuze whom Colenso later encouraged go further to write a history of the Zulu people, to which reference has been made (Fuze 1922).

Assessment of Colenso's Educational Efforts

Though Colenso's own writings and translations were in themselves a great contribution to African education, time devoted to them was one of the reasons why the school at Ekukhanyeni never flourished. Colenso's other difficulties have already been noted: lack of personnel and finance, and the scriptural, theological and political controversy in which he became ever more deeply embroiled. One should not be greatly surprised that the school which had been started with such high hopes came to an end in 1861, only five years after its inception. In the 'Zulu Panic' of that year, it was thought by the Governor that Bishopstowe was particularly endangered because of Mkungu's presence there. Thus, all the boys who had been gathered from their kraals with such difficulty, were scattered once more to those kraals. 'Let us hope', wrote Colenso, 'that the education which they have received will not be lost on them in after life' (Hooker 1953: 55).

The closing of the school coincided with Colenso's visit to England—and when he came back to Natal he did not revive it. In 1865 a number of past and potential pupils requested him to do so. There is no evidence that he did, but we do know that in 1875, as a result of Langalibalele's misfortune, 14 of the chief's sons and nine others were living at Ekukhanyeni. There is no indication, however, that educational activities were undertaken at the time (Winckler 1964:10).

Disappointment at the failure of Colenso's educational schemes is especially keen when one reads the moving accounts of the high esteem in which the Zulu people held him, and the degree of mutual trust that had been built up. Though at the time of his death in 1883 he had few white friends, Zulus informed a travelling evangelist that they had known only one honest white man: 'Sobantu—it is he whom you call Bishop Colenso' (F.E. Colenso 1885: 269).

Francis Colenso recounts a statement made by Cetshwayo which gives further proof of this high level of trust and esteem: 'I have told the Government of Natal this, that whatsoever happens, I and my people have determined ever to consult Sobantu. He is our friend, and we shall tell him everything that we want to. We shall send to him today, tomorrow, and the next day, *Kuze, kube pakade* [literally "forever and ever"—used here to mean "and on till the end of the chapter"]' (F.E. Colenso 1885: 269).

In all his contacts with the Zulus, Colenso, though using the common terms of the time such as 'kafirs', 'savages' and 'barbarians', had treated them as friends and equals, rather than as objects: the work he had done was for their *liberation*, not their *domestication*. In this way he came to deserve another title the Zulus gave him—'Sokululeka' ('the father who brings freedom'). From his first visit to the colony (vividly described in *Ten Weeks in Natal* [Colenso 1855g]) he made evident his fundamental disagreement with the racist attitudes of the colonists who had lost no time in urging him never to 'indulge a Kafir—never shake hands with him. He does not understand it, and will soon take liberties' [Colenso 1855g: 9]). Colenso looked rather for the good qualities of the Zulu people: 'they are not at all wanting as a race, in intelligence' (p. 257). His comment on the feast of the first fruits speaks eloquently of the positive attitude that distinguishes a great educator (p. 93):

> This as now observed, is a purely heathen ceremony, but had undoubtedly a right meaning at the bottom; and, instead of setting our faces against all these practices, our wisdom will surely be, in accordance with the sage advice of Gregory the Great, to adopt such as are really grounded in truth, and restore them to their right use, or rather raise them in the end, still higher by making them Christian celebrations.

Colenso was amazed at the attitude of Daniel Lindley, a missionary for the American Board of Commissioners for Foreign Missions, who claimed that it would take '500 years to produce any sensible effect upon them' (p. 237), and who carefully segregated his own children from the Zulu children on his mission at Inanda.

Even more abhorrent was the attitude of the average settler as described by Colenso's wife, Frances: 'the hatred which the typical colonial bears to the native is quite a phenomenon in the history of mankind. They have never been allowed to make slaves of them which they want to do' (Frances Colenso quoted in Rees 1958: 273). It was an attitude the Colensos had chosen to avoid by living six miles outside Pietermaritzburg.

How should Colenso's educational work be assessed? Certainly his institutional plans were not in any respect particularly original, nor did the curriculum he offered at Ekukhanyeni appear especially liberating; the reasons for its failure have been set out in this article. It is perhaps in his educational philosophy that Colenso is most relevant today. To use his own words: Will education make the Zulu simply a better 'machine for his European Masters' or 'a better and nobler Man'? Colenso was original, in seeing that genuine education is intimately connected with political liberation, and in stressing that teachers who strive for the full autonomy of learners must also be prepared to respect and learn from them.

It is in Colenso's attitude towards those he was educating and the relationship he developed with them that he continues to challenge all who are involved in education.

THE CLASS OF 1856 AND THE POLITICS OF CULTURAL PRODUCTION(S) IN THE EMERGENCE OF EKUKHANYENI, 1855–1910

Vukile Khumalo

Introduction

In one of the informal conversations among residents and visitors at Ekukhanyeni, Alice Werner, one of the founders of African Studies at the School of Oriental and African Studies in Britain, writes: 'Mubi, on one occasion, looking round the Bishop's study, or, probably some of the other rooms whose shelves housed the overflow—remarked, "books are the *izimpetu* (worms) of the house"' (Werner [date unknown]: 13). At one level this metaphor suggests that Ekukhanyeni was 'infested with books', as Werner observed at the time. But there is also a deep meaning of Mubi Nondenisa's statement.[1] His telling observation suggests a particular relationship with books that is rather ambivalent. Partly due to the experience of producing, distributing and reading books and the 'reality' of life at Ekukhanyeni, Nondenisa came to realize that books had a potential to build and destroy—that, literally, books cause trouble. But Nondenisa's association of Ekukhanyeni with books was not limited to residents at the station—an expanding network of writers who regularly sent letters to the mission station from around Natal and Zululand knew the station through its production of books. Moreover, such a statement about books could not have come from anyone but Nondenisa who was known at Ekukhanyeni for his 'pathetic greed for learning', and who had also witnessed what books had done to the house of Colenso.[2] After the publication of *The Pentateuch and Book of Joshua Critically Examined*, Colenso was excommunicated from the Anglican Church, charged with

---

1. Mubi kaNondenisa Mtuli was part of the Class of 1856. He became a teacher at Ekukhanyeni between 1880 and 1900.
2. In this context, 'house' refers to the family in a broader sense (Werner [date unknown]: 13).

heresy and lost all financial support.[3] The book sought to bring into contemporary theological debates the idea that the Bible was not historically true. Of course, this was hardly new in the intellectual debates at the time, but what gave Colenso's assertion local and international attention was that he insisted that William Ngidi, his assistant, had led him to this conclusion.

Because of his conversion, Colenso, a prize-winning scholar at Cambridge and author of one of Britain's most widely used mathematics textbooks, became known as a convert to African ways of life within intellectual and political circles both in South Africa and Great Britain ('Black Philosopher' [CP, Box 126, Miscellaneous Letter Books, III, 1887–88]; see also Etherington 1978; Guy 1983: 174-92). According to one of the leading cultural icons and intellectuals in Great Britain, Matthew Arnold (see Guy 1997: 22), Colenso represented an 'uncritical spirit of our race determined to perform a great public act of self-humiliation'. The shift in Colenso's intellectual thinking, which he attributed to his conversations with William Ngidi, also unsettled political figures within the imperial center. Disraeli (see Brookes and de Webb 1965: 107-108), British minister at the time, commented: 'a wonderful people the Zulus! They beat our generals, they convert our bishops, and they write finis to the French dynasty'. What happened, as Guy points out, was a 'disturbing reversal of the idea of colonizer and colonized which switched dominated for dominant, unlearned for learned, heathen for Christian, savage for civilized, the self for the other' (Guy 1997: 221). This 140-year-old event, while it illustrates the intellectual life at Ekukhanyeni, reminds us that colonial situations were never monolithic and that missionaries' efforts at total transformation of the African political and moral landscape were fraught with ambiguity, contradiction and plain irony (Marks 1986; Landau 1995; Comaroff and Comaroff 1997, II; Cooper and Stoler 1997). The Ngidi and Colenso event, I suggest, was but one episode in a series of critical and

3.   On its first appearance, according to Frances Colenso, the book was regarded as 'one of the most daring ventures undertaken by the house of Longman; few books in Victorian time caused such a sensation. Within six days of its appearance, ten thousand copies, running to four editions, were sold or ordered'. See Rees 1958: 73. For a detailed discussion of *The Pentateuch*, see Guy (1983; 1997). For another take on Colenso's views on the Bible, Robert Thornton (1983: 4) writes that 'Colenso wished to show that much of the Bible was simply the poetic, eulogistic, or folk-tale-like traditions of a pastoral people, and therefore in many respects like the Zulu literature which he had come to appreciate'.

mutually transforming intellectual conversations that took place, initially, between students and the bishop and, later, among students themselves on society, culture, religion and other issues, and is richly recorded in their letters.

In this paper, I will consider one strand of their conversations, namely, the question of what to do with books. The letter-writers from Ekukhanyeni constructed a network through which they shared ideas, and this network came to shape what they called *ibandla* ('sphere'). Here I investigate the inner-dimensions of the network, that is, how letter-writers sustained their correspondence for more than 50 years. The point of entry is the Class of 1856: this group of students, while not homogeneous, saw itself as possessing a 'useful past...that would in time become *lilifa* ['property'] of our children's children and generations to come' (Nondenisa and Fuze in the newspaper *Ipepa Lo Hlanga* 21 June 1901).[4]

Focusing on the 'property' that the members of the Class of 1856 left behind, I argue (1) that the writers (Nondenisa and Fuze—who were part of the Class of 1856) consciously *mbulula* ('dug up') and selected a specific past that they wanted to share with their network of friends, and (2) that by producing and circulating books on the history of the Zulu kingdom and Ekukhanyeni these members sought to expand the readership around South Africa and beyond. And, (3) in the process of circulating books and ideas, this group of former Ekukhanyeni students and their associates came to imagine an audience that had specific ways of reading and particular relationship(s) to the books that they produced.

'Strange Bedfellows':
The Establishment of Ekukhanyeni Education Institution

One of the guiding aims of the founders of Ekukhanyeni School was to produce an elite class of notables that owed its existence to the favour of the colonial state. For an avid Victorian scholar and optimist like John Colenso, establishing the school at Ekukhanyeni would 'raise up...a body of intelligent teachers, who shall be schoolmasters among the numerous villages' (see the letter from Colenso to Grey dated 1 February 1857 [University of Witwatersrand, Department of Historical Papers (UWDHP) AB1606F]). But the bishop was not alone. His sense of optimism found a sympathetic ear in one of the architects of the school, Ngoza Majozi, who

---

4. Some of the questions I ask of this *mbulula* ('dig up' = 'project') on Nondenisa and Fuze are inspired by the questions of David William Cohen (1994).

saw the existence of the school as meaning that 'now the people had got a word to say' (a letter from Colenso to Grey [University of Witwatersrand, Department of Historical Papers (= UWDHP) AB1606F]). Soon the list of participants in this 'raise up' project would increase even further.

Colenso enlisted the support of Theophilus Shepstone, the then Secretary for Native Affairs. Colenso's link with Shepstone provided a means of coming into contact with African chiefs and the colonial government.[5] But neither man had the money to establish the school or the power to influence African families to release their sons. To obtain the former support, Colenso asked Sir George Grey, British High Commissioner at the Cape Colony, for a grant. To Grey this request for financial support could not have come at a better time since his authority was being challenged and his expansionist plans questioned. Grey wanted to impress the Queen and demonstrate to the colonial office that his vision of an expanded British Southern Africa could be achieved by the extension of British influence and civilization through the 'education' of indigenous peoples.[6] Just at the time when Colenso made his request Grey was in Natal making plans to grant land to the missionaries to build mission stations. Through Grey's influence the Natal government granted missionaries land under the Deed of Grant of 1856. The grant gave the mission boards of different denominations powers to control their lands. The character of the mission stations reflected the interests of various mission bodies. Some missionaries emphasized the evangelical aspect of their mission while others, such as the American Board of Commissioners for Foreign Missions (hereafter American Board Mission), encouraged individual land tenure (Bridgman A/608 [American Board Mission Files housed at the Natal Archives Depot (NAD)]).

Due to the concentration of missionary societies in one area between 1850 and 1900, Natal became one of the most heavily evangelized regions of the globe (Etherington 1978: 275). In his book *Preachers, Peasants and Politics in Southern Africa*, Etherington (1978: 5) suggests that:

---

5.   Born in the eastern Cape, Theophilus Shepstone came to Natal in 1847 and was appointed a Diplomatic Agent to the Native Tribes. In 1847, Shepstone established the Locations Commission whose recommendation laid the basis for segregation in Natal. The commission was asked to investigate the possibility of relocating Africans to designated areas. Between 1847 and 1875, Shepstone was a central figure in Natal politics with regard to Native Affairs, and the post stayed within the Shepstone family for a generation—when Theophilus left, his brother Arthur took the post.

6.   For a discussion of George Grey's career at the Cape colony see Peires 1989.

No other quarter of nineteenth-century Africa was so thickly invested with Christian evangelists. The Secretary of the American Board of Commissioners for Foreign Missions estimated in 1880 that the number of missionaries in Natal was proportionately greater than in any other community on the globe two or three times over.

By the turn of the century in Natal alone there were 40,000 communicants and 100,000 adherents to Christianity (Marks 1970: 52). Most of the converts lived on mission reserves, and they occupied about 175,000 acres of land.

When Colenso's request came, Grey promptly agreed to give the school a yearly grant of £500 and a further £1500 contribution towards the building of the Institution (see the letter from Colenso to Hawkins dated 19 October 1854 [NAD]). The school was established on 5849 acres of land commonly referred to as Ekukhanyeni (this name refers both to the school and mission station). Adjoining Ekukhanyeni was the Colenso family farm of 2454 acres known as Bishopstowe (H. Colenso, 1900–1902: 408 [NAD]). In addition to these structures, there were several tenants who paid rent to the Church of England. Both Ekukhanyeni and Bishopstowe were six miles from Pietermaritzburg, the colonial capital. This proximity to the city of Pietermaritzburg was later to prove strategically useful for former students of Ekukhanyeni to facilitate their communication network.

Once established, the school had to get pupils. Shepstone approached Ngoza Majozi, a prominent chief, to use his influence among his people.[7] Majozi at this time had built up his name within colonial circles. He was among the few chiefs who came to greet Colenso in 1854, and on this occasion 'dressed as neatly as an European, with his attendant Kafir waiting beside him' (Colenso 1855g: 46), Majozi was sure to impress and leave his mark in the Lord Bishop's mind (Guy 2001b: 5). Colenso (1855g: 46) noted:

> Ngoza is Mr. Shepstone's head man, and, though not an hereditary chief, has acquired considerable power, and is practically a chief of as much authority as any in the district, which he owes partly to Mr. Shepstone's patronage, partly to his own modest and amiable character. There are,

7.   Ngoza kaLudada Majozi was a chief in Umsinga Division. He was appointed chief while he was working in Durban as a domestic servant. However, he soon found favor with the colonial establishment and became an icon of commercial interests. In the 1860s his picture was used to portray a typical African chief, and circulated in Britain and the English-speaking world.

212 The Eye of the Storm

probably, (by reason of refuges having flocked to him, who had left their own chiefs behind,) more pure Zulus under Ngoza than under other chief in Natal.[8]

Majozi had 300 villages under his control and, unlike most chiefs of his position, he had powers to give people land. When the idea of a school came up, Majozi had just organized a review of his 1000 strong men in honour of a visit from Grey, Colenso and Shepstone to his headquarters (see the letter from Colenso dated 11 August 1855 [Archival record damaged] [NAD]). The review was quite a spectacle and included dance groups that Majozi had arranged to grace the occasion. After this festival, Colenso and Shepstone announced the idea of a school to the community and left for the capital, Pietermaritzburg. The onus was then on Majozi to continue urging people to send their sons to Ekukhanyeni. To persuade the parents, Ngoza enlisted the support of another chief in the district, Zashuke Ngubane.[9] Like his fellow chief Majozi, Ngubane was seen by the colonists as an enlightened, loyal, progressive chief who represented no danger to the colonial government (*The Visit of His Royal Highness* 1861: 16). The two chiefs lived in a location south of the Thukela River and north of Pietermaritzburg.

At first parents, especially mothers, refused to release their children to the school. Their concerns were further deepened by rumours that colonial officials wanted to take their sons to England. Mubi Nondenisa and Magema Fuze (*Ipepa Lo Hlanga* 28 June 1901) recalled 45 years later that when these rumors reached parents there was 'an outcry in the villages'. It took parents ten weeks to send word to Majozi that they had come to realize that formal education was necessary for their sons. To show that he led by example, Ngoza announced that he would send his two sons, Lutshungu and Mdliwafa, to the school (Account of Shepstone's visit to Panda, 5/28/61, SPG D25 [Society for the Propagation of the Gospel in Foreign Parts Files housed at NAD]). The day before the students and their parents left for school, a ceremony was held to bid the children farewell. The following day saw Majozi and Ngubane, on horseback, leading 19

8. For more detailed analysis of this encounter, see Guy 2001b.
9. Zatshuke kaMbheswa Ngubane was a government headman at Umsinga. He took the position after Sidoyi was deposed. Sidoyi had a dispute with colonial authorities concerning the punishment he meted out to those who were suspected of witchcraft. In 1873 Zatshuke Ngubane was appointed to the court that tried Langalibalele Hadebe. When Ekukhanyeni Central School was opened, Zatshuke was among the first parents to send their sons.

boys and their parents to Ekukhanyeni. They arrived at the school in February 1856 (according to the letter from Colenso to Hawkins dated 2 May 1856, 5/28/61, SPG D25). As the two chiefs made their way to Ekukhanyeni, those who did not release their sons held the view that Majozi and Ngubane were 'buying headmanship or Shepstone's favour / *ababeti nokutsho abantu kutengwa ngazo ubuduna ku "Somseu"'* (Nondenisa and Fuze in *Ipepa Lo Hlanga* 28 June 1901). On the day the students and parents arrived at the school a prayer service was held, despite the fact that none of the parents was Christian. Wasting no time in asserting their influence, teachers took pupils to their dormitories immediately after the prayer service and 'dressed' them in a new school uniform. When the pupils came out to greet their parents, according to observers, they were impressed. This display illustrated the notion that once the pupils entered the school they would be transformed into new persons. The taking off of old clothes and donning of new ones symbolized that the students had made a break with a past which was, in the discourse of the time, an 'ignorant dark past' (Colenso to Grey [UWDHP AB1606F]).

Ekukhanyeni was a boarding school. Students came to the Institute for a period of twelve months, which was designed to separate them from their parents and from close contact with their communities. But parents and close relatives were allowed regular visits and 'at first they came frequently, bringing them presents of *amasi* ('sour milk') and other delicacies' (Colenso to Grey [UWDHP AB1606F]). The fact that all the students belonged to notable families meant that parents would take care of them and thus relieve the school of financial difficulties.

At first, the school offered training in agriculture, carpentry, building construction and religious lessons. Unlike the more elite institutions in southern Africa, Ekukhanyeni was not meant to produce a large number of intellectuals, but Colenso hoped that it would produce African teachers who would fill villages. The year the school opened it enrolled 19 boys. The next year it registered 33 students. In 1859 there were some 42 students studying at the Institution (Colenso to Grey [UWDHP AB1606F]). Ekukhanyeni was not the only institution; it had three other satellite day schools in the colony. South of Ekukhanyeni and ten miles from Durban, there was Umlazi day school under Deacon Mackenzie. The school had an average attendance of from 30 to 40 children and some classes took place at the church. This school was at the site of the former American Board Mission School where Reverend Newton Adams and his wife had established an elementary school in 1836. The school had 50 pupils, lessons were conducted in English and 'children were taught to translate the exercises into their own languages' (see the letter from Adams to Kitchingman dated 3 September 1836, quoted in Cordeur and Saunders 1976).

In line with Majozi's request for a mission station and a school, Umsunduzi or Table Mountain mission station was established near his principal homestead (Colenso to Grey [UWDHP AB1606F]). Chiefs such as Majozi saw the advantages they would gain from their relationship with missionaries. One such advantage was letter writing—missionaries wrote letters on behalf of chiefs to colonial officials. To the north, Colenso also tried to start a small boarding institution for Africans living in the town of Ladysmith; ultimately, however, financial constraints hindered the establishment of the school. Evening classes for workers, however, were already underway in 1857 (Colenso to Grey [UWDHP AB1606F]).

In 1858, Ekukhanyeni School admitted eight girls, who were accommodated in the main house with the Colenso family (Nondenisa and Fuze in *Ipepa Lo Hlanga* 23 August 1901). Further west, Langalibalele Hadebe and Pakade Mchunu, two of the most influential chiefs in the midlands, made appeals for schools (Ngidi, evidence before Natal Native Commission [= NNC] 1881–82 [NAD]). As part of the missionary package the schools were to be accompanied by mission stations, but colonial politics in Natal after 1865 did not allow such projects to take off. After Shepstone deposed chief Matshana Sithole and imprisoned Langalibalele Hadebe, Ekukhanyeni sought to challenge the colonial state by investigating the grounds on which the two chiefs were charged. When students (Magema Fuze, William Ngidi and Mubi Nondenisa) and Colenso found the grounds of the government's case flawed, Colenso denounced Shepstone and his regime 'as rotten to the very core' (see the letter from Colenso to Chesson dated 3 August 1875). During the trial of Langalibalele, Fuze, Ngidi and Nondenisa conducted interviews and obtained witnesses.[10] From then on, the Class of 1856 and Colenso became entangled in colonial politics. Because of the time they spent on these trials the students and bishop spent less time on the school premises. As a result of this and other factors associated with Colenso's indictment for heresy, the performance of the school dropped and Ekukhanyeni ceased to occupy a significant place as an educational institution. The consequences of the change in Ekukhanyeni's academic standing was that the government reduced funding, and parents, including William Ngidi and Jonathan Ngidi, stopped sending

10. For a detailed, 384-page treatment of the case of Langalibalele, see Colenso 1874b.

their children. Therefore, the pupils I call here the Class of 1856 were the first and last group of Ekukhanyeni students to receive full tuition. From the mid-1860s the school deteriorated; the colonial government eventually closed it down in 1900.

Digging Up the Past for Coming Generations: The Class of 1856

On 19 June 1901, two former students from the Class of 1856, now in their late 50s and residing in the city of Pietermaritzburg, began writing a series of articles in *isiZulu* that appeared in *Ipepa lo Hlanga* on the character of Colenso, his family and Natal society, that went on for six weeks. The two former Ekukhanyeni students were Mubi Nondenisa and Magema Fuze. As they were writing the articles they were also reprinting old Ekukhanyeni books for publication. The reason for 'digging up' (*mbulula*) the history of Ekukhanyeni and other topics was to 'engrave / *qopa* the great deeds of people who worked for all their lives among black people so that their works could become the property of our children's children and generations to come / *kwemisebenzi yabantu abakulu abesebenza ukupila kwabo konke pakati kwabantu abamnyama ukuze kube lilifa labantwana babantwana betu nezizukulwane zetu'*.[11] After the process of 'digging up', recollecting and recovering the lives they once lived they divided their articles into six parts:

19 June 1901:	*U 'Sobantu'* (John Colenso)	
21 June 1901:	*U 'Sobantu'* (John Colenso)	
28 June 1901:	*U 'Sobantu'* (John Colenso)	
12 July 1901:	*Isimilo sika Sobantu* (John Colenso's character)	
26 July 1901:	*Umuzi Ekukhanyeni* (Ekukhanyeni household)	
23 August 1901:	*Amakosazana nabantwana Ekukhanyeni; Nabafundisi nabelungu abafika no Sobantu* (the daughters and children at Ekukhanyeni; and the white people who came with Colenso)	

By making known this slice of Ekukhanyeni's past they sought not only to take their readers back to the 1850s, but also to transport them to the future of what Natal society could become. Nondenisa and Fuze did not simply write the series of articles on Colenso's life—they located Ekukhanyeni

11. This piece of Ekukhanyeni history was part of a series of articles on the Zulu kingdom, African identity (*Ubuzwe*), John Dube, Booker T. Washington, print media (African newspapers) and many more. Unfortunately the paper went out of business in 1904.

within reach of its neighbours. This is especially evident in their last two articles, in which neighbours feature in a long description of 'important families', among them the Dokotane ka'Nontshebe wakwa 'Camu, Nsimango kaNdengezi wakwa'Mahlase, Nhloyile kaMpongo wakwaDhladhla and many more. The discussion goes on to mention rivers from which the neighbours fetched water, the varieties of vegetation upon which their livestock depended, and the story of the famous dog, Sokugqoka (which translates 'one who likes to wear European clothes'), that Fuze's father, Magwaza kaMatomela, named after an incident that took place in the 1850s when Africans were forced to don European attire. To the two writers all of the above people and things had names. For them, even the vegetation had life, for it nourished the residents of Ekukhanyeni and its neighbours. The two rivers they mentioned had names: they were Umsunduze and Imbindolo. The latter owed its name to William Ngidi, and was where the residents of Ekukhanyeni and their neighbours drew their water. The Umsunduzi River was where the boys, including Shepstone's sons, swam.

To the west of Bishopstowe stood a huge Umkhambathi tree where the church bell hung. Nondenisa and Fuze ended their spatial description by stressing that the tall lush *isiqunga* ('tambootie grass') covered the whole valley of a thousand hills.[12] At first reading, Nondenisa and Fuze's discussion of Ekukhanyeni's relations with its neighbours appears to be a view through rose-tinted glasses. The writers, in their search for a 'usable past' for coming generations, decided to produce a story that would be interesting. In the articles the two writers assert only the idea that they were 'engraving' the history for posterity. But their version of the history of Ekukhanyeni was published in the same newspaper, *Ipepa lo Hlanga*, with two articles that criticized flogging as a brutal practice that failed to reform the convict and to which only Africans were subjected. Similarly, adjacent to their second article on Colenso was another piece decrying the flogging of African prisoners. Not unlike Nondenisa and Fuze's articles, these articles went into details about the effects of flogging and its lifelong impact on the prisoner's body. Furthermore, the six articles came precisely at the time when the municipalities of Durban and Pietermaritzburg proposed racial policies to limit the movement of Africans on sidewalks in the two cities.

I suggest that while the version of Ekukhanyeni history that the two students dug up (*mbulula*), selected and engraved (*qopa*) was meant to

12. This type of grass was used for cleansing.

remind readers of *Ipepa lo Hlanga* of Ekukhanyeni mission station and its founder, it was also aimed at countering the colonial government's attitudes and race policies. The most prominent exponent of the racial policies of the Natal government was James Stuart, the then first Assistant Durban Magistrate. By the turn of the twentieth century, Stuart had come to the conclusion that Africans and Europeans would never co-exist, and through his government position he tried to enact laws restricting Africans' movements in towns and cities. Such laws included, among others, the ruling that 'no natives on the side walks, no natives riding on Trams'. About the latter law Stuart felt quite strongly that:

> Here again is a practice which calls for strong and careful action. The matter appears, at first sight, to be a purely municipal one. This I do not think is the case. It is true the trams are run by and at the expense of the Corporation. The Corporation are, in law, common carriers, and as such have no authority to deny any person the privilege of riding in their cars. But there are other issues in connection herewith which call for special consideration, not so much at the hands of the Corporation, as at those of the Government. I am of the opinion the Supreme Chief should deal with the matter, just as His Excellency is, I think, the proper authority to deal with the question of side-walks. It seems to me eminently desirable that this matter should be taken in hand and a Proclamation issued forbidding Natives to mount the trams as at present managed, and authorizing every conductor to use his discretion as to what persons he allows on the cars. The conductor would, of course, discriminate in the case of nurse-girls or boys in charge of children, or in immediate attendance on their employers, and other particular cases, but the general principle that Natives may not ride on trams should be observed and strictly enforced. It is, to my mind, unreasonable and unnatural for an uncivilized Native to sit alongside Europeans on tram cars, implying equality which does not exist. (*Natal Colony Blue Book* [= NCBB] 1905)

The detailed articles written by members of the Class of 1856 on Ekukhanyeni and its neighbours were in part trying to open a dialogue with this kind of colonial thinking and to show the contradictions between what colonial officials wrote down as law and the reality of their own lives and those of their families. In the articles Ekukhanyeni neighbours had names and were not simply 'natives'. Mission station residents of different backgrounds as well as their neighbours drank from the same Imbodolo River, boys swam together at Umsunduzi River, including those of the segregationist Shepstone, and all the livestock fed on the same lush tambootie grass. This was the Ekukhanyeni that the readers of the *Ipepa lo Hlanga* were asked to imagine.

In the second article the writers talk about the school and focus on the men who sent their sons there in 1856 'against hostile opinions'. The article has a list of 29 names of the men who took their sons to Ekukhanyeni including the two former students' fathers. But the two never talk about the day-to-day workings of the school or the internal squabbles that were so characteristic of boarding school life. One thing they do mention is the place where they spent most of their time—the printing press.

But if the *Ipepa lo Hlanga* version of Ekukhanyeni history was 'romanticized', it seems that that process started as early as the 1860s. In its early years (1856–65), Ekukhanyeni school functioned as intended by its architects. The number of students increased, the school admitted girls in 1858, and the school continued to receive a yearly government grant of £250. Student assignments show that there was open discussion of contemporary problems in the classroom, or at least that pupils could write on a variety of subjects and question the everyday conditions under which they lived. Such an atmosphere might well have been enough to stimulate pupils' imaginations.

To the observer and teacher Alice Mackenzie: 'you should like I am sure to see the black school, about 40 boys of all sizes, and the way they march in and out of chapel reminds me of Rugby' (Mackenzie 1859: 10). Indeed, such scenes had all the signs of progress and were enough to remind her of England. But the marching of boys was not all that was impressive to the eye—in the classroom students were also doing well. Mackenzie, in her 60-page diary, had much to say of the mundane workings of the school. As she writes (p. 11),

> Just now they are working at harvesting, and there has been only one day of school since I came, but that one I was quite astonished. Reading English so nicely and doing sums, taking them down themselves out of the Bishop's Arithmetic books and working them without any help, and bringing their slates to Mrs. Grubbe for correction first like at home.

But at an institution founded on aristocratic hierarchical premises, not every pupil was in the field harvesting. Mkhungo, Zulu king Mpande's son, was in the living room listening to Beethoven and enjoying the company of his tutors. However, the class had some exceptions to the picture above—two students had problems. Mackenzie writes (p. 13):

> One of Mrs. Colenso's pupils is a very bad reader, and quite behind all the others, and Mrs. C. asked me if I would give her a separate hour by herself to which I readily assented, so she is to come in the forenoon always, and we have commenced a thorough drilling. Mrs. Markham's history of Eng-

land being the instrument of torture'. I am also to have Robin [Colenso] reading in the forenoon, and at 12 I am always going to the Bishop to hear him work at the new dictionary with his native assistant William.

Clearly, Mackenzie's diary is well crafted and true to its intentions. What is open to question is how much of Mackenzie's writing was a confirmation of her desires of what the school should be and how much was written for an audience in England. In the latter case, the writings had to paint a rosy picture of the situation at the school and the philanthropic work Colenso was doing for the people in Natal. Unlike the writings of Nondenisa and Fuze, Mackenzie's journal does not declare its 'political' intentions. However, it does reveal that to Mackenzie, success meant that the school functioned in the same way as the schools at 'home' in England.

After considering the recollections of Nondenisa, Fuze and Mackenzie concerning life at Ekukhanyeni, we can now go to the classroom and see what students were writing or asked to write. After three years of student life, Bishop Colenso asked students to write about their experiences at the school. To his surprise, he received incisive commentaries on differences among human beings and segregation at his own church services. In the conclusion of his short essay, Makenjane ka Sotshenge, a 13-year-old student at Ekukhanyeni, asked Colenso a question that would occupy the minds of most people for the rest of the nineteenth century and beyond, namely (as worded in a letter from Colenso to Grey),

> I know not why we differ, since we are made thus by one person. Why is it that some should be white and some should be black?

From all indications, it appears, that the question stunned the Bishop, and he sent the essay to the Cape Governor, Sir George Grey. But neither Colenso nor Grey left a record of their answer(s) to this question. What does such a question tell us about the pupil, the school or Colenso? At the very least, it shows that at the school there existed conditions that allowed the students to pose what was in their minds.

Makenjane was not the only student who commented on life at Ekukhanyeni. Magema Fuze wrote an essay that dealt with mundane activities. In his essay he noted the presence of the bell in their lives as students and the way in which the ringing of the bell punctuated the rhythm of student life, announcing the appropriate time to go for food, classes and church services. Fuze opened the essay by saying that they were happy about the living conditions at the school, but he quickly moved to talk about how the ringing of the bell signified separation. Magema wrote (quoted in Colenso to Grey):

> We are happy at Ekukhanyeni. After our evening meal the bell rings and we go to church. On Sunday morning we go to the chapel to pray. Before midday, the bell rings calling white people to come to church. When they enter the house of prayer they pray and read the news of Jesus Christ, our Lord. When the white people get out of the chapel we have lunch. Thereafter, the bell rings calling black people. Then we go to the chapel. Bishop Colenso announces the words of Jesus Christ, the son of Dio to the people.

This essay raises questions about the kind of life that Ekukhanyeni residents led in the first two years. Could it be that Colenso, while sensitive to issues of race, simply did not stop segregation at his church. Or could it have been that by sending essays to Grey he was challenging British racial policies in South Africa? Whatever the case may be, for Fuze the conditions at Ekukhanyeni seem to have been uncomfortable or at least significant enough to report.

It is important to note that Colenso sent these essays to Grey in order for Grey to see that there was progress at the school. And it was not only essays that he sent to Grey but also more than 15 drawings that originally had been drawn as classroom assignments.[13] The drawings cover a wide range of things—among them dogs, agricultural implements, cows—but here I comment only on two drawings.

Figure 1. *Sketch by Magema Fuze 1858*
(National Library of South Africa in Cape Town. Used by permission.)

13. Mrs F. Colenso taught drawing and painting.

The first drawing is a sketch of a structure or building (see Fig. 1). Its architectural design suggests that it might have been one of the buildings at Ekukhanyeni or was the product of the 13-year-old Magema Fuze's artistic imagination. A glance at the 'sketch' suggests that Fuze must have not only been aware of the mid-nineteenth-century architectural designs but also had a very good sense of nineteenth-century developments in art techniques. I return to this point below.

Figure 2. *Sketch by Ndiane Ngubane 1858*
(National Library of South Africa in Cape Town. Used by permission.)

Like the first 'sketch', the second example, drawn byNdiane Ngubane, evinces a mastery of the art of drawing (see Fig. 2). The figure in the 'sketch' is of a young woman facing away from the artist. A closer look at the figure suggests that she is scantly clad. If the figure in the 'sketch' is a woman, who might she be? Did Ndiane Ngubane draw or trace it from a photo album? Or is the figure in the sketch one of the Colensos? The available information surrounding the production of this 'sketch' suggests that Ngubane was a star art student. His artistic works were shown to residents and visitors at Ekukhanyeni and some sketches were sent to Queen Victoria. Mackenzie (p. 61) writes that

> many of the black boys have a great taste for drawing, and some of the
> pictures of Undiane, Mrs. Colenso's favorite pupil have been sent to the
> Queen, and Her Majesty has sent a very gracious message of approval of
> them, and though Undiane's talent is past the common, still many of these
> boys are very clever at drawing.

Residents were often interrupted to come and observe Ndiane's art pieces.
Mackenzie, again, comments (p. 3):

> Then Mrs. Colenso called me to look at some of her favourate pupil Undi-
> yane's drawings, and wonderful they are indeed, and we had some pleasant
> chat...

It appears that to the bishop such interruptions disturbed mission life and
were quite enough perhaps to warrant Ndiane's expulsion from the school.
Colenso does not give details of Ndiane's case except that he 'left in 1861
when his involvement in an unfortunate love affair had rendered him unfit
for work' (see the letter from Colenso to Hawkins dated 5 July 1861). The
two students' use of the sketch techniques places them in a particular
group of artists, the *avant-garde*. With the emergence of the *avant-garde*
'movement' in the 1830s, the 'sketch' acquired a new meaning that was
associated with 'progressive tendencies' (Harris 2001: 74-75). The quality
of the two drawings suggests that the students had access to latest ideas on
art techniques. And, perhaps, that explains why their works were circulated and attracted a wide and diverse audience.

But, as was said earlier, the Class of 1856 was the last to produce such
impressive works. And, as Nondenisa and Fuze wrote their historical articles in newspapers, they were quite aware of the constraints and limitation
of their message because of the lack of 'proper education' among their
intended readers. The following section demonstrates this.

'Educated in the True Sense of the Word': Education in Natal

Ekukhanyeni school was like most of the educational establishments in
Natal before the turn of the century. The missionary institutions founded
and controlled the schools. However, as time went on well to-do African
communities started their own schools; these were usually referred to as
'family schools' and were headed by female teachers (NCBB 1880). By
1885, however, some of the mission schools as well as the family schools
came under the aegis of Natal government and received a share from a
welfare grant of £5000 (Marks 1970: 55).

The role that the missionaries played in the educational affairs in the colony of Natal before the turn of the twentieth century, however, did vary, as did their practices. Etherington (1978: 282) writes that 'many chiefs invited missionaries to reside near them because they valued their secular services such as letter-writing and intercession with British authorities'. Other chiefs preferred the government-sponsored schools. In 1885 there were about 64 such schools, and by 1901 Natal had 196 schools with 11,051 pupils (NCBB 1880). The curriculum was the same in Natal and Zululand after 1880. Students were taught to read and write in English and *isiZulu*. They also learnt subjects such as geography, physiology, gymnastics, sacred history, history and chemistry. Boys were taught some industrial work, and girls learned sewing, housework and cooking (NCBB). But the emphasis was on languages. For instance, at St Mark's school in Pietermaritzburg African children were also instructed in Latin and Greek (Etherington 1989: 289). And, at the Ladysmith Anglican School in the same year, 42 students attained an advanced level in English, German and Geography, six in English grammar, and two in music. With some schools the problem laid not so much in the content of the subjects taught as in the manner in which they were delivered. For instance, at St John's school in Ladysmith, geography was taught in order to 'constantly reflect upon the infallible truth that Europe, though the smallest in size of the four quarters of the globe, is nevertheless the greatest in spiritual, scientific, and military power' (NCBB 1885: 43). Schools did this to comply with the government's requirement of 'encouraging pupils to conform with European habits' (p. 43). In the case of schools not complying with this requirement, government stopped funding them.

Besides the elementary schools in most parts of the colony, the American Zulu Mission created an advanced College and named it after one of its first missionaries, Newton Adams. Adams College was established at Amanzimtoti, five miles south of Durban in 1852. Students could choose from a number of colleges including Inanda Seminary for girls,[14] Edendale Training Institute and Pietermaritzburg Training School and other schools outside the colony.

After the Natal colonial government was granted greater autonomy by the British in 1893, it changed its policies on African education. This saw a change in government attitudes; part of this shift reflected the views of sugar farmers who wanted cheap labour for the farms. This shift was well

14. Inanda Seminary was established in 1868 and its first principal was Mary Kelly Edwards from Dayton, OH, USA. See Hughes 1990.

captured in newspaper commentaries that characterized educated Africans as 'lazy good for nothing' (Marks 1970: 81). Towards the turn of the century, the emphasis in government schools was on teaching African pupils how to read and write in English and *isiZulu*. Seeing the shift in government's attitudes towards African education, well-to-do *Amakholwa* (Christians) parents criticized the government education system and decided to send their children to racially integrated Cape schools like Lovedale, Grahamstown and Healdtown (Natal Archives Depot, Secretary for Native Affairs Files [NAD, SNA], 1/1/212).[15] Others sent their sons to the United States of America and England. The two first students who went to America were John Nembula and Jeremiah Mali. The former did his medical studies at Chicago Medical College,[16] while the latter trained as a teacher at Howard College and returned to Natal in 1876 to resume teaching at Adams College. (Mali was soon expelled for having had 'a long course of immoral conduct with two young women'—see the letter from Ireland to Clark and Adams dated 14 July 1880 [Archives of the American Board of Commissioners for Foreign Missions, Houghton Library, Harvard University (ABC), 15.4, VIII]). So crucial was the idea of getting children out of Natal that the Ethiopian Church in Natal boasted that it had sent, in 1903 alone, 26 boys and nine girls to American colleges (*Ipepa lo Hlanga* 16 October 1903). To one of the students who went to America, Pixley Ka Isaka Seme, the move to send children out of the Colony of Natal was a clear sign that parents had 'learned that knowledge is power' (Seme 1913: 439).[17]

The dissatisfaction of *Amakholwa* parents with Natal education has been mentioned in the secondary literature (Etherington 1989: 291). However, what has not been fully investigated is the type of education that *Amakholwa* imagined. In an interview with *The Star* newspaper in Johannesburg, Solomon Khumalo, an editor of a Pietermaritzburg-based mission press, *Inkanyiso*, attempted to elaborate on what 'they' meant by 'proper education' (*The Star* 6 December 1895). When he was asked to talk about the type of education that the 'natives' received, he replied:

15. NAD, SNA, I/1/212: 'A Zulu Editor visits the Rand. A chat with him on Mr Marwick appointment and Native Education, December 6th, 1895.' Solomon Khumalo purchased the *Inkanyiso* newspaper from Reverend Green of Pietermaritzburg in 1894. See also Dube 1909.

16. By the 1870s, Nembula was working at a chemist's shop on 308 39th Street in Chicago, IL, USA.

17. Seme wrote this paper in 1906 when he was studying at Colombia University.

Native education in Natal…is not what natives would like it. Natives generally would like to see their children educated. Of course, when I say 'educated' I mean educated in the true sense of the word. Natives will spend almost all their money on the education of their children. But no matter what they do in that way in Natal there is no chance of their acquiring the education for their children which they ought to have.

Khumalo, a graduate of the Training Institute at Grahamstown, clarified this later as follows (NAD SNA, I/1/130):

I mean a proper education—that only mean, one thing, sir. In Natal the highest standard is the fifth; they only oblige the aspirant to read Fourth Royal Reader, to have a sufficient acquaintance with the elementary rules of arithmetic, a smattering of the English language, and well—that's about all. (NAD, SNA, I/1/212)

Khumalo aired his dissatisfaction with the lack of education among native teachers, especially those who taught at family schools. For him it was 'much better for the unfortunate children to stay at home and help their parents than to go wasting their time with such teachers'. The only solution was, Khumalo insisted, to get 'teachers right out from England. We have been thinking of it for a long time, and I think it will soon become an established fact. We shall then have proper education.' This project, however, never materialized. Here Khumalo suggests that what parents needed for their children was higher education. But there is a class element underlying the education concerns. Parents like him, it seems, encouraged the immigration of professional English teachers as opposed to a group of small businessmen and land speculators whom the Natal government disparately needed. But, of course, not all parents shared the need for getting English teachers. Johannes Khumalo had a different take on the subject. As he put it (Khumalo, evidence before NNC 1882–83):

We have schools amongst us, but have difficulty in finding teachers; we would like Native teachers, educated if we could get them, because they would of course understand our language, and it is so difficult to get white people who do.

Parents' views on the specifics of the kind of education they wanted varied because some, like William Ngidi, were more modest; they wanted their children to 'learn how to make chairs, tables, and similar things—in fact, industrial teaching' so that they could open their businesses in the city (Ngidi, evidence before NNC 1882–83; see Guy 1997). For Ngidi self-sufficiency was the first priority. However, even Ngidi was very particular about the kind of education that he did not want his children to receive. Giving evidence before the Natal Native Commission he stated:

> Q: Would the Natives desire more magistrates, especially in locations?
> A: Yes: with a school attached for learning, and one for industrial pursuits but *no* gospel.

Here Ngidi strikes at the core of the civilizing mission's twin foundations: church and school, as espoused by missionaries. Particularly worrying for Ngidi was the terror that the missionaries invoked when preaching the word of God. He questioned the method in which school subjects or the word of God in churches was taught/preached and insisted that he did not 'believe in the preaching of the law as coming with canon to blow up the world'. As he put it: 'I do not like teaching by fear' (NNC 1882–83).

The general view among *Amakholwa* was that most parents wanted their children to learn languages and trades so as to prepare them well for future employment, and that to achieve this 'there should be educational and industrial schools attached to every magistracy throughout the land' (John Khumalo, evidence before NNC 1881–82: 152). And 20 years later, the editor of *Ipepa lo Hlanga*, Mark Radebe, called for the establishment of a Native Ministry for Education (*Ipepa lo Hlanga*, 28 June 1901). Underlying these education concerns was the desire on the part of parents to have their children get what they call 'book learning'. As Johannes Khumalo put it (evidence before NNC 1882–83): 'we would prefer to have industrial schools established amongst us in connection with book learning, etc., as such an education would enable them to earn their own living'. So, in light of the above concerns about 'proper education', it seems parents had realized that their children were not taking full advantage of the available literature from various mission presses since a great number of the available schools in Natal only offered classes up to the fourth grade. Furthermore, from such concerns about 'book learning' the idea of a book began to gather more significance.

If mission station publications created this fetishization or rather high admiration of book learning or books, a number of questions arise: How did the mission presses create the market or readership? Did the publications produce their own readers or publics? Were the presses catering for known expectations? How were these cultural products of the mission stations consumed or read? And, how were the books produced? I address these questions in the next section.

'More Solid and Wholesome Food': The Book

The *Amakholwa*'s fascination with proper education, good teachers and schools extended even to the idea of the book. And one such *Ikholwa* (Christian) was Mark S. Radebe, printer and publisher of *Ipepa lo Hlanga*. Writing about Ekukhanyeni in 1903, Radebe lamented (*Ipepa lo Hlanga* 3 July 1903; see also Ntuli and Makhambeni 1998):

> the good work of writing and publishing books in Zulu language, creditably commenced by the late and much lamented Bishop Colenso, has ceased or slackened.

Among numerous books that Ekukhanyeni Press published between 1855 and 1910 were *Three Native Accounts of the Visit of the Bishop of Natal in September and October, 1859, to Umpande, King of the Zulus* (Colenso 1901 [= 3rd edn]) and *Izindatshana Zabantu* (*People's Stories/Histories*) (Colenso 1859e). The former is an anthology of three accounts written by two students of Ekukhanyeni who belonged to the Class of 1856—Magema Fuze, Ndiane Ngubane—and assistant teacher William Ngidi. The existence and importance of this book is but nominally acknowledged in the historiography of Kwazulu/Natal (Guy 1997), whereas *Izindaba Zabantu* has only appeared in footnotes.

To most of the mission-educated writers and even those who received education at home through private teachers supported by parents, the book represented more than just a number of written or printed sheets fastened together; the book was an agent of change. For them, the cover of a book seemed to contain or conceal something much more significant than an open bi-weekly newspaper or magazine. And, by owning and reading books, the mission-educated readers would not only read for information but also nourish themselves through this 'more solid food'. By the 1890s, the educated section of the *Amakholwa* were calling for a more substantial and diverse coverage of issues. The editor of *Inkanyiso*, Solomon Khumalo, shared this view and, through his paper, urged people not to submit articles solely dealing with religion since such issues were covered in churches. Although his view did not go unchallenged, some writers seem to have moved over to his side. Indeed, soon after his call *Inkanyiso* (on 30 March 1893) announced the launching of a new Zulu Magazine, *Umhlobo waBantu*, to its readers:

> The first number of the new Zulu Magazine '*umhlobo waBantu*' has been issued, and we are glad to know that it has elicited favourable comments from not a few. It supplies a want amongst Natives which has been sorely

felt, and those who care for more solid and whole some food than a newspaper can give them, will find it in the 'Friend of the People'. We recommend all who have not yet seen a copy of this Magazine to posses
themselves of one without delay. It can be had from the office of this paper.

This seemingly 'insatiable' appetite for acquiring 'solid food' suggests
that people might have taken pride in owning magazines and books,
possibly for keeping or display. And such an attachment and demand for
books was not only a late nineteenth-century phenomenon—it dates back
to the early 1860s. Then, Colenso (1865[?]d) remarked that

> One of these lads [the Class of 1856] has come to the station, since my
> return to England, asking for books, and especially for a little book of
> elementary science, which I had written for them in simple English.

Requests for books found ready suppliers at mission stations. Beginning in
the late 1840s, various mission denominations vied for the dominance of
the book market.

Between 1858 and 1910 Ekukhanyeni became an important alternative
center of intellectual life in Natal. Through its Mission Press, the centre
established itself as one of the leading mission publishers in the colony
and beyond. In less than ten years the press had published a *Zulu–English
Dictionary*, *A Zulu Grammar*, *Izindatshana Zabantu* (People's Stories/
History), *Three Native Accounts* and a translation in Zulu of St Matthew's
Gospel (Brookes and de Webb 1965: 106). In two years (1859–60), the
Mission Press had published a number of significant books in both Zulu
and English. Major publications comprised a translated version of the
'New Testament and the books of Genesis, Exodus and I and II Samuel in
the Old Testament, Zulu liturgy, a tract on the Decalogue and Zulu Readers in Geography, Geology, History and Astronomy, as well as sundry
Grammars and general Readers' (p. 105). Members of the Class of 1856
produced most of the books; this enhanced the speed with which Ekukhanyeni published. Continuously setting text in the printing house had an
impact on how students thought about writing, publishing and books.[18]
The effects of that process can be seen in the work of one of the Class of
1856 students, Mubi Nondenisa (the student who, as I noted at the outset,
referred to books as 'worms of the house'). In this production context
Nondenisa's metaphor evokes an ever-present ambience of books or, rather,

---

18. 'From 1865 to 1884 a portion of the rents from lands for Native purposes, paid
into the Native Diocesan Fund', maintained the mission Printing Press. See Harriette
Colenso's evidence before the Lands Commission, 1900–1902: 413.

a persistence of books. And no wonder many of the students deserted Ekukhanyeni in 1861 and only a few returned, but with renewed in enthusiasm: Colenso (1865[?]d) wrote thus about one of them, Magema Fuze:

> ...after twelve months spent at home, [Magema Fuze] has come back to work as a printer upon the mission station; and for three years past, without any overlooker, he has kept himself steadily employed in my absence, printing by my direction a series of books, which I had prepared in Zulu before leaving Natal, and sending to me, month by month, reports of the progress of his labours and sheets of his work. As to the latter, I can only say that they would not disgrace any fair workman in England. They have not only been printed, but corrected and revised, entirely by himself; and there is scarcely a single misprint to be found in any of them. But what I most admire is not the accuracy and neatness of his printing, but the perseverance with which he has hitherto continued at his labours month after month, year after year, during my absence in England...

For Magema Fuze, head printer between 1862 and 1865 (see Harriette Colenso's evidence before the Lands Commission, 1900–1902 [housed at the Don Africana Library, Durban]), the process of producing books gave him the idea of writing his own work.

Ekukhanyeni alone could not cater for an increasing demand for books. A reading of missionary societies' records suggests that at one level the mechanical production of books and periodicals took the form of a competition. For instance, by 1865 the Berlin Missionary Society had completed translations of the gospels of the four evangelists (see Etherington's article 'The Missionary Writing Machine' [2002]). This mission press also used students to do printing and binding (see *The Natal Almanac* of 1880 [Anonymous 1880]: 229]). With regard to the American Board Mission publications, J.L. Dohne and Lewis Grout, who both worked on *isiZulu* orthography between 1850 and 1900,[19] were the two most influential authors. For the American Board Mission, J.L. Dohne in particular occupied a special place in the tally of achievements. As the secretary was to report in 1860,

> For several years previous to 1857, Mr. Dohne was engaged upon a Zulu Dictionary, containing over 10,000 Zulu words etymologically explained, with copious illustrations and examples... When printed, it made a volume of 459 pages, royal octavo.

---

19. Lewis Grout published extensively on Zulu history and language. See the Cumulative Bibliography to the present volume for details of some of his publications.

For Lewis Grout, Dohne's dictionary was 'not only the first dictionary of a South African tongue that can claim any approximation to completeness, but is also a living monument of the author's industry, careful observation and unfaltering perseverance'. And, like Fuze, Dohne showed 'unfaltering perseverance' (*Jubilee of the American Mission* [Anonymous 1886]: 34). This is the kind of language that missionaries used to justify their 'labours', and thus the work of producing books seemed to be the most difficult and yet worthwhile mission.

The decision to publish was influenced by financial constraints. Facing dwindling financial resources from their home countries, missionary societies sought to raise money through publishing for both church services and government schools. Ultimately, however, the decision on what to publish was political. While most missionary societies' publications employed a universalistic approach to religion and problems of faith, others moved from a regional approach to the universal. The latter approach was certainly true for Ekukhanyeni. The Ekukhanyeni Press wanted to show that better understanding of the Bible and issues of faith could be achieved through indigenous understandings of *Umvelingqangi*, the Great One. Hence Colenso's unorthodox position on polygamy. The mission's approach to issues of faith also extended to historical texts. Ekukhanyeni found in the history of the Zulu kingdom issues that could speak to wider historical developments. For instance, a reading of *Izindaba Zabantu* suggests that Ekukhanyeni wanted to show that through the biographies of the Zulu kings and commoners one could understand the history of the region in the same way that amateur historians were writing about political figures in the Metropole.

On the other hand, the American Mission sought a more universalistic approach. Their publications covered continental and international issues other than regional ones. Periodicals (that is, bi-monthly magazines, newspapers, pamphlets etc.) had lengthy sections on Turkey, China, Burma, India, west and east Africa. This coverage of geographically diverse issues reflected the size of American Board Mission itself. For other missionary societies, such as the Berlin Missionary Society and Hermannsburg Lutheran missions the decision about what to publish was shaped by their agreement to co-publish. At one level their decision to pool resources was prompted by the fact that they wanted to maximize outputs and outnumber other denominations. The above discussion of the complex decisions on the production of knowledge is just an overview. For the decision on what themes to cover in mission periodicals might have had more to do with individual missionaries' interests than the organizations under which they worked.

The significant point about the above overview of the explosion of books in nineteenth-century Natal and Zululand is that it indicates that people read books or were familiar with written materials. Furthermore, the fact that most written materials were in a local language hints to the possibility of a wider reading *ibandhla* ('public') than has hitherto been thought. But. again, questions arise: How were hundreds if not thousands of books the mission presses published in both English and local languages read? Were books, newspapers, pamphlets (and also, later, letters) consumed as 'solid and wholesome food'? The following section tries to grapple with these difficult issues.

Ways of Reading: The Presence of the Writer in the Letter or Book

Unlike most human activities, reading does not leave traces behind. It ceases to exist the moment the reader puts down the book. So, in light of this apparently ephemeral nature of reading, how does one write a history of the ways of reading? Here I wish to explore how members of the Class of 1856 sought to exploit nineteenth-century ways of reading to sustain its network.

Ekukhanyeni Press used its conjunctive method of *isiZulu* orthography to influence the way people read the books that it produced. Through letters and lead articles to the *Ipepa lo Hlanga*, *Inkanyiso* and *Ilanga laseNatali*, members of the Class of 1856 and their friends encouraged people to read books, especially those people who had influence in their communities. 'It is disappointing', says an anonymous writer to the paper in 1903, 'to come to church and listen to an uneducated preacher'—'to do that is a waste of time'. The writer's statement is loaded; not only did people have to read, they needed to be educated, and, one assumes here (as Solomon Khumalo earlier insisted), to be educated in the 'true sense of the word'. As we saw earlier only those who heeded the call to acquire 'proper education' or 'book learning' sent their children to overseas institutions of education, but there were those who seized every opportunity to read to those who could not. Young readers were often seen reading in groups. One such witness to such scenes was the Lieutenant-Governor of Natal, J. Scott. Colenso writes (1865[?]d) that one of the Ekukhanyeni students

> was seen by the late Governor of Natal, as he informed me, reading our
> books to the natives around him in his father's kraal.

This suggests that on the occasion in question the Ekukhanyeni student was reading the book aloud to his friends around him. This was but one of the ways in which people 'enjoyed' the activity of reading.

The reading practices might have varied according to class or status/ social position of the reader or listener. Those whose class position allowed them to heed the call of Sangude Zikalala of Pietermaritzburg to all men to enjoy reading and writing in the comfort of the shade might have, indeed, done as instructed (*Inkanyiso* 26 February 1891):

> I say, thank very much for what you are doing with *Inkanyiso*; you're en-
> lightening, even those who do not see they'll come to appreciate/love it
> because of the news it carries. I say, men, do not waste time staring at beer
> pots; if you feel you do not like to work, this work only involves hands,
> sitting in the shade, writing is done by hands.

Zikalala's writing tips are clearly for people of some means, aimed at men who drink beer as a way of passing time or as a leisurely activity. For him, writing was another form of (leisurely) work that did not involve much physical engagement. But Zikalala's insistence that for a writer to *bayitande* ('enjoy' or 'love') writing he needed to be sitting in the shade suggests that he had a particular writer in mind—a writer who had time to kill. Perhaps, partly because of the economy of writing for a newspaper, Zikalala does not specify what kind of shade, that is, whether under a tree or verandah. But this writer is certainly not a teenager and could afford beer.

Still, how were letters or books read? When it comes to letters, it would seem that when recipients read they felt the presence of the writer. Sambana Mtimkulu, responding to his brother, Zatshuke Mtimkulu, on 12 October 1884, wrote: 'we have heard your words my brother just as if it were a person speaking them to us here' (*Uitvlugt* 12 October 1884). Sambana's response suggests that he heard or rather understood the message from his brother. And, this suggests two things: first, that Zatshuke's letter was so clearly written that it was as if he were there with Sambana and company; second, that Sambana read, or probably had someone read the letter to him (them) more than once. The act of reading and re-reading the letter allowed Sambana to follow his brother's message and feel his presence.[20] On the part of Zatshuke, the writing of the letter must have

---

20. In Colenso's time the Zulu language used one word *i-zwa* ('to hear, taste and feel', see Colenso 1905a).

required a particular skill of presentation and skilful deployment of appropriate words. Like most letter writers, Zatshuke might have employed idioms that created visual images. For instance, in the case of Dinuzulu, who polished his writing skills at St Helena, in his first letters he employed idiomatic expression that sought to create specific images in the reader's mind. Dinuzulu writes to his friend Harriette:

> I shall be happy to hear from you that you are all well, for I do not get any letters from you any longer, I shall rejoice to hear that you are in the enjoyment of good health. We have all of us had colds 'which took proper hold of us, you may be sure'. (*isiZulu* proverb)

While the use of idioms or language play might have led novice readers astray or to get lost in the forest of words, for readers known for their 'pathetic greed for learning' getting out of the forest might have involved a sense of satisfaction and, even, bliss.

This sense of 'hearing words' was even more pronounced in the case of the exiles in St Helena. The exiles wanted to be the first to touch envelopes and be the last to handle letters they were sending home. As one would imagine such concerns created dramatic scenes as writers tried to get control of their words and those of their friends.

For all this, a number of questions remain: Can one extend this sort of reading of letters to books? What about the fact that in the *isiZulu* language *incwadi* was used in reference to books and letters in the nineteenth century?[21] Did readers imagine the writer of the book speaking to them? What about texts that contain dialogue? And what about the authority of the person whose 'words' are said to be in the texts? Did words carry the same authority that was invested in the person? In what follows I will take these questions to explore why writers wanted to get hold a copy of the *Three Native Accounts*. I suggest that one of the reasons is that, over time, they had come to establish a relationship with it.

On 12 September 1859, John Colenso, Magema Fuze, Ndiane Ngubane and William Ngidi embarked on a visit to the Zulu king, Mpande, at Nodwengu, his royal palace. The journey took just over a month. To cater for this long journey they took two wagons: a large wagon for storing food, clothing and other accoutrements, and a smaller wagon which Colenso

---

21. In nineteenth century, *incwadi* could mean 'mark or sign, to a person who enquires his way by which he will know whether he is going right or not; token generally, proof; paper, letter, book' (Colenso 1905a). In the 1940s Doke and Vilakazi introduced a new word for book, namely, *ibhuku* (Doke, Malcom, Sikakana and Vilakazi 1990).

The Eye of the Storm

used as a library. Significantly, it was not only the bishop who carried pen and paper. According to Colenso, he had asked the two students and the assistant teacher, Ngidi, to keep journals and record all that they saw on the way to the Zulu king. Some months later Colenso and Ngidi published the journals in book form, and to broaden the readership of the book, the two translated and added a glossary of words used in the text. This became the first book written by students in *isiZulu* and one of the most sought-after books in the nineteenth- and early twentieth-century South Africa. The book was entitled *Three Natives Accounts*. On its first appearance in 1860, the 160-page volume cost three shillings, and was advertised in most newspapers around Natal and Zululand (for instance, *The Natal Witness* 5 June 1860).[22]

What this book did, among other things, was to popularize the conjunctive method of writing *isiZulu* not only among students of *isiZulu* orthography but also to readers of *isiZulu* literature in general. And, as the book was read and re-read in different settings, its proposal/texts thickened to the extent that at an orthography settlement held in 1940; the word-division adopted by Ekukhanyeni in 1860s was found correct for writing *isiZulu* and up until the 1950s *Three Native Accounts* was still used as an examination 'set book' in Zulu (Doke 1958: 235). For language purists in the 1940s the book represented 'one of the four best examples of the purest Zulu'. The book attracted wide interests from schools in Natal. Letters like the one below were often received at Ekukhanyeni before 1910. Mbili wrote:

> Please sir I beg you that you should be able to send me some of those books you have. A Visit to the Zulu King translation glossary and Grammatical Notes. Incwadi yomuhla uBishop WaseNatal ehambela KwaZulu [*The Book about the Bishop of Natal's Visit to Zululand*] and some of other books English–Zulu Gramma best one please. If you get them send me those I ask for them please. If you have not got that please send me two-shilling English–Zulu Dictionary that is all I close.
>
> I remain your humble servant
>
> *Mbili Sinoti*
> C/o Public School.

Demand for the book saw Ekukhanyeni Press publish a third edition of the book in 1901. Magema Fuze and Mubi Nondenisa printed the book using a

22. I thank Professor J. Guy for this reference.

humble printing machine that Ekukhanyeni received from friends in England. A fourth edition came out in the 1920s (Doke 1958: 235).

It was not only Mbili Sinoti who was passionate about books. The following extract from Mahlathini Gumede's letter echoes similar sentiments. Gumede spoke not only for himself, but also for 'all young Zulus', as he called them, who read books. From Johannesburg, Gumede wrote to Miss Harriette Colenso (NAD box 67, A204 [A collection of Colenso letters]):

> Dear Madam, I am very glad to find this present opportunity to write to you and acknowledge you that those books you have sent me have reached me safely and I am grateful for these little books for they are of great importance to me and many of my friends like them very much indeed. So they are welcomed by all young Zulus.

Books 'are of great importance', said Gumede, expressing his delight at receiving them. But how were these important books read or interpreted? What interpretations did readers prefer over others?

One can speculate that some of these books were discussed through letters. And, letter-writers had some sort of consensus on good books to read and circulate.

But what attracted these writers specifically to *Three Narratives Accounts*? I suggest that the style or typography made the reading of the book more accessible to the novice reader. As I show in the examples below, the book was written in short sentences that anticipated its intended audience's reading ability. Combined with the typography, the content of the book allowed the nineteenth-century readers to appreciate not only the protocols and trappings of royalty but also the story or stories that Mpande related to Colenso, Fuze, Ngubane and Ngidi. The fact that some sections in the book are written in the form of a dialogue allowed 'all young Zulus', as Gumede suggests above, to dramatize or assume different roles; this would have been especially appealing to readers who wanted to learn the English and Zulu languages. The two student authors of the book might have also inspired young readers to want to write or imitate their writing styles. It was this appreciation that made the book and the Class of 1856 so central in the letter-writers' imagination at the end of the nineteenth century. Writers from various parts of the colony sent letters to *Ipepa lo Hlanga* and Ekukhanyeni asking for advice and books.

In *Three Native Accounts*, Magema Fuze opens with his story of the journey framed in the discourse of progress. He writes (see *Magema's Story* in Colenso 1901: 118):

That land of kwa'Magwaza, it is that which Umpande gave Sobantu; for
Sobantu had gone to the Zulu country, that there might establish a missionary, and teach those ignorant people of the Zulu country, and cause the
word of the Lord God Almighty to spread among them.

Magema was later, in 1901, to visit his former student Dinuzulu, who was
then on the Zulu throne, to advise him to keep up with the changing times.
Being able to read and write empowered writers to see themselves as
capable of adapting to contemporary situation and also as having control
over their futures. Such a sense of agency characterized most of the contributions to *Inkanyiso Yase Natal*, *Ipepa lo Hlanga* and *Ilanga laseNatal*
at the turn of the twentieth century and helped shape the formation of the
Natal Native Congress, *Iso Lesizwe*.

The significant part in *Three Native Accounts* is Ngidi's accounts of
the journey and specifically the book within a book entitled *Book of the
day we go to Nodwengu*. Ngidi introduces the 'book' by talking about
things that hindered their journey and obstructed their view of Nodwengu,
the king's palace. Ngidi writes (*Book of the day we go to Nodwengu* in
Colenso 1901: 148-49):

> Well, we (*Sobantu* and William) set out from that kraal, at which it (the
> sky) had hindered us (on our journey); we set out, it being now midday. We
> went, we finished a little plain, we went down into the bush; we went, we
> being continually torn by the bush, till at last we crossed the white Imfolozi,
> when the sun was now setting. We went down into a hollow, we went along
> it, when the sun had now set completely. We came out when it was now
> dusk; we saw Nodwengu just over there. We descended the ridge; when we
> came out we saw it, the military kraal of Undabakaombe.

When Masipula, the king's servant, introduced the Ekukhanyeni visitors,
Ngidi exclaimed, 'Ah! And so I saw him, Umpande, son of Senzanga-
kona!' 'Meanwhile that same Umpande is a large man outright, with a
story, and joking' (p. 152). The story and joking that Ngidi found interesting in Mpande was interwoven in kinship networks and the politics of the
Zulu kingdom itself. Ngidi writes (p. 156):

> He asked me, saying, 'You now, where are you from?' I said, ' My father, I
> am one of Ungidi, (son) of Bopela, (son) of Ungcobo'. He said, 'Whose son
> of Mapepesi?' He said, 'Ndabezita! I am son of Mapepesi'. He said, 'O!
> You are a son of Mafuzacolo!' I said, 'Yes, Nkos'. He said, 'So then you
> are just one of mine'. I assented, and said, 'Panther'.

In doing this Mpande was laying claim to the huge Ngidi family in Natal.
Mpande did not end there. He knew how the Ngcobo family under Dube

were removed from the heart of the kingdom. And knowing well the power that the bishop and his men represented, he used them to extend an olive branch not only to the Ngcobo and Mkhize but also Faku further south. Mpande said (p. 156):

> 'O! Mafuzacolo! Mafuzacolo! He did not do valiantly, [not he]!' so he told his story. He said: '(That he came) As to his coming actually into notice with the king, he got to do valiantly about the impi of the Amampondo; when the impi was now arriving here, he was just then getting into notice with the King. And (that he came) as to his coming actually to die, they got to claim land here, at such and such a person's, in such and such a place. So he was killed, he having now come to be accused by them. Inasmuch as you, too, lad, you know that there we, the house of Senzangakona, are a bull with a horn, ah! Ever since it first began (to be so) to Senzangakona.' He said, 'And that kraal of yours, it would not have perished; (but that) we were not present, we the (King's children) Princes. For, you see, that Dube, he came actually to die, not having done wrong in any thing; that Zih-landhlo, he came actually to die, not having done wrong in any thing.'

While extending a hand of peace to all those who had been affected by Dingane's rule, Mpande was quick to assert his family's claim to royalty and its 'right' to rule. He even took this further by inserting himself among well-known southern African kings like Moshoeshoe, Faku and many others. He asked Sobantu (p. 157):

> 'Faku, son of Umgqungqutshe, is he still there?' Said Sobantu, 'He is there'. Said he, 'How then is he now?' Said he, 'O! he is now an old man'. Sobantu asked Umpande, and said, 'Do you know Faku?' Said he, 'Yes, just all, I know them all, and Moshesh, and so-and-and-so; he reckoned them, they were many.'

Did nineteenth-century readers read this dialogue as real words of the king and bishop with their authority? Could young readers have dramatized this exchange for edification? And how did teachers use the book in the classroom? None of this is certain, but what is clear is that students read and re-read this conversation, narrative and power play in nineteenth- and early twentieth-century Natal and Zululand.

Ngidi concluded his narrative with a book of peace in which he commented on the effects of war on social life and urged people to turn their assegais into ploughs. He wrote (p. 168):

> My Brethren, let our weapons,
> Our warlike weapons all,
> Be beaten into ploughshares,
> Wherewith to till the soil;

Our shields, our shields of battle,
For garments be they sewed,
And peace both North and Southward
Be shouted loud abroad.

While books were important to members of the Class of 1856 and their
network of friends, the medium through which they accessed texts was
also just as central to their concerns. As the nineteenth century drew to a
close Ekukhanyeni writers had made a renewed effort not only to protect
isiZulu language from 'extinction' but also to improve its orthography.
Next I will consider their struggles over the control of the inner lives of
written words.

'The Force of Expression' and the Inner Lives of Written Words

From the 1880s, people who sent letters to Ekukhanyeni, *Inkanyiso, Ipepa
lo Hlanga* and later *Ilanga lase Natali* saw language as an agent of change
and thought that by reforming it, that is, improving the structure of sentences and division of words, they would achieve social and intellectual
progress. For Tambuza in Melmoth, acquiring more knowledge of the
isiZulu language and its richness (*ukunota*) meant that he would be enlightened or *ngihlakaniphe incozana* (*Inkanyiso YaseNatali* 1 November 1889).
The discussions on language were held in two newspapers that published
articles in three languages (English, *SeSotho* and *isiZulu*). But the bulk of
the discussion on the *isiZulu* language was in *isiZulu*. The language discussions were characterized by heated debate on how to deal with borrowed
words and whether the adoption of foreign words threatened the existence
of *isiZulu*. Writers expressed different opinions on this issue; for instance,
writers such as T.B. Zulu of Empolweni were of the opinion that borrow-
ing words from other languages would enrich the language rather than lead
to its extinction (*Inkanyiso YaseNatali* 12 February 1891). But what is
striking in these discussions was the absence or omission of the fact that
the *isiZulu* language itself is made up of numerous dialects. This seemed
to have escaped these discussions of committed 'reformers' who sought to
'bring the language up to par with other written languages' (*Inkanyiso
YaseNatali* 12 February 1891 and *Ilanga lase Natali* 11 March 1904). To
achieve their goal, they insisted that Africans should speak and write the
isiZulu correctly. As one such writer, Dambuza Ntabati, insisted that 'it is
with pity and surprise to hear the editor of the Isizulu paper, who writes
faultless English, told me he is learning how to write Isizulu' (*Ilanga
laseNatali* 11 March 1904). But Ntabati's view was not the only one on

language. While other writers advocated the use of *isiZulu*, John Dube, the editor of *Ilanga laseNatali*, encouraged young working 'boys' to learn English (*Ilanga laseNatali* 23 April 1909). To Ntabati and his fellow writers Dube's stance on language was an anomaly because for these writers the *isiZulu* language was about to be extinct unless it was reduced to writing and its grammar improved.

On the question of orthography the foundation had already been constructed, the writers argued, and urged for the adoption and improvement of what had hitherto been called the 'Colenso method' of *isiZulu* orthography. Colenso and Ngidi worked on reducing spoken *isiZulu* into written form between 1855 and 1865. Their collaboration came up with a system that became known as the 'conjunctive method', that is, the joining the prefix and stem to form one word. This method was partly arrived at, argued Colenso, because of the fact that the *isiZulu* language was/is an agglutinative language. The conjunctive method gained popularity through the 'stories'/histories that Ekukhanyeni published between 1855 and 1910 (*Ilanga LaseNatali* 11 March 1904). The conjunctive method was not, however, the only one—a 'disjunctive method' existed that was chiefly used by the American Board Mission.

To counter the missionaries' disjunctive method, opponents suggested the formation of a committee on *isiZulu* language and orthography. One outspoken advocate of the formation of a 'fully' representative committee, or *ibandhla* as he called it, was C.S. Mabaso who worked or lived in Swaziland (*Ilanga LaseNatali* 6 November 1903). For Mabaso, the committee that James Stuart and Reverend W.C. Wilcox organized was not representative.

In 1903 the editor of *Ipepa lo Hlanga* newspaper, Cleopas Kunene, challenged the disjunctive method that Wilcox and Stuart advocated and the way in which English rules of grammar influenced *isiZulu* orthography. For Kunene, the manner in which missionaries translated and made rules about the language distorted basic rules of syntax or, in his words, had caused, 'some very glaring absurdities' (*Ipepa lo Hlanga* 24 February 1904). In order to demonstrate his point, he took some phrases from the translated Bible and subjected them into analysis. For instance, in the following sentence: 'I wished to go yesterday', translated into *isiZulu*: *Ngafisa ukuhamba izolo*. Kunene conceded that 'although the translation is correct according to the English rule, the idea expressed in respect to time is wrong in Zulu'. 'The correct Zulu translation', he continued, 'would be: *Ngifise ukuhamba izolo*. For', he argued, 'it will be seen, that we have two past tenses in our language one which may be said to correspond to the second Greek Aorist'. He felt that the temptation on the part of 'Zulu Grammarians to adopt the English grammar as the standard whereon to formulate Zulu grammatical rules as well as determine the structure of the Zulu words, was far too strong'. For him this had led to 'Grammarians splitting-up words and thus rendering them unintelligibly'. This tendency, according to Kunene, led to students of *isiZulu* who adopted the disjunctive method to find it:

> Very difficult to explain their grammatical construction and necessitates the formulation of illimitable number of unnecessary rules by virtue of their constant occurrence in various ways under different formations.

Underlying Kunene's concerns was that the 'splitting-up of words' disrupted the coherence of the language. This comes out when he wrote that 'in native churches the Zulu Bible is not read as it is written for the simple reason that it would lose the force of expression which is intended to give'. For instance, in the following extract from Reverend Wilcox's *Isizulu Testament*:

> *Ba be se be zwile lokunke kodwa, ukuti, Lowo owa e kade e si zingela u se shumayela ukukolwa, owa e kade a ku cita: Ba m duimisa u Tixo ngami.*

'A comparison with other synthetic languages, with Latin for instance', wrote Kunene, 'will readily decide this issue'. He continued, 'take the first sentence, *'Ba be se be zwile'*—they had heard', and write it as it is spoken, thus, *'Babesebezwile'*—one word—we then find that the Latin equivalent, *'Audiverant'*, is also one word and shows a better comparison'. Kunene saw Greek and Latin as better comparative case to *isiZulu* than English.

However, Wilcox's disjunctive method had found support from James Stuart, the Durban magistrate, and A.T. Bryant, a Roman Catholic priest—both of them keen students of *isiZulu* language. Bryant was so enthusiastic about his method that he saw it as the most original of all methods. At the core of the disjunctive method, Stuart argued, lay the liberation of the *isiZulu* language and that the separation of words would make it easier for the reader to discover at a glance 'without thinking out the meaning' (Stuart 1906a). According to Stuart, the Colenso system relied on accent or spoken language that gave an impression of words as being agglutinated. In fact, what Stuart thought was wrong was the influence of the Class of 1856 on *isiZulu* orthography. For him, this made the language inaccessible. Ultimately, at a conference held in 1905 delegates adopted the conjunctive system with some revisions on inflections.

Conclusion

Newspaper discussions on orthography were more far reaching than it might look, because to the members of the Class of 1856 tampering with words written in the conjunctive method would render communication unintelligible and thus disrupt their network. In addition, writers who defended the conjunctive system hint at the fact that 'splitting-up words' would impact on particular ways of reading that people had come to enjoy and that allowed readers of the Colenso version of the *isiZulu* Bible to extract meaning from text with 'force'. So, in the eyes of the Class of 1856, the advocates of the disjunctive method wanted to deprive them and their friends of the pleasures of reading or the text. And, indeed, more was at stake in the struggle over orthography: if the disjunctive method had managed to substitute for the conjunctive method, Ekukhanyeni would have ceased to be the heart of the land or nation (*Ekukhanyeni lapa kusenhliziyeni yezwe*), as many writers to *Ipepa lo Hlanga* (1 September 1903) saw it. All this would have meant that the income they got from books would have stopped.

The Class of 1856's influence on Zulu politics had an impact on the lack of enthusiasm to adopt the disjunctive method. Through their contributions in English and *isiZulu* newspapers in Natal they managed to shape public opinion. While their impact was limited and constrained because of the lack of financial resources, nevertheless they managed to widen their intellectual influence to the Transvaal. At the turn of the twentieth century, letters from the Transvaal, Kimberley and Swaziland came to Ekukhanyeni requesting books. Such letters continued to arrive until the mission station ceased to exist in 1910.

COLENSO AND THE EMERGENCE OF AN INDIGENOUS BLACK CLERGY
IN SOUTH AFRICA

Abraham Mojalefe Lieta

1. *Introduction*

1.1. *About Colenso*
Bishop John William Colenso's position as the first Anglican Bishop of
Natal was, as is well known, overshadowed by the theological and biblical
disputes which led to his excommunication. The importance of his defence
of Zulu independence and culture against colonial aggression is also
widely recognized today. What interests me in this paper, however, is
Colenso's role in the beginnings of an indigenous clergy among the Zulu
people. Although the American Board of Commissioners for Foreign
Missions began work among the Zulu people as early as 1835, it had met
with little success in obtaining conversions or in building indigenous
leadership of the Church it established, despite its own avowed intention
(see Maclean's paper in this volume). Although Colenso never himself
ordained a single Zulu priest, this paper will argue that his approach to
mission, his teaching and his example contributed to the conditions for the
emergence of an indigenous clergy and indigenous leadership among the
emerging *amakholwa* (a term used to refer to Christian converts among the
Zulu) class.

By the term 'indigenous clergy' I mean to denote those members of the
Church set apart for the purpose of the work of ministry, and who belong
to the original inhabitants of the land. The setting apart is usually marked
by the service of ordination (laying on of hands by the bishop). The term
'indigenous' is used here to refer to locally born ministers of African
extraction.

1.2. *The Role of Catechists and Indigenous Helpers as 'Pre-Clergy'*
Any discussion of indigenous clergy would be incomplete without a
reference to the role played by the early converts and the first indigenous
helpers in the mission of the Church. These helpers were variously called

'native agents', 'Catechists' and 'assistant missionaries'. They served as forerunners and pathfinders for the next generation of believers, from whom the first ordained indigenous clergy were to come (Lenkoe 1994).

These Native agents, who may be considered 'pre-clergy', were involved in a number of activities around the mission station. They were the unsung heroes of the Church's mission. Theirs was a mainly voluntary work. It is reported that they sometimes went to the Church authorities to request that ministry among their people be undertaken. Their work formed a significant part of the activities of the mission in that they held confirmation classes, read the Epistles, enforced discipline, conducted morning services in the absence of the missionary and they also preached (Lenkoe 1994: 79).

1.3. *About Colenso's Views*

It should be stated from the outset that Bishop Colenso himself is relatively silent on the issue of indigenous clergy. My contention is that in spite of the lack of an explicit reference to Black clergy, Colenso demonstrates his support for the emergence of a local Native clergy through his positive attitude to mission work among the Zulu. This attitude is evident in his missionary writings, in the establishment of the Ekukhanyeni school at Bishopstowe as well as in his relationship with William Ngidi and Undiane (properly Ndiane) Ngubane. I maintain that although he did not ordain a single Black person to Holy Orders, he would have ultimately done so, had it not been for the controversy that marred his episcopacy.

It can be argued that it is his missiology which laid the foundation for the emergence of the indigenous clergy in South Africa. That is the legacy left by Bishop Colenso to the Anglican Church. In this article, attention will be paid to the first Anglican clergy of African descent, dating from the establishment of the Anglican presence in Natal until the year 1893.

In order to understand the role of Colenso in this issue, it is instructive to situate his views within the prevailing attitudes of the nineteenth century.

2. *Discussion*

2.1. *Nineteenth-Century Missionary Attitudes*

Behind the missionary policies and practices of the nineteenth century lay the intellectual consensus that is termed 'Eurocentricity'. This was based on the notion of 'diffusionism'. Missionaries, being children of their times, were also affected by these ideologies of racial superiority.

Diffussionism is a belief that Europeans are the makers of history and that cultural processes tend to move out from the European to the non-European sector. Allied to this is the notion that the ethical flow of human causality, innovation and culture from Europe is logical, normal and natural (Blaut 1995: 26).

Blaut further states that diffusionism is grounded into two axioms: that most human communities are not inventive, that a few human activities (or places of culture) are inventive and thus remain the permanent centres of cultural change, and of progress. Taken on a global scale, this gives us a model of a world with a single centre. This centre was taken to be Europe. It had a single periphery. The character of the core was described in terms such as 'inventiveness, rationality, abstract thought, mind, discipline, sanity, and science'. The character of the periphery was described in terms such as 'imitative, irrational, spontaneous, insane, sorcery' (Blaut 1995: 14-16).

There were other similar views on the relation between Europe and other continents. An example is provided by the views propagated by Lucien Lévy-Bruhl (1923), who stated that a fundamental distinction existed between civilized and primitive thought. For him, civilized thought was logical and maintained a critical distance from the object of thought, whereas the primitive thought process functioned through participation and identification with the object of thought (Bediako 1994: 236). The new converts in Africa in the nineteenth century were still regarded as being primitive.

This ethnocentrism can be seen in the many cases of missionary paternalism that one comes across in mission history. For example, we could take the case of Samuel Crowther (the first African to be consecrated as bishop in the Anglican Communion). He achieved this distinction in 1864. His career and personal achievements in the Niger region of Nigeria were quite remarkable. His scholastic ability at Cambridge proved that European scepticism regarding Black intellectual capacity was ill placed. However he was to be humiliated by a new team of the Church Missionary Society who held a low opinion of Black Africans. He ultimately was forced to resign in 1891, and died in 1892 (Bediako 1994: 234, 259).

2.2. *How Colenso Differed from the Others*
Goedhals (quoted in Chidester 1996) notes that the nineteenth-century Anglican mission in South Africa was clearly shaped by the historical forces of imperialism, chauvinism and economic self-interest. The only

exception was Colenso (1997: 39). It is this difference that became his legacy, even right into the next century. His sympathetic disposition was to be the seed that nurtured the emergence of the indigenous clergy in the Anglican Church in South Africa.

His theology was marked by liberalism (as his trial for heresy indicates). He was also a person who did not eschew political engagement. In this regard, one may trace his attitude to politics to the influence of Frederick Denison Maurice on his life. According to Jeff Guy's 1983 study of Colenso, he was introduced to the principles of Maurice by his wife. Maurice's approach is one which led to a personal, felt, religious belief that went beyond argument and external evidence. This developed a faith which was to allow Colenso to accept without qualms the discoveries and theories of the revolutionary age in which he lived (1983: 15).

Maurician theology was a reaction to the narrow and sombre strictures of the evangelicals and the privilege and social responsibility of the conservative Church establishment. It was a romantic reaction to the utilitarian spirit of the age. According to this approach, God's existence is perceived and not proven. He is not found in argument or blind acceptance but in human beings themselves, in their thoughts, actions, desire for good and individual conscience. Maurician theology was, also, partly in reaction to the negative effects of industrialization in Britain (Guy 1983: 16).

It was this theological universalism which motivated Colenso to be involved in the politics of colonial Natal on behalf of the Natives. The key principle was that the amelioration of social ills has to come through social action. This action demonstrates God's love by ministering to his children. This would explain his missionary strategy, which culminated in the setting up of a number of mission stations. This theological universalism, which stressed the existence of God in all humanity, was also behind his willingness to be challenged by William Ngidi on the Bible. Note this quotation from his sermon at the ordination service of Callaway when he stated: 'God's love is not confined to a few, here and there, of His creatures, but extends, like the light and warmth of his glorious sun to all' (Edgecombe 1982: xvi).

It was this positive attitude which led him to listen to the Africans, and to learn from them about their history and religion. Hinchliff notes that Colenso was excited by the possibility of using African religious customs as a foothold for Christianity. He even thought of the idea of officiating at a Zulu feast of the first fruits and, thereby, converting it into a harvest festival (1964: 63).

2.3. *At Ekukhanyeni*
2.3.1. *Focus on missionary strategy*. Colenso believed that mission had to develop an approach, which brought to the heathen the glory of the Christian message and the light in all humanity. This was to replace the conventional message of darkness, division and damnation (Guy 2001a: 22).

His missionary strategy involved the setting up of the mission station at Ekhukhanyeni at the bishop's farm, Bishopstowe. He would then oversee the work of the mission while within walking distance of his cathedral. For him it was important to consider practical training. Mission was for both industrial as well as religious training. Hence there was a carpenter's shop, a forge, brickyards as well as a printing press at Ekukhanyeni. He planned later to include various levels of schooling, a theological college and a hospital. Ekukhanyeni was to be the centre, from which the light would be taken to other areas (Guy 1983: 50-51).

With respect to the main question of that era—how to approach the subject of polygamy—we find that Colenso's intention was gradually to root out polygamy within the next generations of Zulu Christians. This he wanted to achieve by forbidding converts from becoming polygamists after baptism. In this endeavour, the new Zulu Christian leaders had to be exemplary. This explains why he was more strict on this ruling when it came to religious teachers, such as William Ngidi, than to secular workers such as Magema Fuze. While William was expelled from Bishopstowe in 1869 for wanting to marry another wife, Magema Fuze the printer, was allowed to remain even though he had four wives (Colenso 1982: xviii).

Another aspect of his approach to mission is revealed in his intention to resign as Bishop of Natal and take up the bishopric of the diocese of Zululand. This idea of a bishopric for Zululand had been suggested by Bishop Gray. The British government agreed to that move in 1859. That is when Colenso contemplated taking up that position. He mentioned later that it was his intention to ordain William Ngidi as a deacon of Zululand. (see Edgecombe 1982: xxii).

Colenso was later to postpone that move as a result of a visit to Chief Mpande. He felt that he had to wait until the succession issue in the Zulu kingdom had been settled, and the British intentions for Zululand made clearer. In the meantime, he supported the idea of persuading Mpande to recognize Cetshwayo as his heir, and to send a resident missionary to Zululand. Ultimately, this led to the establishment of the KwaMagwaza mission station under Reverend Robert Robertson in 1860 (Edgecombe 1982: xxv). It was from this station that most of the early indigenous clergy of Zululand were to come.

2.3.2. Training programme at Ekukhanyeni. The letter to the main backer of the school, the Society for the Propagation of the Gospel (SPG), which Walter Baugh wrote on 1 April 1856, describes services at Ekukhanyeni. He states that the bishop's sermons were in a dialogue form rather than a discourse:

> After prayers, about 16 or our elder school boys publicly read in the Congregation a portion of the Gospel History, which is afterwards expounded by the Bishop. The exposition partakes more of the nature of a Conversation with the Native Christians, than a discourse. Sometimes the Bishop catechizes the boys and men; at others, the men are requested to ask questions: and so it becomes a season of profit to all present. Much of the good which has been done amongst our people here, I attribute to these daily services. It is impossible to say how much the subject of the morning's conversation upon these occasions, may occupy the minds of the natives present, throughout the day. (USPG Archives, C/AFS/6)

This is an indication that Bishop Colenso respected the views of his hearers. He also describes the school and its pupils, not as faceless 'kaffirs' but as people with names, Mkhungo kaMpande (the son of the Zulu King Mpande), Undiane and Uskelemu (Magema Fuze). The bishop comments about their progress in the following manner:

> What we most need now, is a reading book of Lessons in General Knowledge. Our boys can read fluently, but it is to be regretted, that we have nothing to put into their hands to satisfy their thirst for knowledge. We do all that we can to teach them English, but it will be a long time before they will be able to sit down and read and English book profitably and without much labour. The Bishop has, I am pleased to say, a reading Book compiled and translated in manuscript, of the very kind we require; but the busy state of our Colonial printers gives us no hope of having it printed. Our present expectation is–that the native youths, now making their first attempt at printing, will, in a short time, be able to relieve the Bishop of his manuscript ready for the press. They will commence in a few days to turn out a primer in Kafir [*sic*] for the use of our Church Mission Schools; which, we hope, will be followed by books of greater magnitude. (USPG Archives, C/AFS/6)

If we consider the poisonous letters written on 6 February 1860 by Charles Septimus Grubbe, Baugh's successor at Bishopstowe, in which he justifies the latter's resignation (USPG Archives, C/AFS/6 [14]), one finds a description of a proto-seminary. Grubbe had arrived in July 1858, appointed by the bishop to this station as Principal. He was to be the clerical head of the institution, and a clerical superintendent of the educational work, because the young men at the school 'had now arrived at a point at which it was desirable that they should have higher training, than could be given them by a person who had not been at one of the universities'. Grubbe finds it intolerable that he was not allowed to subject the boys to the kind of schoolmaster's discipline (including beating) common in England at the time:

> The senior boys (Undiane the head boy and two others,) who were the furtherest advanced, and whom I supposed I was wanted to train more than the others, were never put under my care at all. I must frankly say that the extreme favouritism shewn to them, the constant indulgence shewn to them *only*—and the continually shielding them, especially Undiane, from any control or discipline—while they were still reckoned to be in the School. (USPG Archives, C/AFS/6 [14])

Grubbe attributes veiled hints at sexual misconduct to this failure in discipline: 'If they had been either *under* me, or separated from the school altogether, the case would have been different—but they had full opportunity to interfere with the boys without being under my control'. Colenso, it seems, would not tolerate corporal punishment for the young Zulu men at Ekukhanyeni:

> After a time, he made some remarks one evening before others, which seemed to me to imply, that I was unjustly severe towards the boys. That I could not teach them, and could not govern them. If this was his judgement, whether he was right or wrong *in fact*, my course was clear. If he was right, I was clearly unfit to be at the head of the school—if he was wrong I had nothing to do, but to bow to him as my superior and try to find some other sphere of day duty. (USPG Archives, C/AFS/6 [14])

The final insult, for Grubbe, was that Colenso sent the senior boys to a lady teacher to learn mathematics. Undiane's name recurs throughout the letter, and is the focus of Grubbe's wrath, seemingly because Colenso intended him to become himself a teacher at the school and subsequently to be ordained. He writes in a letter to the SPG on the 6 February 1860:

> I believe, in addition, that the real object of the proposal was to place Undiane as a teacher in the school—without being exactly under me—and I was convinced then, and am so now, that if I had voluntarily agreed to that course, I should have voluntarily destroyed my own authority—and any chance of doing any good at all. (USPG Archives, C/AFS/6 [14])

The description of the training included chapel from 09.00–09.45, school from 10.00 to 12.00 and again from 14.00 to 16.00 and, then, chapel again at 19.00. He expressly states that he was to be of 'assistance to catechists in their studies preparatory to Orders' (USPG Archives, C/AFS/6 [14]).

Sadly, the experiment at Ekukhanyeni was prematurely ended by Zulu unrest with colonial domination and then finally by Colenso's excommunication by Bishop Gray and the refusal of the SPG and Society for the Propagation of Knowledge, under Gray's influence, to continue funding the mission station.

2.3.3. *An interesting episode.* An interesting episode is recounted by one of Colenso's earliest converts, Magema Fuze, in his book, the first by an indigenous Zulu person, *Abantu Abamnyama Lap Bavela Ngakona* (1922; translated into English as *The Black People and Whence They Came,* 1979; see also Draper 2000). It demonstrates how revolutionary Colenso was. Even though at that time missionaries were intent on providing new converts with 'Christian' names, he came with a very different approach.

He describes how 'Skelemu' became 'Magema'. William Ngidi suggested names from the New Testament for a new baptism name for Skelemu. The two names that he came up with, first 'Petrose' and second 'Johane' were refused by Colenso. Colenso is reported as having said that he objected to African people being called by foreign names which meant nothing to them. He chose for him the name Magema[1] (1982: iv).

2.4. *Colenso's Relationship with William Ngidi*

A focus on the relationship that Colenso had with William Ngidi will serve to highlight Colenso's contribution to the issue of indigenous clergy. William Ngidi is referred to as Colenso's Zulu philosopher. He was a member of the Ntete people, and had come to Natal from Zululand. He had been baptized by the American missionary Samuel Marsh and later settled at Ekukhanyeni in 1855. He worked for Colenso as an interpreter and helper and, as is well-known, played a an important role in Colenso's thinking on biblical criticism (Edgecombe 1983: xxii) In a letter written on 10 October 1860, Colenso writes that he plans to ordain William and Undiane, satisfied that William's work as a Catechist and Undiane's as teacher are excellently done (USPG-CLR 137 Natal, I, 1858–71).

The key point in this relationship is that Colenso demonstrated *ubuntu* in his relationship with his African converts. He indicated that he respected

---

1. From a discussion with Zulu informants I gather that the name Magema is a praise-song term possibly related to the Ngcobo clan.

the other man's point of view. He also showed that he took their culture seriously, and he was not condemnatory in his approach.

We see this quality of relationship in Colenso's request to Undiane, Fuze and Ngidi to keep diaries regarding their experiences on a visit to Mpande. He asked them to keep the diaries in Zulu. There are very few recordings of the experiences of Native agents during this period. That Colenso made this request is a clear indication of the respect he gave to their views, as well as to the language they spoke. These diaries were later published in Zulu and English as Readers for the school, and were entitled *Three Native Accounts of the Visit of the Bishop of Natal in September and October, 1859, to Umpande, King of the Zulus* (see Edgecombe 1982: xxx).

The relationship he had with William Ngidi is quite unique in the annals of relationships between a missionary and a newly converted indigenous Christian. It was based on mutual respect. It could be that William Ngidi's conversion, which had taken place during his interaction with the missionaries from the American Board of Commissioners for Foreign Missions, gave him enough courage to ask the penetrating questions that he posed to Colenso. He, for his part, showed remarkable openness in dealing with those questions and challenges.

To indicate his positive attitude to the Africans, he quotes extracts of speeches and sermons from the three prominent Africans in his group. He prefaces those quotes with these words: 'and so, too, with my native catechist—these are some of their words, which will show *how thoroughly the Zulu mind is capable of drinking in the true spirit of Christianity* (Edgecombe 1982: 227 [my emphasis]).

Colenso and Ngidi's relationship is that of two men who reached across to one another, across the cultural and language divide. It was developed during the seven years that they worked together in Natal. They discussed at length on the nature of belief and culture. William is celebrated as the Zulu who converted the English bishop. At its most profound level, the relationship was 'a reversal of the idea of coloniser and colonised, which switched dominated for dominant, unlearned for learned, heathen for Christian, savage for civilized, the self and the other' (Guy 1997: 219).

Colenso describes William Ngidi as being a very pleasant and intelligent person. Although initially hired to be a wagon driver he was later to prove himself as being quite capable as an interpreter and translator. This was due to the fact that he spoke the Zulu of Zululand.

Colenso further describes Ngidi as man who

> had an intense thirst for knowledge of all kinds, more especially in things which concerned the Kingdom of God. It was impossible to translate with him a few verses of the Bible, without being carried away by his inquires into conversation upon other matters, far beyond the scope of the text before us. (Guy 1997: 224)

William Ngidi was eager to learn about the divisions within the Church, as well as about the doctrine of eternal punishment. What also attracted these two people was a mutual willingness to challenge and question one another. Colenso was willing to talk freely as well as to question. This appealed to William. He was also attracted by the bishop's liberal interpretation of religious belief (Guy 1997: 224).

William had definite doubts about missionary strategies. He cautioned that missionaries should not be condemnatory and eager to frighten new converts about hell fire but should be gentler. He did not want to believe that the God of love could insist that a polygamist should give up his other wives and children on becoming a Christian. He also questioned the truthfulness of the accounts in the Pentateuch. This led to Colenso's revised approach to biblical criticism (Guy 1997: 225).

Colenso had wanted to ordain William Ngidi but could not do so. He complains that he is unable to 'ordain a thoroughly competent, well-trained, able, pious, native, who had himself helped to translate the whole of the New Testament and several books of the Old Testament...' (Guy 1997: 232).

This was due to the fact that the Church of England required that ordinands should 'unfeignedly believe' in the canonical scriptures, and Ngidi clearly expressed doubts about certain parts of the Bible (Guy 1997: 232).

One may surmise from the relationship between William Ngidi and Bishop Colenso that Colenso's ideal of a proper indigenous clergyman is of one who is of an open and questioning mind, who is aware of the relationship between religion and culture and who was monogamous.

2.5. *The Indigenous Clergy during the Nineteenth Century*
2.5.1. *Colenso's legacy.*
What was the legacy that Colenso left behind? I suggest that it must be found in the number of clergy in Anglican orders that we come across in mission history. Although one cannot draw a straight line between the emergence of indigenous clergy in the Anglican clergy and Colenso, it is quite possible that his influence played a major role. Before 1871 we had no Native Anglican clergyman. What we had

was quite a large number of what could be regarded as 'pre-clergy'—readers, sub-deacons and Catechist-teachers, but no ordained black person. By 1893, the Yearbook of the Church of the Province of South Africa recorded 20 indigenous clergy. Of these, nearly half (9 out of 20) came from the Natal/Zululand region.

Of the four deacons ordained in 1871, three came from Natal and Zululand (Gcwensa, Mbanda and Ngobese). The three were trained by Henry Callaway, himself a protégé of Colenso. He had come to Natal with Colenso as a medical doctor in 1854. Although Callaway was later to become an opponent of Colenso, both in terms of theology and Church-manship and also in terms of Zulu translation, his missionary work was strongly promoted by Colenso. The claim that his move to Springvale in 1858 was in some sense a 'breakaway' or 'independent of Colenso' (as implied by Hinchliff 1963: 63) is very far from the truth, as the SPG correspondence shows. He was required to receive moneys through the diocesan structures and there is no evidence of a reluctance of Colenso to assist in this regard, although they had their differences. He was later to be consecrated bishop for the new missionary diocese of British Kaffraria (later re-named the 'diocese of St John's'). The same support shown by Colenso for Callaway can be observed for Robertson. The idea that he moved to Zululand to 'become independent of Colenso's system' (Hinchliff 1963: 64) is a clear falsification of the evidence found in the SPG archives (for instance Colenso was still writing to urge SPG to send more money for Robertson between 1860 and 1863; see the *SPG Journal* 48: 92, 166, etc.). The result of Colenso's early work, whatever the later outcome of the controversy, was the easy movement of personnel and clergy between St John's and the Maritzburg/Zululand dioceses. For instance, consider the career of William Gcwensa. He was ordained in 1871, was at Springvale up to 1875 and then went to St Andrew's, Pondoland (1875–77).

2.5.2. *Other factors.* Other factors also played a role in fostering this new era of indigenous clergy. For instance, one could point to the example of other Churches in the South African mission field. Of great significance must have been the example of the Presbyterian Church. In 1856 they ordained the very first African in South Africa, the Reverend Tiyo Soga. He was trained and ordained in Scotland and he had a big impact, especially on those who were sceptical of the African's aptitude for pastoral work. We could also look at the effect of the Methodist Church. They were not as hesitant as the Anglicans in entrusting mission work to indigenous Church workers. In 1871 they ordained four Africans as their first fully ordained ministers. These were Charles Pamla, James and Charles Lwama and Bruce Mwama. In the Cape Colony, the Methodist Church accepted 150 Africans as probationary priests between 1866 and 1910. More than 125 of these were ordained (Mills in Hofmeyer and Pillay 1994: 173).

2.5.3. *Within the wider Anglican Church in the Province of South Africa.* We should also consider that the Province as a whole was also wrestling with the issue of Native clergy. This is seen in the appearance of a report on 'The Supply and Training of Clergy and the Formation of a Native Ministry' delivered at the Provincial Synod of 1876. It contained statistics on the Native clergy in the various dioceses.

Three main recommendations were made in the report:

1. that diocesan theological colleges be established;
2. that a theological Faculty for the Province be set up;
3. that the standard for priests be the same as in England. The requirements were to be relaxed in the case of deacons.

The Provincial Synod of 1883 reflected on these measures and noted that the local diocesan colleges had not been successful. The need for a central provincial college was expressed. It also gave out the statistics for the Native clergy in the diocese. These indicated a big jump from the 1876 statistics. Fourteen Native clergy out of a grand provincial total of 218 are recorded. (Provincial Canons and Constitution 1887: 90).

The next set of statistics are obtained from the 1893 Yearbook of the Church of the Province of South Africa, which contained the details of the 319 priests and deacons operating in South Africa. In this year we find 20 Native clergy listed, which constitutes an increase of six from 1876.

3. Conclusion

The place of Bishop Colenso in Anglicanism is a complex one: he was excommunicated for heresy by the Church but was later re-instated, albeit to a powerless role as Bishop of Natal. His trial for heresy is reputed to have been the 'inspiration' behind the well-known hymn 'The Church's One Foundation'. When one considers that he was criticized for being too liberal in matters regarding polygamy, it is interesting to note that the Anglican Church, through the various Lambeth conferences, has steadily moved towards Colenso's position with regard to that issue.

It was among the Africans of Natal that Colenso had great support. Note that an important location in Pietermaritzburg, established in 1906, was named 'Sobantu Location' after his Zulu name *Sobantu*, which means, 'Father of the People'. He captured attention, and gained popularity among the Zulu for the active way in which he championed their causes, in his defense of Cetshewayo and Langalibalele. They found in him a White man who was demonstrated compassion for them, a Christian minister who sacrificed a lot for their sake. It is my belief that it was this sacrifice that attracted people to the Church. It is my contention that his example may have given hope to nationalistic Africans to invest their time and talents in the Church, hoping to be able also to ameliorate social ills. In fact, we read of the 30 or so 'Sobantu' churches, being African congregations that were loyal to Colenso even after his excommunication. Most of them were to be later re-incorporated into the Anglican Church. However, their existence for that limited time is a testament to the adulation that he enjoyed among Africans.

His episcopate held great promise for the Zulu mission. I have mentioned that it was his intention to train his protégés, William Ngidi and Undiane Ngubane, to the level of priesthood. However, they were unable to reach that level. Of great importance is the effect of the existence of the Bishopstowe faction. Here was a safe space where Africans could discuss issues of culture and religion without any of the restrictions of colonialism. I believe that the existence of that space must have attracted indigenous people to the priesthood. For once, the Church could be seen to be divorced from the shackles of colonialism and imperialism.

Bishop John Colenso paved the way for African clergy by treating Zulu culture with respect. He touched the heart of many Africans by his lived Christianity. The name that he was given, *Sobantu*, is recognition of the humanitarian qualities they heard and saw in him.

A Moment in the 'Long Conversation' between African Religion and Imperial Christianity: William Ngidi and John Colenso*

Gordon Mitchell

Tracking the 'Native Informant' has become one of the ways of doing Postcolonial Studies. Instead of assertions of local knowledge serving to enhance the credibility of a literary text, they become the place where the critic pauses to ask questions about interests and power (Spivak 1999). Protestations of innocence denied, texts claiming the authority of the margin, are likened to the process whereby raw materials harvested in distant lands were reshaped, packaged and then shipped back to consumers in Europe. Literature, it is argued, is itself inevitably caught within the history of imperialism. Traces of 'the self-consolidating other' can be, it is argued by Spivak and others, identified through careful textual analysis. Not a great deal of painstaking research is necessary, however, to find Colenso's native informants. He usually introduces them by name.

In Search of True Religion

In his booklet *Ten Weeks in Natal: A Journal of a First Tour of Visitation Among the Colonists and Zulu Kafirs of Natal* (Colenso 1855g), the new bishop describes a tour of the region accompanied by the Governor, Sir Theophilus Shepstone. The main character in the story, however, is indisputably guide and interpreter, William Ngidi (Guy 1983: 187-88; 1997: 236-40). It is he who initiates much of the activity and whose place in dialogues is introduced with 'William said', 'William explained', or 'William answered for me'. The purpose of these extended interviews with the Zulu appears to be to determine 'the impressions of natural religion which they still retain'. Colenso recognizes at the outset that the encounter with Christianity would already have resulted in some changes, but he had hardly

---

* In using the term 'long conversation' I am utilizing the terminology of Jean and John Comaroff (1991: 17-18).

anticipated the range of parallel and sometimes competing oral traditions and vocabularies for the Supreme Being that were available (Chidester 1996: 132-36). How was one to decide between *uThixo*, *iThongo*, *uYehova*, *uDio*, *uLungileyo*, *umPezulu*, *Inkosi pezulu*, *uNkulunkulu* or *umVelinqangi*? Some missionaries had found divine names with attributes, to their mind, closer to the Christian doctrine of God. There was no unanimity, however. Some favoured adopting *uThixo*, in use by missionaries in the eastern Cape, while others favoured the local Zulu *iThongo*. There were also those who regarded these terms as ill equipped for the task and proposed the Hebrew *uYehova* or the Latin, *uDio*. Bent on finding the pre-missionary religion Colenso rejected these efforts. Unlike other missionaries who were concerned with translating the Christian gospel into the vernacular, Colenso saw his task as that of discovering the indigenous God of the Zulu. In the end, faced with a plurality of meanings, he felt he had to make a choice and came down on the side of *uNkulunkulu* and *umVelinqangi*. Although aware that there were those who understood these terms in association with ancestral spirits, he put aside these meanings and declared his to be the normative. The decision to choose two terms could be legitimized by appeal to the Hebrew names in the Pentateuch for God, Yahweh and Elohim. Like Yahweh, *uNkulunkulu* is the creator and shaper of history, and like Elohim, *umVelinqangi* is a more abstract and more remote. As in ancient Israel, the Zulus could have two names with which to encompass the range of divine attributes for the single god. Echoing Paul's appeal to the Unknown God in Acts 17.23-24, Colenso's self-confessed missionary strategy was therefore to question them about their belief in a higher being and then to say that he had come to tell them more about him.

One of the first priests to be ordained by Colenso, Henry Callaway (1817–90), also devoted considerable energy to recording indigenous religious tradition. He however felt that Colenso had made the wrong choice. The debate between these two students of Fredrick Maurice's theological universalism is outlined by David Chidester with gentle irony under two headings: 'Colenso's uNkulunkulu' (1996: 132-36) and 'Callaway's uNkulunkulu' (1996: 153-60). On the basis of his investigations among the Zulu, Callaway argued that *uNkulunkulu* describes their first ancestor and not the unknown god. In 1868, in a letter to William Bleek, Colenso writes: 'I am satisfied that Callaway is all wrong about Unkulunkulu. He has got a "bee in his bonnet" about that subject, and runs wild after Unpengula [Mpengula Mbande] his catechist' (Chidester 1996: 159). Colenso describes consultation on the matter with his own informants who provided him with solid backing for maintaining his position.

The Israelites and African Religion

Colenso was struck by the many similarities between African and Israelite custom. He wrote of the Zulus (1863c: xxi):

> their mode of life and habits, and even the nature of their country, so nearly correspond to those of the ancient Israelites, that the very same scenes are brought continually, as it were, before their eyes, and vividly realized in a practical point of view, in a way in which an English student would scarcely think of looking at them.

To Colenso, the association between the two is more than coincidental and on occasions he does express the opinion that the Zulu are descendants of Abraham through Esau or Ishmael (1861i: 34-35). The possible inference is therefore that for Colenso 'The religion of the Zulu could be understood by reading the Bible' (Chidester 1996: 170). His biblical commentaries would therefore serve as an important source of information for tracing his understanding of African religion.

In the Preface to Part I of his seven-volume study, *The Pentateuch and Book of Joshua Critically Examined*, Colenso describes a vivid scene between a bishop of the British Empire and his Zulu informant, William Ngidi, who was assisting him with the translation of the Bible (Colenso 1863c: vii):

> Here, however, as I said, amidst my work in this land, I have been brought face to face with the very questions which I then put by. While translating the story of the Flood, I have had a simple-minded, but intelligent native,— one with the docility of a child, but the reasoning powers of mature age,— look up, and ask, 'Is all that true? Do you really believe that all this happened thus,—that all the beasts, and birds, and creeping things, upon the earth, large and small, from hot countries and cold, came thus by pairs, and entered into the ark with Noah? And did Noah gather food for them all, for beasts and birds of prey, as well as the rest?' My heart answered in the words of the Prophet, 'Shall a man speak lies in the name of the Lord?' Zech. xiii.3.

> But I was thus driven,—against my will at first, I may truly say,—to search deeply into these questions; and I have since done so, to the best of my power, with the means at my disposal in this colony. And now I tremble at the result of my enquiries...

In his commentary, *St Paul's Epistle to the Romans: Newly Translated and Explained from a Missionary Point of View*, Colenso describes the influence of the informant, this time as questioner (Colenso 1861i: 199):

Such questions as these have been brought again and again before my mind
in the intimate converse which I have had, as a Missionary, with Christian
converts and heathens. To teach the truths of our holy religion to intelligent
natives, who have the simplicity of children, but withal the earnestness and
thoughtfulness of men,—to whom these things are new and startling, whose
minds are not prepared by long familiarity to acquiesce in, if not to receive,
them,—is a sifting process for the opinions of any teacher, who feels the
deep moral obligation of answering truly, and faithfully, and unreservedly,
his fellow-man, looking up to him for light and guidance, and asking, 'Are
you sure of this?' 'Do you believe this?' 'Do you really believe that?'.

Such questioning enables the biblical scholar to uncover the hidden light
in the Bible. For Colenso, 'The time is come, through the revelations of
modern science, when, thanks be to God, the traditionary belief in the
divine infallibility of Scripture can, with a clear conscience, be abandoned...' (1865[?]d: 232). Similarly, Zulu religion cannot be accorded any
infallibility.

The Test of Intelligence and Conscience

At first glance the introduction of a 'very intelligent native' looks like
condescension. This impression is eased when the use of 'intelligent' is
examined elsewhere in the unfolding narrative of his commentary (1863c:
xxiii-xxvii). He writes at length of his concern that the Church in England
is losing the best of its youth because of the refusal to answer questions
with anything other than dogma. For Colenso, those who set the finer
example are the intelligent questioners. He maintains that a common-sense
approach to the text which requires no specialized skill: all that his readers
require is 'an honest, English, practical common sense' (1863c: vi). An
appeal to the ordinary reader to test beliefs appears again in the subsequent
publication of a condensed, popular version of Part I of his *The Pentateuch*
(Colenso 1864b). He was always quick to spring to the defence of his
readers (usually understood as his supporters), and in Part III he writes:

> I respectfully protest against the language which the Archbishop of Canter-
> bury has, apparently, applied to all those, who read my books with interest,
> by summing them up under three categories, as either 'ignorant' or 'half-
> informed' or else 'rejoicing in anything which can free them from the
> troublesome restraints of religion'. (Colenso 1865g)

Colenso is not above poking fun at learned 'refutations' of his exegetical works which parade a complicated array of knowledge but manage
to avoid dealing with common-sense argument. It may be argued that

Colenso's appeal to a popular audience was strategically necessary, faced as he was by a powerful and highly placed opposition. Be this as it may, it must be recognized that fundamental to his theological system was the belief that all people have a religious dimension which is a source of truth. His call to the ordinary reader to test beliefs amounted to a threat to class privilege and control (Guy 1983: 187-88; 1997: 236-40).

The way in which the questions and comments of the intelligent Zulu serve as a touchstone of religious truth in Part I of *The Pentateuch* is brought into sharper focus during his later campaign against dogma. In the conclusion to a series of lectures published in 1873, 'the heathen' are those 'who are not yet drugged with results of past centuries of dogmatic teaching' (p. 369), and he calls for a system of education where 'children shall be supplied with instruction in full agreement with the advanced knowledge of the times, without having their intellects and their hearts and consciences stunted and deformed by the cramping effects of dogmatic teaching' (1873c: 374). Increasingly, the conclusions of his biblical research were influenced by the unhappy experience of High Church politics and motivated by a desire to discredit the priesthood (Rogerson 1985: 236). Colenso describes the influence of the post-exilic priests thus: 'a sacerdotal yoke was fastened on the necks of the people' (Colenso 1873c: 373). In happy contrast to the dogmatic churchmen is the intelligent questioner. The Zulu, with a mind uncluttered by ecclesiastical dogma, serves as the ideal against which truth may be measured. The scene with Ngidi described at the outset of Part I is therefore far from merely offering incidental biographical detail but is central to a hermeneutical approach which fuses African religion and Israelite religion.

While in London fighting for his ecclesiastical future, Colenso attended a meeting of the Anthropological Society on 14 March 1865 where a paper entitled, 'Efforts of Missionaries among Savages' was read by Winwood Reade (1838–75). The central thesis of this paper was, according to Colenso, that during a short stay in Africa 'every Christian negress that he [Reade] met was a prostitute, and every Christian negro a thief'. In the weeks that followed, Colenso responded in three lectures, each containing essentially the same line of argument (Colenso 1865b, 1865[?]d, 1865[?]e). Such is the sense of European racial superiority that Colenso assumes in his audience, a perception of the Anthropological Society which at the time was probably not far off the mark (Poulter 1980), that he finds it necessary to plead on behalf of the essential humanity of Zulus. He does not stop at this but proceeds to present the Zulu as the touchstone of universal religion. When he deals with the idea of eternal damnation, a doctrine in direct conflict with the bishop's own religious beliefs, what settles the argument for him is that the Zulus had never heard of the doctrine before missionaries arrived and were morally shocked by it. To Colenso, the villain of the piece is a certain kind of European missionary who comes to Africa with the confident belief in the infallibility of the religious system that he brings. Colenso finds further evidence of this cultural arrogance in the fact that damnation preaching was found far more often on the mission field than back home in Britain. He continues the attack on notions of European religious superiority by describing in graphic detail the religiously inspired practice of torturing and killing poor old women as witches, a horror from England's not too distant past.

The thesis that he wishes to demonstrate in these lectures is the validity of his understanding of mission. This is achieved primarily by his descriptions of the religious maturity of the Zulu Christians. Colenso frequently quotes from letters sent to him by William Ngidi, which are used to validate Colenso's position. Further to illustrate the beneficial effects of mission, he refers to a report of a sermon preached by Jonathan Ngidi, brother of William. With some pride he relates what he appears to regard as a novel interpretation of a biblical text, and concludes with the words of 'one of our poets':

> No compound on this earthly ball
> Is like another all in all.

In order to demonstrate the validity of such hybridity he argues: 'In like manner there is no accounting for the changes in our religion that have occurred in the course of our admixture with the Latin and other races'. Colenso concludes (1865[?]d: 223-24):

> We know not what may be the special work of the African... Perhaps we may yet have to find that we 'without them cannot be made perfect'—that our nature will only exhibit all its high qualities when it has been thoroughly tried in the case of cultivated black races, as well as white. And surely with our own experience before us we cannot presume to assert that the human family will never be benefited by light reflected even from the thinkers of Zululand.

In his Romans commentary, Colenso likens the Jewish Christians of Paul's day to the British people and the Gentile Christians to those considered to be Heathen (Draper 1999). Critics are thus shamed, and the message then becomes one of respect and tolerance for the newcomers.

There is a particularly striking scene in Colenso's commentaries where Ngidi responds to Exod. 21.20-21, 'If a man smite his servant, or his maid, with a rod, and he die under his hand, he shall be surely punished. Notwithstanding, if he continue a day or two, he shall not be punished: for he is his money' (1863c: 9-10):

> I shall never forget the revulsion of feeling, with which a very intelligent Christian native, with whose help I was translating these last words into the Zulu tongue, first heard them as words said to be uttered by the same great and gracious Being, whom I was teaching him to trust in and adore. His whole soul revolted against the notion, that the Great and Blessed God, the Merciful Father of all mankind, would speak of a servant or maid as mere 'money', and allow a horrible crime to go unpunished, because the victim of the brutal usage had survived a few hours! My own heart and conscience at the time fully sympathised with his.

A study of the role of William Ngidi in the narrative of Colenso's published work demonstrates the fundamental importance of this character, introduced again and again as the decisive factor in his argument.

The Native Informant and Universal Religion

Part I of his commentary on the Pentateuch concludes with two pages quoting the wisdom to be found in other religions in order to illustrate the universality of true religion, in all cultures and in all ages. Thus, far from being on the defensive about allowing the doubts of the Zulu to be taken seriously, Colenso makes use of the notion of a conscience unspoiled by the constraints of dogma, as a test of true religion. Ngidi functions in Colenso's narrative as the spokesperson for that universal religion.

He came to Africa with the belief that truth was to be found in all religions, a belief which he retained to the end. The understanding of God as the father of the whole human family is a conviction that had already become firmly rooted in his thinking, largely influenced by the writings and friendship of Fredrick Maurice (Darby 1981: 66-109). Maurice was a Christian socialist and theological universalist who believed in a universal brotherhood of man and fatherhood of God. The light of God could be found in every human being.

Scholar of African Religion

In his writings Colenso is very interested in recording the results of conversations with the Zulu people, particularly on religious topics. It is likely that his enthusiasm in finding traces of a universal religion makes his reports at times a little unreliable. As Hexham dryly remarks (1987: 159):

> It quickly becomes apparent that rather than simply preserve Zulu oral traditions Colenso sought to obtain specific answers which fit his preconceived views about an innate knowledge of the Christian God to be found among all peoples. Therefore, rather than present Zulu oral evidence what we have is a strange mixture of Zulu comments interpreted and deliberately elicited by a missionary who appears to have known the answers he was seeking before he began.

There is indeed a sense in which the character Ngidi is nothing more than the spokesperson for Colenso's own ideas, introduced merely to clinch an argument. This 'ventriloquism of the speaking subaltern', described by Gayatri Spivak as the 'left intellectual's stock-in-trade' (Spivak 1999: 255), is a critical perspective to which Colenso is certainly vulnerable. For very different reasons contemporaries in England made fun of the Bishop of Natal who 'took a Zulu for a pal'. Former mentor Frederick Maurice in a 'Letter to a Clergyman in South Africa' (Maurice 1885: 510) scolds Colenso for his reliance on 'contemporary—or nearly contemporary—testimony' which is what he calls 'unbelief about nations'. He concludes: 'This worship of mere testimony has been the disease of our theologians and historical students for more than two centuries'.

Critics cannot dispute the high status and authority accorded to the 'native informant' in Colenso's scheme of things. This voice is not confined to Colenso's own narrative, but his informants were also encouraged to speak in their own voices through publications in English and Zulu at the Mission Press (cf. Vukile Khumalo's contribution to the present volume). Anyone looking for an insider perspective or even an attempt at detached scientific description of African religion in the Colenso's works is bound to be disappointed. At best his work of comparison and translation provided a venue where alternative perspectives could emerge, 'a "liminal space" in which the hegemonic ideology of British colonialism was subverted and out of which forms of resistance and consciousness could emerge' (Draper 1999: 13). Similarities between the ancient Israelite and the Zulu made it possible to understand and give a measure of credence to customs such as polygamy (Colenso 1855e). The parallel Hebrew names for God, Elohim and Yahweh could help Zulus, Colenso would have us believe, understand what they really meant by *umVelinqangi* and *uNkulunkulu*. The inner spiritual struggle of Pauline theology is matched by the *uGovana*, 'which prompts him to steal and lie, commit murder and adultery' and the *uNembeza*, 'which 'bids him' as a native would say, "leave all that"' (1861i: 156).

This comparative work inevitably resulted in the selection and attempted standardization of diverse African religious traditions, a privileging of some and the suppression of others. Ironically, the very shift in Israelite religion he lamented, that from an inner spirituality to a systematically organized canonical text, was exactly the kind of change to which he himself contributed in nineteenth-century Natal.

Part IV

FAMILY AND SOCIETY

'THE TWIN PILLARS OF HEATHENISM': AMERICAN MISSIONARIES,
BISHOP COLENSO AND ZULU CONVERTS IN CONFLICT—
POLYGAMY AND *UKULOBOLA* IN NINETEENTH-CENTURY NATAL
AND ZULULAND, SOUTH AFRICA

Iain S. Maclean

Introduction

The late Anglican Church historian Peter Hinchliff in his perceptive theological study of the first Bishop of Natal, *John William Colenso* (Hinchliff
1964), observes that Colenso's downfall in large part can be attributed to
his remarkable ability to alienate friends and constituents. Thus, in a
surprisingly brief period of only a few years in the mid- to late 1850s, he
had managed to become embroiled in conflict with precisely those groups
of people that would have given him support. Hinchliff states that 'He
began by quarreling with the missionaries, then with the laity, then with
the clergy of his diocese, and finally with his brother bishops' (p. 54).

The latter conflicts are well known: the controversies with the church
councils in Natal; the delation for heresy by his Dean, James Green, and
the subsequent involvement of the Bishop of Cape Town, Robert Gray,
and indeed the Anglican hierarchy in England. In fact, for perhaps obvious
reasons, these conflicts have received most of the subsequent scholarly
attention. This is understandable since these conflicts resulted in Bishop
Colenso's teachings being declared heretical, lengthy legal processes, the
formation of the Church of the Province of South Africa, the protection of
the defeated Zulu peoples, and ongoing evaluation of Colenso's contributions to critical biblical studies.[1] Perhaps for these compelling disciplinary

1.   Consequently, the scholarly (and popular) focus has primarily been on Colenso's
biblical researches, Episcopal authority and support for the rights of the defeated
Zulus. For example, examine the standard histories of the Church of the Province of
Southern Africa such as that by Hinchliff 1963 or the more recent studies by Guy 1983
and 2001.

and institutional factors, the first conflict, that with the (primarily American) missionaries over the question of admitting polygamists to baptism, has received less, if scarcely any attention. It is the aim of this study to address this partial lacuna in the study of the life and work of the first Bishop of Natal. The primary sources for at least the American side of this conflict, is the archive of the American Board of Commissioners for Foreign Missions (ABCFM), housed in the Houghton Library of Harvard University.[2] The archive includes not only the American missionaries' comments and evaluation of the conflict, but also copies of all Bishop Colenso's printed tracts dealing with the subject, material sent back by the American missionaries to the ABCFM offices in Boston, Massachusetts.

The present study will first set the historical context for this the first conflict between Bishop Colenso and the missionaries, Americans of Congregational and Presbyterian backgrounds who formed the American Zulu Mission (AZM) in Natal. Then, the conflict or rather debate is outlined and, in the process, the observation made that polygamy was only one part of a larger Zulu social understanding of marriage and family relations, one that included specific social roles and the practice of *ukulobola* (see below). The missionary conflict over the practice of polygamy revealed not only the missionaries' own perceptions of proper marital relations, but also their assumptions regarding the best means of mission in a non-Christian or pagan culture. Ultimately these perceptions rested on how the missionary evaluated such a culture: Bishop Colenso offered a positive evaluation, while the American missionaries concluded that these practices were in effect the 'twin pillars of heathenism', and had to be rejected by every convert. The conflict over polygamy continued among the American missionaries even after Bishop Colenso withdrew by 1861 in order to prepare his defense against charges of heresy. This conflict continues up to 1879, now among and between the missionaries and their Zulu converts. The issues raised brought the indigenous voice into the conflict, though only Bishop Colenso and some of the AZM missionaries listened. Bishop

2.   This source material is from the American Board of Commissioners for Foreign Missions Archives. Publication is by permission of the Houghton Library, Harvard University, and the Wider Church Ministries of the United Church of Christ. I must thank the assistant curator of manuscript, Dr Charles Coakley, for his generous assistance. The Letters and Papers of the American Board of Commissioners for Foreign Mission, housed in the Houghton Library, Harvard University, are indicated in the present study by the initials ABC, followed by volume number, Letter number and, where known, date.

Colenso included Zulu observations in his published works on the subject of polygamy, while the AZM missionaries printed Zulu converts' 'Letters to the Editor' objecting to missionary policy on polygamy and *ukulobola*, in the columns of their Zulu-language newspaper. At the end of this article it is noted that in deciding on this issue for their converts, the AZM missionaries acted largely against the directives of their own ABCFM General Secretary, Rufus Anderson. The doubts of and reservations of their own policy, particularly by a women missionary, Katie Lloyd, are also noted. Finally, Rufus Anderson's evaluation of indigenous cultures was perhaps closer to Bishop Colenso's than that of his own missionaries, and his mission theory one that has proved to be strikingly contemporary.

The first Christian missionaries to the Zulu nation, which was, up to the time of its defeat by the British in 1879, one of the largest Sub-Saharan African empires, were not British, but in fact Americans.[3] The first missionary was Daniel Lindley, a graduate of Union Theological Seminary in Richmond, a Presbyterian, and a missionary of the interdenominational ABCFM. Lindley, together with several colleagues, had actually preceded Bishop Colenso in Natal by many years, the ABCFM mission to southeastern Africa having begun as early as 1835 and resulting in numerous mission stations in Natal alongside the Zululand frontier by the 1840s. Following the 1843 Britain annexation of Natal, an Anglican mission was created with the appointment, in early 1853, of the first Anglican bishop of Natal, John William Colenso. Colenso, a great visionary and scholar, arrived shortly afterwards in 1854 on a tour of inspection. The report he subsequently published of his episcopal visit contained remarks critical of the AZM handling of both polygamy and *ukulobola*.

The Zulu practices of polygamy and *ukulobola* (the traditional Zulu exchange of cattle between a groom and his father-in-law[4]), were described

3.   Captain Allen Gardiner, RN, retired, was in Port Natal from December 1834 to October 1835 seeking permission from the Zulu chief Dingaan to open a mission station in Zululand. This was refused, permission only being granted to open a mission in Port Natal, a place he named Berea. He then left for the Cape and proceeded from there to England to recruit Church Missionary Society missionaries, returning in May 1837 with the Reverend Francis Owen.

4.   The Zulu term *ukulobola* is often translated as 'bride-price', a rendering which limits its meaning. The term *ukulobola* marked the transfer of one kin member into another and most importantly, potential offspring, *ukulobola* serving as 'child-price'. The related term *ukulobolisa*, the causative form, meant the requesting of *lobola* by the senior member of a woman's family. This was not clearly perceived by the early missionaries, who primarily coming from the North American, abolitionist context,

by one AZM missionary in a letter to the General Secretary of the ABCFM as the 'twin pillars of heathenism',[5] and so had to be rejected by any Zulu candidate for baptism. It was this opposition to these central features of Zulu culture that were questioned by Bishop Colenso.[6] In the debate, which was initiated in 1855, by published responses to Colenso's criticisms, the AZM, Bishop Colenso and the Zulu converts themselves all took stances that were ultimately based on what each conceived to be the Christian marriage, the ideal home and the rights and status of women. Underlying these stances were differing exegetical approaches to Scripture and to the understanding of the relationship between the gospel and culture. When the AZM finally, in 1879, laid down as conditions for baptism, prohibitions of these practices, the dominant role of the American missionaries' cultural norms in formulating mission policy becomes patent.

Bishop Colenso had opposed such views on the basis of differing conceptions of the gospel, Zulu culture and the relationship between the two, conceptions that were exposed in the polygamy conflict, and were plainly set out in his 1861 *Commentary on St. Paul's Epistle to the Romans Newly Translated and Explained from a Missionary Point of View*.[7] While such a paternalistic approach by the AZM missionaries might be taken as typical for the age, the stance adopted by some of the American missionaries and

equated the *ukulobola* practice with slavery and the 'buying of a bride'. See for instance the 1860 manuscript by Josiah Tyler, 'Women in Zulu Society' (ABC 15.4, VI, Letter 114). For a modern anthropological approach see Krige 1950: 120-23, 177. The issue is complicated by the fact that explanations are so divergent. On the whole question of interpretation and of child-price, see Jeffreys 1951.

   5.   David Rood and Hyman A. Wilder, 'On Behalf of a "Society of the Zulu Mission"', a letter addressed to the General Secretary of the ABCFM, Dr Rufus Anderson, 25 November 1867 (ABC 15.6, Letter 45.28).

   6.   The British had annexed the area of the southeastern African coast between British Kaffraria, north to the Tugela River in 1843, though Letters Patent from the Crown establishing an Anglican Bishopric of Natal were only granted on 23 November 1853. The newly consecrated Bishop John William Colenso arrived in Port Natal on 30 January 1854.

   7.   The views set out in this commentary, which was published by Colenso at his mission station in Zululand, underlie his stance towards Zulu culture assumed in the polygamy debate. See the article by Jonathan Draper (1997) which explores this relatively unknown work. Unlike even the work of John and Jean Comaroff (1991, 1997) on European missionaries, which traces the dialectical play between missionary and convert, but which fails actually to provide the indigenous voice, Colenso, and indeed (in some instances to be noted below) the AZM, record the Zulu voice and viewpoint.

their parent body, the ABCFM in Boston, MA, was strikingly different. From letters directed to the AZM and from published reports it is clear that some individual missionaries, including a missionary spouse, Mrs Katie Lloyd, and the ABCFM (far ahead of its time) opposed the AZM's prohibitions of polygamy and *ukulobola*. The ABCFM, through its governing Prudential Committee and its Secretary Rufus Anderson, declared both in the 1850s, and again a quarter century later, that the missionaries were overstepping their bounds, were imposing American cultural norms, and failing to create an autonomous Zulu national Church. Rather, both Anderson and the ABCFM declared that such cultural issues need to be decided by the Zulu converts themselves, and not by the American missionaries. So, for example, in Anderson's 1845 Sermon *The Theory of Missions to the Heathen*, he points out that since Americans are accustomed to identifying Christianity with 'the blessings of education, industry, civil liberty, family government, social order, the means of a respectable livelihood, and a well-ordered community' they run the risk assuming that 'our idea of piety and our idea of the propagation of the Gospel are clothed in social and doctrinal forms that we identify with the Gospel itself' (reprinted in Beaver 1967: 73-74). Anderson notes in the same sermon that missionaries often try to mix the 'sublime spiritual object' with another less noble aim, that of 'reorganizing, by various diverse means...the structure of that social system of which the converts form a part'. He is even more specific in a later sermon in 1851 (quoted in Phillips 1968: 253) stressing that:

> It has seemed to be the mistake of some, that the great object of American missions should be to reproduce our own religious civilization in heathen lands, and just in the precise social and religious forms which that civilization has in this country. It may be that the Gospel will produce just these results, in the process of time, all over the world; but that is not the proper object of gospel missions. Their object is to proclaim salvation for immortal souls, through repentance and faith in the Lord Jesus...

He clearly perceives the dangers inherent in assuming an identification between the Christian message and American culture, so much so that he questions mission policy that seeks to evangelize through establishing schools or even teaching in English. He thereby rejects the typical accompanying motives of much nineteenth-century mission theory—that of civilizing or educating the indigenous peoples according to Western norms. These latter points are reiterated in Anderson's now almost forgotten work, *Foreign Missions* (1869: 97-99), which also notes the dangers of English education in alienating converts from their culture, and also hindering the spread of the missionary message—a position that predates the thesis of Lamin Sanneh (1989) concerning the role of the vernacular in the spread of Christianity in Africa.[8]

To return to the American mission to the Zulus, the debate, indeed conflict among Christian missionaries, and between them and their converts, over marriage customs, reveals in microcosm many of the major issues that faced the American nineteenth-century missionary movement. These included: the role of missionary cultural norms in the mission project; accommodation (or not) to differing gender roles and expectations; indigenous family arrangements; the role of indigenous converts in ecclesiastical governance; and the place of indigenous versus English language education of indigenous peoples. The AZM experience reflected most of these issues, but the present study will focus only on the ones that became critical for the missionaries, those surrounding the proper gender and marriage roles of women. The Zulu case offers a vivid example of how cultural norms surrounding marriage and gender roles influenced missionary hermeneutic and practice and ultimately led to the failure of the AZM. It is clear that the majority of the AZM missionaries, despite their deep empathy with the Zulus, failed or refused to differentiate between the gospel and their own cultural norms surrounding the nature of marriage and gender roles.[9] Despite the lack of clear scriptural statements on the continued practice of polygamy and *ukulobola* and what their own reformed tradition, including Calvin himself, taught concerning the acceptance of polygamy in first generation converts, the AZM missionaries valorized their own Nineteenth Century marriage customs. This attitude and its consequent results eventually alienated converts and potential converts alike and contributed to the AZM's failure to establish an autonomous, national Zulu Church. This failure revealed the growth and strength of the African converts' critical self- and culture-consciousness[10] and was to pave the way for the rise of indigenous churches independent of the missionaries altogether.

---

8.   On language and mission, see Sanneh 1989 (particularly, the Introduction and Chapter 3).

9.   Christensen and Hutchinson (1982: 167-78) deal with a similar phenomenon a generation later.

10.   It is noteworthy that Bishop Colenso attributed the origins of his source-critical work on the Pentateuch to attempts to answer the questions of a Zulu convert, William Ngidi.

An examination of these conflicts surrounding polygamy and *ukulobola* from a reading of the published tracts by Colenso, Wilder and others, as well as the surviving correspondence, primarily preserved in the archives of the ABCFM, exposes much of the missionaries' understanding of culture and their attitudes towards gender which contributed to their failure to fulfil the original aims of the AZM. First, however, it must be asked why the conflict and resultant uncertainty over polygamy erupted with Bishop Colenso's criticisms when the AZM had been faced with the practice since their arrival in Zululand in 1835? The answer to this question lies in the early history of the AZM, when it failed to reach the Zulu kingdom itself and its initial optimistic attitude towards Zulu power and culture shifted to a more pessimistic stance, one that condoned describing elements of Zulu culture as 'pillars of heathenism'.

An Errand into the Wilderness, 1835–55[11]

The first American missionaries to the Zulu were part of a two-pronged effort by the ABCFM, acting on the advice and encouragement of Dr Phillips of the London Missionary Society, stationed in Cape Town, to send missionaries to an unevangelized people. The Directors of the ABCFM declared in their 1834 Letter of Instructions to the first missionaries that:

> We aim rather to exert general and enduring influences to reach and mould the elementary and fundamental principles of society, and rear up Christian communities which, with the ordinary blessing of God, shall be able to stand and flourish without foreign aid.[12]

The ABCFM missionary vision was to reach an entire people and establish a Church that would eventually be independent of both home Church and other mission influences, and that would become the instrument of Christianizing the whole nation. The missionaries were to regard themselves as temporary missionaries and not as pastors, for the future Zulu Church was to be pastored, supported and propagated by the Zulus themselves. Rufus Anderson, Secretary of the ABCFM, clearly stated that:

---

11. This term comes from the title of Perry Miller's (1956) classic work on the self-conception of the New England Puritans, *Errand into the Wilderness*, used also by Norman Etherington (1970: 62-71).

12 'Prudential Committee of the ABCFM, "Instructions of the Prudential Committee"', ABC, II/I/I, 22 November 1834.

'the vocation of the missionary who is sent to the heathen, is not the same with that of the settled pastor' (Anderson 1845: 5; also Beaver 1967: 73-88).

The party sent out from Boston in 1835 was to divide upon arrival in Cape Town.[13] One group (comprising Mr Daniel Lindley, Mr Venable and Dr Wilson and their wives) moved North overland to work among the Matabele under Chief Mzilikazi, while the other (comprising Mr Grout, Mr Champion and Dr Adams) proceeded by sea to Port Natal and there set up a mission station in Zululand.[14] Both missions initially failed. The Matabele mission, after a sixth month delay in Cape Town due to the outbreak of the Sixth Frontier War, travelled North to settle beyond Kuruman at Mosega among the Matabele. The mission never overcame Mzilikaze's hostility to Christianity and the joint catastrophes of disease and of the Matabele defeat by the Afrikaner Voortrekkers. By July 1837 the missionaries had trekked down to the coast to join the other group of American missionaries in Natal. This latter group, after a year's delay, had arrived in Port Natal in 1837 and set up two stations, one at Umlazi, the other (Ginani) at the Umsinduzi River beyond the Tugela, in Zululand. The new arrivals from the interior set up another two mission stations in Zululand. However, within a year of their arrival, the Afrikaner Voortrekkers entered Natal and a cycle of warfare broke out between them and the Zulus, resulting in the missionaries' flight to the Cape Colony. In 1839, Wilson, Venable and Champion returned to America. Lindley, Adams and Grout returned to Natal in 1839, only to endure the succession struggles in Zululand in which the successful contender, Prince Mpande, exterminated rival clans as well as all of Grout's potential converts. Grout abandoned his station, moved into Natal, opposed the Zulu state and adopted a pro-British imperialist stance, believing that only the destruction of Zulu power would enable the mission to grow. The remaining missionaries were by 1841 in Cape Town en route back to the USA when they were persuaded by local clergy and missionaries to return to Natal (Grout 1864: 213-14).

13. The missionaries were so directed by the board in its instructions given them at the Park Street Church, Boston, MA. 'Prudential Committee of the ABCFM, "Instructions of the Prudential Committee"', ABC, II/I/I, 22 November 1834 (reprinted in Kotzé 1950: 46-52).

14. Zululand itself comprised the areas north of the Tugela and bound by the Drakensberg Mountains to the west and the sea in the east.

It was only a decade after the AZM arrival, in 1846, that the first convert, an old woman named Umbalasi, was baptized (Grout 1864: 215; Etherington 1978: 92; Welsh 1971: 43). By this time the British had finally annexed the land between British Kaffraria and the Tugela River, and imposed colonial rule over Natal. Under these calmer conditions the missionaries gathered many refugees from Zululand on their mission reserves. By 1854 they had twelve mission stations, 31 missionaries with three Zulu assistants, nine churches and schools. They also had published Zulu texts. However, there were only about 100 converts (Du Plessis 1911: 219-32, 368-75).[15] The low number of converts was in part due to increasing Zulu hostility to the missionaries and their message, perceived by many traditional Zulu (correctly) as largely condemnatory of their customs. This was pointed out by Bishop Gray of Cape Town, who, reporting on a visit to Lindley's mission station, stated (Gray 1852: 52-54):

> when [Lindley] first came here, the heathen flocked around him…but when they found that the gospel would interfere with their heathen customs and practices, they held several meetings and resolved that they would have nothing to do with the religion of Christ.

The American missionaries had required their converts to reject polygamy and to reject all but one of their wives prior to baptism, though they entertained differing views on the value of the related practice of *ukulobola*. Indeed, Grout, three months after his arrival in Zululand, in a letter to Anderson in 1841, noted that among the Zulus 'though polygamy is universal, they are not licentious'.[16] This generous and generally correct observation was to change dramatically as the missionaries encountered growing hostility among potential and actual Zulu converts. Zulu sexual mores came to be regarded as corrupt, licentious, and a major cause of opposition to the missionaries and their message; hence the description of the two most prominent marital customs, *ukulobola* and polygamy, as the 'twin pillars of heathenism'. Further, a complicating factor was the fact that the colonial Secretary for Native Affairs, Theophilus Shepstone had recognized both polygamy and *ukulobola* under colonial law by Ordinance 3 of 1849. Shepstone himself disapproved of polygamy, but regarded the missionary opposition to such practices as exaggerations which failed to take into account the legal and property rights of wives and so disregarded

---

15. According to Grout (1864: 221-22), the American Zulu Mission had 150 converts by 1854 and 190 by 1857.

16. A letter from Lewis Grout to Rufus Anderson (ABC 14, Letter 62, 1841).

traditional social and political order (Welsh 1971: 71-73). The missionaries opposed Shepstone's approach to these Zulu customs and increasingly there were reports of the excommunication of men who took a second wife.[17]

The First 'Pillar of Heathenism': The Polygamy Debate 1855–69[18]

The conflict among and between the missionaries, not to mention the rising Zulu opposition, over the monogamous baptismal requirement became public when John William Colenso, after an initial tour of the colony in 1854, having interviewed both missionaries and Zulus, returned to England and there published in 1855 his *Ten Weeks in Natal*. In this work he set out his theology and approach to Zulu culture—which were often in sympathy with Shepstone's views and in contrast to the AZM's approach. He accused the AZM of overly stressing sin, hell and damnation, and of entertaining negative views of Zulu beliefs and customs (Colenso 1855g: 61-64).[19] Such views, he stated, are seen in the Americans' rejection of the perfectly acceptable native term for God, *uNkulunkulu* and their substitution of the neutral term, *uThixo*, a term that functions without 'pagan connotations' (see Colenso 1855g: 57-60),[20] and their policy of requiring monogamy as a baptismal prerequisite. He elaborated on the last-mentioned practice in his *Remarks on the Proper Treatment of Cases of Polygamy* published the same year. Colenso's published remarks were

17. William Mellen, 'A Report of Umtulumi Station for the Yr ending 1855' (ABC 15.4, V [Mellen Correspondence], Letter 111).

18. The colonial and the missionary debate was extensive. The focus in this paper is on the issue as it was treated by the American Zulu Mission and Bishop Colenso. Various Colonial Commissions dealt with the subject in 1848 (*Proceedings and Report of the Commission Appointed to Inquire into Past and Present State of the Kafirs in the District of Natal* [1852–53]) and in 1881 (*Report and Evidence of the Natal Native Commission, 1881–1882* [Pietermaritzburg, 1882]). The Natal Evangelical Alliance issued its findings in *Polygamy and Women-Slavery in Natal: Report of Special Committee of Natal Evangelical Alliance* (Durban, 1861).

19. See the report made by the American missionary, William Mellen, on Colenso's comments on the American's beliefs and preaching on subjects such as hell, damnation and sin (ABC 15.4, V [Mellen Correspondence], Letter 12).

20. Further detail on the American missionaries' position is given in the 115-page manuscript by Henry Callaway, on the use of *uNkhulunkulu* and *uThiko*, fowarded by W. Mellen to the ABCFM (ABC 15.4, VI, Letter 121). This was also published as *uNkhulunkulu* (Natal: J. Blair, 1868).

perceived as a direct attack on the policy and practice of the AZM missionaries. This initiated a public, and fortunately, published debate, the extent of which can be gathered from a brief covering letter that the missionary protagonist, Lewis Grout, sent to the ABCFM general secretary, Rufus Anderson, in which he lists the published material on polygamy and *ukulobola* that he sent to the ABCFM.[21] Grout further notes that he would have sent a copy of 'bro. Wilders's Review' (i.e. Wilder 1856), but has 'none by me at the moment'. He also noted, but did not include, an anonymous twelve-page pamphlet he had written in 1856 under the pseudonym 'A Protestant Dissenter', entitled *An Apology for the Toleration of Polygamy in the Converts from Heathenism.*

On Colenso's return in the middle of 1855 to Natal, he was visited by two American missionaries, William Ireland and William Mellen, one of whom later reported that Colenso 'avows his intention to admit polygamists to the communion' and also, with some hyperbole, that he 'would have no objection to baptizing a man who had a whole score of wives'.[22] Colenso then wrote his *Remarks* in response to hostile correspondence in 'Natal journals of late' (1855e: 3) which arose out of the comments he had made on the subject in his *Ten Weeks in Natal*. In an earlier publication (1855g: 139-42) Colenso had questioned the existing missionary rule that a man put away all his wives but one before baptism. Now he argued that this rule should be done away with altogether. In place of the inflexibility of the American missionaries' approach, Colenso advocated a gradualist approach to the conversion of both individuals and society. The great strengths of Zulu society, its family and kinship systems, needed to be preserved and gradually transformed. Colenso advocated baptizing polygamists, with their wives and children, but on the condition that no more wives would be taken. The succeeding generation's sons would of course only take one wife. Colenso was not alone in suggesting such a gradualist

21. See the letter from Lewis Grout to Rufus Anderson dated 25 June 1857 (ABC 15.4 [Grout Correspondence], Letter 84). The items referred to are Colenso's *Remarks on the Proper Treatment of Cases of Polygamy* (1855e), 'our reply' (i.e. Grout's [1855] *A Reply to Bishop Colenso's 'Remarks on the Proper Treatment of Cases of Polygamy as Found Already Existing in Converts from Heathenism'* [Grout wrote under the pseudonym 'An American Missionary']), Colenso's *Letter to an American Missionary* (1855d), and 'our answer' (i.e. Grout's subsequent [1856] *An Answer to Dr. Colenso's 'Letter' on Polygamy*).

22. Correspondence of W. Ireland to R. Anderson 'Report of the Ifumi Mission Station for the Year Ending 1855' (ABC 15.4, IV, Letter 279). The quotations come from an Appendix dated 1 August 1855.

approach to cultural transformation. He was supported by the English theologian and social reformer, F.D. Maurice, who, in correspondence with Mrs Colenso, had stated, 'That the bishop is right in his view of polygamy, I can have no doubt. And if so, it must be a great and useful duty to state his conviction' (Maurice quoted in Cox 1888, I: 65). Archbishop Whately of Dublin expressed his support for Colenso (Woolsey 1858: 425-26), as did other Anglican missionaries. Henry Callaway, one of Colenso's deacons, strongly opposed his views in his (Callaway's) *Polygamy: A Bar to Admission into the Christian Church* (1862: 3; cf. Colenso 1862a: 81). In addition, Colenso's position was supported in South Africa by the Reverend Canon Grubb, the Reverend Robert Robertson, John Armstrong, a former Bishop of Grahamstown,[23] and by the Lutheran missionary Dr August Hardeland.[24]

Colenso emphatically denied that he was condoning polygamy, and stated rather that he questioned 'whether the method, at present adopted by the Missionaries, of requiring a man, who had more than one wife, to put away all but one, before he could be received to Christian Baptism, was the *right* way of accomplishing this end' (1855g: 3). Colenso thus challenged the American missionary practice of refusing to baptize polygamists, arguing that it was 'unwarranted by the Scriptures, unsanctioned by Apostolic example or authority, condemned by common reason and sense of right and altogether unjustifiable' (p. 3). A survey of Colenso's work shows that his argument was developed from Scripture and from the actual Zulu social context. After trawling the Scriptures and noting the clearly polygamous practices of the Hebrew kings, he argues that Deut. 21.15-16, if taken with the Decalogue, implies that having more than one wife is not the sin of *adultery* (1855e: 3 [Colenso's emphasis]). He then argues that in the New Testament period the Jews practiced polygamy by divorcing a wife in order to marry another[25]—what might be called 'diachronic polygamy'. So in Mt. 19.8, the phrase 'and shall marry another' is

23. Armstrong was Bishop of Grahamstown from 1853–56. He was succeeded by Henry Cotterill who held the bishopric from 1857–71. Cotterill, an evangelical, initially supported Colenso until the publication of Colenso's controversial *Commentary on Romans* in 1861.

24. Dr August Hardeland was sent out to Natal in 1860 by Louis Harms, founder of the Hermannsburg Mission Society, to take up the position of Superintendent of Missions.

25. He refers to Josephus, *Antiquities* 17.1; Justin Martyr, *Dialogue against Trypho* c.134; *The Apostolic Constitutions* and works by St Basil and St Chrysostom.

construed as providing the motive for the divorce and so confirms his interpretation. He concluded that Jesus' statements in the gospels on the subjects of marriage and divorce are aimed not at what we might call 'synchronic polygamy', but rather at a divorce practice that was in effect diachronic polygamy. In the Zulu social context, Mt. 5.31-32, which condemns unlawful forms of divorce, is interpreted to mean that if missionaries force a man to put away his other wives, he is in effect forcing them into adultery. Colenso argued that Jesus condemns such practices and not polygamy at all. Likewise, the phrase 'let a bishop be the husband of one wife' (1 Tim. 3.2) according to Colenso's reading of Patristic and Protestant commentators, implies that some synchronic polygamists were at least admitted to baptism. In support of this position, he quotes from Daniel Whitby, John Wesley, Thomas Scott, Dr James Macknight, John Calvin and Peter Martyr.[26] Colenso concludes his argument from Scripture by declaring that to force a Zulu convert to 'put away his wives, we are doing a positive "wrong", perhaps to the man himself, but certainly to the woman, whom he is compelled to divorce' (Colenso 1855g: 150).

Colenso then proceeded to examine under five headings, the effect such a policy would have on Zulu society. First, it would disrupt the family and also the kinship system. Second, it reveals a lack of sensitivity for the humanity and natural feelings of the Zulus. He offers examples showing that 'Kafirs have a sense of feeling as highly developed as whites', and indeed, 'an equal sense of justice' (1855g: 16). Third, he inquires if any consideration has been given by missionaries to the plight of the wife/wives and children put away under such a policy? Fourth, have the missionaries knowledge of anyone who has actually given up his wife/wives? On what grounds was this actually accomplished? By putting away all but the most favored, all but the oldest, or by some other arrangement? How could such be accomplished morally? (1855g: 18). Colenso raised the question of the social problems such a ruling on polygamy would occasion if it were actually enforced throughout the colony. He also enquired, given the Zulu resistance to the AZM missionary policy, what would become of the hope

26. His sources included the Anglican divine Daniel Whitby (1804), the Methodist John Wesley (presumably Wesley's *Explanatory Notes upon the New Testament* [date of specific edition unknown]), the Calvinist commentator Thomas Scott (1812), the Church of Scotland New Testament scholar James Macknight (possibly Macknight's *A New Literal Translation, from the Original Greek, of all the Apostolical Epistles with a Commentary* [date of specific printing unknown]), and the exegetical works of the Protestant reformers John Calvin (1856a) and Peter Vermigli (1576).

of creating a Christian society? (p. 20). Colenso asks if 'any *chief* man converted' (p. 19) and what the effect of such a rigid anti-polygamy policy might have on the ideal of the national conversion of the Zulus. For unless chiefs converted (with their wives), little could be done to reach the peoples subject to these chiefs, who simply forbade missionaries from working in their territories.[27] This of course was what had happened, with the AZM outside of Zululand proper, and the consequent limitation of their mission to ministering solely to refugees from the Zulu kingdom.

Lewis Grout, writing under the pseudonym 'An American Missionary', began his *A Reply to Bishop Colenso's 'Remarks on the Proper Treatment of Cases of POLYGAMY'* (1855) by noting that in the whole preceding 45-year history of the ABCFM, only one polygamist had ever been baptized. Basing his response on works on polygamy authored by Rufus Anderson (1845 and 1848: 62-80), he proceeds to quote the following (Grout 1855: 6 [italics in original]):

> Polygamy stands on a very different footing from that of slavery. Little difficulty is apprehended from it in gathering native churches. The evidence that polygamists were admitted into the church by the Apostles, is extensively and increasingly regarded as inconclusive by the Board. *We nowhere find instructions given, in the New Testament, to persons holding this relation; nor is there evidence of the practice having existed in any of the churches subsequent to the apostolical age.* The committee believe that no positive action of the Board, in relation to this subject, is needed or expedient. *Unsustained as the practice is by any certain precedents in the apostolical churches, and unauthorised by a single inspired injunction,* the native convert will rarely be able to prove the reality of his piety, should he persist in clinging to it, or refuse to provide for the education of his children, or for the support of their mothers, if he may be permitted to regard the mothers as his wives.[28]

Grout then proceeds through the Old Testament and New Testament references used by Colenso, rejecting his interpretations of these texts. He focuses on Colenso's treatment of New Testament passages and denies his claim that polygamy was tolerated either in the New Testament or in the

27. In fact, cases of polygamy were exceptionally rare among converts, who came primarily from exiles in Natal colony from the Zulu succession wars and who consequently had few resources. The social and economic status of the Zulu converts is fully described in Chapter 4 of Etherington's 1978 study.

28. A similar position is advocated by Henry Venn in his 'Appendix' on the subject of polygamy, appended to the Church Missionary Society, *Proceedings of the Church Missionary Society for Africa and the East* (1857: 207-12).

early Church.[29] Grout, however, seems primarily concerned to refute Colenso's charges that the American missionaries' approach is contrary to 'common sense'. Grout brings forward a 'slippery slope' argument, claiming that Colenso's conclusions prove too much. Could not Colenso's argument for tolerating polygamy be applied to other vices such as drunkenness? (An American Missionary 1855: 32). Grout then proceeds to offer examples from the experience of missionaries to counter Colenso's claim to 'common sense'. He contrasts the American position with that of the Natal Lutheran Mission that baptized one polygamist, an experiment which ultimately failed as the convert took more wives.[30] Grout then gives examples of converts who gave up wives—examples that reveal much about missionary expectations of converts and of their understanding of the place of men and women in Christian society. For instance, in highlighting the exemplary convert John Mavuma of Inanda, Grout declares that he is (An American Missionary 1855: 44):

> A humble devoted consistent Christian, now an old man, yet working hard, he performs for himself and for his family much of the labour which other men (polygamists) extort from their plurality of wives, *alias* female slaves, while they themselves lie basking in the sun, lounge from kraal to kraal, or waste their days in the endless litigations which their polygamy has engendered.

The polemical stance against Zulu culture is clear. Prominent is the missionary assumption that Western gender divisions of labor are the only norm and that conversion means the acceptance of such norms. Traditional Zulu society is viewed as morally deficient as men 'extort' labor from their 'plurality of wives' who are really nothing but 'female slaves'. Such men do not display the virtues of working to provide for their families, but instead are lazy (pejorative terms such as 'basking', 'lounging' and 'waste') and litigious. Grout argues that the reason 'why the Gospel is disliked by the natives in their heathen state' (quoting Colenso 1855g: viii) goes beyond the missionary prohibition of polygamy, to a flawed moral

---

29. It is interesting to note that Grout does not deal with the reformed authorities utilized by Colenso and uses instead the works of the German Church historian Johann August Wilhelm Neander and the American biblical scholar, Dr Timothy Dwight, Professor of Divinity at Yale University.

30. Ironically, in light of its failure, this was the example of a baptism of a polygamist used by Colenso in his *Ten Weeks in Natal* (1855g: 138-40). The missionary involved was the Reverend Carl Posselt of the Berlin Missionary Society, stationed at Emmaus, near the Ukahlamba Mountains.

sense, one that is the result of 'superstitious notions and practices', indeed of the *servile beastly estimate and condition* in which they hold, and strive to keep, the *female sex*', their 'love of *sensuality*, and of *indolence* and of inordinate gain, and, as a consequence of these, their polygamy' (An American Missionary 1855: 49). This is an integral part of heathen society which holds

> ideas and practices which rob woman of all her dignity, rights, and duties, as man's companion, and as an intelligent moral being; and reduce her, as far as possible, to the state and character of a mere slave—an object of merchandise—an object of brutal lust... 'My wives and my daughters', says the native, 'are my cattle, my oxen, my cows, my horse, my plow, my wagon. I bought my wife and paid for her...' (p. 52)

Grout's negative evaluation of traditional society is sharply shown in his description of a native family who abandoned the mission station, not because of prohibitions on polygamy he claims, but rather through adherence to superstitions. He describes a family's departure as follows (An American Missionary 1855: 51):

> and, as soon as they could arrange their affairs, they left their upright houses to decay, left the station and Missionary, threw off their clothes, and returned to Kafir huts, and to all the darkness and pollution of heathenism in a Kafir kraal.

These are descriptions which are clearly dependent upon the missionary's own cultural experiences of slavery and assumptions concerning dress, housing and work ethic. The AZM missionaries were strongly abolitionist and Daniel Lindley himself had great reservations in sending his two daughters for education back to his family in the American South because they were slave owners.[31] Consequently, their frequent evaluations of polygamy and comparison of the practice with slavery, is understandable. Another possibility for the missionaries' opposition to polygamy could be the rise of American Mormonism and their recent revelation legitimating the practice of polygamy—a practice that was to spark the so-called 'Mormon Wars' in 1858. However, I have not been able to discover a direct link between this unfolding American phenomenon and the AZM missionaries.[32] Western housing, clothing and educators are associated

---

31. See Smith 1952: 40-43, 291-92.

32. The Mormon practice of polygamy did much to arouse opposition and indeed contributed to the formation of the Protestant Women's 'Anti-Polygamy' Crusade. See Iversen 1997. This work covers a slightly later development, but the issue emerged in

with light and purity, while all that is traditional Zulu is cast in terms of darkness and impurity. The remainder of Grout's *Reply*, in its negative and culturally-bound demonization of Zulu culture, examines the actual practice of polygamy and its effect on women, men and family life, concluding that the practice is against God's word, that a (synchronic) polygamist is not married, but rather living in a continual state of adultery with all except the first wife.

In the same year that Grout's pamphlet appeared, another American missionary, Hyman Wilder, published his *Review of 'Remarks on the Proper Treatment of Cases of Polygamy'* (1856). His method of rebuttal follows that of Grout's. Drawing on the exegetical works of classical Protestant divines,[33] he challenges Colenso's interpretations, and argues that polygamy was a temporary and imperfect arrangement which led, in the case of the Old Testament figures, to great domestic troubles. Here again emerges the concern for a set pattern of domestic arrangements, an assumption of a particular cultural norm for marital affairs. Wilder concedes that even if the Old Testament had condoned polygamy, this was but a pale reflection of what was to come in the Christian dispensation. Wilder categorically rejects Colenso's interpretation of Jesus' words in the Gospel of Matthew. He agrees with Grout that any present-day accommodation to polygamy is but the beginning of multiple concessions and that it is immoral forever 'since, where it has been practiced, it has depended upon war and slavery for its support, and the evil consequences...have uniformly borne testimony against it' (Wilder 1855: 12). Wilder further

the 1850s and bore implications not only for marriage, but as the title above indicates, the ideal domestic arrangement.

33. The authorities he included where Thomas Williams, commentator for *The Cottage Bible and Family Expositor: Containing the Old and New Testaments with Practical Expositions and Explanatory notes* (Hartford: D.F. Robertson and H.F. Sumner, 1834) and of Old Testament books such as his, *The Song of Songs, which is by Solomon* (Philadelphia: W.W. Woodward, 1803); Dr Justin Edwards (1787–1853), leader in the American Temperance Movement and commentator for *The Family Bible: Containing the Old and New Testaments* (New York: The American Tract Society, c. 1851–56); Dr John Kitto wrote extensively on the geography of Palestine and the history and customs of the peoples of the Bible; Andrew Fuller wrote on the subjects of Indian mission, Christology, practical Christianity and religious toleration; Professor George Bush was a commentator on the Old Testament (Pentateuch and apocalyptic), as well as author of works on Christology and the Trinity; Bishop Robert Lowth was an Oxford biblical scholar known for his *Lectures on Hebrew Poetry* (1787); Bishop John Henry Hopkins, First Protestant Episcopal Bishop of Vermont, and Timothy Dwight, New England Churchman and President of Yale College.

charged Colenso with inconsistently condoning the continued practice of polygamy and for claiming that while polygamy is an offence, it is not thereby a *sin in the sight of God* (Wilder 1855: 5, quoting Colenso 1855g: 13). In this, however, he misreads Colenso's attempts to deal only with the case of polygamous first generation converts. Colenso had after all quoted Calvin (1856a: 78, 1856b, II: 381) who accepted just such a distinction between 'what is permissible' and a sin.

   The final round of charges and counter-charges came with Colenso's *A Letter to an American Missionary From the Bishop of Natal* (Colenso 1855d) and Lewis Grout, William Ireland and William Mellen's[34] *An Answer to Dr Colenso's 'Letter' on Polygamy*.[35] Both works go over the same scriptural texts, adding nothing original to the exegetical discussion, but providing inadvertently substantial information on the social and cultural contexts of Zulu marriage customs. Significantly, Grout and his co-authors devote much space to 'the true account of kafir Marriage & their Consequences', including extended discussion of the colonial commission on polygamy in 1847,[36] and of the terms *ukutenga* ('to buy') and *ukulobola*, with further sections entitled 'More on the Mode, Ease, and Joy of Putting Away Polygamy', and 'More on the Vile Nature and Fruits of Kafir Polygamy and its Attendants'. As the scriptural arguments proved inconclusive, more weight is clearly being given to the alleged moral consequences and depraved conditions of traditional society. These statements are made as if the AZM missionaries had not read what Colenso had perceptively pointed out in his earlier work (1855d: 48) referring to Grout (An American Missionary 1855: 38), that,

> In every one of those expressions of mine, which you have quoted, there is
> a reference to the rights of the wife and children, not to the mere feelings,
> or sensual desires, of the husband.

---

34. Contained in correspondence of Daniel Lindley to Rufus Anderson dated 16 November 1855 (ABC 15.9, AFR Miscellanies, I, 1843–73). He notes that they are 'furiously at work responding to Colenso'.

35. Issued anonymously under the pseudonym, An American Missionary (1856).

36. The Natal Native Commission Report of 1847 on Polygamy heard evidence on the subject and on the practice of 'buying wives' from natives themselves, from civil magistrates and from diverse missionaries. The Reverend Newton Adams, Daniel Lindley and J.L. Döhne, formerly of the Berlin Mission, and who had joined the American Zulu Mission in 1849, all made submissions to this commission. *Proceedings and Report of the Commission Appointed to Inquire into Past and Present State of the Kafirs in the District of Natal*, VII: 44, 73.

Colenso's criticism was never answered. In fact, Colenso had examined Grout's booklet with the non-Christian Zulu Chief Zatshuke, with Theophilus Shepstone acting as interpreter. The chief did not recognize the traditional Zulu marriage practices from the AZM missionaries' descriptions. In response to specific questions, Chief Zatshuke answered that the Zulus do marry for life, that they do not send their wives away when they are old and infirm, and that they do not actually 'buy and sell' their wives like cattle (Colenso 1855d: 59)[37] as many whites think. He further explained that if a woman leaves a man's kraal, the cattle are returned only if the woman was not at fault. The cattle cannot be returned, though, if the woman has borne a child.[38] The AZM missionaries never seemed to reckon with what would happen to 'excess wives' put away by a potential convert. In fact, ironically, the AZM missionaries seemed to assume that the very extended kinship system they so vigorously condemned would somehow absorb and care for the material and social needs of such women and their children. If *ukulobola* had been handed over, the woman could leave, but her children, by Zulu law, would be their father's and would have to be left behind with him.

This inter-missionary debate ended shortly after this exchange as Bishop Colenso became embroiled in heresy charges (which included his stance on polygamy [Colenso 1855d: 57-60][39]) brought against him by his own Dean, James Green, and the Reverend Dr Henry Callaway, and necessitated his presence in England from 1862 to 1865 in order to conduct his defense.[40]

---

37. He also quotes a colonial magistrate, Mr Fynn, on the meaning of the Zulu term *ukutenga* ('to buy'), often used interchangeably with *ukulobola*. Fynn confirms that it refers to trading, but not to marriage.

38. What Colenso does not observe or mention is that if the woman leaves, even voluntarily, if the *lobola* has been paid, she has no claim on the children. They remain with the husband. Conversely, if no *lobola* had yet been paid, the children remain part of the womans' family. See Jeffreys 1951.

39. He also notes that the polygamy issue will be discussed by a Conference of the South African Church and then referred to the Convocation of the Province of Canterbury in England. Colenso's stance was a factor in the charges brought against him for heresy, necessitating his writing (1862a).

40. In 1866, the Church Congress in Wakefield (England), chaired by Bishop Lightfoot further discussed the polygamy question. Finally, at the 1888 Lambeth Conference it was resolved that polygamists not be baptized until they 'conform to the law of Christ', though their wives, dependent upon local circumstances, might be baptized. This decision was to be accepted by all Anglican provinces as well as by other

The Second 'Pillar of Heathenism':
Ukulobola *and Paternalistic Solutions, 1861–79*

If the controversy over the first 'pillar of Heathenism', the practice of
polygamy, had primarily been conducted among the missionaries, largely
in terms of how particular scriptural passages were to be interpreted, that
over the second 'pillar of Heathenism', the custom of *ukulobola* and
ukulobolisa, was one conducted between the Americans and their own
converts who were deeply concerned about the status of their marriages,
their daughters and their extended families within traditional Zulu society.
While the giving and receiving of cattle for wives was a widespread
African custom, intricately interwoven with African cosmology and kinship systems, the missionaries understood these customs, in the words of
David Rood, as follows:

> The giving of cattle for a wife is expressed in the native language by the
> term *ukulobola*. The receiving or demanding of cattle for a daughter is
> called *ukulobolisa*. This is the causative form of the word *ukulobola*. It
> means, 'cause cattle to be given for a wife'.[41]

Another American missionary, Josiah Tyler had written a position paper in
1860 to the Board of Commissioners entitled 'Zulu Women in South
Africa',[42] in which he described the life of a typical Zulu woman and the
practices of polygamy, *ukulobola* and *ukulobolisa*. The focus of these evil
practices, according to Tyler (p. 8), is 'the Zulu father…much opposed to
his daughters living at a missionary station and adopting Christian and
civilized habits'. Consequently, young women were kept away from missionaries and so remain in a state of 'ignorance and heathenism'. He goes
on to relate how the Zulu girl, when of marriagable age, 'is sold by her
father, or oldest brother if the father be dead, to be the wife of one who

denominations such as the Presbyterians, Methodists, Lutherans and sustained by the
International Missionary Conference at Tambaram in 1938.

41. A letter from D. Rood, stationed at Amanzimtoti, on behalf of a 'Society of the
Zulu Mission' to Dr N.G. Clark, Foreign Secretary of the ABCFM dated 25 November
1867 (ABC 15.4, VI, Letter 45, pp. 1-2). See similar definitions given by another missionary, Alfred T. Bryant, under the entry '*lobola*' in his *A Zulu–English Dictionary*
(see Bryant 1905: 360).

42. Josiah Tyler, 'Women in Zulu Society' (ABC 15.4, VI, Letter 114 [the title is
incorrectly given as 'Essay on the Position of Women in Zulu Society', in Etherington
1978: 63 n. 4]).

will pay for her the greatest number of cattle' (p. 5).[43] He continued to relate that 'I am sorry to say that rarely is the preference of the Zulu girl consulted by her father when he is about to give her up in marriage'. In effect, says Tyler, the father wishes to obtain the greatest number of cattle in order to secure another wife, for 'his whole heart alas is wedded to polygamy that has been called with truth the "cursed idol of the Zulus"' (p. 6). The missionaries viewed these customs as being responsible for what they saw as the menial and inferior position of the Zulu woman, who performed the manual and agricultural labor. Tyler concludes that they are in a 'condition of abject slavery...to their husbands' (p. 12). Here the conflict is directly expressed: for the Zulu the question is one of the legitimacy of marriage in the wider Zulu society; for the missionary the question is the eradication of the excessive sexual desires of the Zulu male and the eradication of 'female slavery'. Again, the AZM missionaries saw the Zulu women perform manual labor and associated this with lower, even slave status. This becomes transparent in Tyler's contrasting of heathen Zulu women, to those who are

> well instructed girls and married women in Natal who can ply the needle with dexterity, who make clothing for themselves and others who can read and write and who have adopted many of the customs of civilized life. These of course offer a pleasing contrast to the great multitude who live in ignorance, superstition and filth. (pp. 13-14)

In the absence of clear scriptural references, the debate largely revolved around the alleged moral consequences of these customs. The cultural and gender presuppositions involved in the earlier debate now loom much larger in the missionary discourse and were now brought into question by their own Zulu converts. Educated and given a written language by these same missionaries, the Zulu converts now read the Scriptures in Zulu and discovered that these selfsame Scriptures had little to say on the issue of *ukulobola*. A partial record of this conflict between missionaries and converts is preserved in the monthly Zulu newspaper *Ikwezi*.[44]

43. Similar criticisms, though more sharply, are offered by H. Wilder in his letter to the ABCFM dated March 1868 (ABC 15.4, VI, Letter 126).

44. The newspaper, *Ikwezi* (*Morning Star*) succeeded the earlier *Inkanyezi Yokusa* (also 'Morning Star') which was begun under H. Wilder at Umlazi in 1850. *Ikwezi*, a monthly paper of 4-6 pages, first appeared in April 1861. David Rood notes that the newspaper 'is full of letters on this issue' (in a letter from D. Rood, 'On Behalf of a Society of the Zulu Mission' to the General Secretary of the ABCFM dated 25 November 1867 [ABC 15.4, VI, Letter 45, p. 44]. The following articles and letters to the

The conflict functioned at various levels, the most prominent being the personal, as Zulu converts struggled to resolve contradictions between their own inherited customs and new practices brought by the AZM missionaries. By the early 1860s the original converts now had daughters of a marriageable age, or, in some cases, sisters or other female relatives inherited, according to Zulu kinship laws, at the decease of close relatives. In the latter case, non-Christian families often expected or even demanded *ukulobola*. Many Zulu converts had inherited obligations from non-Christian family members, and, due to tribal solidarity, felt obligated to accept or hand over cattle to make *ukulobola* for such female family members. Thus, fathers as well as relatives were expecting the exchange of cattle and many of the converts were arguing for the morality of the practice. Further, if a man had not made *ukulobola*, his wife's non-Christian family could claim the children as their own. Another level was the colonial government's recognition of Zulu customary law, which required payment of cattle to legalize a marriage. Ironically, there also existed a level of external critique from traditional Zulu society that complained that mission stations were hotbeds of moral laxity if not license, as they rejected traditional courting, betrothal and marriage customs. Without such customs, the Zulus regarded converts' marriages and the subsequent offspring as illegitimate.

Besides the rounds of articles and letters on the issue in the pages of *Ikwezi*, the Zulu Christians at their Annual Meetings, the *Isikhumbuzelo*,[45] raised objections to the missionary stance on *ukulobola* and rejected missionary charges that Zulus bought women like cattle or slaves or that the custom was a commercial transaction. Unlike the earlier debate over polygamy when they presented a united opposition, the American missionaries were divided on this issue: some were totally opposed to *ukulobola* and subjected practitioners to Church discipline, while others in practice

Editor (*Ku 'Mhleli we' Kwezi*) were consulted: John Caluza, 'Letter to the Editor', December 1862; J. Ximwa, 'Letter to the Editor', December 1862; J C 'Letter to the Editor', January 1863; B.H., 'Letter to the Editor', January 1863; Leader article, *Ukulobola*, May 1863; G.C., 'Letter to the Editor', September 1863; J.N. Qaba, *Umbuzo Ngokulobola*, September 1863; John Vimbe, *Ngokulobola*, January 1864; J.N. Adams, *Ngokulobolisa*, February 1864; J. Caluza, *Ukulobola*, March 1864; G.C., 'Letter to the Editor', February 1863; S.G., 'To the Editor of Ikwezi', with reply by the Editor, March 1863.

45. Arthur Fridjof Christofersen (1967: 54-55) describes the origins of this annual meeting (which as early as 1851 was discussing *ukulobola*) as distinct from the general Annual meeting, called the *umkhondlu*.

ignored it, either for principled or pragmatic reasons. The controversy came to a head at the AZM's Annual Meeting in 1867, when three resolutions were submitted: first, that *ukulobola* is contrary to humanity and retarded the progress of civilization and Christianity; second, that it is the duty of all members of the mission to eradicate the practice from the churches; third, that those who follow the custom should be subject to ecclesiastical discipline. The first two were passed while the third was dropped due to intense opposition. A council of five missionaries and 20 Zulus was set up to consider the issue, but ultimately this became deadlocked, with the missionaries divided and the Zulus arguing in favor of the custom.

One of the longest-serving AZM missionaries, Daniel Lindley, who had not previously spoken on the issue, had sided with Aldin Grout in the mission meeting called later in 1867 to discuss the three principles enunciated at the Annual Meeting. There, upon the vote for the third resolution calling for disciplinary action, Grout had declared that all his converts at the Umvoti mission station supported *ukulobola* and that if required to enforce such discipline, he would resign from the mission. Lindley now openly declared that he viewed the practice as 'the foundation of the structure of native society', and one which was 'productive of a world of good. If today one word from my mouth would instantly annihilate the custom, I would not speak that word' (Lindley quoted in Smith 1952: 393). The AZM missionaries then chose David Rood and Hyman A. Wilder to draft a report to send to the ABCFM General Secretary in Boston, now Anderson's successor, George Clark. This report was duly conveyed in Rood's letter of 1867 (Rood and Wilder 1867). This 47-page letter clearly states that the majority of the AZM missionaries understand *ukulobola* and *ukulobolisa* respectively as bride-price, and as the mercenary selling of daughters. This was not the only correspondence sent to Boston, as Rood and Wilder allude to others having written to the ABCFM. Katie Lloyd's letter on the issue was one of the letters mentioned as having been sent independently to the committee. In addition to Lloyd's letter, others were also sent by Rood himself, by H.A. Wilder[46] and of course, earlier in 1860, Josiah Tyler, had written a lengthy essay on *ukulobola* and *ukulobolisa*. Rood and Wilder's letter makes it clear that

---

46. See the letters from David Rood to N.G. Clark (ABC 15.4, VI, Letter 125), and from Hyman A. Wilder to N.G. Clark (ABC 15.4, VI, Letter 126 [this letter comprises 13 pages that are now almost illegible]).

the committee of the AZM wished the ABCFM to make a decision, as the missionaries were unsure that they could obtain unanimity among their own number on this issue.[47] In addition to the points made in the essay submitted by Tyler, this co-authored letter argued for a unanimous position to be taken on these issues, which it proceeded to describe. Thus, fully one half of this lengthy epistle is devoted to describing how *ukulobola* functions in Zulu society. The latter half moves to 'notice some of the objections to this custom and to give reasons why we think it should not be allowed in our churches' (Rood and Wilder 1867: 22-23). Two major reasons are advanced, namely, its mercenary character at the present time, and the 'evil and degrading influence it has upon the people'. The description of the practice as 'mercenary' arose naturally from the missionaries' understanding of it as a purely commercial exchange between the senior male guardian and the potential spouse. The second reason advanced, that of its negative moral effects, comprised the following objections: first, the union so created is not in fact a marriage; second, the woman is degraded to a servile state and so becomes subject to the mercenary and sexual passions of the man; third, the woman is expected to deny her own choice and submit to her father's choice and that the condition of the women in such unions is one of drudgery and slavery (pp. 27-36). In fact, the letter concludes by expressing the missionary fear that *ukulobola* is but the thin edge of the wedge to reintroduce polygamy into Churches as men take new wives as their aged ones retire to their eldest son's kraal (pp. 36-38). However, a differing perspective comes from Katie Lloyd,[48] who worked among Zulu women at the mission school. She directs her criticism here specifically against Hyman A. Wilder, who was regarded as a champion of 'civilization' and 'Americanization' and who was opposed to the development of an indigenous Zulu literature (Smith 1952: 392). Wilder's letter to the ABCFM was directed specifically against the practice of *ukulobolisa* by converts, claiming that it had a powerful negative moral impact on both men and women. Indeed, he held that the practice was not only mercenary, but that it was 'the chief obstacle to the civilization and christianization of the natives'. He went further, claiming that not only did it discourage men

47. Though the Anglican, Lutheran, Methodist and Presbyterian missions in Natal and elsewhere in southern Africa accepted the practice of *ukulobola* without deleterious effects.

48. Katie Parker was the widow of Charles Hooker Lloyd, who died in 1865. She was to marry Daniel Lindley's son, Newton Lindley in 1870, returning with him to the USA in 1872.

from manual labour, but that it was a 'chief source of crime' and of 'forni-
cation, adultery...witchcraft and murder'. In fact, according to Wilder,
'*ukulobolisa* is *ukutenga* (to buy)'.[49] Lloyd rejects this simplification of the
practice and indeed its near demonization of Zulu culture and writes, in
part of a letter to her mother, that:

> I fear we as a mission have tried too much to make Americans of our
> Zulus... Very many things they give up when they become Christians are
> merely making them more like our nation... I cannot help feeling...that
> their marriage custom of paying cattle is to the young Zulu girls the greatest
> protection they have against the immorality of the nation, while it insures to
> the women good treatment and care... When a woman is married the cattle
> are a surety in the father's hands of her good treatment... In case she is
> abused he can come and protect her and in case of need he returns his
> pledge, the cattle, and gives his daughter the shelter of her old home. I have
> thought it would be well if white women's fathers had the power to aid
> them that a Zulu father has, when I remember suffering and ill-treated
> wives in New York. The women themselves on the stations without excep-
> tion realize this and therefore desire that the custom continue. I would say
> once for all that the girls in marrying choose the husband they love as much
> as we do in America, and the women are no more slaves than you are to
> father or I was when Mr. Lloyd was living.[50]

Here again we have a critique similar to that made by Colenso, that the
American missionaries focus entirely on the male motivation, their alleg-
edly sexual turpitude in addition to the laziness engendered by the 'twin
pillars of Heathenism'. This is one of the few positive stances taken by an
ABCFM missionary on this traditional custom.

The reply from the ABCFM comprised two responses. The first came
the following year addressed to the 'Zulu Mission' from the 'Prudential
Committee' (PC 1868[51]). This was followed by the Prudential Committee's letter the following year addressed directly to the 'members of the
Zulu Churches' (PC 1869[52]). The first response, addressed directly to the
missionaries, acknowledged that it was not a definitive reply as there did

49. See the letter from H. Wilder to the ABCFM dated March 1868 (ABC 15.4, VI,
Letter 126, parts I, IV-VI).

50. See the letter undated from Katherine Lloyd to Mrs Parker (ABC 15.4, VI,
Letter 127).

51. PC 1868 = 'Prudential Committee of the ABCFM Letter to the Zulu Mission',
2 June 1868 (ABC 15.4, VI, Letter 128).

52. PC 1869 = 'The General Secretary, Dr N.G. Clark, Letter to the Members of
the Churches Connected with the American Zulu Mission', 9 March 1869 (ABC
Foreign Letters 2.1.1, XXXV): 204-12.

not seem to be unanimity among those in Natal as to what the terms actually meant. The committee had of course by this time received not only Rood and Wilders' letter, but also individual communications from Katherine Lloyd, Hyman Wilder and Josiah Tyler. The Prudential Committee reiterated its understanding of the missionary task in four principles. First, they stated that: 'Our proper work as a missionary body, engaged in carrying forward the divine plan for the reconstruction of a fallen race, is to introduce the new divine life, not the forms it shall assume'. They proceed to note that Christian morality as developed in the West cannot be suddenly 'transferred at once to a heathen land' (PC 1868: 3). Second, they declared that: 'The new life which it is our single object to inspire in the hearts of men, is best nurtured by love and kindly sympathy, rather than by authority'. Thus, 'we must not expect to bring up our native Christians to our standard at once. Your work is not to make American but Zulu Christians' (p. 5). Third, they stated that the task of the missionary is 'to bring men to Christ, not to change their social customs, their national usages or to lead them to adopt the practices of civilized nations'. Finally, they stressed that the ABCFM is not an ecclesiastical body and has no control over the native churches (p. 6). Consequently, the General Secretary, Clark, pointed out that the missionaries enjoy only temporary relations with the native churches precisely as missionaries. They are not pastors and have no authority over them (p. 8). The second response was an eight-page letter addressed directly to the Zulu Churches by Clark himself. The latter half of this letter comprised a brief description of the Christian ideal of marriage, the equality of male and female and the dangers of transgressing this ideal by the practices of polygamy and *uku-lobola*. However, these are all customs which Clark is sure 'the gospel of Christ will change' (PC 1869: 210).

Conclusion

The most striking aspect of the Prudential Committee's two letters is the contrast they present to the AZM in their understanding of the missionary task. The ABCFM had set up the AZM as a mission to an independent nation, ostensibly in new missionary territory, independent of other missions and colonial authorities. The missionaries themselves, to be distinguished from settled local pastors, were to create an independent, national Zulu Church, one capable of ruling and propagating itself under the direction of a Zulu clergy. Virtually all of these elements failed to materialize. First, the American missionaries basically remained within Natal and never managed to penetrate Zululand itself and were in fact prohibited from doing so by the Zulu monarchs who regarded Christian converts as de facto non-Zulus and incapable of paying homage (*ukukhonza*) to the monarch. Second, Natal swiftly fell to colonial intruders, initially to the Afrikaners and then to the British, the latter imposing indirect rule which relied upon keeping traditional chiefs and customs, such as polygamy and *ukulobola*, largely undisturbed. Third, not only had the AZM to contend with the Anglican Bishop of Natal, John William Colenso, as the Wesleyans under James Archbell (who arrived in 1841 [subsequent bracketed dates indicate the year in which the mission was initiated]), the Norwegian Mission under Schreuder (1844), the Berlin Missionary Society with Döhne (1847), the Roman Catholic mission (Oblates of Mary Immaculate) under Bishop Jean Francois Allard (1852), and the Hermannsburg Mission (1854), all of whom differed in their approach to traditional marriage customs. Thus any sense of there being a single but with a host of competing missionary societies such national Zulu Church or even a unified missionary front on theological and practical issues, soon disappeared.

The missionaries of the AZM never managed to implement their original vision and their handling of the 'twin pillars of heathenism' shows that they were hindered in part by their own cultural perceptions and assumptions which influenced their understanding of Zulu society and its marriage customs. The ensuing conflicts, particularly with their own converts, led them to exercise illegitimate authority as pastors, and thereby to move beyond their mandate as ABCFM missionaries. The AZM missionaries also impeded the growth of an independent African clergy, fearing the intrusion of one or more of these 'pillars of heathenism', and in fact only ordained their first Zulu clergy in 1878. Consequently, after the voices of moderation, Katie Parker, Daniel Lindley and Aldin Grout were gone,[53] the AZM missionaries, contrary to congregational principles and the directives of the Prudential Committee of the ABCFM, passed formal regulations for all the mission stations called the 'Umsinduzi Rules'.[54] The first three rules prohibited any convert from practicing polygamy, *ukulobola* or *ukulobolisa*, while the fourth and fifth rules required abstinence from the production and consumption of alcohol (African beer), and

53. By this time Daniel Lindley had returned to the USA where he died in 1873; Katherine Lloyd had remarried and likewise returned to the USA, as had Aldin Grout. By 1878 David Rood had rejected the rigid AZM position (Welsh 1971: 261-62).

54. See the General Letter dated 27 May 1880 (ABC 15.4, VIII). All five rules are also given in Christoferson 1967: 62-63.

from the smoking of *intsangu* or wild hemp. Missionary unwillingness to compromise on the 'twin pillars of heathenism', polygamy and *ukulobola*, and on other cultural customs (beer-drinking) meant finally, as Bishop Colenso had predicted, not just a negative judgment upon Zulu social values, but the inability of the AZM to found a national Zulu Church. In fact, indigenous Zulu leadership, particularly after 1880, moved out of the European mission locations in order to found their own African Indigenous or Independent Churches (Sundkler 1948: 1-32). Ironically, then, the AZM missionaries, through their refusal to follow ABCFM policy and their own cultural opposition to their Zulu converts, contributed to the establishment of Zulu churches independent of missionary control.

JOHN WILLIAM COLENSO AND THE ENIGMA OF POLYGAMY

Livingstone Ngewu

1. The Definition of Parameters

Soon after John William Colenso was appointed and consecrated the first Anglican Bishop of Natal in the middle of the nineteenth century he decided to spend some time trying to acquaint himself with the new diocese. During this initial tour of the diocese, he interviewed a number of Zulus as well as missionaries of the American Zulu Mission (AZM) who had come to Natal under the auspices of the American Board of Commissioners for Foreign Missions (ABCFM). The information he gathered was not just for his edification—Colenso wanted to use it so as to solicit financial assistance for the building up of the new diocese. To this end, he published in 1855 a book entitled *Ten Weeks in Natal: A Journal of a First Tour of Visitation Among the Colonists and Zulu Kafirs of Natal* (Colenso 1855g). The contents of this seminal work stirred up a hornet's nest, and thus Colenso soon found himself embroiled in many storms of controversy, not least of these was the perception that he was advocating the somewhat permissive practice of admitting polygamists to Communion. For some of the missionaries of the AZM who had been in the region before Colenso (described in Maclean's contribution to the present volume), polygamy and *lobola* (a deal that the bridegroom's family made with the bride's family to guarantee that the bride would be subsumed by the subsuming family and that all children born to the bride would belong to the bridegroom's family) were the 'two pillars of heathenism', which had to be denounced by any convert to Christianity. This paper is an attempt to review Colenso's pragmatic and accommodative approach to the enigma of polygamy. This will be done against the backdrop of an uncompromising attitude of some missionaries towards polygamy. Those missionaries who were resolute in their opposition to some African practices did so on the understanding that such practices were not just *contra bonos mores*, but also that they were at variance with the principles of the gospel as they understood them.

On the whole European missionaries who came to plant Christianity in Africa seem to have fallen into three broad categories. The first category consisted of missionaries who were quite accommodative in their approach to African norms and practices. These missionaries tried to bring the gospel into harmony with most facets of African culture. They were certainly not agents of assimilation or integration but sought to protect and promote diverse cultural expressions. In an era in which Africans were misconstrued as heathens/pagans this approach could have been perceived as no less than an outrageous heathenization/paganization of Christianity. In some cases those missionaries who sought to protect cultural expressions of their converts soon found themselves subsumed by the culture of such prospective converts. In 1806, James Read, a London Missionary Society agent in the Eastern Cape, married a young Hottentot girl (Mostert 1993: 346). Three years later a 58-year-old missionary, Jan van der Kemp, married a 17-year-old slave girl whose black parents came from Madagascar. It has been aptly suggested that actions of missionaries like Read and van der Kemp deepened their 'personal identification with the people they served...by marriage' (p. 346). Such 'miscegenation' was denounced by a number of colonists and missionaries. Read must have alarmed his critics even more when he committed adultery and his paramour bore him a baby boy (p. 440). Read is a classic example of those missionaries who were captivated by the culture of their converts.

The second classification of missionaries consisted of those who adopted a disjunctive model where the gospel was made to stand aloof from, and diametrically opposed to, African culture. The gospel was perceived as an instrument of judging culture. While such missionaries tended to see Christianity as coterminous with Western culture, nevertheless, they were inclined to dismiss African culture as incompatible and incongruous with Christianity. The missionaries of the ASM belonged to this class. This is borne out by their unfaltering opposition to baptizing polygamists except on condition that each convert put away all but one of his wives. Needless to say, that a number of African converts who complied with this stipulation became disillusioned with their culture and suffered from acute identity crisis. Thus the African culture disintegrated and Africans 'lost the social cohesion which had been the strong point of their tribal system' (Vilakazi, Mthethwa and Mpanza 1986: 9). These missionaries created settlements for their converts and such African settlers became known as 'the mission people' (Peires 1981: 76). The price that such converts had to pay for embracing new religion was denunciation of their culture and thus they became cultural renegades as was the case with Tiyo Soga of the eastern Cape who refused to undergo the circumcision rite (D. Williams 1978: 12, 19).

The third division of missionaries consisted of those who adopted a gradualist approach to individuals seeking conversion. These missionaries did not subscribe to the notion that every facet of African culture was necessarily incompatible with the gospel, but preferred to choose and 'baptize' into Christianity those facets of African culture which they held to be innocuous. John William Colenso belonged to this category. Colenso grasped the nettle by suggesting that if a polygamous man wanted to embrace Christianity, he should be baptized together with his wives without putting away his supernumerary wives. Colenso stands out as one missionary who was determined to ensure that Christianity was planted in the fertile soil of cultural interaction. Colenso saw it as begging the question to assume that the Zulu people would bear the fruits of the Spirit even before they read the New Testament.

2. *The Growing Storm of Controversy*

Jeff Guy (1983: 50) observes that when Colenso arrived in Natal he had 'no practical experience of colonial life', 'pontificated on the nature of African personality' and 'treated blacks with sentimental optimism, tolerating barbarities and encouraging disrespect'. A close study of Colenso's dealings with the Zulus thus depicts him as having had initially, if one were to read this observation in reverse, a profound respect for the Zulu cultural norms. Colenso might also be seen as being averse to using the gospel as a means of disrupting the Zulu kinship system as he found it. He did not, however, confine himself to the issues of polygamy and *lobola* but went on to critique the strategy employed by the AZM missionaries. He found them to have laid undue stress on their negative views of Zulu customs.

These missionaries had insisted that polygamous converts should put away all their wives but one as a prerequisite to baptism. They do not seem to have taken pains to find out why Zulu men took multiple wives. Of the first three missionaries of the AZM to work in Natal in the 1830, it was Aldin Grout who had expressed his view that polygamy and promiscuity were not coterminous (Grout 1841: 3). However, such an insightful observation does not seem to have ever been used by any of the American missionaries as a point of reference in dealing with the problem of polygamy.

Soon after his return from England, Colenso was paid a visit by two American missionaries, William Ireland and William Mellen, who were distraught by Colenso's apparent determination to baptize polygamists without requiring them to drive away their supernumerary wives. While in his *Ten Weeks in Natal* (Colenso 1855g) Colenso had questioned the propriety of requiring polygamous men to give up their ancillary wives, in his *Remarks on the Proper Treatment of Cases of Polygamy* (Colenso 1855e), which he also published in 1855, he argued that this requirement should be stamped out by the missionaries. He clearly saw that the missionary policy of the AZM showed a lack of sensitivity for both the feelings and the humanity of the Zulu people. It is interesting to note that the views of the American missionaries in Natal were at variance with those of some of the ABCFM as enunciated by the Secretary of the governing Prudential Committee, Rufus Anderson. Anderson had claimed that the missionaries of the AZM had become impervious to the cultural mores of the Zulus (Beaver 1967: 73-74).

What was evident in the controversy over the baptism of polygamous men was the preoccupation of the missionaries of the AZM with salvation of individual souls at the expense of one's family. Apart from undermining Zulu culture, this position also tended to regard Zulu women as expendable chattels who could be sent away at the drop of a hat. It is not necessary here to highlight the fact that these American missionaries were least concerned about the conversion of women who were trapped in polygamous marriages. There is no doubt that such a policy would have created a class of castaway women known as *amadikazi* or *oomabuyek-wendeni*—detached women who are not expected to have any moral restraints. This problem would have been compounded by the children of such detached women. Once the bond between such children and their fathers had been severed, the children would have fallen into a category of illegitimate children known as *imigqakhwe*.

3. *The View of the Anglican Church on Polygamy*

It was Colenso's ardent wish that the Anglican Church should work out guidelines under which polygamous people may be baptized and become full members of the Church. Five years previously the General Secretary of the Church Missionary Society, Henry Venn, had 'issued a memorandum which laid down the policy that polygamists should not be accepted into membership in the Church' (Baeta 1968: 224). It is likely that Colenso found such a prohibition too callous and his experience among the Zulu people in Natal impressed upon him the need for the Church to pronounce on the matter.

It was with this in mind that, in 1862, Colenso wrote a discourse to the Archbishop of Canterbury, Longley, in which he proposed how the Anglican Church should deal with 'converts from heathenism, who may have more than one wife at the time of their conversion...' (Colenso 1862a: 1). He clearly discerned that Christian missionaries in Southern and Central Africa were torn between two conflicting principles, each compelling in its own way. On the one hand there was the need to ensure that the standards of religion and morality were not lowered. On the other hand there was 'the cause of justice and mercy' (p. 77). Colenso chose the latter and in so doing appealed to Scriptures, the Apostles and Tradition. Despite his impassioned plea for toleration of polygamy there was no reference to it at the consultation of the Anglican Bishops, which was held at Lambeth in 1867, nor in the consultation, which was held in 1878. The question of polygamy was too peripheral an issue compared to the heavy matters facing the Anglican Bishops during the first two consultations.

It was not until 1888, in the Third Lambeth Conference, that the Anglican bishops addressed the problem of polygamy. This Lambeth Conference passed an ambiguous resolution, that was a distillation of a Report of the Committee Appointed to Consider the Subject of Polygamy of Heathen Converts. In submitting their report the members of the committee raised, *inter alia*, three pertinent points (*Lambeth Conferences* 1948):

a.   They affirmed 'distinctly that Polygamy [was] inconsistent with the law of Christ respecting marriage'.

b.   They argued that no polygamists had ever been baptized in the early Church even if such polygamous alliances had been contracted before conversion.

c.   They also reported that they considered it far better to withhold baptism from polygamous persons until they accepted the law of Christ.

It was within this framework that a resolution on polygamy was formulated. The resolution clearly stated that 'persons living in polygamy be not admitted to baptism, but that they be accepted as candidates and kept under Christian instruction until such time as they shall be in a position to accept the law of Christ' (Resolution 5[A] Lambeth 1888—see *Lambeth Conferences* 1948). This raises the question of how a person who was living in a polygamous alliance was expected to demonstrate his/her acceptance of the law of Christ beyond a declaration that he/she accepted Christ. Was it accidental or deliberate that the bishops consistently referred to the law, rather than the grace, of Christ?

An Encyclical Letter issued by the bishops attending the Third Lambeth Conference, defined decisively the law of Christ in so far as marriage was concerned. The bishops wrote that the 'sanctity of marriage as a Christian obligation implies the faithful union of one man with one woman until the union is severed by death. The polygamous alliances of heathen races are allowed on all hands to be condemned by the law of Christ' (*Lambeth Conferences* 1948: 108). From this it can be inferred that a polygamous convert would be understood to have accepted the law of Christ only when he put away all his wives but one.

It would probably not be too far-fetched to surmise that the decision of the bishops who were assembled at Lambeth in 1888 was, to a very large extent, influenced by the knowledge that Colenso, the heretic, had championed a lenient rather than an austere treatment of polygamous converts. It is important to note that by 1888 the problem of Natal had not been completely resolved. In 1867, 56 of the 73 bishops at Lambeth who voted on the Colenso affair had declared their 'acceptance of the sentence pronounced upon Dr Colenso by the Metropolitan of South Africa and his Suffragans, as being spiritually a valid sentence' (Stephenson 1978: 39). Twenty-one years later the bishops of the Anglican Church distanced themselves from the views of Colenso on the matter of polygamy.

4. *Colenso's Realistic Approach to the Issue of Polygamy*

Colenso had encountered a number of incidents in which polygamist men (while 'polygynist' is the technically correct term, for convenience I will continue to use 'polygamist' to refer to men with multiple wives) wanted to embrace Christianity. He was aware that elsewhere the practice of the Church required each polygamous man to put away all his wives but one. In the case of a woman who was in polygamous relationship, she was required to separate herself from her husband before she could be baptized. Colenso reckoned that such abrogation would result in multitudinous hardships for the jilted wives and their children. In order avoid the breaking up families, he proposed what he referred to as 'the lesser evil of the two' which would have made it possible for those converts who were in polygamous relationships to be baptized without having to put away their companions. However, such a convert would be required not to take an additional wife or wives after his conversion (Colenso 1862a: 6). Lest he be misunderstood as promoting polygamous relationships, Colenso provided a disclaimer that polygamy was 'at variance with the whole spirit of Christianity...and must eventually be rooted out by it'. He also emphasized the need for Christian Ministers to work untiringly towards 'its extirpation throughout the world...' (pp. 2-3). Unless Colenso's Letter to the Archbishop of Canterbury (1862a) is read against the backdrop of this crucial disclaimer, one might run the risk of dismissing his writing on the subject as promoting the continued practice of polygamy.

A number of missionaries, not just in Natal but also in other parts of Africa, had dismissed polygamous marriages as non-marriages at all. Indeed, they were seen as unpardonable adulterous relationships. Africans held a different opinion—a polygamous man was never perceived to be committing adultery with any of his wives. One needs to note that in African communities there 'was no sense of moral outcast and sexual delinquency was easily forgiven', except in cases where a married woman committed adultery (Mostert 1993: 455).

In dealing with the question of polygamy among the Zulu people Colenso elicited a number of texts from the Old Testament and came to the conclusion that in Hebrew Scriptures 'eminently pious men' who were polygamous were not censured by God (Colenso 1862a: 4). In essence, what Colenso proffered was a subtle parallelism between the lives of the Jews as contained in the Old Testament on the one hand, and the lives of the Zulus before the preaching of the gospel on the other. He could see that it was difficult to reconcile if the baptismal prerequisite for practicing polygamists to put away all their wives but one. This would make it difficult to explain King David's lascivious lifestyle, 'the man "after God's own heart" [and the lifestyle of Abraham], the "father of the faithful" who were both polygamists...' (p. 7).

Colenso's analysis of the New Testament texts becomes somewhat convoluted. He argued that a fair number of the followers of Jesus were poor and thus 'were content with one wife from necessity as much as from choice' (Colenso 1862a: 14). He also found it puzzling that even though Jesus censured divorce most severely, he never censured polygamy. While in Lk. 16.18 Jesus is alleged to have said that a man who put away his wife and married another committed adultery against her, Colenso pointed out that in this text Jesus did not say anything about a man who did not put away his wife but simply went ahead and married another. Colenso's painstaking analysis of the Gospels drew him to the conclusion that Jesus did not find polygamy an anomalous practice worth suppressing.

He found two texts particularly compelling in support of his exposition—namely, 1 Tim. 3.2 and Titus 1.6—both of which determine the moral boundaries of Church leadership. While the texts lay down the ground rule that a person who is called to be either a bishop (presbyter) or a deacon should be the husband of one wife, nothing is said about those who do not aspire to such positions. From these texts Colenso drew the inference that some men who had more than one wife must have been admitted into the Church by baptism. Unless there were polygamous believers among the Christians, such a prescription would not have made sense at all. After examining the various biblical texts, Colenso came to the conclusion that the extreme dislike that European people exhibited towards polygamy had more to do with 'Roman laws, customs, and opinions...[than with] religious feeling' (Colenso 1862a: 26).

Colenso was of the view that monogamy evolved over a long period. A natural consequence of this evolution was socialization as well as habituation. A clear example of this process was the religious practice of the people of Armenia, Ethiopia and Abyssinia. The missionaries who preached Christian religion to the people of these states did not require their polygamous converts to embrace monogamy as an essential ingredient of conversion.

5. *Colenso's Silenced Voice*

It has been aptly observed that so 'long as the Church ignored polygamy, it was forced to ignore discussion of social morality, for the majority of social bonds existed through polygamous relationships' (Webster 1968: 227). Those missionaries who, like Colenso, broached the subject of polygamy could be seen as having taken a 'vital step towards indigenization' (Webster 1968: 227). It is hard to see how the nineteenth-century missionaries could be so doctrinaire not just on the matter of polygamy but also on a whole array of indigenous cultural expressions. This rigidity can be attributed to a view that, ultimately, 'national culture was an integral part of each Protestant religion as it had developed historically. Calvinism was either Scottish or Dutch, Lutheranism German or Swedish, just as Anglicanism was English, and, unconsciously, (the missionaries) thought of Christianity as necessarily national' (Brown 1960: 198). From this it could be surmised that since in Europe the practice of polygamy had become obsolete, converts to European forms of religion were expected to adhere tenaciously to European norms and values. To have accepted a European form of Christianity without the entire aggregation would not have been good enough. Together with Christian religion, African converts were expected to accept European imperialism as part of the baggage. Henry Callaway alluded to this when he reminded Colenso that in deciding the status of African marriages, the Europeans should never pay heed, and allow themselves, to be influenced 'by the laws and customs of ignorant and unenlightened savages' (H. Callaway 1862: 20).

African polygamous converts who wanted to embrace Christianity but loathed putting away their wives devised a mechanism of dealing with the problem. Some simply appeared to have dispensed with all their ancillary wives but continued to have clandestine relationships with such supernumerary partners. A man who had been known to have a number of wives was suddenly forced to see them furtively to avoid detection by hawk-eyed missionaries. Relationships, that were understood to be honest and above board were suddenly declared to be sinful. Callaway imprecated polygamy and allowed himself to be carried away in his invective when he said that if Africans found it pleasant to have many wives it was a misplaced pleasantness. It was 'the pleasantness of having wives to till the ground, that he may have plenty to eat; to make beer for him, that he may get drunk, and call his friends in crowds to get drunk with him, and in their drunkenness, in a kind of Bacchanalian orgies, to enact obscenities, the details of which we cannot write' (H. Callaway 1862: 25).

As soon as polygamy was demonized, some Africans chose to traverse between the two worlds: the sacred world of the missionary on the one hand, and the unhallowed world, which had been the matrix of all his humanity on the other. Thus conversion had nothing do with justification by grace but everything to do with justification by compliance to the demands of the missionary. The need to appear 'just' in the eyes of the missionaries forced a number of Africans to become quite obsequious, all for the sake of the gospel as interpreted, or rather misinterpreted, by those missionaries who believed in a complete break with the culture of the convert.

Colenso intimated that he was aware how disruptive this putting-away of superfluous wives was to family life. He had been informed by one missionary that a certain man who had to dispense with one of his two wives when he embraced Christian religion never renounced sexual intercourse with the jilted woman. After some time the man slipped back so as to live with both wives (Colenso 1862a: 62).

Colenso could not be completely silenced and consigned to the realm of quietude, as converted polygamists who surreptitiously visited their wives under the shroud of darkness were the living icons of what he championed.

Human beings who converted to Christianity primarily out of fear of the missionaries than the forgiving love of Christ continued their practices. While Colenso would have helped in the extirpation of polygamous practices, the lethal criticism of his opponents only succeeded in sweeping the problem under the carpet.

It is worth noting that the question of posterity was very important for a number of Africans. When a married man died without offspring, it was considered an inescapable duty of one of his brothers to *ngena* the widow. The greatest tragedy that could befall an African man was to die without a baby boy. Thus his line would die out and his name would be forgotten. This tragedy could, however, be redeemed. A brother of the deceased man could deputize for him and give his wife a baby boy. Since they were both sons of the same father, the seed was essentially the same. This custom, known also as levirate marriage, makes sense when seen in this light. It was a means by which a man restored some form of immortality to his diseased brother and rescued his name from oblivion. All the children born out of this *vinculum matrimonii* would be regarded as the deceased man's offspring. One missionary informs us that Xalisa's husband died and left her with a little girl. 'Xalisa was…claimed to wife [*sic*] by Xala, her late husband's brother' (G. Callaway 1926: 61-62). Some polygamous marriages were contracted out of necessity rather than out of desire.

There were those converts who decided that the demands of the gospel were too cumbersome. These converts tended to pick from Christian religion what suited them and left the mainline churches to start their own congregations. It is interesting to note that it was in Colenso's diocese that Isaiah Shembe's movement began. The members of the sect called themselves 'Nazarites', with their headquarters at Ekuphakameni. In Isaiah Shembe's sect, polygamous practices were not frowned upon by any of the members. Colenso, on the other hand, refused to allow baptized Christians to acquire more wives than they already had before their baptism.

6. Colenso's Flaws

A tribute to Colenso as having taken an urgent stride towards indigenization does not by any means portray him as a paragon. Throughout his exposition, Colenso was primarily concerned with the problem of polygamous men and had very little to say about women who were living in polygamous alliances. Colenso (1862a: 79) wrote that he was willing 'not to act at variance with the general practice'. Here he begins to stand out like a solicitor who realizes that his/her solicitation has not swayed the judge and begins to proffer extenuating circumstances to mollify his/her client. Colenso gave himself away by intimating that he would defer baptism until there was a significant reduction of a man's wives 'by natural and providential causes, to one' (1862a: 79).

Callaway's response to Colenso was even more lethal in his attitude towards wives who were living in polygamous alliances. Callaway robbed them of their status as wives and reduced them to the status of *amadikazi* or *oomabuyekwendeni*. It was Shepstone, the Secretary for Native Affairs in Natal, who had once asked an apposite question: 'Why attempt to destroy their self-respect, by inducing them to believe, contrary to fact, that they are not (wives)?' (G. Callaway 1926: 93). Since Callaway denied them the status of wives they were dispensable. He suggested that it would be uncouth of a converted polygamist to drive away his wives, while it was 'his duty to separate from them... The man may take his one wife; the others should be set completely at liberty... And of course the put-away wives might marry of their own accord' (H. Callaway 1862: 96-97). Just like in Colenso we see in Callaway that a man's salvation takes precedence over that of his wives. Putting-away or separating from one's wives meant one and the same thing, which amounted to getting rid of one's wives.

Colenso's tergiversation towards the end of his letter to Archbishop Longley portrayed that there was no fundamental difference between him and Callaway. Both were advocates of monogamy. While Callaway encouraged polygamists who wanted to embrace Christianity to chase away, or separate from, their superfluous wives, Colenso's solution was to wait for fate in the form of death to intervene. Callaway claimed that as a result of a lack of 'solemn obligation' polygamous alliances did not provide the quintessential bonding between a man and his wives, and if there was any bonding at all it existed more in 'imagination' than in reality (H. Callaway 1862: 11-12). Callaway made two bold assertions: first, that among Africans divorce was 'an easier matter than marriage' and, second, that married Africans separated 'one from the other for the most trivial causes' (pp. 15, 19). For Colenso, a polygamous marriage contracted before one's conversion was a marriage *par excellence*.

It is interesting to note that for Shepstone there was absolutely no doubt about the validity of polygamous marriages. He did not sympathize with those who would 'teach a heathen, as a duty enjoined by our Christian religion, that (a man) must injure another, to benefit himself—that he must commit an unlawful act...and a reckless sacrifice of the interests of others, to further his own' (Colenso 1862a: 92).

304   *The Eye of the Storm*

7. *The Vindication of Colenso*

The problem of polygamy was revisited by the Lambeth Conference of 1988 and the resolution, which had been passed hundred years previously was rescinded. The reason for this *volte-face* is not too hard to find. Unlike the Lambeth Conference of 1888 that of 1988 consisted of a fair number of African and Indian bishops who had first-hand information on the problem of polygamy. Apart from this, the 1988 Lambeth Conference was confronted with a whole array of sexual problems and the Bishops must have wanted to deal decisively with the problem of polygamy and the diction of the resolution was a blatant vindication of Colenso.

1. The resolution that the bishops passed could have been drawn by Colenso because two of its four clauses encapsulated all what Colenso had put forward some 106 years ago. Resolution 26 of The Lambeth Conference 1988 on Church and Polygamy said:

2. This Conference upholds monogamy as God's plan, as the ideal of relationship of love between husband and wife; nevertheless recommends that a polygamist who responds to the Gospel and wishes to join the Anglican Church may be baptized and confirmed with his believing wives and children on the following conditions:

3. that the polygamist shall promise not to marry again as long as any of his wives at the time of his conversion are alive;

4. that the receiving of such a polygamist has the consent of the local Anglican community;

5. that such a polygamist shall not be compelled to put away any of his wives on account of the social deprivation they would suffer.

8. *Closing the Stable Door*

With the Lambeth Resolution of 1988 any discourse that purports to refute Colenso's position on the question of polygamy would almost amount to locking the stable after the horse has bolted because the matter has now been laid to rest. There is no doubt, though, that the Lambeth Conference of 1988 marked a significant shift from the emphasis on justification by law in 1888 to justification by grace. In a sense the Lambeth Conference of 1988 could be said to have lived up to the parable of the wheat and the tares.

9. The Unfinished Business

The Lambeth Resolution of 1988 provides only a partial solution to the problem of polygamy. It provides useful guidelines for people who are in polygamous alliance before their conversion to Christianity. There are those Africans who are baptized as infants and grow up as Christians. These contract monogamous marriages and pretend to disdain polygamy even though they have no qualms about acquiring a bevy of mistresses. There are also those Christian Africans who contract polygamous marriages later on in life. Do such Africans fall outside the pale of Christ's salvation? Some of the Christians who relapse into polygamy contend that Christianity embraced them before they embraced it. These are people who are baptized as infants and become regular in their church attendance either out of parental obligation or because it is fashionable to do so. That is an acute problem that needs to be addressed but unfortunately it falls outside the scope of this paper.

THE TRIAL OF BISHOP JOHN WILLIAM COLENSO*

Jonathan A. Draper

1. *Introduction*

When Bishop John William Colenso received a summons to attend a trial for heresy from his Metropolitan, Robert Gray, he chose not to attend, but to appeal immediately to the Privy Council against Gray's right to hold such a trial. This decision was presented to Gray's court by Dr Bleek, the Lutheran Curator of the Grey Library. His trial and conviction for heresy hit the British public at the same time as his enormously controversial *Commentary on the Pentateuch*. Colenso promoted his critical challenge to the inerrancy of the Old Testament vigorously, while he waited patiently for the result of the Privy Council's judgment. Their rejection of the validity of Gray's Letters Patent of the Crown and hence of his right to try in a court of law the Bishop of Natal, whose Letters Patent were valid in their finding, gave Colenso a moment of respite from the storm which had hurtled around him. But it was only a respite, as he well knew. Like the stubborn captain of the *Nan-Shan* trapped in the eye of the storm, in Joseph Conrad's short story, *Typhoon*, Colenso held to his principles as the only way forward through the coming crisis:

> 'Don't you be put out by anything', the Captain continued, mumbling rather fast. 'Keep her facing it. They may say what they like, but the heaviest seas run with the wind. Facing it—always facing it—that's the way to get through. You are a young sailor. Face it. That's enough for any man. Keep a cool head.'

Colenso's unshakeable trust in the triumph of truth and justice sustained him in both his struggles over the Bible and doctrine and also over the rights of the Zulu people. He believed that the truth would prevail in the

* This paper was written with the assistance of a grant from the USPG to enable me to conduct archival research in their archives at Rhodes House, Oxford. I am very grateful for their generous support and encouragement.

end. Bishop Robert Gray, his implacable opponent, declares in a letter dated 11 June 1865 to his ally at the Society for the Propagation of the Gospel (SPG) in London concerning him, 'I never met with a more unscrupulous man' (USPG Archives D-24b-8128). Gray succeeded in destroying Colenso as a Churchman by silencing his voice, making sure there was never the possibility of an appeal against his excommunication in a legal court, and by using his class position as a son of the Bishop of Bristol, who had married into the landed gentry, to influence powerful people in England. Whether his theology was right or wrong, however, there is no doubt that Colenso was a man of impeccable integrity, acting out of a sense of duty to the truth. If anything, he was not so much 'unscrupulous' as over-scrupulous, like Conrad's sea captain. Yet he was excommunicated from the Anglican Church in South Africa by the Metropolitan, Robert Gray, and this judgment remains in force to this day.

This paper raises again the issue of the trial that condemned Colenso, arguing that an injustice has been done which needs to be addressed for the sake of the integrity of the Church by which he was excommunicated. It is important for the Church to recognize its own historical limitations and fallibility. There is no doubt about Bishop Robert Gray's sincerity and passionate conviction of the justice of his cause. Nevertheless it is time to recognize that the way he proceeded with his trial of Colenso was a mistake that inflicted considerable pain on Colenso and his family and considerable damage on the Church itself in Natal and Zululand.

My feeling is that any 'exculpation' of Colenso, or rescinding of the pronouncement of excommunication, should not be based primarily on a reconsideration of whether he is or is not heretical in his theology. There is unlikely to be any unanimity as to what constitutes heresy today, any more than there was in Colenso's time. Elsewhere in this volume, sufficient evidence has been produced to show that Colenso remains within the bounds of acceptable diversity in the Anglican Church, as this is expressed today. In his own day he certainly stood on the boundary, or as we would say today, 'on the cutting edge of theology'. Yet, even then, he was not alone. The authors of the *Essays and Reviews* published in 1860, some of whom were prosecuted but exonerated in court in England, some of whom later became significant and influential Churchmen, were in broad agreement with Colenso on the need for transformation in Church and theology in their day. By 1889, with the publication of a further collection of essays, *Lux Mundi*, the kind of position adopted by Colenso had become established, albeit still controversial, within the Church. Today, Colenso's ideas are not only acceptable within the broad stream of Anglican unity and diversity, but are enthusiastically endorsed by many as visionary and courageous, though there are still many who would reject them now as the majority did in his own day. It seems that he was right in his claim, 'I am not conscious that in any of my published writings I have transgressed the limits allowed to the clergy of the National Church, by whose laws only I am bound, to whose authority only I will be responsible' (Colenso's Letter to Gray of 1 January 1866).

Certainly, there is a need for continuing exploration and evaluation of Colenso's theological, biblical and hermeneutical positions. He was right in some matters and wrong in others, but he remained within the mainstream of Christian thought and not outside it. It is remarkable therefore, that a Church court could solemnly and publicly find him guilty of heresy and even more remarkable that the Dean of the Cathedral in Pietermaritzburg could feel no qualms in solemnly reading out the sentence of excommunication in Bishop Colenso's own cathedral, pronouncing him a 'heathen and a sinner', separate from the Church and presumably condemned to burn in the hell whose existence he himself rejected. It is this extreme intolerance on the part of the hierarchy in the Church of the Province in Colenso's case that really falls outside the bounds of acceptable Anglican diversity and not the thinking of Colenso himself. Moreover the process of his trial and excommunication itself was, this paper will argue, irregular and outside the norms of due process and fundamental justice.

2. *The Case of Reverend William Long*

The trial of Bishop Colenso did not happen in a vacuum. It follows on from and is affected by the trial and appeal of Reverend William Long, a clergyman from Mowbray who had refused to attend the Synod called in 1856 by Bishop Robert Gray, on the grounds that he had no authority to call it. When he continued to defy Gray, he was tried and dismissed from his benefice. Colenso appealed to the Crown against Gray's right to try him, as expected, the Crown and Cape Town referred the matter to the Privy Council in England. Despite his protestations to the contrary, Gray's decision to defend the case in the Privy Council constituted a recognition of the appellate jurisdiction of the Privy Council in matters relating to the Church in South Africa (Hinchliffe 1964: 152-53). The ruling of the Privy Council (*Privy Council* 1863) in the matter of Long was delivered on 24 June 1863, upholding the rights of Long and finding against the authority of Gray to hold an ecclesiastical court in the Cape. Indeed, it found that Gray's Letters Patent of the Crown, creating him Bishop of Cape Town and Metropolitan of South Africa, were invalid. It held that Letters Patent of the Crown could run only in England or in a Crown Colony, but that the Cape had become self-governing between the issuing of Gray's first Letters Patent in 1847 and the new Letters Patent in 1853. Hence the Crown had no jurisdiction in the Cape, except through the colonial legislature, and the validity of Gray's old Letters Patent ended with his resignation of them in 1853 without the Crown having any power to issue new ones: 'it is quite clear that the Crown had no power to confer any jurisdiction or coercive legal authority upon the Metropolitan over the Suffragan Bishops, or over any other person' (*Privy Council* 1863). Therefore *Gray had no coercive jurisdiction* over the Church of England in South Africa (the Church of the Province of South Africa having not yet been constituted) beyond that of the leader of a voluntary society.

However, the Privy Council did provide Gray with a way out of the impossible dilemma this placed him in as Metropolitan, namely, the principle of the authority of a Visitor sitting *in foro domestico*, which already applied to cases between members of dissenting churches in England, who were not bound by the laws relating to the Church of England. This grants them the status of a voluntary society and their disciplinary proceedings the status of an internal legal tribunal with the right to enforce adherence to their own constitution. Under these provisions, the proceedings of such a Visitor must nevertheless be 'conducted with that attention to the rules of substantial justice and that strict impartiality which were necessary to be observed by all tribunals, however little fettered by forms' where care must be taken 'to secure, as far as possible, the impartiality and knowledge of a judicial tribunal' (*Privy Council* 1863). Here, the Privy Council found that Gray had not acted entirely impartially as judge, nor had he passed sentence on the basis of 'the only charge he had been summoned to meet' but on 'what are termed repeated acts of disobedience and contempt by Mr Long, instead of on the single charge which he was called upon by the citation to meet'. Hence the Privy Council did not consider the proceedings to have been properly conducted. This is important, because the trial of Colenso conducted by Gray, even if it were considered as proceeding *in foro domestico*, would be obliged to pay substantial attention to the criticisms of the Privy Council concerning his handling of the case against Long. His hearing would have to meet the conditions of fundamental justice, regardless of the questions of the belief systems espoused by a private society, if that was the basis of the court's claim to legitimacy.

3. *The Trial of Bishop Colenso*

On 18 May 1863 Bishop Gray summonsed Bishop Colenso to appear before a metropolitan court on a charge of heresy brought by Dean Douglas of Cape Town, and Archdeacons Badnall of George and Merriman of Grahamstown. Although Gray claims that 'The clergy of Natal' were the ones who presented the bishop for erroneous teaching (Letter to the SPG, 8 June 1863 [USPG-CLR-115-180-84]), it is strange that the case was presented by those not under the authority of the Bishop of Natal and therefore not directly affected by the alleged heresies, but rather by the Cape bishops, on the grounds that the books had been distributed in the Cape. He was instructed to appear on 17 November 1863. The ruling of the Privy Council in the matter of Reverend Long was handed down on 24 June 1863. Despite its ruling that he had no legal jurisdiction as Metropolitan, Gray persisted with the trial. He does not take account of the criticisms of the Privy Council concerning his conduct in the case of Long. Instead he repeatedly complains about the 'wrongs of the Privy Council':

> But it [the Privy Council ruling] mentions a number of points connected with the trial, and misrepresents every one of them, in a way to arouse feeling against myself, so to make it appear that I was unfair to Long, and wholly unfit to have the conduct of Colenso's trial. I have pointed out some of these in a letter to the Church Court of Mowbray, which *the Guardian ought* to insert, as it inserted in a leading article the judges attack upon me; but there are others which I did not touch upon which are not creditable to the accuracy or fairness of the Court. But enough of this judgment. It is a disastrous one for the Church. (Letter to Bullock, 2 September 1863 [USPG-D-24b-11065])

Gray already indicates his intention to defy the ruling, taking up the decision of the Privy Council concerning the Church's status as a voluntary society, but not registering its comments concerning the requirements of fundamental justice in such a disciplinary hearing *in foro domestico*:

> While refusing to recognize the Church here as a body, so regarding it as consisting only of certain individuals who enter into a contract with each other, it regards us as bound by an unknown quantity of English law. It leaves us quite uncertain what law it chooses to regard as residing upon us. Everything here is vague and indefinite. I believe the true state of the case to be this. No statute law prevails here. It is expressly excluded by treaty. We carry along with us the Church's own laws—accepted or framed by her, and none other. But if so, these not only authorize but require the Bishop to summon his Synod—allow of the presence of the laity—require the Priest

to attend the Synod—and make its decisions the laws of the Diocese,—or Province. All this the Judgment denies, and it places all Colonial Churches, who cannot or will not go to Parliament for an act in a worse position than the heathen Emperors placed the Church of their day. They recognized (as the Courts in America do at this day) the Church as a body—so pronounce the decision of its Synod to be the laws of that religious association. (*Privy Council* 1863)

He makes it clear in a further letter to Bullock on 18th December 1863 (USPG-D-24b- 2102) that 'I do not mean to defend either my jurisdiction, or my doctrine in a Civil Court, if I should be assailed in that directly. I will not do so, on principle'.

The problem with Gray's position here is that he did not have any authority to hold a trial except on the basis of the authority granted him as Metropolitan by Letters Patent, which he never renounced publicly. He did, in any case, defend his position before the Privy Council in the appeal concerning the trial of Colenso, thereby recognizing the jurisdiction of the Privy Council in the matter. He did not, as Colenso did with regard to Gray's court, protest the validity of the jurisdiction of the Privy Council in England. Second, he is still basing his authority as Metropolitan on his Letters Patent of the Crown in his official notification of excommunication to Colenso of 13 December 1865:

I put this prominently forward because it seems to have been the course decided upon by the Crown and the Church, at the foundation of the See, and marked out in the Letters Patent... Because it expressly provided in the Letters Patent founding the several Sees of this Province that the gravest spiritual causes in this portion of the Church shall be finally decided by Bishops only. (*Letters from the Archbishop of Canterbury et al* 1866: 15-16)

Third, he failed to pick up the second half of the judgment in the case of Long, namely, that his hearing, even if it has only the status of that of a voluntary society, was still bound by the rules of fundamental justice and was still subject to appeal to a court of law. Basically, Gray considered he had been wronged in the matter of the Letters Patent by judges acting 'out of hatred to all spiritual authority'. Gray utilized the principle of voluntary association as a means of defiance without considering its legal implications as he wrote in a letter to Bullock on 15 October 1863:

The World cannot best the Church in such as case as this, if the Church is true to herself. Civil Courts may control property, but they cannot bind the conscience, or restrain the exercise by the Church of her Spiritual functions. These the World did not give, and cannot take away. Nothing has so disheartened me as the low worldly view that Churchmen take of their respon-

The Eye of the Storm

sibilities to Christ in such a case as this. *The Guardian* is really sickening. Really is it not so, that Christ in our day bids fair to be sold over again for 30 pieces of silver—and the Church is ready to believe what the Lord Chancellor tells it shall be its Creed? (USPG-D24b-5183)

The change of status forced on an (unwilling) Metropolitan did not absolve him of civil accountability before the courts, even in matters spiritual.

3.1. *The Status of a Court Acting* in Foro Domestico

For instance, as the Privy Council pointed out in its judgment in their ruling on Gray's trial of Colenso, the Bishop of Natal could not be considered subject to a hearing *in foro domestico*, since he had never given consent to the coercive authority of Gray. Colenso's Letters Patent were drawn up on 23 November 1853 and he was consecrated on 30 November 1853, while Gray's (defective) Letters Patent, which included the proviso of powers of coercion over other bishops as Metropolitan, were drawn up only on 8 December 1853, 15 days after Colenso's Letters Patent were drawn up and eight days after Colenso had been already consecrated. As the Privy Council rightly points out, there was no possibility that Colenso knew of, or was party to, the powers of coercion granted to Gray at the time of his consecration and of his taking of the oath of canonical obedience to Gray, since they exceeded the powers enjoyed by an English Metropolitan in his Province at the time. Hence it was not just or reasonable to expect him to submit to a court convened under terms to which he was not party. Thus, even if Gray's authority derived from his position within a voluntary society, he could not exercise it over one who had not legally and voluntarily placed himself under his authority. This Colenso did not do, despite Gray's pronouncement in his judgment against him that he had 'recognized both the office and the jurisdiction' of the court at his consecration (*Trial Reports* 1863: 340).

3.2. *Trial* in Absentia

Bishop Colenso was tried *in absentia*, having already indicated his rejection of the jurisdiction of the court. It was for this reason that he chose to send a legal representative, Dr Bleek, who was not even Anglican, who simply presented his position and gave notice of Colenso's intention to appeal any judgment Gray might make. Bishop Gray tried on several occasions to draw Dr Bleek into the proceedings in order to make it appear as if Colenso presented some kind of defence (*Trial Reports* 1863: 40, 258-59, 272), but Bleek made it quite clear throughout that he would do nothing which might be construed as a recognition of the jurisdiction of the court. The outcome of the appeal fully justified Colenso's position in law. Yet the Privy Council did not make any finding in the matter of the substance of the charges of heresy presented against Colenso, since it was not asked to do so and did not consider it necessary to go further than a declaration that the trial was null and void in law. However, the effect of this decision by Colenso not to appear before Gray was that he was never given a legal forum to defend his theological position against the attacks on him by the High Church party in South Africa. He was never heard in his own defence. Gray's court in Cape Town in its judgment explicitly excluded any right of appeal for Colenso. Instead, Gray allowed that Colenso could submit himself to the mercy of the Archbishop of Canterbury. It was a legal choice that Gray exploited astutely to proceed with the excommunication of Colenso on the basis of a court whose legal status was overturned.

3.3. *The Impartiality of the Presiding Judge*

Colenso was tried by Gray as presiding judge when Gray had already publicly and privately, in letters I have read, declared Colenso guilty. When he first read the *Commentary on Romans*, Gray had already declared in 1861 that 'on the Inspiration of Holy Scripture, Justification (all heathen, etc., are "righteous and accepted before God from their birth"), Original Sin, the Sacraments, the Judgment, Eternal Punishment, Universal Salvation—he has propounded opinions at variance with those of the Church' (Lewis and Edwards 1934: 162). This means that he could not have served as an impartial judge. Again, in a letter to Reverend Bullock of the SPG dated 10 August 1863, months before the trial, he writes of his determination to ignore the Long judgment, but also speaks of the 'Natal business' as presenting a 'fresh anxiety'. In this context he discusses the dangerous growth of 'liberalism' among the Dutch clergy and his determination to stamp it out in his own Church:

> I reckon that about two fifth of the Dutch Clergy, are liberals, i.e. more or less rationalistic. They are to have another Synod in October to expel liberalism that is spreading. Thank God not one clergyman as far as I know holding a spiritual office in this Province sympathizes with their views, nor do I think that more than a very few of our laity do; but the public do in some measure, especially the Dutch portion of it, do. And this brings such subjects as Inspiration—the Atonement—the perfect Divinity and humanity of our Lord, into public discussion, must admit I hope the good, do not a little learn. May yet over-rule it all for good. We have an anxious time

before us; but I believe, happen what will, Bishops and Clergy, at least, will
do what they believe their duty as the great head of the Church requires.
(USPG Archives D-24-no reference number)

It is obvious that these questions that he sees as so dangerous and needing
to be rooted out in the Dutch Church and his own are the very ones of
which Colenso is charged and found guilty. Gray could in no way act as an
impartial judge under such conditions.

In a letter to Bullock on 19 November 1863, in the middle of the trial,
he inveigles against Bishop Shelby for not attending the trial because it
undermines the 'cause' (that is, of destroying Colenso): 'It is the greatest
flaw in our proceedings that he is not here. I hate that shrinking from
responsibility in the cause.' Further, he comments on the submission of the
prosecution: 'The Dean has made a noble address. For oratory, grandness
of subject, argument, theology, clarity of style it is equal to anything I ever
heard. There are few even in Europe who could have made such an
address.' Finally, he ridicules Colenso's choice of representative: 'The
Bishop appears by Dr Bleeks, an unbeliever, I believe' (USPG Archives
D-24-12531). In a further letter to Bullock on 18 December 1863, two
days after the judgment had been delivered, Gray writes that, 'We bishops
have worked together as Brethren. Our documents are our joint production.
We have worked apart many hours daily for five weeks, and compared
notes each day, and revised each other's productions' (USPG Archives
D-24-2102). The assessors hardly represented independent judgments,
though it is unclear to me how much this might be allowable between
presiding judge and assessors in a court of law.

The judgment of the Privy Council in the case of Long had already
declared Gray to be a problematic judge, since he was not impartial in the
case, having already become emotionally involved, and also since he had
no legal training. This applies every bit as much in the case of Colenso—
probably more so. The judgment argued that although Gray did not have
authority under British law to judge, nevertheless, even if the matter were
that of a voluntary association and therefore that he had 'to act with the
authority of a Visitor sitting *in foro domestico*', it remains a valid legal
question whether the proceedings were conducted with attention to the
rules of substantial justice and strict impartiality which are necessary to be
observed by all tribunals, 'however little fettered by forms'. Hence 'care
should have been taken to secure, as far as possible, the impartiality and
knowledge of a judicial tribunal'. With regard to Gray's procedure the
Privy Council comments:

Here the Bishop was not merely in form but substantially the prosecutor, and a prosecutor whose feelings, from motives of public duty as well as from the heat necessarily generated in the purest minds by a long and eager controversy, were deeply interested in the question. It was, perhaps, necssary that he should preside as the Judge before whom the cause was heard, and by whom the sentence was pronounced; but he should have procured, as a Bishop in England under such circumstances would have done, the advice and assistance, as Assessors, of men of legal knowledge and habits, unconnected with the matter in dispute, and have left it to them to frame the decision which he would afterwards pronounce. But instead of adopting this course, he selected as assistants three gentlemen, all Clergymen sharing his own opinions on the subject of controversy, and all themselves members of that Synod which Mr Long was accused of treating as illegal.

There were changes of procedure for Colenso, but most of the same legal comments would be valid in Colenso's case.

As Colenso himself points out in his letter to Gray in a reply to his notice of excommunication, while he himself writes with the utmost respect for the views and convictions of others, even when he considers them to be wrong, Gray has continued to use insulting and *ad hominem* language concerning him:

> Whatever 'supposed' heresies you might detect and deplore in my writings, yet I consider that the tone of every one of my books, from the Commentary on the Romans to the last volume on the Pentateuch, ought at least to have protected me from being publicly charged by you—in the house of God—in my own cathedral church—with 'reckless arrogance, like that which marked the infidels of the last century', with 'using the language of the boaster and the scorner', with 'being led captive by the Evil One', with 'having forsaken the Living Word of God'. I utterly deny that I have 'given any just ground' for these imputations. (*Letters from the Archbishop of Canterbury et al.* 1866: 7)

The two other bishops in this case could scarcely be regarded as impartial. They were both members of the High Church faction of the Church of England to which Gray also belonged. Bishop Twells, in particular, was capable of quite bizarrely partisan behaviour, as in the case of his visitation to the Diocese of Natal in October 1867, which ended in a public scandal. Cotterill had corresponded with Colenso in 1857 about his rejection about the legality of Gray's coercive jurisdiction. Yet he agreed to play the role of assessor bishop in a court he had rejected in private correspondence. He would not allow Colenso, in his own defence, to publish the letters he had written to that effect and Colenso was too honourable a man to proceed without his permission:

And as I cannot do what the Bishop of CT [Cape Town] has done, who has taken my private letters, written (as he says in his *Statement*, p. 6, which a friend has just sent me, though it was published at the beginning of the year in England) when 'we were brothers, our correspondence was unceasing and most confidential',—letters beginning 'My dear Brother', and ending 'Yours affectionately', in reply to his own, using the same terms,—and has 'preserved them', as he says, 'in his registry' for public purposes, I am debarred from making that free use of these [letters from Cotterill] which I had hoped and desired. I will say, however, that we freely imparted our thoughts to one another about the said clause, which I had just seen for the first time, when I received in Oct., 1857, from Bp Gray, a copy of the 'Acts and Constitutions' of his first Synod, at the end of which his Letters Patent were printed. We agreed that it was of the utmost consequence that we should not in any way admit the principle, that the Metropolitan was *episcopus episcoporum*; and we resolved that, if he should at any time exercise jurisdiction over us, we must require him to proceed by a regular process, and issue a final sentence *such as would form the ground for an appeal to an Ecclesiastical Court in England*. We repeated to each other again and again that the obedience we owed to him as Metropolitan was simply '*canonical*' obedience, 'all *due* obedience', and that he had no right to interfere with either of us, except we overstepped the bounds *of English ecclesiastical law*,—that we must in a spirit of love and meekness, but with much firmness, resist the Bishop of Cape Town's claims,—he had certain precedents, and due reverence and obedience *according to law*, but we must stand on the position that our episcopal rights and authority were as good as his. We both rejected the designation adopted by the Bishop of Cape Town, 'the Church in this diocese in union and full communion with the United Church of England & Ireland'. (*Pamphlet of the Natal Church Clergy Fund* 76 of February 1868 in USPG Archives)

In other words, the two assessor bishops and Gray himself as presiding judge were all caught up in the dispute themselves and were not sufficiently impartial to judge the matter in a manner consonant with fundamental principles of legal justice. Jones (1987: 193) comments of Colenso: 'Convinced, though perhaps unfairly, that he could expect no justice from Gray or the systems he controlled, he appealed directly to the Crown-in-Council, that is, the Judicial Committee'. It seems, on the contrary, that Colenso had every reason to 'expect no justice' from Gray and his courts.

3.4. *The Use of Private Correspondence in the Trial*
Despite the fact that Colenso was forbidden to use correspondence from Cotterill to himself in his own defence, letters he had written to Gray, the

presiding judge, personally, as 'My Dear Brother', were used as evidence in the trial against him. Worse, they were presented either as evidence against him or as evidence for Colenso's own defence, in an attempt to give legitimacy to the trial—whichever suited. Surely this would constitute a compromising of the impartiality of the judge in any trial. Seven letters from Colenso to Gray were brought forward by Gray as evidence. What is worse, they were mostly only 'extracts', so that the whole context of the passages was excluded (*Trial Reports* 1863: 33-36).

In particular, a substantial letter he had written to Gray on 7 August 1861 (*Trial Reports* 1863: 244-58), in a conciliatory manner, attempting to explain himself to Gray, was presented by Gray as evidence for the defence, when Colenso had specifically refused to defend himself on the grounds that he did not recognize the court's jurisdiction:

> The Bishop of Cape Town said: The case for the prosecution having been closed I call upon the Registrar to read a letter of the Bishop of Natal which he has put in his defence, and to which he has called the special attention of the Court. The letter to which it is a reply is on the table for the use of the prosecuting clergy if they desire to have it. (*Trial Reports* 1863: 244)

In the letter, Colenso shows himself to be respectful of the right of Gray to differ from his opinions, even if he misunderstands some of them. He agrees that the matters are of fundamental importance and concern, and begs Gray to accept that he too is acting out of the deepest religious sincerity and conviction:

> My dear Brother,—I thank you sincerely for your letter on the subject of my Commentary on the Epistle to the Romans. I cannot be surprised at your writing so earnestly and seriously, holding the views that you do on some of the points that I have discussed. But, as you will have learned from my last letter, it is too late now to stop the publication of the book, even if I desired to do so. Whatever you may think it right to say or do in the matter, I am quite sure that you will only act from a sense of duty to what you believe to be the truth, which compels you to set aside all personal feelings, in obedience to a higher law. In writing what I have written, and publishing it, I, too, have done the same, though conscious that I should thereby cause pain to yourself, and others, whom I entirely esteem and love. It is true that you have mistaken some of my expressions; others (forgive me for saying it) you seem to me to have misjudged. But in respect of others, I am well aware that my views differ strongly from yours; though I believe that I have said nothing in my book which is not in accordance with the teaching of the Bible, or which transcends the limits so liberally allowed by the Church of England for freedom of thought on such subjects. (*Trial Reports* 1863: 244)

This letter was then submitted to the court and Gray turned to Bleek, who was present as an observer, and seeks to involve him at this point (obviously to strengthen the idea that this letter represents Colenso's defence). Bleek denies that he has any instructions or role in the matter beyond what he has already presented:

> I do not, my Lord [desire to say anything on behalf of the Bishop]. But may I make one personal remark? I came here for a threefold purpose. First, for the purpose of protesting, and secondly,—in the event of your Lordships, notwithstanding that protest, assuming jurisdiction—to read a letter, and thirdly, to give notice of appeal. I have no instructions to do anything further. But I see it has been stated by the Registrar that some of these papers have been inspected by me. The Registrar, it is true, showed me some papers, but I stated to him at the time that this must not be construed into my having allowed, in any way, on behalf of the Bishop of Natal, the admissibility of these papers. I could not do so, as I had no authority, and I must protest against its being supposed that I did. (*Trial Reports* 1863: 259)

Despite this protest, Gray continued the exchange, offering to make any papers or information available to Bleek if he requests it, despite his repeated refusals! The prosecution then argued that, despite Colenso's absence, nevertheless the letter to Gray constitutes a sufficient defence:

> Had he been present, I have no doubt he would have said a great deal; but at the same time I think we must regard this document which I have now printed before me as being in reality the substance of all that he could have said. (*Trial Reports* 1863: 260)

At the same time, it is held to have actually strengthened the case for the prosecution:

> I must say that, to my own mind, and, I believe, also to the minds of those who are associated with me, instead of in any degree weakening our case, or refuting or setting aside our arguments, it has, upon very many of the main and important points, confirmed and strengthened them. (*Trial Reports* 1863: 260)

For the presiding judge of a court to admit as evidence for the defence something written in a private letter to himself by the accused, without his permission, and which is used only to strengthen the case for the prosecution, since it is not cross-examined for the defence, is a gross violation of judicial procedure.

3.5. The Use of 'Cumulative Charges'

One of the legal procedures for which the Privy Council censured Gray's court in the case of Gray vs. Long was that he did not proceed only on the basis of the charge for which Long was summonsed, but on actions of Long external to or subsequent to the charge, so that the case was cumulative rather than specific:

> Mr. Long was cited for refusing to give the required notice, but the sentence was not grounded entirely on this charge...and from the language of the Bishop in delivering his Judgment it may be inferred that the sentence against Mr. Long was not founded entirely on the only charge which he had been summoned to meet. (*Privy Council* 1863)

This opinion of the Privy Council is affirmed again in its judgment in the trial of the authors in *Essays and Reviews*, Brodrick and Fremantle, that 'the accuser is, for the purpose of the charge, confined to the passages which are included and set out in the articles as the matter of the accusa-ion' (*Letters from the Archbishop of Canterbury et al.* 1866: 26-27). Gray specifically uses the argument of 'cumulative evidence' in his judgment:

> Now language such as that which I have quoted has constrained me to declare that the teaching of the Bishop on the great subject of the Atone-ment was not so at variance with that of the Church as to call for any con-demnation, did it stand alone. There are, however, other passages in his work besides those complained of, which show that he uses the words 'atonement', 'redemption', 'sacrifice', 'satisfaction', 'propitiation',—which are, so to speak, ecclesiastical and historical words,—in a sense of his own; that he does not mean what the Church intends by them, and that while using them, he repudiates some portion of the truth which they teach. (*Trial Reports* 1863: 346-47)

This makes it clear that in some, at least, of the charges, Gray would have been forced to acquit Colenso if he had simply been tried on the basis of the charges as given. Evidence which should have been ruled as inadmis-sible by the court forms the basis of part of his judgment. Gray acts *ultra vires* as the presiding judge in this instance, and should have known that if he had taken account of the findings of the Privy Council in the matter of Gray vs. Long.

3.6. Refusal of Leave to Appeal

In view of the extremely controversial nature of both his court and the subject matter of the judgment, it would have been a fundamental require-ment of justice, in my opinion, that the accused be given leave to appeal the judgment. Where there is even a modicum of doubt concerning the jurisdiction of a court, the constitutionality of a judgment or the admissibility of evidence, there should indeed be a recommendation that the matter be taken on appeal. This should particularly be so where the accused has made the matter the basis of his defence, and did not appear in person or by proxy. In this case, Gray was in no doubt as to the dubious nature in terms of the law of the jurisdiction he was exercising. Even if he had based his right to hold the court on the basis of the Church's status as a voluntary society, something entirely new and untested arising out of the Gray vs. Long finding, he should have recommended that the procedure and findings of the court be tested by a competent higher court in terms of the new situation.

Colenso had made it quite clear that he intended to appeal. However, Gray in response concluded his judgment with a refusal of the right of appeal:

> The Bishop of Cape Town: I cannot recognize any appeal except to His Grace the Archbishop of Canterbury, and I must require that appeal to be made within fifteen days from the present time. (*Trial Reports* 1863: 405)

Gray made it quite clear that this appeal could only be to the Archbishop himself in person (who was avowedly and publicly supportive of Gray and hostile to Colenso even before the trial was convened) and not in an ecclesiastical court. Previous attempts to prove heresy in English ecclesiastical courts had shown the difficulty of doing so, and that the English courts insisted on a very specific charge based on contravention of the 39 Articles and Formularies alone, without allowing the kind of elaborate arguments from the early Church Fathers, liturgy, councils and creeds of the early Church favoured by Gray's Cape Town court. Colenso himself was quite willing to accept an appeal to the Archbishop of Canterbury, but not in his personal capacity, but in an ecclesiastical court competent to try such matters:

> I am quite ready to submit my writings, in accordance with the provisions in your own Letters Patent, to the Archbishop of Canterbury—not, of course, to the Archbishop in person, for that would be a mere idle form, since His Grace has repeatedly, and even within the last month, condemned me unheard, and evidently, as I have said, without having even read my books. But I am ready to submit them to the Archbishop of Canterbury, sitting in his Ecclesiastical Court, before which the case of any clergyman of his province, and of every dignitary below a Bishop, might be brought by appeal. But your own counsel, Sir H. Cairns, admitted that there must lie

from the Archbishop a further appeal to the Crown; and, as you are also aware, the Privy Council laid down the law that for us to make an agreement with one another to ignore the supreme authority of the Crown in such a case, would be an *illegal* act on our part. I am not prepared to violate the law of the land for the purpose of supporting ecclesiastical authority. I reserve, therefore, my right of finally appealing to Her Majesty; and surely, as I have said, you cannot be justified in assuming beforehand that in such a case as this, involving questions of *doctrine*, a Commission would be appointed consisting only of lay judges. The duty of a loyal subject would seem to be to await and see what would actually be done, and then, if felt to be necessary as a 'matter of conscience', to protest against the *constitution* or the *decision* of such a court, and to disregard and disobey it, taking the consequences. (*Letters from the Archbishop of Canterbury et al.* 1866: 12)

It is quite clear that Gray was unwilling to allow an appeal to the Ecclesiastical Courts, despite the belief of Bishop Tait of London, who later Archbishop of Canterbury, and Gladstone, the British Prime Minister (Jones 1987: 194), that this was the correct course of action, because he believed he would lose. In this he was correct, as demonstrated by the judgment of the Privy Council in the case of the *Essays and Reviews* authors Williams and Wilson, whose sentence by Judge Lushington was under appeal at the time of Colenso's own trial. The Privy Council acquitted them of all counts in February 1864. Their case paralleled Colenso's own case in many important respects, as both Gray and Colenso recognized. Colenso wrote to Shepstone:

I need not say that it sweeps away at a stroke the whole farrago of the Bishop of Capetown's judgement... And on every single point of the nine (on which they have condemned me) which has been under discussion in the English courts, either in the Gorham judgment, or Lushington's, or this last of the Privy Council, *I* am justified and they are condemned. (Cox 1888: 249)

Gray, for his part, wrote to Bullock on 4 April 1864 on hearing of the judgment, 'This judgment covers all that Colenso has written' (*USPG Archives D-24b*). Hence, it was on the basis of his recognition that he would lose any appeal to an Ecclesiastical Court in England which led Gray to refuse Colenso right of appeal. It was the knowledge that he already had the support of the Archbishop of Canterbury that led him to confine right of appeal to the Archbishop personally and not the Archbishop in a competent court.

In sum, Gray's actions as presiding judge in pronouncing sentence and denying right of appeal were determined less by a determination to see justice done than to see that his party won their battle against the liberalism he saw embodied in Colenso. In denying Colenso right of appeal, he was denying Colenso justice. Certainly, Colenso was able to appeal against the jurisdiction of Gray's court and win his appeal. He retained his office as Bishop of Natal. But he was never given the opportunity to defend himself against the condemnation for heresy pronounced against him by Gray as presiding judge of the court that was declared 'null and void' by the only competent authority in law to decide the matter, the Privy Council. This had far-reaching and devastating consequences for Colenso and for the Diocese of Natal.

4. *The Pronouncement of Excommunication*

Despite the decision of the Privy Council that Gray's court had no jurisdiction, Gray proceeded on the basis of his judgment to excommunicate Colenso. Dean Green read out the sentence of greater excommunication in St. Peter's Cathedral on 5 January 1866. Gray began in earnest to persuade the missionary societies and the hierarchy in England to back him in appointing a new bishop. Colenso was condemned unheard and without right of appeal by a court declared incompetent to try him. While the majority of the hierarchy in England did not protest, there was a significant group of people who did not agree with this move. These included Bishop Tait of London, who was to succeed Longley as Archbishop of Cape Town and who believed that legal opinion should be consulted, and the Archbishop of York, who was of the opinion that Gray's action was illegal (*Correspondence of the Most Reverend the Lord Archbishop of Canterbury* 1868). Indeed, Tait and Thirlwall only agreed to attend the First Lambeth Conference in September 1867 when Archbishop Longley gave his express promise that the case of Colenso would not be discussed, while York absented himself as a gesture of support for Colenso. At the Lambeth Conference, Gray also publicly accused the Bishops of Ely and Lincoln as to blame for Colenso's heresies. Only 76 of the 144 bishops attended, none from Australia. Bishop Thirlwall of St David's held the Archbishop to his promise not to discuss Colenso, despite tumultuous demands from Gray and his party. Despite frequent assertions that Colenso was condemned by the first Lambeth Conference, this was not the case. According to the copy of the minutes made and printed by William Benham in 1878, a document was circulated by a group of bishops after the close of the Lambeth Conference, though no signed copy of this document exists

(*Lambeth Conferences* 1878: 58). The various committees, including one on the appointment of a new bishop for Natal, were only 'received' without being debated or voted on, due to the steadfast refusal of Thirlwall to allow Colenso onto the agenda. Gray's party haled the First Lambeth Conference as a victory, whereas it was in point of fact entirely ambivalent on the matter of Colenso.

What happened at Lambeth was characteristic. Gray proceeded by mobilizing the conservative Church hierarchy in England against Colenso and by winning over the missionary bodies, in particular the SPG and the Society for the Propagation of Knowledge. The Colonial Bishoprics' Fund refused to pay until the British Courts forced them to reinstate Colenso's stipend after he appealed to the Chancery Court under the Master of the Rolls, Lord Romilly. Then Colenso was, to a very real extent closed down by being starved of funds. Gray, the son of the Prince Bishop of Bristol and the son-in-law of English landed gentry, found no difficulty in winning over the establishment, and painting himself as the hero of orthodoxy against the *parvenu*, lower middle class and quixotic Bishop of Natal. The case was made especially vigorously in the committees and public meetings of the missionary societies. So, a General Meeting of the SPG of 20 February 1863, with Gray present, moved to 'withhold its confidence from him until he shall be cleared from the charged notoriously incurred by him', refused to re-elect him a Vice-President of the Society and placed the funds granted to the Diocese of Natal under a committee chaired by Dean Green, Colenso's greatest enemy in the diocese (USPG-USPG *Minute Book* 48: 324-25). Fresh clergymen under this system were specifically exempted from the jurisdiction of Colenso, and those SPG missionaries who remained faithful to Colenso, such as Reverend A. Tönnessen, had their salaries removed (*Minutes of General Meeting of 20 April 1866* [USPG-USPG *Minute Book* 49: 210]). When Colenso protested that the society's constitution required SPG missionaries to submit to the duly constituted ecclesiastical authority where they served, the society changed its constitution to exclude Natal (USPG-USPG *Minute Book* 49: 210). Gray persuaded the SPG to switch its support for Ekukhanyeni to pay white clergy ministering to the settlers instead, out of the existing grants:

> You will see also that I allow nothing for the resumption of mission work at the Bishop's Station, Ekukanyeni, and nothing, I understand ought to be allowed. I am told by intelligent men of business that that fine property, upon which thousands have been thrown away, ought to produce a considerable revenue. One shrewd man of business said £1500 a year. I believe that your grant of £1900 a year would maintain your existing work, accomplish

that which I have pledged myself to, and pay the passages out of the men
that are needed;—and I will do my best, so long as there is no Bishop to
work with you and with your Board to this end, if you will trust me and
work generously with me. (Letter from Gray to Hawkins, 27 May 1864;
USPG.CLR 115.213-223)

The same pattern can be seen in the SPK's minutes, which had funded
Colenso's printing press and school at Ekukhanyeni. After 1863, grants
are made to individual clergy without reference to the bishop and, after a
row over the exact status of Colenso and the Diocese of Natal, the Society's
General Meeting of 1 October 1867 resolved that 'in the Society's Alma-
nack for 1868, no mention be made of the Diocese of Natal' (SPCK.MS
A1/50.302). Despite the formation of the Church Clergy Fund on 31 May
1866, to attempt to provide the funding necessary for Colenso to continue
to run the diocese, with considerable success initially, the long-term effect
of the missionary societies policy was to stifle Colenso's work completely.

In terms of the theological questions on which Colenso had been tried
and found guilty, the hierarchy responded with ridicule and/or silence
(Guy 1997). Few are as explicit as a letter from a missionary at Bishop's
College in India to Reverend Ernest Hawkins of the SPG, who was
preparing a commentary on Genesis countering Colenso, 'I very much
shrink from noticing errors *directly*, because I am sure that, be the answer
as complete as may be, there is often more effect produced by the objection than by the reply' (USPG Home Correspondence. H1). Alongside this
strategy of fighting Colenso by ridicule while keeping silent on the major
issues, ran a determined strategy to keep the matter of Colenso's guilt or
innocence for heresy out of the courts, denying him any right of appeal.

5. *Conclusion*

Whether or not Colenso was a heretic, which is debatable, even more
today than in 1863, the trial was, in my opinion, seriously flawed, particularly when leave to appeal was denied. The problem is grave enough that
one could argue that since insufficient attention was paid to 'the rules of
substantial justice' and that, in view of the likelihood that there did not
exist 'that strict impartiality which [is] necessary to be observed by all
tribunals, however, little fettered by forms', the judgment might be set
aside by the Church of the Province of Southern Africa today on the basis
of the principles of 'natural justice'.

This would leave the matter of the substantive charge of heresy still unsettled. But then it never was settled in the lifetimes of the two adversaries, Colenso and Gray, and probably never will be. In the matter of Gray's conduct in the trial and his excommunication of Colenso, I would only say that his motives were high minded and his intentions sincere, but his judgment poor. It seems inappropriate that Gray should have written privately to Colenso at the time of his excommunication recognizing him as a 'man of honour', while publicly pronouncing him as 'a heathen and a sinner' who was led by the devil. There is no doubt either, that Colenso was inflexible and determined in his pursuit of what he considered to be matters of principle. Summing up the two men, Hinchliffe (1964: 126) writes: 'Like Colenso, Gray is a controversial figure. He is conventionally represented as saint and hero or narrow bigot; just as Colenso is represented as courageous liberal or wicked heretic. In neither case is the picture a just one.' In the end, Gray's work in the organization of the institutional Church and his formulation of the constitution of an independent South African Anglican Church was of fundamental importance, not only for South Africa, but also for the development of the Anglican Communion. On the other hand, Colenso's vision and struggle in terms of the issues around the Bible, theology, colonialism and the mission of the Church with respect to other religions and cultures continue to provide inspiration for the Church today in South Africa and beyond. The relative value of their work could not be and should never have been a matter to be settled by a court of law.

'THE BRAVEST WOMAN I HAVE EVER KNOWN':
FRANCES COLENSO (1816–93)

Mandy Goedhals

Frances Colenso[1] once remarked, somewhat dismissively, that history is 'what is generally supposed to have happened and therefore useful to know. As for what did happen—it is nonsense to expect to find it out' (Rees 1958: 12). This is hardly encouraging to anyone attempting a study of her life. Moreover, Frances' own assessment of her life would make feminists frown and certainly does not promise much of interest to posterity. After John Colenso's death in 1883, she referred to her husband as 'my Lord and Master, my superior in every way, morally and intellectually' (p. 374) and described her life as 'a mere appendix to his' (p. 380). On the basis of this evidence, she seems to fit quite comfortably into nineteenth-century expectations that women would be socialized to act and think in a way that would receive acceptance from men, to fulfil a role which would support male leadership and to submerge themselves in other's needs and interests (Conn 1995: 78).

Why then, did her daughter Harriette describe her mother as 'the bravest woman I have ever known'?[2] Frances Colenso described herself as 'shy and retiring', but also commented that she had never been 'so sweetly silly and simpering' (Rees 1958: 350) as she appeared in an early photograph. Although she shrank from revealing 'sacred feelings' (p. 407), Frances had a keen insight into her own personality and recognized a strand of toughness and independence. She was not a natural rebel, and did not lightly cast off family expectations, social convention and her own somewhat timid nature, but the search for an expression of her own spirituality

---

1. For biographical information see Rees 1858; Guy 1983: 3-36, and index references in Guy 2001a; Nicholls 1995: 480-81. Her full forename was Sarah Frances, but her family knew her as Frances—I have followed this convention in my discussion.

2. The words appear in an account of her mother's death in 1893. The quotation is taken from Guy 2001a: 353.

was a strong impulse in her. Throughout her life, she was sensitive to a male tendency to seek domination and to humiliate those who were regarded as subordinates: it was a pattern of behaviour she experienced in religious and educational institutions (Guy 2001a: 14) and later encountered in Church and State. Frances' way was never open confrontation, but throughout her life, she resisted expressions of patriarchy and power and the infliction of mortification that went with them, although it was difficult for her to do so. This was the path she followed long before she met John Colenso: her devotion to him was not born of blind loyalty but because she shared his questioning of biblical fundamentalism, clericalism and Eurocentricism, and the brutality of colonialism and imperialism. Hers was a courageous struggle of heart and mind against her own fears and social expectations, which continued into the frailty of her old age. Frances Colenso left no published works systematically setting out her views on politics or theology, but she left a generous legacy in the hundreds of letters she wrote. Jeff Guy has called them an 'incomparable record' (Guy 2001a: 438) of the history of Natal and Zululand. The letters also set out her informed and vigorous religious opinions, her love for her family and home, her delight in the beauty of Ekukhanyeni, the recognition and acceptance of loss which her choices brought, the humorous and uncomfortable events of daily life, her belief that what people needed was *'plenty of love'* (p. 14). As Frances herself reminds us, we cannot know or understand all of the life of another human being. There is probably much that she chose not to reveal and certainly much that we do not understand, but her letters reflect, not the emotional and intellectual passivity expected of women of her time, but the religious spirituality of a 'human life energised by an inner drive for self-transcendence, for moving beyond self-maintenance to reach out in love, in free commitment to seek truth and goodness…in relation to the divine mystery as Source and Incarnate Word and life-giving Spirit' (Conn 1995: 77).

Frances Colenso was born on 3 June 1816, the eldest child of Frances and Robert Bunyon. Her maternal grandfather, Thomas Bignold, was a founder of the Norwich Union insurance company, so she was born into middle-class respectability and comfort. Frances had three siblings: Harriette, just a year younger, Ellen and brother Charles, whom Frances always found rather stolid. Charles was educated at Harrow and Cambridge, his sisters at an academy for young ladies in Cheltenham. In early adolescence, Frances began to question the expression of Christianity taught and practised in her family. The Bunyons were members of the established Church of England, and within it, devout Evangelicals,[3] with the earnestness and emphasis on personal conversion and salvation through the atoning death of Christ associated with evangelical faith. From a theological point of view, Evangelicalism upheld the verbal inspiration and sole authority of the Scriptures and had close connections with Calvinism: human beings after the Fall were no longer free and all works outside Christianity were sinful, while even within Christianity, the evil was only covered by the saving death of Christ. Like Calvinists, Evangelicals emphasized the omnipotence of God as set against the degraded and depraved nature of human life and effort: the threat of damnation hung over all.

When she was 70, Frances still recalled vividly: 'O, how I did suffer in my early days from the Calvinistic, so-miscalled Evangelical doctrines in the midst of which I was brought up' (Rees 1958: 404). She expressed some of her painful reflections in a letter from school to her mother when she was 14, after the death of a fellow pupil, Helen Fenton. For someone who usually revelled in the use of language, the phrases are trite and stilted, as if quoting the words of a teacher: 'Mrs Fenton has born up all the time with the most admirable Christian firmness'. The letter contains extraordinarily pious expressions of evangelical belief:

> O how unimportant is everything but the one thing needful, and yet unless the Holy Spirit teaches us this, how little effect do the most solemn, loudest warnings produce upon us, they only harden our hearts more and more. (p. 20)

The only thing that does ring true in the letter is an agonized parenthesis, in which she explains to her mother that all the tenets of faith beloved of Evangelicals have no meaning for her:

> (Dear Mama, pray for me, for I do find it so very difficult to come to Jesus. I cannot feel the reality of religion. I cannot love the Saviour or feel that he is *my* Saviour nor even feel the weight of my sins.)

It was not in Frances' character to withdraw from a task once she had embarked on it, although we know nothing of the different stages of her struggle out of evangelicalism. Frances always found her own search for meaning painful, hampered as she was by her personal reticence, reinforced by her acceptance of a gender ideology that women were not only

3.   See the entry 'Evangelicalism' and the cross-references in Cross 1978: 486. Linda Wilson (2000) examines evangelical spirituality among women, although largely outside the Church of England.

physically but mentally weaker than men, a view to which she adhered until the end of her life.[4]

Frances did have the advantage of living in an age in which religious orthodoxy was being questioned,[5] and so could find literature which answered the kind of questions she was asking. By her mid-twenties, she had been drawn to the teachings of Samuel Taylor Coleridge (1772–1834), poet, philosopher and theologian (Cross 1978: 312), although we do not know what in his diffuse writings attracted her. Coleridge was interested in seminal ideas rather than in setting up a system: he distinguished between abstract and superficial knowledge which he called 'understanding', and a higher form of knowledge which he called 'reason', through which people were able to respond with all their being. For Coleridge, the Bible was neither an infallible book nor evidence for the truth of Christianity. Rather the authority of the Scriptures lay in their power to draw people to faith and repentance, to hope and adoration. All this was a far cry from the Evangelicalism of Frances' youth.

In March 1842, Frances wrote to F.D. Maurice (Vidler 1961: 83-99), who was Professor of English Literature and History at King's College London and who had been influenced by Coleridge, asking for 'a little tract' setting out the value of Coleridge's ideas. There was no sense of pretentiousness or self-importance about what was for her a necessary search for truth: when she plucked up courage to write to Maurice she noted that it 'is, however of very little importance what any one thinks of me' (Rees 1958: 27). She was doing something unusual among women and sought to disguise this, even from herself, by adopting the modest tone expected of her sex. She explained, without any indignation, that Maurice's views would be treated with respect when she encountered queries about Coleridge's work, whereas the voices 'of young ladies talking about philosophy, or a philosopher, would not be listened to, even if they ventured to raise them' (Rees 1958: 27). Presumably she knew this from personal experience.

4. For example, in 1884, when her daughter Harriette was negotiating for the appointment of a Church of England bishop to succeed her father, Frances referred to her daughter's 'little weak woman's hand' and was afraid that 'the manifold letter writing should be too much for her head' (Rees 1958: 381). There are also references to her opposition to women's suffrage and political participation in (pp. 208, 409).

5. Vidler (1974) discusses a range of the debates and controversies, including Coleridge and Maurice.

Frances had already read Maurice's own books, and found them 'deeply interesting' (Rees 1958: 27). Maurice was the son of a Unitarian minister, and unhappy divisions in his own family drew him eventually to the Church of England as part of the Catholic Church in which people could be brought together in unity and community, free from parties or sects. As he explained in *The Kingdom of Christ* (1836), this did not mean uniformity: he believed that divisions in Christendom and parties in the Church of England represented aspects of truth, although they were in error where they claimed exclusive truth for themselves. Like Coleridge, he saw the Scriptures as a witness to God's unfolding purpose for the universal human community with Christ as the head, into which all people are born. Frances' letter produced a copy of the desired tract and led to a friendship that influenced her life and that of John William Colenso whom she met in Cambridge while visiting her brother Charles later that year.

John Colenso and Frances Bunyon saw a great deal of each other during the two weeks that Mrs Bunyon and her daughters spent in the university town, and Mrs Bunyon invited him to visit them in London afterwards. Frances was obviously delighted to find that John took her religious opinions seriously, and before his second visit to her London home, he reminded her teasingly that he was 'only coming to *see you*, remember, and all at Highgate—not for any *very severe* conversation upon Hume and Coleridge' (Guy 1983: 24). But religion loomed large in their concerns, and meeting Frances was important for Colenso's own development, as he found himself drawn more and more towards the thought of F.D. Maurice. She recalled in 1883:

> it is true enough that I *first* turned his attention to the study of Coleridge and Maurice. I shall never forget finding him one morning, an hour before breakfast time, in the little room between the drawing and living rooms, with a volume of Maurice in his hands, and his whole soul in his face, as it often was, with a wrapt assent and consent to what he had been reading, and a full conviction that he would find perfect sympathy on this point in me— the *foundation* indeed of all our sympathy and love. (Rees 1958: 425)

She wrote this in a letter to her friend Mrs Lyell, emphasizing that this personal memory was not for publication: probably Frances felt it would reflect adversely on Colenso if it were known that he owed some of his religious opinions to his wife.

Although they were engaged to be married in 1843, financial difficulties and the death of Frances' father delayed their marriage until 1846, when John Colenso took up the living of St Mary's at Forncett in Norfolk.

Frances' married life in Norfolk and the early years of the mission in Natal follow a conventional pattern, determined by her husband's choices and concerns. At Forncett, husband and wife were occupied with parish work, Frances carrying out the work of unpaid curate (Rees 1958: 32), as well as building what her husband longed for, a 'Home, where I could taste its real character, or test its capabilities for joy or sorrow' (Guy 1983: 12). Like other wives whose husbands felt a vocation to work as a missionary, Frances had to decide in 1853 whether to support her husband in his work and agree to go to Natal. Her sister Harriette had also married a clergyman, Frank MacDougall, who had been consecrated Bishop of Borneo in 1847, and they sailed east that year, leaving behind their two-year-old son Charles and taking baby Harry with them. By 1851, Harry was dead, as were three more children, Edward, Thomas and Robert (O'Connor *et al.* 2000: 316). In spite of her devotion to Colenso, Frances could not do as her sister had done and would not go until she was sure it would be safe for her children, Harriette Emily (born 1847), Frances Ellen (1849), Robert (1850) and Francis Ernest (1852). 'The difficulty of the whole thing is… Harriette's motherhood being swallowed up in her wifehood' (Rees 1958: 424), she later remarked. But once in Natal, where her fifth child, Agnes Mary, was born four months after their arrival in 1855, she threw herself into the work, and one of the women missionaries at Ekukhanyeni described her as

> such a worker, at the same time fancying she does nothing. She is governess to all her own children, and many others who are here, and besides is constantly overseeing the troop of black girls, and indeed the whole population up here comes to her as their mother, in any kind of sickness or trouble, for she is their doctor as well…in fact, I cannot tell you half of what she does, but you may believe it is plenty, being at the head of such an establishment as this; and then besides all, she is fond of music, drawing, and poetry and flowers, and everything beautiful in nature. Above all, she is in love with the (African) people. (Rees 1958: 41)

One aspect of Africa about which Frances never felt comfortable was traditional African dress. In spite of her reservations about the imposition of Western civilization on Africa, she was relieved that Christianized Africans were 'decently clothed' and made knee length tunics for her African servants (Rees 1958: 96), as well as running a sort of trouser library (p. 398) for African men who needed to go into Pietermaritzburg. Certainly, the beauty of the place added a new dimension to her delight in creation and she especially loved the view of Table Mountain which faced their house at Bishopstowe 'like a majestic altar, and always peaceful and benignant, from its early morning aspect of soft deep ultramarine shadows wreathed with white mists, to the evening glory of the opposite sunset in which it shines iridescent, with the crown of red rocks round its brow showing opaline, as if from within' (Cox 1888, I: 77). The house, of stone and wood and brick, with gables and pitched roof, grew by degrees (Guy 2001a: 30). In 1868 Frances wrote to a friend in the middle of the Natal summer, endeavouring to share the charm of her home. Her bedroom was 'a perfect grotto, and the creepers over the verandah before the window, vine with its clusters, and a luxurious plant, an impomoea, with honey-scented flowers, make a green blind which we almost wish we could draw up, at least Papa does, complaining that they keep out the morning sun which else would wake him to his work' (Rees 1958: 195).

For Frances, coming to Natal had meant separation from family and friends, but also involved sacrificing an aspect of her life which did not apply to most missionary wives, the intellectual life that was important to her. Few clergy in South Africa would have been able to discuss theology with their wives in the way that Colenso could, but being in Natal would have increased Frances' dependence on her husband for this kind of intellectual stimulation. She would certainly have understood the issues regarding mission and biblical criticism that faced him early on in his work and must have shared in his reflections as he sought an answer. Frances showed no resentment that her husband's career determined the context in which she lived her life and their shared faith and the contribution she could make was very important to her. When the wife of a French missionary explained that she had liberal sympathies while her husband was orthodox, so that she took 'care not to meddle herself with doctrines!', Frances found this inconceivable: 'How do people manage?' (Rees 1958: 217). But she was used to reading and thinking for herself and the fact that she held no official position in the Church allowed her freedom that Colenso did not enjoy. Her husband certainly did not attempt to limit or compete with her reading and thinking, and she recalled that, when asked about metaphysics, 'he used to say with a smile, dear angel, that he left that to me!' (p. 424). Although she identified closely with her husband's work, the ways in which she did this were not always conventional.

In 1862, the Colenso family went to England and returned to Natal at the end of 1865. By 1862, Colenso and the Bishop of Cape Town were already at odds, and by the time the Colensos returned to Bishopstowe, Colenso had published his volume on the Pentateuch and had been pro-

hibited from officiating in English dioceses and condemned as a heretic by
the South Africa bishops. Colenso's position also led to a painful estrangement from F.D. Maurice, who had officiated at their wedding. More than
20 years later, Frances remembered this meeting, and her own part in the
encounter:

> I did hope that one whom I had looked on as a prophet would have found us
> a standing point for our faith quite distinct from historical beliefs, but, no, I
> was present and my blood ran cold when he, whom I had always regarded
> as a Saint, as nearer to God than any other man, actually said that if he
> could not believe that Moses wrote the Pentateuch, he could not believe in
> God at all, or in 'the powers of the world to come'...
>
> I was driven at last to exclaim in despair, 'O, Mr Maurice, it is too dreadful
> to hear such words from your lips!'—for there was no reasoning, no
> stooping to our weaker powers, no persuasion, nothing but denunciation—
> 'suppress your book and resign your bishopric!'
>
> For all the bitterness of that time, the suffering of it, which we kept very
> much to ourselves I still remember F.D.M. with reverence and affection,
> and so did my dear Lord. Mr M.'s intellect was no doubt gigantic, but he
> was rather tyrannical. I think he might have taken a little more pains with
> us, instead of casting off at once with something like contempt. (Rees
> 1958: 395-96)

What this account makes clear is that Frances understood the theological
issues that were at stake, and expected to be treated as an intelligent
participant: she was not there merely to support her husband out of loyalty.
The Colensos' theological position also led to estrangement from Frances'
family (Rees 1958: 77). Her sister Harriette in particular felt 'repelled' by
what she regarded as Frances' refusal to recognize 'the Deity of the Lord
Jesus' (p. 182). Here again, the problem was not that Frances was loyal to
her husband, which her mother and sister would have understood and
accepted, but that she herself held views that they regarded as heterodox.
Although John and Frances lost important relationships at this time, they
did make new friends. The geologist Sir Charles Lyell and his wife Mary
made them welcome in their London home and introduced them to eminent political, literary and scientific figures. Both Mary and her sister
Katherine Lyell, who had married brothers, were generous friends to
Frances and she corresponded regularly with Mary who died in 1873, and
with Katherine until her own death in 1893 (pp. 86-87).

Colenso's supporters felt that he should return to Natal in the wake of
the Privy Council judgment. Although she may have hoped that their stay

would not be permanent, Frances was glad to get back to Natal: 'O how lovely the land looked, stretching out its arms as it were, the promontories enclosing the inner bay, to receive us to its quiet bosom' (Rees 1958: 93). Colenso's determination to assert his claim to the see involved not only more legal wrangling but preaching twice in St Peter's on a Sunday, and long visitations around the diocese. Frances herself worshipped at the Zulu service in the Ekukhanyeni chapel on a Sunday. Here, Jonathan Ngidi[6] preached for between half an hour and forty minutes to Christian converts and people from neighbouring homesteads. She commented wryly: 'I understand him partly, but not well enough to bring him up for heresy if he uttered any' (p. 96). Why did Frances attend this chapel service and not St Peter's? A practical reason was that her husband preached at morning and evening services in Pietermaritzburg, and she would have had to remain there the whole day if she had accompanied him. Perhaps her absence caused some comment—at one stage, there was a rumour abroad that she and her husband were at odds (p. 311). But Frances was also expressing some of her own needs by remaining behind: something of the simplicity of the chapel service, membership of a worshipping community where quibbling over words had no place, appealed to her. She found Pietermaritzburg society superficial (pp. 217, 227, 242) and was glad not to be 'in the midst of gossip' (p. 106) while 'the beauty and the healthfulness of this dear place…are transcendent'. As a result of her experience as a young woman, she dreaded an institution where one group wielded power over others, and more recent experience gave her a somewhat dim view of the institutional Church as she saw it developing in southern Africa: 'a free church in the mouths of the High Church party means one in which the clerical party do as they like, and the laity are to be obedient' (p. 236). So great was her antipathy that when her sons, Frank and Robert began to conduct a service in English at Bishopstowe, she wrote that she had not the 'least wish' to see them among 'religious teachers' unless something mighty 'took possession of their souls and then it would be a call to a kind of martyrdom' (p. 180). She always felt grieved that her husband did not receive recognition for his work of biblical scholarship, and was particularly indignant at the English bishops when a time came that biblical criticism was widely recognised and accepted. 'Yet they don't come forward as they ought and say—you were right and we were wrong and

6.   Jonathan Ngidi was a teacher at Ekukhanyeni. His brother William Ngidi was a printer at the mission and assisted Colenso with the work of translation (Guy 2001a: 19-21, 44).

we retract all our hard words against you! Oh no—we always knew that—only you expressed it so coarsely, we were shocked at you!' (p. 256). All of this constitutes quite a telling critique.

The family said a daily office together, of Colenso's own compilation, based on St Augustine and Theodore Parker (1810–60) an American Unitarian (Cross 1974: 1034). For Frances this was an intensely moving part of her day:

> When Papa is away I try to read them just to our own little party, but I am sorry to say it is sometimes too much for me, and I am tempted to suppose that public readers must divest themselves of all feeling and act as mere machines or else how could they get through! (Rees 1958: 219)

Simplicity of domestic worship expressed something of her understanding of God. Her own personal creed was also simply expressed: 'to cling to the thought of a heavenly Father, to see the true God revealed in the Son of Man, to look to the Spirit of [our] Father as the fountain of [our] own spiritual life' (Rees 1958: 378), but she also enjoyed an intellectual challenge. She read whatever theology she could lay her hands on, and not only the works of the like-minded: 'Without being in the least influenced or persuaded by what Renan[7] says, one must be interested—provoked too sometimes. I don't think he is quite so great a thinker as he opines himself to be' she remarked (p. 118). She enjoyed a book (she did not record the title) by J.A. Froude,[8] 'for I have read it quarrelling with it half the time, which is pleasantly stimulating' (p. 152). One edition of *The Theological Review* 'was a string of pearls. I tried in vain to keep it for Sunday but I had not the strength of mind to keep it till then' she told Katherine Lyell who had sent it in a parcel from England (p. 184). The Ascension she found difficult to cope with: 'I confess, I always felt something more grotesque than sublime, in the vision of a human being suspended in mid air, when it visited my mind's eye' (p. 402). She opposed practices of what she called the 'Ritualistic Party', particularly what she called worship of the 'Flesh in which the Word was manifested' (p. 135) although she described the doctrine of the incarnation as 'rational, adorable' (p. 155). She was interested in *Ecce Homo*, published in 1865, which presented

7. J.E. Renan (1823–92), French philosopher and theologian, whose *Vie de Jesus*, published in 1863, denied the supernatural in Christ's life and ignored the moral aspects of his preaching. The publication of *Vie de Jesus* caused a sensation and led to his removal from a professorship at the College de France (Cross 1974: 1173).

8. The historian James Anthony Froude (1818–94) visited southern Africa in 1874–75 on a government mission to investigate the possibilities for federation.

Christ as a moral reformer rather than the Christ of the creeds (Cross 1974: 439), but felt that the book did not grapple with the difficulties of understanding Christ as true God and true man. But, like a good controversialist, she avoided the difficulty too, by criticizing the High Church position instead of explaining her own:

> they are clearly urging on what is in ecclesiastical terms a *heresy*, for they are always denying the Humanity of Christ. They can't bear anything which is clearly deducible from it. They are nearly saying that he only seemed to perform the functions of mortal life, to be weary, or to suffer, or to sleep or to die. (Rees 1958: 115)

A distinctly Protestant document, which criticized devotion to the Virgin Mary on the grounds that God is a jealous God, also aroused her anger. Her lengthy response gives some insight into her experience of God:

> O heaven and earth! The Father of Spirits, the Fountain of Law, the Strength of Beauty, of Order, the Maker of all…will be jealous if we pray to the Virgin Mary![9] If we do not give Him the honour due to him, he will be angry with us!! I don't know how to contain myself when I think of it. We have laboured for many years to expound to ourselves the words—'He is a jealous God'—and discovered in them a care for us, a will that we, whom he made for Himself, should not cast away the best, the bloom of our hearts on some mere creature—for our sakes and because His will was our satisfaction, our perfection, and it was labour, the words were hard, they were not easily beaten into shape—but what can we do with these? Do not worship Mary, because God is a jealous God, who will not give his honour to another! Surely no creature, the most perfect, is another; as far as it is perfect, God is in it. But people talk on these subjects without a moment's thought, and, oh what nonsense they do talk. (Rees 1958: 155)

Probably, much of what she read was discussed with Colenso, although she also used the times he was away to read voraciously, and these extracts from her letters reflect a zest for theology and a relationship with God that owe nothing to her husband's opinions.

9.   This quotation as a whole reflects the Maurician view that Anglicanism embraces a range of theological positions, each of which reflects an aspect of Christian truth, which is denied when any view claims exclusivity for its own opinion. Christians do not of course pray to the saints but ask the saints to pray with and for them. Confusion on this matter arises from the changing use of the word 'to pray', which originally meant 'to ask', and was not restricted only to prayer. Mary is honoured for the child she bore rather than worshipped. Asking the saints for their prayers has historically been practised by Roman Catholics, the Orthodox, and by catholics within Anglicanism. (Wakefield 1983: 349-51).

Natasha Erlank (1999: 98) has argued that Jane Philip shared the work of her husband Dr John Philip and that they were both superintendent of the London Missionary Society between 1819 and 1847, when he died. Frances was aware that other clergy wives did the same, and commented humorously and not altogether disparagingly of Sophy Gray at the time of the first Lambeth Conference in 1867: 'Will the Bishops' wives come to look after their husbands? Or will they stay behind to look after the flocks? Mrs Capetown is equally valuable in either capacity, I believe. She is not at all popular, but that is rather a proof of her efficiency' (Rees 1958: 49). It could not be said of Frances Colenso on the other hand that she had done the work of the Bishop of Natal. She was not keen on tasks often regarded as the purview of clergy wives. Her own particular household duty was sewing, 'clothing the family just decently', which she loathed and could not quite believe her own dictum that 'drudgery for those we love loses its character' (p. 174). A bazaar to raise money for church funds drove her into a pathetic state of anxiety, but her daughters proved excellent organizers and saleswomen, and all she had to do in the end was act as chaperone while they managed the Colenso stall (p. 220). Although no dab hand at the practicalities, she understood very clearly that the reason for the bazaar lay in the economic dependence of women: 'the charity is on the part of those who work for the Bazaar and not at all of those who buy at it. Some of them, I am sure, made a very good thing out of it' because they purchased 'the results of ladies' labour which cannot be turned into money in any other way' (p. 221). Although she understood the factors that limited women, Frances found it difficult to relate to many settler women. She thought they were far too susceptible to clergy influence: 'This is the way with women! I am sorry to say they are a great hindrance to progress' (p. 237). Her attitude, which is perhaps less than generous, is a reminder that women do not constitute an identical mass. Many women still exercise influence in the Church indirectly through their husbands or in spheres traditionally open to women, and are challenged by women whose experience and training has given them a sense of autonomy and an expectation that they may speak on issues formerly reserved for men.

Although Frances Colenso did not share the practical work involved in her husband's office in the way that Jane Philip and Sophy Gray did for their husbands, much of what Colenso achieved he was only able to accomplish because his wife made it possible. The private arena of the Colenso home impacted on John Colenso's public efforts in significant ways. Not only did Frances Colenso come with him to Natal, but she consistently supported his work. After his death, Frances wondered if she might have prolonged her husband's life by insisting that he take better care of his health, but reminded herself that 'he would have been so grieved if any care of himself had hindered everything possible being done for his poor clients that I cannot regret having religiously adhered to my own law to myself, i.e. never to thwart him or worry him' (Rees 1958: 374).

The late 1860s and early 1870s were an important turning point for Frances herself and for the whole Colenso family. Frances clearly hoped to return to England. She felt that there was no major purpose in remaining as Colenso had established his position as Bishop of Natal (Rees 1958: 199). She also felt 'sick of the struggle' (p. 131). Her sons were to go to England to further their education (p. 193), and Frances must have been anxious about her daughters' future. The 'social excommunication' under which they lived (p. 370) was hard to bear. 'The departure of one rational being from our little circle is quite a calamity' (p. 207), she wrote, as most people she met were 'without an idea' (p. 217). Clearly, she was not a bland and sweetly smiling episcopal wife: she had exacting standards for those she met. Perhaps she was a bit of a snob as well as being shy, and might have made more of an effort to relate to other women at the level of their own interests instead of standing aloof.

But if Frances was hoping for a new development in the life of the Colenso family, the change that came brought with it even greater isolation for her family than they had already experienced, as Bishop Colenso took on the cause of the Hlubi chief Langalibalele against the colonial authorities.[10] Frances told her brother, Charles Bunyon, in 1874, at the time she received the news of her mother's death: 'John is again at issue with the world in which he lives. It is useless to say to him, would it not be wiser to leave things to take their course... John *can not but* lift up his voice against injustice' (Rees 1958: 282). Clearly Frances knew her husband and had tried to reason with him, and perhaps she gave up rather than quarrel. Colenso's criticism of colonial policy alienated white members of the Church of England and she told Charles: 'these are dark days for us' (p. 286). It was one of the few times that Frances wrote anything that could be construed as disloyal to John Colenso. There is no record of Frances' struggle to come to terms with the new circumstances that faced

---

10. On Langalibalele, see Guy 1983: 196-246.

her, which required her to subordinate her own wishes and which pro-longed her stay in South Africa. Although Frances' eyesight was fading (Rees 1958: 337, 380) and it was their daughter Harriette who worked most closely with her father in the Zulu cause (p. 320), Frances understood the issues of truth and justice that were at stake (p. 282), made them her own, expounded them eloquently in her letters to England and shared the obloquy visited on her family as a result of their friendship with the Zulu.

In May 1875, Sir Garnet Wolseley visited Bishopstowe. Wolseley had come to Natal as Special Commissioner appointed by the Colonial Office to reform the system of African administration in Natal, in the wake of inadequacies exposed by the colonial conflict with Langalibale, and his subsequent travesty of a trial. From the time of his arrival in Natal, Bishop Colenso had admired the policy of Theophilus Shepstone, the Secretary of Native Affairs, towards the colony's African population. Trust and confi-dence between the two men were shattered by Shepstone's role in Langa-libalele's trial. Colenso worked to overthrow what he regarded as a denial of British justice and took the case to England where the Secretary of State for the Colonies promised to right the wrong. The bishop expected to be heard when Wolseley arrived, but Shepstone was important to imperial plans for confederation in southern Africa and could not be abandoned. Wolseley had already resolved to exclude the bishop's influence from shaping colonial policy towards Africans.

His visit to Bishopstowe was not a success. He considered the behaviour of the family 'in very bad taste' while the house and grounds were 'in bad order'. The real problem for Wolseley was that 'all the lot have Kaffir on the brain & [seem] to be really mad on the subject viewing everything from one side alone and being incapable of taking a broad view on any matter where the interests of Kaffirs are in any way concerned' (quoted in Guy 2001a: 46). Wolseley's most unfavourable opinion was reserved for Frances Colenso, whom he considered a 'drivelling idiot and tolerated by her family as such'.

Frances Colenso was clearly not a drivelling idiot, but perhaps she was less admiring than he required of the 'balls and entertainments' (Rees 1958: 315) he staged to impress colonial society, and more outspoken than he expected on Zulu affairs. Representations of women were central to the process of constructing male identity in the colonial period. For men of the nineteenth century, their image of themselves derived partly from the fact that they saw themselves as protecting British women from the sexual threat constituted by indigenous men (Erlank 1999: 96). Frances Colenso did not fit into this worldview at all. She never saw African men (whom she always spoke of as men and not in any diminutive) as a threat to herself or her daughters (Rees 1958: 101, 183), and perhaps this challenged Wolseley's own understanding of himself and provoked his ungallant expressions about her.

In the 1870s, the failure of the Colensos' efforts on behalf of Langalibalele and then their work to expose the cynicism with which the Zulu were driven into war in 1879 left them all 'disappointed, indignant and sick at heart' (Rees 1958: 321) and the outbreak of war sent them into mourning (p. 341). They found that the postal service had become 'out of joint as far as we are concerned—such is the consequence of meddling with politics' (p. 318). Frances was afraid that political differences would add Katherine Lyell to her painful list of lost friendships (p. 370): 'I am really very anxious to write to you and that you should not give up writing to me, but these are hard and heavy times, and I hardly know how to give you any idea of how things look to us' (p. 345). In spite of her fears, she could not always stifle her natural vehemence and the indignation she felt. She was disgusted at what she regarded as the immorality of colonial behaviour and asked: 'is it quite certain that the civilisation of Western Europe is good for Eastern Africa?' She also pointed out that the Zulu had never launched any reprisals on Natal and told Katherine Lyell: 'I declare that I am ashamed to look black people in the face or to remember that I am an Englishwoman' (p. 343). With Zulu affairs uppermost in her mind, she wrote to Mrs Lyell about the lovely Natal plants and her efforts to paint in spite of failing eyesight; about books (including Darwin's work on earthworms); and their grandson Eric, with whom she galloped down the passage and fell flat on her face, whereupon he kissed it better and charmed them all (pp. 355, 362, 372).

John Colenso's death in June 1883 was a sudden and devastating blow, which removed the centre of her life. Family and friends urged that Frances and her daughters should return to England.

In the end, they remained, although not in the house at Bishopstowe, which was destroyed in a fire in September 1884. Harriette managed to save her father's notebooks (Rees 1958: 382), but furniture, books, paintings and clothes were destroyed, and Frances wrote 'it is rather trying, *even to us*, to reflect on all the valuable and pretty things which are burnt' (p. 388). Frances Ellen, the middle Colenso daughter, who already showed signs of tuberculosis, moved to Durban while the other three Colenso women settled into a ramshackle and rat-ridden set of buildings, with a leaking thatched roof and no ceilings, few floor boards and brown paper for window panes (Guy 2001a: 117-18). In the midst of it all, books were still Frances' 'cravingest want' (Rees 1958: 386). Characteristic reticence may have prompted Frances to write soon after the destruction of Bishopstowe:

> I think the people are all somewhat surprised at our cheerful aspect, but since he is gone who was the soul of it all, it seems almost suitable that the place should be, as it were wiped out and dwell in our loving memory as He ever does. (Rees 1958: 384)

The words, however, do carry a ring of hope, of ending, but also beginning. The three women continued with their activities on the mission (where Agnes ran a school and dispensed medicine and Harriette burnt fire breaks and collected rents), and with what probably seemed their somewhat eccentric lifestyle. One night, Agnes woke her mother to watch a lunar eclipse, went and delivered a lecture on the subject to men working on the mission, after which she and Frances stayed up until two o'clock in the morning to see the Morning Star—'a lively and delightful night' in Frances' estimation (Rees 1958: 386). Her daughters saw to it that she dressed with some nod to fashion, but she seemed attracted to the idea of an eccentric old age:

> I think possibly, that after all, knitting (stockings) may be the best pastime for one's declining days—but I do not know whether I could carry the stitches in my head. I must try. One cannot, I suppose be allowed to smoke. I never tried, but I think that I should like it. (Rees 1958: 394)

By the late 1880s, Frances could no longer walk easily, having broken both legs in the 1870s (Rees 1958: 355). Local children, black and white, knew her interests and brought her bunches of flowers (p. 425). Life was, she acknowledged to her brother, 'somewhat rough' and would not suit 'you children of the upper civilisation, but there are reasons, more than one, why it suits us' (p. 395).

The reasons were interconnected. First, Frances was determined to see the continuation of her husband's work, his contribution to biblical scholarship recognized and the Church of England in Natal provided with a new bishop. Nor could she bear to abandon the Zulu cause to which John Colenso had given his life.

The second factor determining that they would remain in Natal was Harriette's involvement in her father's work since the early 1870s, where Frances had 'neither memory, nor patience nor knowledge of Zulu to do

The Eye of the Storm

what she has done for him' (Rees 1958: 320). As Guy (2001a: 32) rightly points out, for the Colenso daughters (and for Frances herself) the liberal education they had received, and their real intelligence and ability led to no independent existence, no career and income. Although their lives were circumscribed by their father's choices for his own life, the nature of his work offered them a really worthwhile cause, one they could not have chosen easily for themselves but which the fact that they were their father's daughters made possible.[11] Although they earned no money of their own, Colenso left his estate to his wife and daughters, and this legacy they also expended in defence of the Zulu (Guy 2001a: 271, 278, 300, 306).

John Colenso fought against racial inequality in southern Africa, and this perhaps developed into some breakdown of inequalities in gender relationships as well, particularly where Harriette was concerned. Harriette took a lead in attempting to persuade the members of the Church of England in Natal to elect a bishop to succeed Colenso. Her mother commented: 'She has some weight as Her Father's daughter in talking to one and another and putting leading ideas into their heads, but being only a woman she cannot openly take the lead, however competent to do so' (Rees 1958: 380). One can see in Frances a struggle between the way of viewing women's role with which she had grown up, and a reaching out towards a different understanding. As always, she found the change and challenge difficult, but would not turn from what she believed to be right, however painful. The fact that Harriette was continuing her father's work made it easier for Frances to cope with her daughter's activities (p. 381). Frances came to rely on her completely: 'My Harry is *wise*, else I should not pour out to her my folly, my indignation' (p. 424). But it was still foreign to Frances that a woman should take on the burdens that Harriette did, and she could only explain it by using masculine imagery; Harriette was not a strong and independent woman but 'such a man of business' (p. 421). The cause of the Zulu royal house, of Cetshwayo and Dinuzulu, became Harriette's concern, although, like her father, her way was to listen, support and suggest, never to dictate. In 1889, Harriette thought that for the sake of Dinuzulu and others imprisoned on St Helena, she should go to England. Her mother had always dreaded the sea voyage and clearly did not want to go—'I am more infirm than you imagine' (p. 426). She was shocked that her daughter proposed to speak in public, yet would bear

11. On Frances Ellen and Agnes Mary Colenso, see Nicholls 1995: 482-84, and references in Guy 2001a.

it for the sake of her father and the Zulu, and could even see the funny side of the situation: 'do if you *wish to*, my precious child, but what will Uncle Charles say?' (p. 426).

But it is also clear that the Zulu cause had become Frances' own, as she wrote to Katherine Lyell, 'our hearts are still in Zululand' (p. 400). She was worried that if they went to England they would not return to Africa 'and what would our poor natives do then? No, no, we should be lost without them and they without us' (p. 426)—words that reflect a deep sense of mutuality in human relationships. Nearly 30 years in Africa had left their mark on her. When Dinuzulu had come to their house to hand himself over to the colonial authorities in November 1888 (pp. 422-23), she knew how to entertain him with great courtesy, and shortly before her death, she recalled seeing both her husband and Cetshwayo in a dream (Guy 2001a: 354), a far cry from her youth in the young ladies' academy in Cheltenham.

From 1890 to 1893, Frances and her daughters were in England among family and friends, although she understood that the causes closest to her heart were embarrassing to many of her family (Guy 2001a: 314). When the three women returned to Natal in September 1893, she was 77. After a short time in Pietermaritzburg, they went back to the dilapidated cottage, which she called 'little Bishopstowe'. Frances was soon unwell and quietly and suddenly, just before Christmas in 1893, she died.

It might be tempting to suggest that Frances Colenso would be more comfortable in the Church at the beginning of the twenty-first century than she was in her own time. Not only has the Church come to understand that the search for justice and truth that she shared with John Colenso and her daughters is part of Christian mission, but also, by ordaining women, the Church provides scope for women of her intellectual ability and dedication. The volume of which this essay forms part is an attempt to recognize the achievement of John Colenso for which she hoped, and to acknowledge ways in which the Church may have acted unjustly in the past. But it is important not to colonize or domesticate Frances Colenso in this way. Even in a more democratic age and one in which women are ordained to the priesthood, there are still clergy who believe that bishops have high status and laity low status, that clergy exercise absolute authority in their parishes and have the right to silence even informed theological opinion, where it does not coincide with their own preconceptions. Clergy talk about 'allowing' women's ministry, as if it is a concession to rules and not a move towards wholeness. It is convenient but inaccurate to attribute such attitudes exclusively to 'High Church' clergy. Fundamentalism and authoritarianism persist and make exclusive claims, which narrow and deny the nature of Anglicanism. It remains difficult too for anyone, even bishops, to admit that they have made a mistake. Such attitudes seem to preclude any kind of ministry that is mutual: the traffic is one-way, from clergy to laity. Contemporary women find themselves accused not necessarily of being drivelling idiots but of being quarrelsome or difficult because they question or challenge male leadership. Sometimes the Church is as insensitive to culture and to deeply felt symbols as were the missionaries in the nineteenth century, even while criticizing those missionaries. Individuals who love God and the Church still find themselves silenced or humiliated because of the uncomfortable truths they speak. At the end of *St Joan*, Bernard Shaw suggests that although the Church has tried to right a past wrong by canonizing a woman previously condemned as a heretic, it is certainly not ready to be confronted with the living woman once again. Frances Colenso lived in an age which assumed that hierarchical race, class and gender relationships in State, Church and family reflected the divine order: we understand that the doctrine of the Trinity supports 'only relationships that are mutual and collaborative, and social structures that are collegial and interdependent' (Conn 1995: 91). Although hampered now by assumptions of female dependence and by her own feelings of insecurity, Frances Colenso lived in a way that challenged the restrictive conformity of her times with enormous courage and perseverance and offered to her contemporaries and to us the richness and complexity of her story.

THE COLENSO DAUGHTERS:
THREE WOMEN CONFRONT IMPERIALISM

Jeff Guy

Introduction

This essay originated as a lecture given to the Arts Students Council at the University of Cape Town in May 1980 in a series called 'Women in Society'. Looking at it again, nearly a generation later, it struck me that while gender studies are now established in South Africa and women's struggles are a familiar aspect of general education, the nature of these struggles, the contradictions and difficulties which they necessarily involve still need to be asserted and re-examined, and a book on the significance of the Colenso family's lives in South Africa provides just such an opportunity.

Although I have shortened the text I have not made any major alterations to the substance of the original lecture—in spite of being tempted to rewrite some of the passages in the light of greater experience and exposure to feminist studies over the past two decades. It must therefore be read in the historiographical context in which it was produced—that is at a time when historians of southern Africa were first trying to incorporate women, with their own dynamic and within the social context created by their being women, into historical research and writing. The essay's origins as an oral presentation must also be kept in mind.

The Colenso Family in Natal: 1853 to 1932

The essay deals with three sisters, the daughters of John and Sarah Frances Colenso. It concentrates on their eldest child, Harriette Colenso, and discusses her two sisters only in passing. After outlining her life and that of her family I examine certain aspects of it in some detail in an attempt to grasp something of its dynamics and reveal the contradictions that entrapped her.

John William Colenso was born in 1814, into a middle-class, but finan-cially impoverished, family. At Cambridge he excelled in mathematics, was ordained in the Anglican Church, and became a parish priest in Norfolk. Here his two older daughters were born, Harriette Emily in 1847, and Frances Ellen in 1849. Colenso was then invited to go to Natal as its first bishop and he visited the colony in 1853 before the mission was established in 1855. In that year another daughter, Agnes Mary, was born and together with two sons, made five children in all.

The Colensos lived at Bishopstowe, part of the mission station Ekuk-hanyeni, a few miles outside Pietermaritzburg. It was from here that their father planned to spread the light of progress and Christian belief among the people of Natal. There was to be industrial and an agricultural training, a college for the sons of chiefs, together with basic secular and religious instruction. The bishop soon became expert in *isiZulu* and his translations of biblical texts were printed by Africans trained at the Ekukhanyeni press, and he pursued his objectives in African education with a forthright energy not always appreciated by other missionaries or Natal's settlers. His wife, Sarah Frances, was bright, informed, with a wry sense of humour. But she was also was intensely reserved and found the colonial society of Pieter-maritzburg far too rough for her Victorian, evangelical sensibilities. She withdrew, gathering her daughters around her, determined that they should have some experience of the artistic and intellectual world of the metro-pole which meant so much to her.

As a result the Colenso sisters spent their formative years sharing in colonial life, but also apart from it. They were closer in many ways to the Africans on the mission station than they were to their white contem-poraries. Their education was sound, and their interests were wide, and as soon as they were old enough they began teaching in the mission school. Bishopstowe might have been at the edge of the empire, but it was also in touch with the intellectual life of Europe. Their father the bishop kept himself informed about the scientific advances of the age, and he and his wife counted among their friends and acquaintances some of the great intellectual figures of the Victorian era.

He was an honest and outspoken man, and his attempts to present Chris-tianity to his African flock as a loving, universal religion brought him into conflict with his peers and his superiors. He challenged the idea that the heathen would burn forever in hell and that members of polygamous households could not join the Church. Listening carefully to the opinions of the Zulu who helped him with his biblical translations, and being well informed about the latest thinking on geology and biology, he argued, in a book which caused one of the great religious controversies of the age, that the Bible was a mixture of legend and historical fact, and contained, but was not, the word of God. He was found guilty of heresy by his brother bishops and, when he refused to retract his comments, he was excommunicated.

He challenged the legality of his excommunication and although there was a judgment in his favour, he was deprived of funds, the Anglican Church in South Africa split, and Colenso was forced to spend years in violent theological and legal disputes which absorbed much of his talent and energy.

It was in this atmosphere of furious debate and intense commitment that his daughters grew to maturity. The Colenso family was widely considered to be an asset to the colony. Controversial, yes, but also, by virtue of Bishop Colenso's work, a phenomenon which attracted world interest—a fact not resented by the occupants of a small and obscure colony. The family's strong sense of moral purpose is revealed by the fact that, in 1873, the Colensos alienated most of their remaining colonial supporters by protested vehemently against their treatment of Langalibalele and the Hlubi in the so-called Langalibalele rebellion. Shocked at the colonists' violence and brutality the bishop travelled all the way to London to bring the details to the attention of the British government.

From this time on the bishop and his daughters were deeply involved in political matters affecting the relations between Africans and the colonial or imperial authorities. Much of the hard work fell on Harriette, who was in her mid-twenties at the time of the Langalibalele affair. Her *isiZulu* was excellent and she interviewed African witnesses, transcribed the evidence, wrote letters and petitions for her father. Her Zulu name was *Udlwedwele*, which means 'her father's staff, his guide and helper'.

Their political stance on the question of the treatment of Africans was a liberal one, except that, after 1873 at least, it had a degree of honesty and perception usually lacking in colonial times. They strongly supported British rule, believing that it was beneficial, just and based on a God-given truth. It was the duty of an English bishop to ensure that the subject peoples were, as far as it was possible, treated justly and guided firmly towards the higher level of civilization represented by British rule.

Events like the Langalibalele affair, during which colonists and officials acted with injustice and brutality, shocked him deeply and he protested in the hope that Britain would rise to its true calling and intervene. But, as the 1870s drew to a close, the Colenso family received an even greater shock than they had at the time of the Langalibalele affair. The first stirring of the mining revolution persuaded Britain to advance the cause of progress on the sub-continent by bringing under control the most obstructive of southern Africa's pre-capitalist communities. The Boer republic of the Transvaal was annexed in 1877, and, to the horror of the Colenso family, Britain invaded the Zulu kingdom in 1879.

With the help of his daughters Colenso tried to publicize the fact that the Zulu had been attacked without justification. For him, the blame lay with local officials, Sir Theophilus Shepstone and Sir Bartle Frere in particular, who, by distorting the South African situation in their reports, had persuaded the imperial government to agree to violent intervention. The Colensos analyzed newspaper articles, official documents, tested them against evidence collected from Zulu informants and the mission printer, Magema Fuze, printed their conclusions for circulation among friends and supporters. When the Zulu king, Cetshwayo kaMpande, was exiled, the Colensos began to agitate for his restoration. Frances wrote a number of books exposing the iniquity of the officials and the suffering of Natal and Zululand's Africans. Harriette took over more and more of her father's correspondence on political matters and, with Agnes, interviewed numerous Zulu informants while keeping them informed of developments taking place beyond their borders.

But they had no success. Although the Zulu king was returned to his country in 1882, largely as a result of the Colensos' efforts, peace did not come to the Zulu kingdom. Disappointed and exhausted, the bishop died in 1883 and his daughters pledged themselves to carry on their father's work for Cetshwayo kaMpande's followers, the Usuthu. However, civil war broke out in Zululand and thousands were killed. In many people's eyes the Colensos were the white agitators responsible. In 1884 the Zulu king died. Natal took over a portion of Zulu territory in the south and soon afterwards Boers invaded the remaining portions from the northwest. Not only public but also personal tragedy continued to affect the Colenso family. In 1887 Frances Colenso died of tuberculosis at the age of 38. She was working on Zulu matters to the last, trying to publicize the injustice with they had been treated by the British and the Natal officials. In the same year Britain annexed what was left of the country, and when leading members of the Zulu royal house, including young Dinuzulu, Cetshwayo's son, protested, they were charged with treason.

In 1888 and 1889 Harriette and Agnes organized the defence of these Zulu leaders. Harriette travelled to Zululand herself, giving encouragement to the prisoners, and paying for their legal defence from her inheritance. She was still convinced that if only the British government and

British public knew the facts about what was happening in Zululand they would try to rectify the situation. While she may well have saved the chiefs from the gallows, she was not able to save them from being exiled to St Helena. Harriette, Agnes and their mother went to England where Harriette travelled the country speaking to liberal and radical clubs, women's organizations, and lobbying MPs. But it was no good; she was unable to effect any substantial change in British policy towards the Zulu although the princes were returned from exile in 1897.

Neither Harriette nor Agnes married. They lived together as missionaries of the Church of England in which position they were constantly appealed to by Natal Africans, particularly those who had fallen foul of the law. Harriette's grasp of legal matters was widely recognized, and more than once her interventions saved Africans from being hanged. In 1908, in the aftermath of the Bhambatha rebellion, the Natal ministry—dominated by 'the crazy party' as Harriette called it—once again charged Dinuzulu with High Treason and once again it was Harriette Colenso who organized the defence.

The trial of Dinuzulu was her last great public intervention. Soon afterwards the Church of the Province of South Africa succeeded in evicting the sisters from their home at Bishopstowe and they moved to Pietermaritzburg. They kept in contact with Africans, however, and became friends and advisers of some of the leading men who in 1912 founded the South African Native National Congress, later the African National Congress.

But by this time they were beginning to age and money was short. They gathered around them a group of African retainers and moved to the outskirts of Pietermaritzburg, where they died, recluses, in 1932 at the ages of 85 and 77.

The Sweep of History

So much for the bare bones of the story: three daughters of a controversial Anglican bishop, who adopted his liberal tenets and attempted to persuade the imperial and colonial authorities to treat Africans with justice and to consider their rights, intervening to protect them when they could. They failed in this: and in the 60 years bracketing the turn of the twentieth century their status changed from being leading members of colonial Natal to a forgotten couple in the Union of South Africa. It is a tragic story and, at the same time, an inspiring one, of three women fighting for the right against great obstacles.

Now in the rest of this essay I want to put some flesh on the historical bones, and to suggest some ways of understanding the Colenso daughters; of conceptualizing them as women of a particular class and during a specific historical period; of understanding the contradictions in which they were caught, contradictions which made their lives, which began with such high hopes, end in failure.

We can begin by looking at the times in which they lived in a broader perspective, using the longest lived of all three, Harriette, as the main figure, but remembering that she was two years older than Frances and eight years older than Agnes. Harriette was born in 1847. That is the year before the writing and publication of the *Communist Manifesto*, and the year liberal revolution swept Europe. She was four at the time of the Great Exhibition of 1851, the event usually associated with the flowering of competitive industrial capitalism, with British power at its height and leading all rivals. Within a decade diamonds had been discovered in South Africa and imperial statesmen began to envisage a union of southern African states as a framework for future economic and political development. One of the consequences was the further conquest of African societies to serve settler society and capital. Harriette was in her twenties when she had the vivid personal experience of the suffering caused by the crushing of the Langalibalele and the Hlubi. The British invasion of the Zulu kingdom was an early indication of the aggressive imperialism which soon came to dominate the age. And throughout the 1880s and 1890s, as Harriette moved to middle age, she experienced, personally, the terrible effects of aggressive, expanding capitalist forces on non-capitalist peoples, as they lost their land and their lives, and control over the products of their labour. She had turned 50 when imperialism reached its height in southern Africa with the conquest of the Ndebele and Shona and the creation of Rhodesia, followed by the conquest of South Africa by Britain in the South African war. She had a particular antipathy for Cecil John Rhodes, the man who bribed and slaughtered his way to power and riches, and said publicly that he preferred 'land to niggers'. With the creation of the South African state in 1910 the dominance of the capitalist system was complete. In her sixties Harriette continued to protest at the effect of this on Africans and she wholeheartedly supported the foundation of the South African Native Congress in 1912. As an elderly women she watched horrified at the First World War, and she died at 85 during the first truly global capitalist depression.

It is this great arc formed by the rise and decline of British imperialism which coincides with the ebb and flow of Harriette Colenso's life and which gives it its form. Born when British capitalism was at its height, reaching maturity when European imperialism was at its most blatantly aggressive and directly expansionist, and dying when its contradictions were manifesting themselves on a worldwide scale.

The Grip of Imperialism

To understand the Colensos we have to appreciate that the bishop and his family came to Natal as supporters and propagators of this imperialist system. As the family of an English bishop they were leaders in society, and their lives were to be an example to others. And they were proud of this position and accepted the responsibilities it imposed on them with utmost seriousness. Harriette was ten years old and her father's mission station was well established when David Livingstone told the cheering undergraduates at Cambridge 'I go back to Africa to try to make an opening for Commerce and Christianity. Do you carry out the work I have begun. I leave it with you.' Colenso's task as a missionary bishop was just this: to direct the dissemination of the ideology of British capitalism in southern Africa, its religion, its political ideals, its supporting structures in law and education, its social values, the ideal of individual labour, the sanctity of the nuclear family. We can see this ideology at work on the bishop's mission station in its early years, with its chapel, the printing press, the African apprentices, the brickyards, watermill, the Colenso daughters teaching in the school, the tenant farmers working the mission lands, the enrolment of chiefs' sons who were going to make their school at Ekukhanyeni the Harrow of South Africa.

The goal was the creation of communities of individualistic, commodity-producing, commodity-consuming families. It was this which underlay the missionary ideal, exemplified so clearly in the illustrations in the missionary journals of well-dressed, well-scrubbed, beaming African families, leaving their square cottages for the Sunday morning service—and it was so different from the reality of the sprawling traditional homesteads, the polygamous families, communal labour, with its low level of commodity production and high level of self-sufficiency. And the ideal was never realized. First, the white settlers objected strongly to the process. They wanted to exploit African labour for their own use, oppressively and directly, by driving Africans off their land and out of agricultural production. Second, the conversion of tribal production to individual production was a difficult and largely unsuccessful endeavour, a venture that was resisted by the majority of Africans, which caused great physical and social distress, and which was very often implemented through violence. The Colensos supported the lofty aims but protested at the lowly means, when in fact both were part of the same process. The Colensos believed more deeply, honestly and intelligently in the essential justice of British expansionism and that this had the support of a loving God. Out of these contradictions between the ideology of imperialism, and its reality in southern Africa, between the noble ideal and the brutal fact, out of the attempt to reconcile the irreconcilable, came the tragedy of the Colensos' lives.

Bishops Colenso's religious teaching shows clearly how he attempted to cushion the blow that capitalism, through Christianity, was making on African lives—the blow that he himself, as a missionary bishop, was called upon to deliver. He came to the conclusion that could not break up polygamous families and make wives destitute as a precondition for a person's acceptance into the Christian Church. He also found it impossible to insist that a formal, ceremonial public demonstration of faith was a sufficient entrance qualification to the Church. In Colenso's eyes the Christian way of life was demonstrated by the manner in which one lived, not by mere forms. And he refused to use the fear of eternal suffering to drive heathens into the Church. Then, in an incident which became famous in the history of the conflict between scientific and religious beliefs in the Victorian age, Colenso stated publicly that his discussions with his Zulu assistant William Ngidi had persuaded him that the Old Testament could not be accepted as the literal word of God: that it contained, but was not, religious truth. A missionary bishop who did not insist on monogamy, and therefore did not destroy the system of communal labour which underpinned polygamy, who believed there could be salvation outside the Church, who did not assert that non-believers would suffer for eternity, and who did not accept the bible as infallible? Colenso, as we know, was driven out of the Church.

It was inevitable that such questioning of the accepted ideas of the time had to move beyond matters of belief and into the political world. This came in 1873, when the Natal government used violence against Langalibalele and his people, and then, in 1879, with the invasion of the Zulu kingdom and the exile of the Zulu king. Colenso shocked his white congregation with the vehemence and eloquence of his sermons as he urged his congregation to consider not just the losses they had suffered themselves, but the losses suffered by their Zulu enemies as well.

But, in spite of the huge personal costs he had to pay for opposing the ideas and actions of Britain towards Africans, Colenso hardly questioned his role, Britain's role, imperialism's role in southern Africa, nor did he cease to believe that the British system was the political manifestation of justice. His protests, his bitter quarrels with officials, his newspaper debates, his official interventions, were all premised on an ideal of British honesty and justice and the belief that British rule, honestly executed, was for the benefit of its subject peoples. The horrors which he saw all around him in the last ten years of his life were aberrations, the consequence of political expediency, the personal ambitions of colonial administrators, which had to be exposed so that the fountainhead of British justice, the British people and their parliament, could rectify the situation and make amends. He was unable to see that he was protesting about, not an aberration, but the very essence of Imperialism.

A Patriarch's Legacy

I have spent some time on Colenso's ideas because they were accepted, indeed they were taken over, by his daughters. On his death in 1883 they took up his banner. This was of course courageous and admirable. Southern Africa at this time was desperately in need of literate, articulate supporters of African rights, of people drawn from the upper reaches of society, who had the ear of governors, journalists, officials and the humanitarian lobby. However, not only were the number of people with such qualities minute, but they were also male—a reflection of male domination, of patriarchy in the Victorian family. Colenso's vision of himself, and his destiny, was at every stage of his life imposed on his family. It was his decision to leave England for Africa. His wife hated the idea—her sister, also the wife of a missionary bishop (in Borneo), had watched five of her children die in six years. Colenso's decision to pronounce on matters of religious belief and on imperial politics brought vituperation on him and on the heads of those around him. And Colenso's passionate commitment to justice lived on after his death in his daughters. Again this is admirable and inspiring; and yet it imposed a terrible responsibility on them which—because they were women—demanded from them greater sacrifices than those experienced by their father and their brothers.

Except for a short and extremely stimulating spell at a progressive school in England, all three Colenso daughters were educated at home. They had a wide range of interests: Harriette in geology, botany and the Classics; Frances in mathematics, art and writing; Agnes in languages, nursing and entomology. At home they had supervisory domestic as well as educational duties, and the girls spent much of their time in the classrooms at Ekukhanyeni. They had friends in Pietermaritzburg, they attended the most important social occasions, and they were visited by the leading members of colonial society. But the bishop's controversial opinions, his time-consuming duties, and their mother's aversion to colonial society meant that they were isolated—unable to travel without a chaperone and very dependent on their father as a consequence. Harriette and Agnes, the eldest and the youngest of the children were both shy, although Harriette was capable of overcoming this when necessary. As they grew older, they grew closer and closer; Frances described them as being like husband and wife. In fact they never married and died within months of one another. Frances had more than one romantic association with men in the colony, but her last—with a Colonel Durnford—was tragic. Durnford, who was already married, was later to die during the British invasion of Zululand. After his death, many people felt that Durnford was responsible for the disaster at Isandlwana.

Thus, although born into a loving home, a home which provided them with great intellectual stimulation, it was still a Victorian home, a bourgeois home which dominated and oppressed its female inmates. In the Victorian family a woman passed from the control of one man to that of another; from her father to her husband. Attempts to break out of this groove were met with a phalanx of material and ideological strictures: the loss of reputation and respectability on the one hand and the loss of financial support on the other. A woman's means of subsistence lay in the control of men—husbands or fathers. As far as bourgeois women were concerned labour outside the household was not allowed; training for a profession, therefore, was not considered, and any unwillingness to marry meant not only being viewed with ridicule or animosity as an old maid, but also the real possibility of a lonely and often poverty-stricken old age.

The Daughters' Dilemma

Bishop Colenso inflamed his daughters with a passion for justice, political agitation, and a belief in the integrity of the British imperialist system, which persuaded them to continue his work after his death. It was a terrible and contradictory legacy: 'a woman's place was in the home', and women were expected to be demure and obedient to authority and their their menfolk. None of the Colenso daughters married, a fact not unrelated to their reputation as controversialists. They were unable to promote their cause and earn a salary as professional men might have done. And, at the same time, they found that agitation against injustice—paying lawyers, publishing pamphlets—cost money. With great courage they provided the funds from their own inheritance, their one source of independence. The road the Colenso sisters chose was a hard one—but it was hard especially because they were women. They had to accept a contradictory legacy: their mission was to reform an ideology which could not be reformed; to act in a world which frowned on independent action by women; to publicize a point of view without adequate means for publicity; to maintain social respectability while consuming its means—money. This was the legacy they received from their liberal, intelligent and loving father. And they accepted the moral imperatives willingly, indeed as a privilege, even as it wreaked havoc with their lives.

I don't want to give the impression that all three daughters were the same. While they were united in embracing their father's political ideals all three had very distinct personalities. Frances, in particular, was a rebel, quarrelled with her family and distressed her mother, often in differences in opinion over women's sexuality. Part of Frances's anger and vehemence sprang form the fact that she was seriously ill with the tuberculosis which was to kill her in 1887. She worked energetically, desperately, knowing that her time was short—publishing a number of books on British policy in Natal and Zululand. Her political differences with her sisters were extremely significant because they show her moving away from the Colenso point of view. She never in fact rejected her ultimate faith in Britain, although it was sorely tried, but she did begin to see violence as the very essence of colonialism. In 1884 she wrote:

> I see a terrible future for South Africa not very far ahead, the spread of a Boer empire over the whole, and the establishment of a horrible slavery of the blacks. As things are going what is to prevent it? See how the Boers are creeping on, on every side! …Our little English colonies are struggling for 'independence'. Once they get it they will make common cause with the Boers for all evil, and I firmly believe that, as things are going now three or four generations more will see a race of Boers with a mixture of the sort of British Colonists who fraternises best with the Boers independent of Europe, establishing a slavery before the horrors of which the recollection of the Southern States of America will pale. (Guy 1979: 215)

At this time, in the mid-1880s, when Natal and the Transvaal were attempting to annex Zululand, Harriette also depicted what was happening with a radical clarity unique at the time:

> The English and Dutch are conspiring together to finally crush out the Zulu and to divide the spoil. And if the Zulu make an attempt to stand for their liberty, they will be mercilessly butchered by either or both of these civilised and Christian nations. And I want you to understand the real nature of the transaction and the cruel injustice of thus wiping out the national existence of the Zulu people, by robbing them of their country... (Frances Colenso, quoted in Guy 1979: 235)

But there were differences in their responses as well. For Frances, dying in a sanatorium in England in the late 1880s, but working to publicize the injustices occurring in Zululand to the end, the only answer was resistance:

> Better to die to a man, as the brave men they have always shown themselves to be fighting for their rights, than to die out slowly as a degenerate race in the wretched unhealthy corner left to them... Better for our poor friends to die to a man; than to be made subject to any rule by colonists, or that brings them into contact with the colonists. There are many worse things than death. (Frances Colenso, quoted in Guy 1979: 237)

But Frances was writing this from England. Harriette was in Natal, in direct contact with the Zulu leaders who were asking her for advice, asking her to employ lawyers, to write petitions, and she could not answer them:

> When grey headed men put their case earnestly to me, and ask what can be said against it, I can only cover my eyes and admit that there is no answer—no real honest answer... (Frances Colenso, quoted in Guy 1979: 235)

And indeed for the liberal in a colonial situation there was no answer. As she wrote in another letter:

> My very existence as my Father's daughter tends to hold the Zulus back from resorting to force...but force might, who can tell, have been their best chance. I could not advise them to fight because I could not share the responsibility or the consequences—because I could not sufficiently judge of their chance of success, because as an Englishwoman I had no right to believe that England would not in the end—when she heard the truth—do right. (Frances Colenso, quoted in Guy 1979: 237)

A moving statement on the liberal dilemma. With all her knowledge of the suffering and violence in Zululand, and the hopelessness of the situation, she could still only hope that England would intervene—if, somehow, she could persuade those in power to act with justice.

A Dream of Justice

A few years after this Harriette once again tried to get Britain to hear the truth. In 1888 and 1889 Dinuzulu, son of the last Zulu king, and his uncles, were brought before the courts of Zululand and charged with murder and High Treason. Harriette was convinced not only of the innocence of the accused, but also of the guilt of the colonial officials in Zululand who had provoked the Zulu into defending themselves. Her faith in the facts of history, if she could only make them public, and in the essential justice of the British legal system, revived once again. If only the British public and parliament knew the truth they would respond and demand that justice be done to the Zulu chiefs. Filled with a new enthusiasm she organized and paid for their defence. Her intervention and courage raised the morale of the Zulu, who flocked to her camp in what was then the very wild frontier town of Eshowe. It was perhaps the high point in Harriette Colenso's life. She successfully persuaded the Zulu leaders that they had a chance to regain some of their independence by appealing to the law and the English sense of justice. In 1889 she and her aged mother and sister went to England to promote the cause of the chiefs. She hated public speaking but, when pressed, was most effective. She wrote pamphlets, lobbied MPs, and travelled the country addressing liberal, radical and women's organizations. But she was largely ignored by those in control of state policy and her attempt awaken the conscience of England failed. As her brother wrote to her: 'A complete change has come over the spirit of our dream'.

It was the turning point in Harriette Colenso's life: the Colensos' dream was indeed crushed in the 1890s. This is not to say that she stopped fighting or that she showed publicly signs of weakness or loss of faith. But her hopes of success in the material world, the world of politics, and of men, were irreversibly diminished. Beneath the brave and resolute exterior there are signs of a deep bitterness, the result of the hardly admitted realization that change for the better was impossible. The best that could be hoped for was limited reform, and for the majority of South Africans the conditions of existence were likely to get worse.

The South African Native Affairs Commission

I want to demonstrate this and other aspects of Harriette Colenso's character by considering the evidence she gave in 1904 to the South African Native Affairs Commission. It was out of a feeling of responsibility that she reluctantly agreed to appear before this Commission, which was trying to formulate a South Africa-wide 'native policy' after the South African war. While the evidence given before the Commission is important, much of it makes depressing reading. Some of the Commissioners and many of the witnesses were convinced that they 'knew the native' whose irrationality, backwardness and laziness was best answered by making him experience the advantages of wage labour.

Harriette Colenso had her answers to such views. A favourite device was to deflate the complacency of the questioner by exposing the hypocrisy implicit in her interrogator's racial attitudes (South African Native Affairs Commission 1905: questions 23,911-13):

Commissioner:	Do you believe in the total prohibition of liquor to the natives?
Harriette Colenso:	Yes, just as soon as ever you can bring it in for Europeans...
Commissioner:	So in fact you are not in favour of total prohibition to the Natives at present?
Harriette Colenso:	You cannot carry it out. I would like to see prohibition for all of us.

Or, to take another example (South African Native Affairs Commission 1905: questions 24,062-64):

Commissioner:	Has contact with civilisation generally improved the Native population so far as you know?
Harriette Colenso:	It is rather hard on civilisation, is it not, to put it in that form.
Commissioner:	Do you mean that to call what the Native has seen of civilisation is hard on civilisation?
Harriette Colenso:	Take the lower end of Church street—all the bad living, the prostitution, that goes on down there. Is that civilisation?
Commissioner:	Are not those the concomitants of civilisation?
Harriette Colenso:	Then I think all that sort of thing has injured them greatly.

The way she deflected the commissioners' questions greatly annoyed them. There was very little meeting of minds, and disagreement even over the way the questions were formulated. They turned eventually from men ostensibly there to gather information to interrogators, wanting to argue, disagree, and to score points. Thus, when a commissioner asked if she would give Africans the vote (South African Native Affairs Commission 1905: questions 23,987 and 23,990), her reply was 'When they asked for it...'

Commissioner:	In your opinion, [do] you think the day of enfranchisement is a long, long way off for the Zululand and Natal Native?
Harriette Colenso:	No, I do not say it is long way off, and I may say this, that the more we break up their own system, the more we shift them from the land and agriculture for their own uses and drive them to industrial centres, and drive them out to work for other people, the more we hasten on the time when they must have the franchise; it is inevitable.

And finally let us consider an exchange in which the questions are formulated in such a way that Harriette Colenso finds them impossible to answer (South African Native Affairs Commission 1905: questions 24,004-06, 24,009-12). Instead she expresses her views on the nature of good government, and in so doing turns her answers into challenges on the expertise and the status of her interrogators:

Commissioner:	Do you think the Chiefs themselves have no longer the power to give trouble in South Africa?
Harriette Colenso:	I do not think it was ever the Chiefs individually who had that power… And I think, on the whole, it has been generally we Europeans who began it, when there has been trouble.
Commissioner:	Is there not very much greater security for life and property among the native people now than before we ruled them?
Harriette Colenso:	In some parts of the country but not in others I should say.
Commissioner:	Surely there is no part of the country where one Chief could rise up and make war on another Chief, and devastate his country, and carry away his stock and his women.
Harriette Colenso:	No, if you speak of conquest of the country, ours is the latest conquest.
Commissioner:	[I]s it not the case that the conquest that you speak of left the fruits of conquest to the conquered and that we simply gave them the benefits of good government.
Harriette Colenso:	It is a question if they have had government since 1879.
Commissioner:	At any rate we have protected them being preyed upon by themselves or by other people.
Harriette Colenso:	No, I am afraid it is not so by any means.
Commissioner:	Look at Natal.
Harriette Colenso:	Natal we did not conquer from Native inhabitants and see how we have appropriated it.
Commissioner:	Will you indicate to me for a moment what would be the result to the Natives of Zululand and Natal if the British power were withdrawn tomorrow?'

Harriette Colenso: I could not say that, I could not answer such a question as that.

Commissioner: Would the country be in shambles or would it not?

Harriette Colenso: I could not tell you that; it would depend on the circumstances. I do not say for an instant that we have no right here. We have a very great right here, but every right if you turn it over, is a duty. There is as much duty in the question as right.

And there with her back to the wall speaks the daughter of Bishop Colenso, the nineteenth-century liberal, with his ideas of the duties which rested so heavily on the backs of the ruling classes. Here again I would argue lies the contradiction of the Colensos' lives. By 1904 there can have been few whites in southern Africa with a more intimate experience of African suffering and more sympathetic to the African predicament. Harriette Colenso had seen women and children smoked out of the Drakensberg caves during the Langalibalele rising, her Zulu friends had died in the Zulu civil war, she had sat for hours in the cells of Eshowe, Durban, Pietermaritzburg, on the island of St Helena, taking statements, giving comfort, passing messages for men and women, some of whom had been goaded into resisting the system, others whom she knew were quite innocent. She had seen the Natal peasantry impoverished and dispossessed. However, at the same time she knew that it was pointless placing herself beyond the pale of colonial society—that she must protest publicly and within the law, and thereby make her voice heard. And this meant talking to men of high status like the members of the South African Native Affairs Commission. And yet they did not understand her; she was a woman, a liberal, an old maid with eccentric ideas about the natives. And as long as duty, responsibility, to the political system in which she lived was the foundation of her political and moral philosophy so she would be trapped in this contradiction. And because she was unable to shift from the belief that radical political action lay in the realm of petition and protest, she failed to discern the real nature of colonial politics as the struggle between irreconcilable interests.

A Way for the Future

In 1906 the nightmare of the Zulu or Bhambatha rebellion occurred—a despairing rising against oppression which left 4000 Natal Africans and 26 Natal militia dead. This was followed by the attempt to pin the responsibility for the rising on Dinuzulu and once again he was accused of High Treason, and once again Harriette organized the defence, and paid for a considerable part of it. He was found guilty of three of the 23 counts against him and exiled once again. The Dinuzulu trial was Harriette Colenso's last great public intervention.

In 1910 the Union of South Africa came into being, denying political rights to Africans. But Harriette was greatly heartened by the creation of the South African National Congress in 1912. Here, she felt, was an organization that might well effectively oppose the system of racial tyranny entrenched in the Act of Union, and demonstrated so soon and so fundamentally in the Natives' Lands Act of 1913. Harriette was a strong supporter and friend of many of the farmers, preachers, teachers, lawyers and journalists who founded the Congress. She knew and respected John Dube, the first president, Josiah Gumede and Pixley Seme. Sol Plaatje dedicated his classic *Native Life in South Africa* to her.

But Harriette Colenso was now growing old. She and her sister had been evicted from Bishopstowe by the Church of the Province and they moved into Pietermaritzburg. Harriette turned 70 during the First World War, a conflict that so horrified her that when she was approached to assist in writing a book on Zulu history she replied that she could never concentrate on such a task while such horrors were taking place. Moreover she doubted whether the layers of deceit and untruth which lay so deep on past events could now be removed. Money was short and the sisters left Pietermaritzburg moving to the outskirts of town to Sweetwaters. Here they lived in a cottage looked after by, and looking after, a number of African retainers. Gradually Harriette and Agnes withdrew from the world. Their trips into town, in long old-fashioned dresses and wide-brimmed hats, followed by a train of Africans carrying their effects, grew fewer and fewer.

They had lived together for so long, and the world now appeared increasingly hostile. Agnes Colenso said: 'Its the parting I dread when one of us is taken'. She feared that an attempt would be made to split them up, to place them in a hospital or a home. By the end of the 1920s Harriette was bedridden, and then Agnes became partially paralyzed and was only able to use her arms to drag herself along the floor. They were determined, however, to remain on their own—neighbours were driven away, notices put up in the garden warning off visitors, and the windows barred. On one occasion a doctor had to break into the house to sew up a gash on Agnes' head. In 1932 Harriette Colenso died. Agnes was found with the body but refused to leave the house. A few months later she herself died, in the words of a neighbour, in the way she wanted, 'like a Kaffir'. The African retainers who had kept watch for so long disappeared into the locations, and as a neighbour's servant said to his employer: 'The wind will now blow on them, as it blows on us'.

Society had taken its revenge on these two women who stepped out of line. During the course of their lives the Colenso sisters had moved from the highest echelons of society, where they had mixed with some of the great figures of their time, to a poverty-stricken old age. In the end, they were treated as cranks. The warning to unmarried women who involved themselves in radical politics was clear.

The sadness of the Colenso daughters' lives, and their old age, was a direct consequence of their being women. Already by the 1930s men who had publicly criticized imperial policy were being officially recognized and gaining honours as people who had been 'ahead of their time'. Often the consequences of their attacks on the *status quo* had been ameliorated by the fact that they tended to be professional men, drawing a salary. This was not so for lady missionaries, in a tiny schismatic church, with nothing but a small pension. For a woman to take a radical position was hard in practical terms—and also emotionally. Society frowned upon women who stepped beyond the bounds of the home, who did not marry, and who challenged any part of the structure, whether political or personal. The lives of the Colenso sisters show that in human affairs there is a direct and intimate link between the intensely personal and the broadest forces of the age. And this of course is one of the most important messages of women's studies.

I would like to finish by quoting a short letter by Harriette to John Dube, first president of the South African National Native Congress. In itself it is not an important document and merely concerns the making an appointment. But, for me, it evokes the strength of Harriette Colenso as much as her speeches and pamphlets. And it contains a vision of the future—of a better future. It is a Victorian letter, written within Victorian conventions. It is from a white woman to a black man written at a time when such communication was unusual to say the least. It gives advice and yet is never patronising. It has clarity, strength and honesty, intelligence, perception—all qualities which this woman had in abundance, and which, because they were held by a woman of those times, made her long life a tragic one.

Ekukanyeni
(144 Boshoff St)
30 Aug. 1913

Dear Mr. Dube,

I understand that you are likely to be in P.M.B. on or about Sept. 10, for the Meeting of Congress on that date. If so I shall be very glad if you can look in on me here one day, letting me know a little (an hour or two) beforehand, that I may be at home when you come.

There are several matters that I think we may usefully discuss, & there are things to be done in connexion with the Lands Act. But to begin with I want to be sure that you realize how much more important a fact than even the Lands Act, is the existence of the Congress. Before, the Abantu were dumb, now they have found their voice, & John Dube has largely helped in finding it. This makes a difference for all the future. Perhaps you are too deep in the darkness of the Lands Act to perceive the difference as yet, but I see it clearly, & you will do so before long. I am, Dear Mr Dube,

Yours faithfully

H.E. Colenso

Part V

BIBLIOGRAPHY

COLENSO BIBLIOGRAPHY*

Compiled by Fiona Bell
(Assisted by Emily Krige, Margie Gray and Brenda Nsanzya)

1. *Introduction*

A bibliography of this nature draws upon a wide variety of sources for its content. Not only have the bibliographies supplied by the contributors to this publication proved useful, but also the work of bibliographers, researchers and writers from the past has also been used as a foundation upon which to build. Mention must be made of the bibliography by B.D. Fraser, compiled in 1952, which has provided a sound and invaluable basis for the lists presented here. Due to time and funding constraints, the compilers were restricted to using the libraries and archives of the Province of KwaZulu-Natal, South Africa, as their main source. Happily, KwaZulu-Natal can boast perhaps the greatest concentration of original, Colenso-related documents in the world. The relevant archives include the Killie Campbell Africana Library and the E.G. Malherbe Library of the University of Natal, the Don Africana Library of the Ethekwini Munici-pality in Durban, the Pietermaritzburg Archives Repository (formerly the Natal Archives), the Alan Paton Centre and main library of the University of Natal, Pietermaritzburg, the Natal Society Library and the Archives of the Cathedral of the Holy Nativity in Pietermaritzburg. It should be noted that the Special Collections of the Natal Society Library have recently been transferred on permanent loan to the Alan Paton Centre. Various database searches were undertaken to gain a wider coverage. SABINET Online and CD-ROM database searches such as First Search on World Cat were also completed. The compilers found numerous errors in catalogues,

* We would like to thank the following for their assistance in the compilation of this bibliography: the staff of the archives and libraries, for their help; the administrative staff and colleagues in the School of Human and Social Studies, University of Natal for their assistance and Jennifer Verbeek for her advice and support.

databases and lists—every effort was made to correct these to avoid them being perpetuated.

The bibliography has focused on published works and has been divided into two main parts. The first part, 'Works by John William Colenso', is a chronological list of Colenso's published works, including his sermons, textbooks and some of his letters. The chronological arrangement was aimed at giving researchers an understanding of the pattern and themes in his writings through the years. This arrangement does, however, lead to a 'scattering' of the various editions of a particular work over a number of years, which, it is hoped, will not be too frustrating for the user (see, for example, *The Natal Sermons*). A concerted effort has been made physically to check each item listed in this section of the bibliography and to provide locations for each item. The items marked with an asterisk have been seen at the particular location indicated.

The second part, 'A Select Bibliography of Works on John William Colenso', is an attempt to update and consolidate contemporary and later published sources about Colenso, his life and his work. The sources included are those which are directly on the topic of Colenso, edited works containing a chapter on Colenso and those which have devoted a number of pages to him (such as biographical reference works). Numerous works contain many brief references to Colenso, but do not focus on him particularly; as such, these have been excluded. These parameters determine that it the second list presented below should rightly be labelled a 'select bibliography'. (Note that the locations of the items listed in the Select Bibliography are not supplied.)

Throughout the two parts of the bibliography an attempt has been made to list each known edition or version of a work. If the same work has been published by two different publishers they are listed as separate items, whether published in the same year or not.

Due to the limitations mentioned above the following types of material have been excluded:

1. Audio-visual material,
2. Newspaper articles,
3. Official government documents,
4. Photographs,
5. Unpublished papers and manuscript collections.

For the serious researcher there are other locations identified outside South Africa where materials on Colenso are housed. In the United Kingdom these are the SPCK Archives, Cambridge University Library, the USPG Archives, Rhodes House, Oxford, and the Archives of the Aboriginal Protection Society. In the United States the ABCFM Archives, Houghton Library, Harvard University, should be consulted.

2. *Works by John William Colenso*

In the list of Colenso's works the following abbreviations are inserted in square brackets after references (where appropriate) to indicate the current location of the listed items:

APC	Alan Paton Centre, University of Natal, Pietermaritzburg
CPSA	Church of the Province of South Africa, Cathedral of the Holy Nativity, Pietermaritzburg
DA	Don Africana Library, Durban Municipal Library
ELC	Evangelical Lutheran Centre, Lutheran Theological Institute, Pietermaritzburg
ESSAL	Evangelical Seminary of Southern Africa Library, Pietermaritzburg
JL	Jesuit Library, Pietermaritzburg
KC	Killie Campbell Library, University of Natal, Durban
NM	Natal Museum, Pietermaritzburg
PAR	Pietermaritzburg Archives Repository
UND	University of Natal, Durban, E.G. Malherbe Library
UNPA	University of Natal, Pietermaritzburg, Archives
UNPL	University of Natal, Pietermaritzburg, Main Library
VM	Voortrekker Museum, Pietermaritzburg

2.1 *Works by Colenso Alone*

uncertain [Prayers for morning worship] (place and publisher unknown). [KC*, APC*, PAR]

1826[?]–1933 *J.W. Colenso Papers* [manuscript] (43 files, 11 v. [bound], 1 box; [place and publisher unknown]). [The Colenso Collection comprises about 2400 items, mainly correspondence to and from Bishop Colenso.] [KC*]

1849 *The Elements of Algebra Adapted for Teachers and Students in the University* (London: Longman). [UNP]

1851 *A Key to Algebra: Part I* (London: Longman, 2nd edn). [APC*]

1852[?] *Psalms and Hymns, for Use in the Church of England, at Home and in the Colonies: Selected and Arranged by the Lord Bishop of Natal* (London: George Bell). [APC*]

1854a *The Good Tidings of Great Joy, Which Shall Be to all People: A Sermon Preached in the Cathedral Church of Norwich, on Sunday, August 13, 1854 on the Occasion of Ordaining Henry Callaway, M.D. ...Missionary Among the Heathen in the Diocese of Natal* (London: Bell). [UNP]

1854b *Sermon Preached...March 26, 1854, in...Maritzburg, on the Occasion of the Admission of a Candidate to Deacon's Orders, Published by Request* (Durban: J. Cullingworth, Mercury Office). [DA]

1854c *Village Sermons* (Cambridge: Macmillan, 2nd edn). [KC*]

1855a *Arithmetic Designed for the Use of Schools* (London: Longman, Brown, Green & Longmans, new edn). [KC*]

1855b *An Elementary Grammar of the Zulu–Kafir Language: Prepared for the Use of Missionaries, and Other Students* (London: Clay). [KC*]

1855c *The Elements of Algebra Adapted for Teachers and Students in the University* (London: Longman, Brown, Green & Longmans, 4th edn). [KC*]

1855d *A Letter to an American Missionary from the Bishop of Natal* (Pietermaritzburg: James Archbell). [The letter was written in response to Reverend Lewis Grout's *A Reply to Bishop Colenso's 'Remarks on the Proper Treatment of Cases of Polygamy, as Found Already Existing in Converts from Heathenism'*.] [KC*]

1855e *Remarks on the Proper Treatment of Cases of Polygamy, as Found Already Existing in Converts from Heathenism* (Pietermaritzburg: May & Davis). [APC]

1855f *Sermon Preached at Pietermaritzburg...September 1855, at the Admission of a Deacon to the Order of the Priesthood...* (Durban: Natal Mercury Office). [DA]

1855g *Ten Weeks in Natal: A Journal of a First Tour of Visitation Among the Colonists and Zulu Kafirs of Natal* (Cambridge: Macmillan). [KC*, APC, UNP, VM, PAR, NM, CPSA*]

1855h *IVangeli Eli-Yingcwele Eli-baliweyo G'uMatu* (*The Holy Gospel which is Written by Matthew*) (reprinted, with some alterations, from the translation published by the American Missionaries; London: Richard Clay).

1856[?]a *Commencement of a Zulu school* (place and publisher unknown). [A photocopy of article from: *The Mission Field* July 1856 and August 1856: 156-65; 173-78.] [KC*]

1856b *Incwadi Yokukuleka jenga-so isimiso seBanhla las'England* (*The Prayer Book According to the Tenets of the Church of England*) (Emgungunhlovu [Pietermaritzburg]: May & Davis).

1856[?]c *Zulu School in Natal* (place and publisher unknown). [A photocopy of article in *The Mission Field* (October 1856): 232-32.] [KC*]

1857a *Izindaba Zokupila kuka'Jesu-Kristu indodana ka'dio unkulunkulu Inkosi yetu* (*A Narrative of the Life of Jesus Christ, the Son of Dio God our Lord*) (Pietermaritzburg: May & Davis).

1857b Letter dated 1 February 1857 to Sir George Grey giving an account of the first year of work at Ekukanyeni Mission Station, 1856–1857, in Grey Collection, National Library of South Africa, Cape Town.

1858a *A Key to Algebra: Part I* (London: Longman, Brown, Green, Longmans & Roberts, new edn). [APC*]

1858b *Minutes of the Proceedings of the Conference of the Clergy and laity of the Church of England in the Diocese of Natal, ...April 20, 1858...* (printed at the Native Industrial Training Institution, Ekukanyeni). [DA]

1858c *Two Sermons on Spiritual Eating in the Holy Eucharist, Preached in... Maritzburg* (Pietermaritzburg: May & Davis). [DA]

1859a   *An Elementary Grammar of the Zulu–Kafir Language* (Ekukanyeni, Natal: Mission Press). [KC*, APC]

1859b   *The Elements of Algebra: Designed for the Use of Schools: Part I* (London: Longman, Green, Longman & Roberts, 14th edn). [APC*]

1859c   *First Book in Zulu–Kafir: An Introduction to the Study of the Zulu Language* (Ekukanyeni: Church of England Missions).

1859d   *First Steps in Zulu–Kafir: An Abridgement of the Elementary Grammar of the Zulu–Kafir Language* (Ekukanyeni, Natal: Mission Press). [KC*]

1859e   *Izindatyana zabantu kanye nezindaba zas'eNatal* (EmGungundhlovu: May & Davis). [KC*]

1859f   *Plane Trigonometry: With the Use of Logarithms: Part I* (London: Longman, Brown, Green, Longmans & Roberts, new edn). [KC*]

1860a   *First Lessons in Science Designed for the Use of Children and Adult Natives* (2 vols. in 1; Pietermaritzburg: May & Davis). [KC*]

1860b   *First Lessons in Science Designed for the Use of Children and Adult Natives: Part II* (Pietermaritzburg: May & Davis). [APC*]

1860c   *First Steps of the Zulu Mission (October 1859)* (Missions to the Heathens, 39; London: Society for the Propagation of the Gospel in Foreign Parts). [KC*, APC]

1861a   *The Elements of Euclid (the Parts Usually Read in the Universities) from the Text of Dr Robert Simson, with Geometrical Problems for Solution* (London: Longman, Green, Longman & Roberts, new edn). [APC*]

1887 [1861]b   *First Lessons in Science* (London: Ridgway).

1861c   *First Lessons in Science Designed for the Use of Children and Adult Natives: Part I* (Ekukanyeni: Industrial Training Institution, 2nd edn). [APC*]

1861d   *Holy Communion: A Sermon* (London: Hatchard). [The cover title reads *The Lord's Supper.*] [KC*]

[1861]e   A Letter to His Grace the Archbishop of Canterbury Upon the Question of the Proper Treatment of Cases of Polygamy as Found Already Existing in Converts from Heathenism (Ekukanyeni: Mission Press; Pietermaritzburg: P. Davis). [A letter dated Natal, March 1, 1861.] [KC*, DA]

1861f   *Letter to the Laity of the Diocese of Natal* (London: Longmans, Green, 3rd edn). [DA, APC]

1861g   *The Message which Came Unto All Men: A Christmas Sermon Preached in the Parish Church of Wynberg, Cape of Good Hope* (Cape Town: A.S. Robertson). [KC*]

1861h   *St. Paul's Epistle to the Romans: Newly Translated and Explained from a Missionary Point of View* (Cambridge: Macmillan).

1861i   *St. Paul's Epistle to the Romans: Newly Translated and Explained from a Missionary Point of View* (Ekukanyeni: Mission Press). [KC*, UNP, APC]

1861j   *Zulu–English Dictionary* (Pietermaritzburg: P. Davis). [KC*, APC, UND]

1862a   *A Letter to His Grace the Archbishop of Canterbury, Upon the Question of the Proper Treatment of Cases of Polygamy, as Found Already Existing in Converts from Heathenism* (London: Macmillan). [A photocopy of pamphlet in the Pusey House Library, Oxford.] [APC]

1863 [1862]b   *The Pentateuch and Book of Joshua Critically Examined: Part I* (New York: Appleton). [KC*, UNP*]

1862c   *The Pentateuch and Book of Joshua Critically Examined: Part I* (London: Longmans, Green, 2nd rev. edn). [APC]

1863 [1862]d   *The Pentateuch and Book of Joshua Critically Examined: Part I* (London: Longman, Green, Longman, Roberts & Green). [With: *The Pentateuch and Book of Joshua Critically Examined: Part II* (London: Longman, Green, Longman, Roberts & Green, 1863).] [KC*]

1862–65   *The Pentateuch and Book of Joshua Critically Examined: Parts I-V* (5 vols.; London: Longman, Green, Longman, Roberts & Green). [KC*]

1862–71   *The Pentateuch and Book of Joshua Critically Examined: Parts I-VI* (6 vols.; London: Longmans, Green). [APC*, UNP (Has pts I, II, III, VI only)*]

1863a   *Extracts from the Two Works Published by the Bishop of Natal* (London: Church Review)

1863b   *Notes by the Bishop of Natal on an Examination of Part I of His Work on the Pentateuch by the Rev. Dr. M'Caul* (London: Longmans, Green). [Bound with: *A Letter to the Laity of the Diocese of Natal* (London: Longmans, Green, 1864); *Remarks Upon the Recent Proceedings and Charge of Robert Lord Bishop of Capetown...* (London: Longmans, Green, 1864); and various works by other authors.] [UNP*]

1863c   *The Pentateuch and Book of Joshua Critically Examined: Parts I-VII* (London: Longman, Green, Longman, Roberts & Green, 5th rev. edn). [PAR*]

1863d   *Trial of the Bishop of Natal for Erroneous Teaching: Before the Metropolitan Bishop of Cape Town, and the Bishops of Graham's Town and the Orange Free State as Assessors* (Cape Town: Cape Argus). [KC*, APC, CPSA]

1864a   *Abraham's Sacrifice: A Sermon for Claybrook Sunday-School* (London: Longman). [Includes two extracts from his works *On the Fear of Death* and *On the Reading of the Scriptures*.] [KC*]

1864b   *Bishop Colenso on The Pentateuch: Part I* (London: Longman, People's edn).

1864c   *A Letter to the Laity of the Diocese of Natal* (London: Longman, Green, Longman, Roberts & Green).

[1864]d   *A Letter to the Laity of the Diocese of Natal* ([London: Spottiswoode]). [A photocopy of pamphlet in Pusey House Library, Oxford] [APC*]

1864e   *Remarks Upon the Recent Proceedings and Charge of Robert Lord Bishop of Capetown and Metropolitan at his Primary Metropolitical Visitation of the Diocese of Natal* (London: Longman, Green, Longman, Roberts & Green). [KC*, DA]

1865a   *Foreign Missions and Mosaic Traditions: A Lecture* (London: Macdonald). [Another longer version of this lecture appeared under the title: *On Missions to the Zulus in Natal & Zululand: A Lecture*. The lecture deals with the value of Christian missions to the heathen, Bible criticism and the Zulus.] [KC*]

1865b   *Foreign Missions and Mosaic Traditions: A Lecture* (London: Murray). [Another longer version of this lecture appeared under the title: *On Missions to the Zulus in Natal & Zululand: A Lecture*. The lecture deals with the value of Christian missions to the heathen, Bible criticism and the Zulus.] [KC*]

[1865]c   *Natal Sermons: A Series of Discourses Preached in the Cathedral Church of St Peter's, Maritzburg* ([Pietermaritzburg]: [Davies for J.W. Colenso]). [The title on the spine reads *Bp. Colenso's Sermons*. This volume contains first and second series: the first sermon was delivered on 12 November 1865; the last sermon was delivered on 27 May 1866.] [UNP]

1865[?]d   *On Missions to the Zulus in Natal & Zululand: A Lecture* (London: J. Kenny, [printer]). ['Read at the Marylebone Literary Institution, Edward Street, Portman Square, on Tuesday, the 23rd of May, 1865'. 'Reprinted from the *Social Science Review* for June, 1864'. Reprinted in J.W. Colenso's *Bringing Forth Light* (1982): 203-38.] [KC*, DA]

1865[?]e   'On the Efforts of Missionaries Among Savages' [A bound photocopy of article in *Journal of the Anthropological Society* 3 (1865): 248-89.] [KC*, DA]

1865f   *On the Judicial Functions of Metropolitans, and on the Appeal of Bishop Colenso* (London: Rivingtons).

1865g   *The Pentateuch and Book of Joshua Critically Examined* (London: Longmans, Green, People's edn). [Contains pts I-V 'corrected and condensed'.] [APC*]

1865h   *Preface and Concluding Remarks of Part 5 of the Pentateuch and Book of Joshua Critically Examined...Printed Separately by Request* (London: Trübner & Co.). [DA]

1865[?]i   *Sermon Preached in St Paul's Durban...November 12, and in Maritzburg... November 26, [1865]* (Pietermaritzburg: P. Davis [printer]). [DA]

1866[?]a   *The Case of Bishop Colenso: Rolls Court, Nov. 6, 1866, Before the Master of the Rolls: Colenso v. Gladstone and Others*, I ([Pietermaritzburg: J.W. Colenso(?)]). [KC*]

1866b   *The Elements of Algebra Designed for the Use of Schools: Part II* (London: Longmans, Green, new edn). [With: *A Key to Algebra: Part II* (London: Longman, Green, Longman, Roberts & Green, 1863, new edn).] [KC*]

1866c   *A Letter to the Members of the United Church of England and Ireland in the Diocese of Natal* (Pietermaritzburg: P. Davis). [KC*, DA]

1866d   *Natal Sermons: A Series of Discourses Preached in the Cathedral Church of St Peter's, Maritzburg* (London: Trübner & Co.). [KC*, UNP, DA]

[1866]e   *Natal Sermons: Fourth Series* (place and publisher unknown). [No title page: title taken from spine.] [UNP]

1866f   *[Natal sermons]*. Third and fourth series (place and publisher unknown). [Contains sermons preached from 3 June to 23 December 1866.] [APC*]

[1866–67]   *[Natal sermons. Third series, no. 1-26]* (7 pts.; place and publisher unknown). [KC*, UNP, DA]

1866g   *Reply...to 'Remarks by the Rev. W.O. Newnham...on Some Portions of Bishop Colenso's Teaching and its Tendencies'* (Pietermaritzburg: P. Davis). [DA]

1866[?]h   *A Sermon Preached in...Maritzburg...January 7, (1866)* (place and publisher unknown). [DA]

1866[?]i   *A Sermon Preached in the Cathedral Church of S. Peter's, Maritzburg on Sunday Evenings, Feb. 4 and 11, 1866* (Natal Sermons, First series, 13; [Pietermaritzburg: P. Davis]). [KC*]

1866[?]j   *A Sermon Preached in the Cathedral Church of S. Peter's, Maritzburg on Sunday Morning, Feb. 11, 1866* (Natal Sermons, First series, 14; [Pietermaritzburg: P. Davis]). [KC*]

1866[?]k   *A Sermon Preached in the Cathedral Church of S. Peter's, Maritzburg on Sunday Mornings, Jan. 28 & Feb. 4, 1866* (Natal Sermons, First Series, 12; [Pietermaritzburg: P. Davis]). [KC*, DA]

1866l   *Two Sermons Preached by the Lord Bishop of Natal in St. Paul's, Durban,*
            on Sunday, November 12, 1865, and in the Cathedral Church of St.
            Peter's, Maritzburg, on Sunday, November 19, 1865, and on Sunday, November 26,
            1865 (London: Trübner & Co.). [KC*]
1867a   *The Argument of the Bishop of Natal before the Supreme Court of the*
            Colony of Natal...September10, 1867 (London: Trübner & Co.). [DA]
1867b   [Correction of Statements Made by the Bishop of Cape Town]: Letter to
            the Editor of *The Times*, dated 9 December 1867 ([Pietermaritzburg:
            J.W. Colenso]). [Draft print with hand-written amendments.] [APC*]
1867c   *Lecture Delivered by Request of the Working Men of Durban...February 25*
            1867... (Durban: Natal Printing Co., Herald Office). [KC]
1867d   *Natal Sermons: A Series of Discourses Preached in the Cathedral Church of*
            St Peter's, Maritzburg (London: Trübner, 2nd edn). [Contains first series.]
            [UNP*, APC, CPSA]
1867e   [*Natal Sermons*. Fourth Series, no. 1-20] (5 pts.; place and publisher un-
            known). [The sermons were issued in sets of four, each set bearing the title:
            Four sermons preached in the Cathedral Church of St. Peter's, Maritzburg.
            (One KC copy is bound with: *Three sermons preached in the Cathedral*
            Church of St. Peter's, Maritzburg).] [KC*, DA]
1867[?]f   *Published for the Information of the Clergy and Laity of the United Church*
            of England and Ireland in the Diocese of Natal (Pietermaritzburg[?]:
            publisher unknown). [Includes correspondence between Bishop Colenso and
            churchwardens of St Andrew's Church, Pietermaritzburg, and summonses
            issued by the bishop on 26 March 1867 to the reverends James Green,
            Thomas Gleadowe Fearne and James Walton.] [KC*]
1867[?]g   *Reply of the Bishop of Natal Delivered before the Supreme Court on Thurs-*
            day, November 14, 1867 (place and publisher unknown). [From the case of
            the Bishop of Natal vs. Rev. J. Walton and Rev. J. Green.] [KC*]
1867[?]h   *A Sermon Preached in the Cathedral Church of St. Peter's, Maritzburg, on*
            Sunday Morning, October 20, 1867 (place and publisher unknown). [KC*,
            APC, DA]
1867i   *Three Sermons: Preached in the Cathedral Church of St. Peter's, Maritz-*
            burg (place and publisher unknown). [Bound with *Natal Sermons: Fourth*
            Series (no. 1-20).] [KC*]
1867j   *To the Clergy and Laity of the United Church of England and Ireland in the*
            Diocese of Natal (place and publisher unknown). [APC*]
1868a   *Natal Sermons: Second Series of Discourses Preached in the Cathedral*
            Church of St Peter's, Maritzburg (London: Trübner & Co.). [KC*, APC
            (Covers sermons from 4 March to 27 May 1866)*, UNP]
1868[?]b   *The Elements of Algebra: Designed for the Use of Schools: Part I*; to which
            is prefixed *A Sketch of the History of Algebra* (London: Longmans, Green,
            new edn). [APC*]
1869[?]   *The Elements of Algebra Designed for the Use of Schools: Part I* (London:
            Longmans, Green, new edn to which is prefixed *A Sketch of the History of*
            Algebra). [With: *A Key to Algebra: Part I* (London: Longmans, Green,
            [186?], new edn).] [KC*]
1870a   *Address Delivered by the Bishop of Natal at the Fifth Session of the Church*
            Council of the Diocese of Natal, May 31st, 1870 (Pietermaritzburg: P.
            Davis). [KC*, DA]

1870[?]b   [Letter addressed to C.J. Harford and dated Bishopstowe, 8 September 1870] (Pietermaritzburg: P. Davis). [Originally published as an appendix to: *Correspondence between the Bishop of Maritzburg* (Church of the Province of South Africa) and C.J. Harford (Church of England).] [KC*]

1870–79[?]   *Review of Bishop Colenso on The Pentateuch, etc.* ([New York]: Holman).

1977 [1871]   *Abstract of Colenso on the Pentateuch: A Comprehensive Summary of Bishop Colenso's Argument, Proving that the Pentateuch is not Historically True; and that it was Composed by Several Writers, the Earliest of Whom Lived in the Time of Samuel, from 1100 to 1060 B.C., and the Latest in the Time of Jeremiah, from 641 to 624 B.C. To which is Appended an Essay on the Nation and Country of the Jews;* [by] J.W. Colenso [and] W.H. Burr (New York: Sold by the American News Co.).

1871a   *First Steps in Zulu: Being an Elementary Grammar of the Zulu Language* (Pietermaritzburg: P. Davis, 2nd edn). [APC]

1871b   *Izinncwadi zika' Samuele ezimbili, eyokuqala neyobubili* (Bishopstowe: Mission Press; Maritzburg: P. Davis).

1871–74   *The New Bible Commentary by Bishops and Other Clergy of the Anglican Church Critically Examined* (6 vols.; London: Longmans, Green). [KC (Vols. 1-5 only)*, DA, PAR (Pts. IV-VI only)]

1873a   *Contributions to the Criticism of the Pentateuch* (Bishopstowe: [Mission Press]). [Notes by Colenso on an essay by W.H. Kosters.] [DA]

1873b   *Dr. Colenso versus the Bible: 'Correspondence' Reprinted from the 'Witness': With Additions from Bishop Thirlwall and Others* (Pietermaritzburg: P. Davis. [Correspondence between 'Reviewer', Dr. Colenso and S.N. Waterhouse with additions. 'The critique upon the book entitled "The Pentateuch and Moabite stone", led to it...'-Pref.] [KC*]

1873c   *Lectures on the Pentateuch and the Moabite Stone* (London: Longmans, Green, 2nd edn). [Appendices: 'I. The Elohistic narrative'; 'II. The Original Story of the Exodus'; 'III. The Pre-Christian Cross, Its Universality and Meaning.] [KC*, UNP, APC]

1874[?]a   *Defence of Langalibalele: With Additional Evidence and an Appendix Bringing Down the History of the Case to the Latest Date* ([Bishopstowe(?): Mission Press(?)]). ['Name of author does not appear in book, but the command paper C.1121 for 1875, contains a commentary on this publication (pp. 20ff) by Sir Theophilus Shepstone, Secretary for Native Affairs at this time, and Bp Colenso is held to be the author'-SABIB. Volume 1.] [KC*]

1874b   *Langalibalele and the amaHlubi Tribe: Being Remarks Upon the Official Record of the Trials of the Chief, His Sons and Induna, and Other Members of the amaHlubi Tribe* (London: Spottiswoode [printer]). [KC*, APC]

1874[?]c   *Sermon Written for Westminster Abbey, December 21st, 1874.* [Detached from: *The Contemporary Review* 25 (1874[?]): (327)-35.] [KC*]

1875[?]a   *The History of the Matshana Enquiry: With a Report of the Evidence; as taken down by the Bishop of Natal and the Reverend Canon Tonnesen* ([Bishopstowe: Mission Press]). [KC*]

1875b   *Izindab'ezinhle ezashunyayelwa ku'bantu ng'uJesuKristo inkosi yetu kanye nezinncwadi ezalotywa ng'Abapostole bake (The Good News which was Proclaimed to Humanity by Jesus Christ our Lord together with the Letters which were Written by his Apostles)* (Maritzburg, P. Davis).

1876a   *Arithmetic Designed for the Use of Schools: To Which is Added a Chapter on Decimal Coinage* (London: Longmans, Green, new edn, thoroughly rev.). [KC*, APC]

1876[?]b   *Izindab'ezinhle Ezashunyayelwa Ku'bantu ng'uJesu-Kristo Inkosi Yetu Kanye Nezinncwadi Ezalotshwa Ng'abapostole Bake (The Good News Preached to People by Jesus Christ Our Lord Together with the Letters Written by His Apostles)* (Pietermaritzburg/Durban: P. Davis; Bishopstowe: Magema [printer]).

1876c   *Lectures on the Pentateuch and the Moabite Stone...* (London: Longmans, Green, 3rd edn). [UNP]

[1878–88]   *[Digest of Zulu Affairs]*. Series 1-9; continued after his death by his daughter, Harriette Emily Colenso (9 vols. in 5; [Durban]). [Photocopy of original published: Bishopstowe: Mission Press, 1878–88.] [KC*]

1878[?]a   *Zulu–English Dictionary* (Pietermaritzburg: Davis, new rev. and enlarged edn). [KC*, UNP]

1879a   'Letters on Cetywayo's Overtures of Peace', *Aborigines' Friend* June: 149-53. [KC]

1879[?]b   *What Doth the Lord Require of Us?: A Sermon Preached in the Cathedral Church of St. Peter's, Pietermaritzburg, on Wednesday, March 12, 1879, the Day Appointed by Authority to be Kept as a Day of Humiliation and Prayer, in Consequence of the Great Disaster at Isandhlwana on January 22nd, 1879* ([Bishopstowe(?): Mission Press(?)]; Pietermaritzburg: P. Davis). [KC*, UNP (Copy has no title. Begins 'A sermon...'), APC, DA]

188?   *Bishop Colenso's Commentary on Frere's Policy* (place and publisher unknown). [This item consists of series I and II of Colenso's *Digest of Zulu Affairs* ([Durban: 197?]).] [KC*]

1880   *Four Sermons Preached in St. George's Cathedral Church, Grahamstown; together with An Address to Candidates for Confirmation* (Grahamstown: Sheffield). [KC*, APC, DA]

1881   *Umzimba ozwayo; ikitshwe ng'uSobantu enoWilliam-Ngidi* (Pietermaritzburg: Davis). [KC*]

1882a   *Address Delivered by the Right Rev. J.W. Colenso, Lord Bishop of Natal, at the Seventh Session of the Church Council of the Diocese of Natal, Held at Durban, October 17th & 18th, 1882: Together with the Rules to be Observed in the Diocese of Natal, as Revised at the Said Session* (Pietermaritzburg: P. Davis). [KC*, APC*, DA]

1882b   *Exodus* (Bishopstowe: publisher unknown).

1882c   *First Steps in Zulu: Being an Elementary Grammar of the Zulu Language* (Pietermaritzburg: P. Davis, 3rd edn). [KC*]

1882[?]d   *Sir Bartle Frere's Last Attack on Cetshwayo*; [by] Sir H. Bulwer and Bishop Colenso (London: publisher unknown). [Includes text of letters written by Sir Bartle Frere, Francis E. Colenso and Bishop Colenso concerning the restoration of Cetshwayo and the state of affairs in Zululand.] [KC*]

1883   *Three Sermons Preached in...Maritzburg* (Pietermaritzburg: P. Davis). [DA]

1884[?]a   *The Course of Political Events in Zululand: From October 1881 to 16th June 1883: Official, Colonial & Zulu Statements, Analysed and Compared* ([Bishopstowe(?): Mission Press(?)]). [Spine title: *The Zulu nation: Extracts from the Blue Book*. Part of Colenso's *Digest of Zulu affairs*. Series II

(1878–88). Concluding remark on p. 884 signed H.E. Colenso, Bishopstowe, May 20, 1884 states: '...The Digest of papers on Zulu Affairs must therefore be considered to be closed...'] [KC*, PAR]

1884b   *Zulu–English Dictionary* (Pietermaritzburg: Davis, new rev. and enlarged edn). [KC*, APC]

1890   *First Steps in Zulu: Being an Elementary Grammar of the Zulu Language* (Pietermaritzburg: P. Davis, 4th edn). [KC*, UNP]

1894a   *Address to Candidates for Confirmation...October 21, 1880, Reprinted in 1894, as a Christmas Gift to Members of his Flock Who Have Recently Been Confirmed* (Pietermaritzburg: Munro Bros.). [A sermon.] [KC*]

1894b   *The Pentateuch and Book of Joshua Critically Examined* (London: Longmans, Green, new People's edn). [Contains Parts I-V.] [APC*]

1895a   *Amazwi ka Sobantu: okululeka akitshwe olimini lwamaNgisi ng'uDhlwedhlwe ka Sobantu: kanye no Dinuzulu ong'uMamonga ka Cetshwayo betanda ukusiza abantu baoyise* (Pietermaritzburg: Munro Bros., 1895). [A sermon.] [KC*]

1895b   *Praying for Rain: A Sermon Preached by the Late Lord Bishop of Natal, Right Rev. John William Colenso, in the Cathedral Church of S. Peter's, Maritzburg, on Sunday, November 17th, 1878* (place and publisher unknown). [APC]

1897   *Izindab'ezinhle Ezashunyayelwa Ku'bantu ng'uJesu-Kristo Inkosi Yetu Kanye Nezinncwadi Ezalotshwa Ng'abapostole Bake* (The Good News Preached to People by Jesus Christ Our Lord Together with the Letters Written by His Apostles) (London: J.M. Dent & Co. [printed and published for Miss H.E. Colenso] [2nd edn]).

1898   *A Shilling Arithmetic Designed for the Use of Elementary Schools* (London: Longmans, Green, new edn). [APC]

19??   *ZULU Pamphlets. Volume I* (place and publisher unknown). [A photocopy of a collection of pamphlets, by various authors, on the Zulus and their status. Originally bound together, presumably by Harriette Colenso, in 2 vols. entitled: *Zulu Pamphlets*. Includes: 'What doth the Lord require of us?' by J.W. Colenso.] [KC*]

1901   *Inncwadi ka'Bunyane okutiwa ukuhamba kwesihambi (Zulu).* Translated by John William Colenso (Pietermaritzburg: Vause & Slatter).

1902   *Genesis: A Commentary on the Book of Genesis* (2 vols.; Pietermaritzburg: Vause, Slatter). [Contents: pt. 1. *Amazwi okucansisela, kanye namazwi alotshwa kuqala*; pt. 2. *Amazwi ngokuxutshwa kwawo endulo*.] [KC*]

1903   *First Steps in Zulu: Being an Elementary Grammar of the Zulu Language* (Pietermaritzburg: Vause, Slatter, 4th edn). [APC]

1904   *First Steps in Zulu: Being an Elementary Grammar of the Zulu Language* (Pietermaritzburg: P. Davis, 5th edn). [KC*, UNP, APC]

1905a   *Zulu–English Dictionary* (Pietermaritzburg: Vause, Slatter, 4th authorized rev. and enlarged edn). [KC*, UNP, NM, APC*]

1905b   *Zulu–English Dictionary* (Pietermaritzburg: Shuter & Shooter, 4th rev. and enlarged edn). [UNP]

1967 [1905]   *Zulu–English Dictionary* (Farnborough, Hants.: Gregg, 4th rev. and enlarged authorised edn). [JL]

1918   *Three Sermons Preached in the Cathedral Church of S. Peter's, in 1883* (Pietermaritzburg: City Printing Works). [UNP, APC]

1920   *Amazwi ka Sobantu (Bishop Colenso): awashumayela ebandhleni lake
labelungu ngonyaka wokugoduka kwake* (1883) (Acindezelwe: publisher
unknown). ['Akitshwe olimini lwamaNgisi ng'uDhlwedhlwe ka Sobantu,
nabamsizayo, 1919'. A sermon.] [KC*]

1923   *Praying for Rain: A Sermon Preached in the Cathedral Church of S. Peter's,
Pietermaritzburg on Sunday, November 17th, 1878* (Pietermaritzburg: City
Printing Works, 3rd edn). [KC*]

[1978]   *Izindaba zas 'eNatal* ([Durban]). [Bound photocopy, p. lxxxi-cxxvii.] [KC*]

1982   *Bringing Forth Light: Five Tracts on Bishop Colenso's Zulu mission* (ed.
Ruth Edgecome; Killie Campbell Africana Library Reprint Series, 4; Pieter-
maritzburg: University of Natal Press; Durban: Killie Campbell Africana
Library). [Consists of reprints of the following by J.W. Colenso: *Church
Missions Among the Heathen in the Diocese of Natal*; *The Good Tidings of
Great Joy, which Shall be to all People*; *First Steps of the Zulu Mission
(October 1859)*; *Three Native Accounts of the Visit of the Bishop of Natal in
September and October, 1859, to Umpande, King of the Zulus*; *On Missions
to the Zulus in Natal and Zululand*.] [KC*, UNP, ELC, ESSAL, NM, PAR,
UNPA, CPSA, UND]

2003   *Commentary on Romans* (edited with an Introduction by Jonathan A. Draper;
Pietermaritzburg: Cluster Publications).

2.2. Collaborative Works by John William Colenso and Others

Hunter, John

1873   *Key to Colenso and Hunter's Introductory Algebra* (London: Longmans,
Green). [KC*]

188?   *A Key to Colenso's Arithmetic* (London: Longmans, Green, new edn). [KC*]

Kuenen, A.

1865   *The Pentateuch and Book of Joshua Critically Examined; Translated from
the Dutch and Edited with Notes by J.W. Colenso* (London: Longman,
Green, Longman, Roberts & Green). [KC*, UNP, PAR*]

La Touche, James D.

186?   *A sermon; by James D. la Touche [of] The Society for the Propagation of the
Gospel and the Natal Diocese: Extracted from the Natal Herald of March
7th, 1867. An Extract from the Bishop of Natal's Pastoral Address to the
Clergy and Laity of the United Church of England and Ireland in the
Diocese of Natal. Bishopstowe, 25 March 1867* ([London(?): Natal Church
Committee(?)]). [One of a number of leaflets published by Bishop Colenso's
supporters in London, to present Colenso's cause in the church controversy
in Natal. A fund was started and a note on this pamphlet invites subscrip-
tions to be sent to the Natal Church Committee in London.] [KC*]

Maurice, Frederick Denison

1886   *The Communion Service, from the Book of Common Prayer: With Select
Readings from the Writings of F.D. Maurice* (ed. J.W. Colenso (London:
Macmillan, new edn). [UNP]

Oort, H.

1865   *The Worship of Baalim in Israel: Based upon the Work of Dr. R. Dozy 'The
Israelites at Mecca'; Translated from the Dutch and Enlarged with Notes*

[1852]

and Appendices by John William Colenso (London: Longmans, Green).
[KC*, UNP, APC]

PSALMS and Hymns for Use in the Church of England, at Home and in the Colonies; Selected and Arranged...by the Lord Bishop of Natal (London: Bell). [APC]

1901

Three Native Accounts of the Visit of the Bishop of Natal in September and October, 1859, to Umpande, King of the Zulus: With Explanatory Notes and a Literal Translation and a Glossary of all the Zulu Words Employed in the Same: Designed for the Use of Students of the Zulu Language (trans. and ed. by J.W. Colenso; Pietermaritzburg: Vause, Slatter, 3rd edn). [KC*, UNP, APC]

Vijn, Cornelius

1880

Cetshwayo's Dutchman: Being the Private Journal of a White Trader in Zululand During the British Invasion; Translated from the Dutch and Edited with Preface and Notes by J.W. Colenso (London: Longmans, Green). [Pages 83-192 consist of Colenso's notes. Appendices: 'The Zulu Military System'; 'A Protest Against the Zulu War'.] [KC*, APC, PAR, VM, UND]

1969 [1880]

Cetshwayo's Dutchman: Being the Private Journal of a White Trader in Zululand During the British Invasion; Translated from the Dutch and Edited with Preface and Notes by J.W. Colenso (New York: Negro Universities Press). [Reprint of Longmans, Green 1880 edn.] [UNP*]

1988 [1880]

Cetshwayo's Dutchman: Being the Private Journal of a White Trader in Zululand During the British Invasion; Translated from the Dutch and Edited with Preface and Notes by J.W. Colenso (London: Greenhill).

3. A Select Bibliography of Works on John William Colenso

Alpha

1853

Bishop Colenso and the Pentateuch or, The Bible in the Gospels: A Vindication of the Historical Character of the Old Testament (London: Wertheim, Macintosh & Hunt).

Angus, J.

1863

Our Progress Statistical and Spiritual: A Paper Read at the Autumnal Meeting of the Baptist Union...Manchester Oct. 9, 1872 (Manchester: Palmer & Howe).

Arnold, Matthew

1863a

'The Bishop and the Philosopher', *Macmillan's Magazine* 7 (February).

1863b

'Dr Stanley's Lectures in the Jewish Church', *Macmillan's Magazine* 7 (February): 327-36.

[The above articles are republished in Fraser Neiman (ed.), *Essays, Letters, and Reviews by Matthew Arnold* (Cambridge, MA: Harvard University Press, 1960).]

Ashpitel, F.

1978

The Increase of the Israelites in Egypt Shewn to be Probable from the Statistics of Modern Populations: With an Examination of Bishop Colenso's Calculations on This Subject (Oxford: John Henry & James Parker).

Barber, S.R.

1975

'The Development of J.W. Colenso as a Missionary Bishop' (unpublished Masters dissertation, Pietermaritzburg, University of Natal).

Barnes, R.

1866　　　*Remarks on the Judgement of the Judicial Committee: In the Case of the Bishop of Natal* (Exeter: Roberts; London: Hatchard).

Beke, C.T.

1862　　　*A Few Words with Bishop Colenso on the Subject of the Exodus of the Israelites and the Position of Mount Sinai* (London: Williams & Norgate).

1863　　　*A Few Words with Bishop Colenso on the Subject of the Exodus of the Israelites and the Position of Mount Sinai* (London: James Madden, Williams & Norgate).

Benisch, A.

1863　　　*Bishop Colenso's Objections to the Historical Character of the Pentateuch and Book of Joshua (Contained in Part I)* (London: Jewish Chronicle).

Biley, E.

1865　　　*The Elohistic and Jehovistic Theory Minutely Examined with Some Remarks on Scripture and Science: Having Especial Reference to the Fourth Part of 'The Pentateuch, etc., Critically Examined by the Right Rev. J,W. Colenso, D.D., Bishop of Natal* (London: Bell & Daldy).

Bost, T.E.

1863　　　*A French Pastor's Estimate of Bishop Colenso's Work on the Pentateuch, Parts I and II* (London: Longman).

Brooke, A.

1947　　　*Robert Gray: First Bishop of Cape Town* (Cape Town: Oxford University Press).

Brookes, E.H.

1936　　　*A Century of Missions in Natal and Zululand* (Durban: E.H. Brookes).

Brookes, E.H., and C. de B. Webb

1987　　　*A History of Natal* (Pietermaritzburg: University of Natal Press, 2nd edn).

Browne, E.H.

1863　　　*The Pentateuch and the Elohistic Psalms: In Reply to Bishop Colenso: Five Lectures Delivered in the University of Cambridge* (London: Longman, Green).

1978　　　*The Pentateuch and the Elohistic Psalms: In Reply to Bishop Colenso: Five Lectures Delivered in the University of Cambridge* (London: Parker, Son & Brown).

Brunel, I.

1868　　　*Remarks on the Proceedings at Capetown in the Matter of the Bishop of Natal* (London: Rivingtons).

Burnand, F.C.

1863　　　*Bishop Colenso Utterly Refuted, and Categorically Answered* (London: Richard Hatton).

Burnett, B.B.

1947　　　'The Missionary Work of the First Anglican Bishop of Natal, the Right Rev. John William Colenso, D.D.; between the Years 1852–1873' (unpublished Masters dissertation, Grahamstown: Rhodes University).

1955　　　*Anglicans in Natal* (Durban: Churchwardens, St Paul's [1950, 1954]).

Callaway, H.

[1862]　　*Polygamy: A Bar to Admission into the Christian Church* (Durban: John O. Brown).

Chadwick, O.
1970   *The Victorian Church Part II* (London: Adam and Charles Black).
Chamberlain, W.
1863   *A Plain Reply to Bishop Colenso Respectfully Addressed to the Layman of England* (London: Wertheim, Macintosh & Hunt).
Chesson, F.W. (ed.)
1881   *Cetywayo and Langalibalele: The Bishop of Natal's Interview with the Ex-Zulu King* (Westminster: P.S. King).
Cheyne, T.K.
1893   *Founders of Old Testament Criticism* (London: Methuen).
Chidester, D.
1996   *Savage Systems: Colonialism and Comparative Religion in Southern Africa* (Cape Town: University of Cape Town Press).
Church Council of the Diocese of Natal, Session
1858   *Report of a Committee Appointed by the Church Council to Consider...the Secession of the Rev. Canon Jenkins, and the Rev. R. Robertson* (Durban: Natal Printing Co.)
Church of England in Natal Defence Association
1903   *Addresses by Counsel Against the Late Church Properties Bill* (place of publication unknown: The Association).
Church of the Province of South Africa
[1865]   *Letters and Articles in the Case of Dr. Colenso, Extracted from English Publications, with Introductory Remarks* (Cape Town: Saul Solomon, Printers).
1887   *The Constitution and Canons of the Church of the Province of South Africa as Revised, Amended and Confirmed by the Provincial Synod, held at Cape Town* (Cape Town: College Press).
Clark, J.
1976   'Colenso's Greatest Sermon', *Natalia* 6 (December): 12-23.
Cockshut, A.O.J.
1959   *Anglican Attitudes: A Study of Victorian Religious Controversies* (London: Collins).
1964   *The Unbelievers: English Agnostic Thought, 1840-1890* (London: Collins).
1966   *Religious Controversies of the Nineteenth Century: Selected Documents* (London: publisher unknown).
Colenso, F.E.
1885   'Attacks on J.W. Colenso', *The Eagle* (St John's College, Cambridge) 13.
Colonial Office of Great Britain
1868   *Copies of the Judgements of the Supreme Court of the Colony of Natal in the Case of the Bishop of Natal against the Dean of Pietermaritzburg...* (place and publisher unknown).
Constitution and Canons of the Church of the Province of South Africa
1887   *The Constitution and Canons of the Church of the Province of South Africa as Revised, Amended and Confirmed by the Provincial Synod, Held at Cape Town, 1887* (Cape Town: College Press, Zonnebloem).
Cookesley, W.G.
1863   *An Answer to the Second Part of Bishop Colenso's Objections to the Authenticity of the Pentateuch* (London: Upham & Beet).

380 *The Eye of the Storm*

Cotterill, H.
1864   *Opinion Delivered by the Bishop of Grahamstown as Assessor in the Trial of J.W. Colenso, Dec. 14th, 1863* (London: Bell & Daldy).

Cox, G.W.
1888   *The Life of John William Colenso, D.D., Bishop of Natal* (2 vols.; London: W. Ridgway).
1896   *The Church of England and the Teaching of Bishop Colenso* (London: Kegan Paul).

Cumming, J.
1863   *Moses Right, and Bishop Colenso Wrong: Being Popular Lectures in Reply to the First and Second Parts of 'Bishop Colenso on the Pentateuch'* (New York: J. Bradburn).

Darby, I.D.
1977   'Anglican Worship in Victorian Natal' (unpublished Masters dissertation, Pietermaritzburg, University of Natal).
1981   'The Anglican Diocese of Natal: A Saga of Division and Healing', *Natalia* 11 (December): 43-46.
1982   'The Soteriology of Bishop John William Colenso' (unpublished doctoral dissertation, Pietermaritzburg, University of Natal).
1984   'Bishop Colenso and Eucharistic Theology', *Journal of Theology for Southern Africa* 46: 20-28.
1989   'Colenso and Baptism', *Journal of Theology for Southern Africa* 67: 62-66.

Davidson, P.
1863   *The Pentateuch Vindicated: From the Objections and Misinterpretations of Bishop Colenso* (Edinburgh: Elliot).

De Kock, W.J. (ed.)
1968   *Dictionary of South African Biography* (Cape Town: Nasionale Boekhandel), I: 177-81.

Deist, F.
1984   'John William Colenso: Biblical Scholar', in J.A. Loader and J.H. Le Roux (eds), *Old Testament Essays* 2 (place and publisher unknown).
1999   'Colenso, John William (1814–83)', in J.H. Hayes (ed.), *Dictionary of Biblical Interpretation* (Nashville: Abingdon Press), I: 203-204.

Doke, C.M.
1940   'Bantu Language Pioneers of the Nineteenth Century', *Bantu Studies* 14: 207-46.

Draper, J. A.
1998a   'Hermeneutical Drama on the Colonial Stage: Liminal Space and Creativity in Colenso's Commentary on Romans', *Journal of Theology for Southern Africa* 103: 13-32.
1998b   'Archbishop Gray and the Interpretation of the Bible', in J. Suggit and M. Goedhals (eds.), *Change and Challenge: Essays Commemorating the 150th Anniversary of Robert Gray as First Bishop of Cape Town (20 February 1848)* (Johannesburg: CPSA): 44-54.
2000a   'The Bishop and the Bricoleur: Bishop John William Colenso's *Commentary on Romans* and Magema Fuze's *The Black People and Whence they Came*' in G.O. West and M.W. Dube (eds.), *The Bible in Africa: Transactions, Trajectories, and Trends* (Leiden: E.J. Brill): 415-54.

2000b   'Bishop John William Colenso's Interpretation to the Zulu People of the
             Sola Fide in Paul's Letter to the Romans', *Society of Biblical Literature
             2000 Seminar Papers: One Hundred Thirty-Sixth Annual Meeting, Novem-
             ber 17-21, 2000, Opryland Hotel, Nashville, Tennessee* (SBLSPS, 39;
             Atlanta: Scholars Press): 465-93.
Drew, G.S.
1863   *Bishop Colenso's Examination of the Pentateuch Examined* (London: Bell &
             Daldy).
Droogleever, R.W.F.
1992   *The Road to Isandhlwana: Colonel Anthony Durnford in Natal and Zululand
             1873–1879* (London: Greenhill Books).
Du Plessis, J.
1911   *A History of Christian Missions in South Africa* (London: Macmillan).
Edgecombe, R.
1980   'Bishop Colenso and the Zulu Nation', *Journal of Natal and Zulu History* 3:
             n.p.
Edgecombe, R. (ed.)
1982   *Bringing Forth Light: Five Tracts on Bishop Colenso's Zulu Mission* (Pieter-
             maritzburg: University of Natal Press; Durban: Killie Campbell Africana
             Library).
Elder, W.A.
1866   *An Address by…(the) Rector of St. Thomas' Church, Verulam, Delivered on
             the Occasion of the Lawless Intrusion of Dr. Colenso into that Church…
             September 30th, 1866* (Durban: Adams).
Eldridge, C.C.
1978   *Victorian Imperialism* (London: Hodder & Stoughton).
Etherington, N.
1978   *Preachers, Peasants and Politics in Southeast Africa 1835–1880: African
             Christian communities in Natal, Pondoland and Zululand* (London: The
             Royal Historical Society).
Fowler, C.H.
1864   *Colenso's Fallacies: Another Review of the Bishop of Natal* (Cincinnati, OH:
             Poe & Hitchcock).
Fraser. B.D.
1952   *John William Colenso: A Bibliography* (Cape Town: School of Librarian-
             ship, University of Cape Town).
Freshman, C.
1864   *The Pentateuch its Genuineness and Authenticity Proved and Defended by
             Facts and Arguments against the Hypothetical Theories and Conjectural
             Criticisms, Historical and Literary, of Bishop Colenso* (Toronto: A. Green).
Fuze, M.M.
1922   *Abantu Abamnyama, Lapa Bavela Ngakona* (Pietermaritzburg: City Printing
             Works). [See the next entry for the English translation.]
1979   *The Black People and Whence They Came: A Zulu View* (trans. H.C. Lugg;
             ed. A.T. Cope; Pietermaritzburg: University of Natal Press; Durban: Killie
             Campbell Africana Library).
Gellner, E.
1974   *The Legitimation of Belief* (London: Cambridge University Press).

382 *The Eye of the Storm*

Gordon, R.E, and E. Gericke
  1973   *Macrorie, Gentle Bishop of Maritzburg: The Natal Career or William A.K. Macrorie, Bishop of Maritzburg, and his Confrontation with John William Colenso, Bishop of Natal, 1869-1891* (Pretoria: Simon Van der Stel Foundation).
Gray, C. (ed.)
  1876   *Life of Robert Gray, Bishop of Cape Town...Edited by his son...* (London: Rivingtons).
Gray, R.
  1863   *Trial of Bishop of Natal for Erroneous Teaching* (London: G Street).
  1864a *Journal of a Visitation of the Diocese of Natal in 1864* (London: publisher unknown).
  1864b *Judgement delivered by the Bishop of Cape Town on the 16th Dec., 1863 in the case of the Right Rev. J.W. Colenso, D.D. (Bishop of Natal)* (London: Bell & Daldy).
  1867   *A Letter to the Members of the Church in the Diocese of Cape Town* (Cape Town: Pike and Byles).
  1867   *A Statement Relating to the Facts which have been Misunderstood and to Questions which have been Raised in Connexion with the Consecration, Trial, and Excommunication of the Right Rev. Dr. Colenso* (London: Bell & Daldy).
Gray, R. et al.
  1867   *Correspondence of the Most Reverend the Lord Archbishop of Canterbury, the Most Rev. the Lord Archbishop of York, the Right Rev. the Lord Bishop of London, with the Bishop of Capetown Concerning the Appointment of an Orthodox Bishop to Natal* (London: Rivingtons).
  1868   *Correspondence of the Most Reverend the Lord Archbishop of Canterbury, the Most Rev. the Lord Archbishop of York, the Right Rev. the Lord Bishop of London, with the Bishop of Capetown: Concerning the Appointment of an Orthodox Bishop to Natal* (London: Rivingtons).
Greaves, A. (ed.)
  1999   'Bishop Colenso's Speech. Preached in the Cathedral Church of St Peter's, Pietermaritzburg on Wednesday, March 12th 1879', *The Journal of the Anglo Zulu War Historical Society* (December): 47-51
Green, W.H.
  1863   *The Pentateuch Vindicated from the Aspersions of Bishop Colenso* (New York: J. Wiley).
Greenslade, S.L. (ed.)
  1976   *The Cambridge History of the Bible*. III. *The West from the Reformation to the Present Day* (Cambridge: Cambridge University Press).
Gregg, F.
  1892   *The Story of Bishop Colenso: The Friend of the Zulus* (London: Sunday School Association).
Grout, L.
  1855   *A Reply to Bishop Colenso's 'Remarks on the Proper Treatment of Cases of Polygamy as Found Already Existing in Converts from Heathenism'* (Pietermaritzburg: May & Davis).
  1856   *An Answer to Dr. Colenso's 'Letter' on Polygamy* (Pietermaritzburg: May & Davis).

1869   *Colenso on the Doctrines: A Review and Analysis of St. Paul's Epistle to the Romans* (place and publisher unknown).

Gurney, A.
1864   *The Faith Against Free-Thinkers, or Modern Rationalism, as Exhibited in the Writings of Mr Buckle, Bishop Colenso, M. Renan and the Essayists* (London: n.p.).

Guy, J.
1979   *The Destruction of the Zulu Kingdom; The Civil War in Zululand, 1879– 1884* (London: Longman).
1983   *The Heretic: A Study of the Life of John William Colenso, 1814–1883* (Johannesburg: Ravan Press; Pietermaritzburg: University of Natal Press).
1991   'Learning from History: Religion, Politics, and the Problem of Contextualization—The Case of J.W. Colenso', in C.F. Hallencreutz and M. Palmberg (eds.), *Religion and Politics in Southern Africa* (Uppsala: Scandanavian Institute of African Studies): 185-93.
1997   'Class Imperialism and Literary Criticism: William Ngidi, John Colenso and Matthew Arnold', *Journal of Southern African Studies* 23.2: 219-41.
2001   *The View Across the River: Harriette Colenso and the Zulu Struggle Against Imperialism* (Chalottesville: University of Virginia; Oxford: James Currey; Cape Town: David Philip).

Hattersley, A.F.
1940   *Portrait of a Colony: The Story of Natal* (Cambridge: Cambridge University Press).
1951   *Portrait of a City* (Pietermaritzburg: Shuter & Shooter).

Henfrey, Anthony W.
1999   'What Doth the Lord require of Us? Bishop John William Colenso and the Isandlwana (1) Sermon Preached in the Cathedral Church of St Peter, Pietermaritzburg, March 12th, 1879', *The Journal of the Anglo Zulu War Historical Society* (June): 41–51.

Herd, Norman
1976   *The Bent Pine: (The Trial of Chief Langalibalele)* (Johannesburg: Ravan Press).

Hinchliff, P.
1962   'John William Colenso: A Fresh Appraisal', *Journal of Ecclesiastical History* 13.2: 203-16.
1963   *The Anglican Church in South Africa: An Account of the History and Development of the Church of the Province of South Africa* (London: Darton, Longman & Todd).
1964   *John William Colenso, Bishop of Natal* (London: Thomas Nelson).
1986   'Ethics, Evolution and Biblical Criticism in the Thought of Benjamin Jowett and John William Colenso', *Journal of Ecclesiastical History* 37 (January): 91-110.

Hirschfelder, J.M.
1864   *The Scriptures Defended being a Reply to Bishop Colenso's Book on the Pentateuch and Book of Joshua* (Toronto: Henry Rowsell).

Hoare, W.H.
1863a   *The Age and Authorship of the Pentateuch Considered.* II. *In Further Reply to Bishop Colenso* (London: Rivingtons).

1863b   *Letter to Bishop Colenso: Wherein his Objections to the Pentateuch are Examined in Detail* (London: Rivingtons).

1863c   *Letter to Bishop Colenso, Wherein his Objections to the Pentateuch are Examined in Detail: with Additional Remarks on Part II* (London: Rivingtons; Cambridge: Deighton, Bell & Co.)

Holyoake, G.J.

1817–1906   *A Zulu's Answer to Dr. Cummings. The Colenso Controversy: The View of the Kafirs Involved in it. The Missionary Meaning at the Bottom of it. A Reply to Dr. Cumming's 'Moses right; Colenso Wrong'* (place and publisher unknown).

1863   *Cumming Wrong; Colenso Right. A Reply to the Rev. Dr. Cumming's 'Moses Right; Colenso Wrong'* (London: Farrah & Dunbar).

Hooker, M.A.

1953   'The Place of Bishop J.W. Colenso in the History of South Africa' (unpublished doctoral dissertation, University of the Witwatersrand, Johannesburg).

Jarrett-Kerr, Martin

1989   'Victorian Certainty and Zulu Doubt: A Study in Christian Missionary Hermeneutics from Shaka to Colenso', in D. Jasper and T.R. Wright (eds.), *The Critical Spirit and the Will to Believe* (London: Macmillan): 145-57.

Jones, T.H.

1987   '*Ex Africa Semper Aliquid Novi*: Colenso Revisited', *Ecclesiastical Law Journal* 24: 188-95.

Judgment by the Judges of the Supreme Court of the Colony of Natal

1868   *The judgement delivered by the judges of the supreme court of the colony of Natal, in the case of the Bishop of Natal v. The Rev. J. Green, on January 9, 1868* (place and publisher unknown).

Kay, W.

1865   *Crisis Hupfeldiana being an Examination of Hupfeld's Criticism on Genesis: As Recently set Forth in Bishop Colenso's Fifth Part* (Oxford: John Henry and James Parker).

Knight, J.C.

1863   *The Incredibilities of Part II of the Bishop of Natal's Work upon the Pentateuch: A Lay Protest* (London: Samuel Bagster).

1978(?)   *The Pentateuch Narrative Vindicated: From the Absurdities Charged against it by the Bishop of Natal* (London: Samuel Bagster).

Kuenen, A.

1865   'De Kerkelijke Beweging in England', in *De Gids*, III.1-30: 185-216.

1884   'John William Colenso', in E.D. Pijzel (ed.), *Mannen van Beteekenis in Onze Dagen* (Haarlem: Tjeenk Willink): 1-28.

La Touche, James D.

186?   *A Sermon* (publication details uncertain, but possibly London: Natal Church Committee).

1867   *Lambeth Conference* (London: Rivingtons).

1948   *The Lambeth Conferences (1867–1930): The Reports of the 1920 and 1930 Conferences, with Selected Resolutions from the Conferences of 1867, 1878, 1888, 1897 and 1908* (London: SPCK).

Lambeth Conferences

1929   *The Six Lambeth Conferences 1867–1920* (London: SPCK).

Larsen, T.

1997   'Bishop Colenso and critics: the strange emergence of Biblical criticism in Victorian Britain', *Scottish Journal of Theology* 50.4: 433-58.

2003   'Colenso, John William', in Hans J. Hillerbrand (ed.), *The Encyclopedia of Protestantism* (New York: Routledge): *s.v.*

forthcoming   'John William Colenso', in Jeffrey P. Greenman and Timothy Larsen (eds.), *Reading Romans: Encounters with the Epistle to the Romans through the Centuries.*

Layman of the Church of England

1863   *The Historic Character of the Pentateuch Vindicated: A Reply to Part I of Bishop Colenso's ' Critical Examination'* (London: William Skeffington).

Le Roux, J.H.

1993   *A Story of Two Ways: Thirty Years of Old Testament Scholarship in South Africa* (Pretoria: publisher unknown): 91-107.

Letters and Articles in the Case of Dr Colenso

1865   *Letters and Articles in the Case of Dr. Colenso, Extracted from English Publications, with Introductory Remarks by the Dean of Cape Town* (Cape Town: Solomon).

Letters from the Archbishop of Canterbury *et al.*

1866   *Letters from the Archbishop of Canterbury, the Bishop of Capetown, and the Bishop of Natal: With Some Observations on the Archbishop of Canterbury's Reply to the Bishop of Natal* (London: Trübner & Co.).

Leverton. B.J.T.

1965   'The Colenso Papers', *Lantern* 14 (June): 46-51.

Lewis, C., and G.E. Edwards

1934   *The Historical Records of the Church of the Province of South Africa* (London: SPCK).

Linden, I.

1985   'The Heretic—A Study of the Life of John William Colenso 1814–1883', *Journal of Southern African Studies* 12.1: 136-37.

Lorimer, D.A.

1978   *Colour, Class and the Victorians: English Attitudes to the Negro in the Mid-Nineteenth Century* (Leicester: Leicester University Press).

Lund, T.

1863   *A Key to Bishop Colenso's Biblical Arithmetic* (London: Longman).

McCallum, H.K.H.

1966   'A Figure of Controversy: The First Bishop of Natal' (unpublished Bachelors dissertation, Pietermaritzburg, University of Natal).

McCaul, A.

1863   *An Examination of Bishop Colenso's Difficulties with Regards to the Pentateuch; and Some Reasons for Believing in its Authentic and Divine Origins* (London: Rivingtons).

M'Caul, J.B.

1862   *Bishop Colenso's Criticism Criticised in a Series of Eight Letters Addressed to the Editor of the 'Record' Newspaper; with Notes and a Postscript* (London: Wertheim, Macintosh & Hunt).

M'Caul, Reverend Dr

uncertain   *Notes on the Bishop of Natal on an Examination of Part I of his Work on the Pentateuch* (London: Longmans).

MacDonald, D.
1863(?)   *An Examination of Bishop Colenso on the Pentateuch* (London: publisher unknown).
MacKenzie, A.
1859   Journal Written while at Bishopstowe (unpublished journal, Killie Campbell Library).
McSweeny, M.
1867   *Two Visions: The Pope and Old Nick; The Pan-Anglican Synod and Bishop Colenso* (London: E. Truelove).
MacWhorter, A.
1863   *The Memorial Name: Reply to Bishop Colenso* (Boston: Gould & Lincoln).
Mahan, M.
1863   *The Spiritual Point-of-View: or, The Glass Reversed; An Answer to Bishop Colenso* (New York: D. Appleton).
Mann, J. H.
1863   *The Pentateuch and Writings of Moses Defended against the Attacks of Dr. Colenso* (London: James Nisbet).
Marsh, J.B.
1862   *Is the Pentateuch Historically True?: Containing all Bishop Colenso's Arguments in Favour of the Rejection of the Pentateuch and Book of Joshua—The Learned Doctor's Misquotations of Scripture exposed, and a Humble Review Attempted in Vindication of the Truth of the Pentateuch* (Manchester: John Heywood; London: Simpkin, Marshall & Co.).
Marcshall, J.G.
1863   *A Full Review and Exposure of Bishop Colenso's Errors and Miscalculations in his Work, the Pentateuch and Book of Joshua Critically Examined* (London: W. Freeman).
Mitchell, G.
1997   'A Hermeneutic of Intercultural Learning: The Writings of John Colenso', *Old Testament Essays* 10.3: 449-58.
Moon, R.
1863   *The Pentateuch and Book of Joshua Considered with Reference to the Objections of the Bishop of Natal* (London: Rivingtons).
Morris, D.R.
1966   *The Washing of the Spears* (London: Cape).
Mosothoane, E.
1991   'John William Colenso: Pioneer in the Quest for an Authentic African Christianity', *Scottish Journal of Theology* 44.2: 215-36.
Muller, R.
1990   'Two Cornishmen Abroad—The Controversial Colensos', by A.L.Rowse. *Contemporary Review* 26, 1489 (February): 110-11.
Neil, W.
1963   'The Criticism and Theological Use of the Bible, 1700–1950', in S.L. Greenslade (ed.), *The Cambridge History of the Bible Vol. III: The West from the Reformation to the Present Day* (Cambridge: Cambridge University Press).
Nicholls, B.
1991   'Colenso Letters', *Natalia* 21(December): 17-31.
1997   'The Colenso Endeavour in its Context' (unpublished doctoral dissertation, Pietermaritzburg, University of Natal).

Oarker, F.
  1863   *Replies to the First and Second Parts of the Right Reverend the Bishop of Natal's 'Pentateuch and Book of Joshua Critically Examined'* (London: Bell & Daldy).

Ollivant, A.
  1863a   *A Letter to the Clergy of the Diocese of Llandaff: In Reference to the Critical Examination of the Pentateuch by Bishop of Natal* (London: Rivingtons).
  1863b   *A Second Letter to the Clergy of the Diocese of Llandaff: In Reference to the Second Part of the Critical Examination of the Pentateuch by the Bishop of Natal* (London: Rivingtons).

Page, J.R.
  1863   *The Pretensions of Bishop Colenso to Impeach the Wisdom and Veracity of the Compilers of the Holy Scriptures Considered* (London: Rivington, Waterloo Place).

Palmer, G.
  1990   'Good and Cornish', *Times Literary Supplement* No. 4531 (February 2).

Parsons, G.
  1997   'Rethinking the Missionary Position: Bishop Colenso of Natal', in J. Wolffe (ed.), *Religion in Victorian Britain*. V. *Culture and Empire* (Manchester University Press): 135-75.
  1998   'A Forgotten Debt: John Colenso and the Life of Blanco White', *Faith and Freedom* 51: 96-116.
  2000   'Friendship and Theology: Unitarians and Bishop Colenso, 1862–1865', *Transactions of the Unitarian Historical Society*: 97-110.

Porter, J.L.
  1863a   *Bishop Colenso on the Pentateuch* (Belfast: C. Aitchison).
  1863b   *The Difficulties of the Pentateuch Explained: With Especial Reference to Bishop Colenso's Recent Work* (Leeds: J. Hamer).
  1867   *Position of the Church of England in the Colonies Legally Defined; Being the Judgement of the Master of the Rolls in the Case of the Bishop of Natal versus the Trustees of the Colonial Bishoprics of Fund* (Cape Town: Van Der Sandt De Villiers).

Pritchard, C.
  1863   *Vindiciae Mosaicae: A Letter to the Rt. Rev. Bishop Colenso, in Reply to his Arguments against the Veracity of the Pentateuch* (London: Bell & Daldy).

Privy Council
  1863   *Judgment of the Lords of the Judicial Committee of the Privy Council on the Appeal of the Rev William Long v. the Right Rev Robert Gray, D.D., Bishop of Cape Town, from the Supreme Court of the Cape of Good Hope: Delivered June 24, 1863.*
  1864   *The Case of the Bishop of Natal: Judgment of the Lords of the Judicial Committee of the Privy Council upon the Petition of the Lord Bishop of Natal, referred to the Judicial Committee by her Majesty's Order in Council of the 10th June, 1864; delivered 20th March, 1865.*

Procter, W., and J. Usher
  1863   *Bishop Colenso's Principal Objections to the Historic Truth of the Pentateuch: Anticipated and Answered More than Two Hundred Years Ago by Archbishop Usher* (Alnwick [England]: Mark Smith).

Rees, W. (ed.)
1958   *Colenso Letters from Natal* (Pietermaritzburg: Shuter & Shooter).
Resolutions
1865   *Resolutions Agreed to at a Meeting at Pinetown (Pinetown, Wednesday, May 31st, 1865, held in the Church of St. John Pinetown* (Pietermaritzburg: Barfield, Keith).
Reynolds, J.
1869   *The Bishop of Natal and his Anglican Assailants: An Essay and Critique on the Leading Aspects of the Natal Church Controversy* (Durban: Cullingworth).
Ridge, S.
1994   'A Sifting Process: the Truth, Language and Bishop Colenso', *Journal of Theology for Southern Africa* 88: 21-33.
Rivett, A.W.L.
1890   *Ten Years Church Work in Natal* (London: Jarrold).
Rogers, H.
1863   *A Vindication of Bishop Colenso* (Edinburgh: A. & C. Black).
Rogerson, J.W.
1978   *Anthropology and the Old Testament* (Growing Points in Theology; Oxford: Basil Blackwell).
1984   *Old Testament Criticism in the Nineteenth Century: England and Germany* (London: SPCK).
Rogerson, J.W. (ed.)
2001   *The Oxford Illustrated History of the Bible* (Oxford: Oxford University Press).
Ross, F.A.
1857   *Dr. Ross and Bishop Colenso: or, The Truth Restored in Regard to Polygamy and Slavery* (Philadelphia: Henry B. Ashmead).
Rowse, A.L.
1989   *The Controversial Colensos* (Cornwall: Dyllansow Truran).
Russell, G.
1899   *The History of Old Durban; and Reminiscenses of an Emigrant of 1850* (Durban: Davis).
Saayman, W.A.
1993   *Christian Mission in South Africa: Political and Ecumenical* (Unisa. Manualia Didactica, 11; Pretoria: University of South Africa).
Savile, B.W.
1863   *Bishop Colenso's Objections to the Veracity of the Pentateuch: An Examination* (London: W. Freeman).
Scherer, E.H.A., and J. Harris
1863   *The Confessions of a Missionary: Being a Defence of Bishop Colenso* (London: Longman, Roberts & Green).
Scholder, K.
1990   *The Birth of Modern Critical Theology: Origins and Problems of Biblical Criticism in the Seventeenth Century* (London: SCM Press [translation of the original German work, published in 1966]).
Scott, W.A.
1863   *Moses and the Pentateuch: A Reply to Bishop Colenso* (London: W. Freeman).

Silver, A.
1863   *The Holy Word in its Own Defense: Addressed to Bishop Colenso and All Other Earnest Seekers after Truth* (New York: D. Appleton).
1872   *The Holy Word in its Own Defence: Addressed to Bishop Colenso and All Other Earnest Seekers after Truth* (Boston: T.H. Carter).

Spencer, S.O'B.
1987   'Colenso, John William', in *British Settlers in Natal: A Biographical Register, 1824–57*. IV. *Cadle–Coventry* (Pietermaritzburg: University of Natal Press): 137-41.

Spry, W J.
1862   *Bishop Colenso and the Descent of Jacob into Egypt: An Analysis* (London: Wertheim, Macintosh & Hunt).

Stephenson, A.M.G.
1978   *Anglicanism and the Lambeth Conferences* (London: SPCK).

Stone, J. L.
1863   *Reply to Bishop Colenso's Attack upon the Pentateuch* (San Francisco: Bell & Lampman).

Sugirtharajah, R.S.
2001   'Colonialist as a Contentious Reader: Colenso and his Hermeneutics', in the Sugirtharajah's *The Bible and the Third World: Precolonial, Colonial and Postcolonial Encounters* (Cambridge: Cambridge University Press): 110-39.

Sundahl, D. J.
1996   'Bishop Colenso on the Pentateuch', *First Things* 59 (January): 26.

Thomson, W.
1868   *Speech of the Most Rev. William Lord Archbishop of York...on the Intended Consecration of a Second Bishop of Natal: [Delivered] to the Convocation of the Province of York, on Friday the 7th of February 1868* (London: Murray).

Thornton, R.
1986   *Bishop Colenso, Zulu Ethnography and the 'Higher Criticism'* (Cape Town: University of Cape Town, Centre for African Studies).

Todd, C.H.
1865   *Observations on the Judgement of the Judicial Committee of the Privy Council, in the Case of Bishop Colenso v. the Bishop of Capetown* (London: Rivingtons).

Trial of the Bishop of Natal
1863   *Trial of the Bishop of Natal for Erroneous Teaching Before the Metropolitan Bishop of Cape Town and the Bishops of Graham's Town and the Orange Free State as Assesors* (Cape Town: Cape Argus).

Trollope, Anthony
1974a   'The Clergyman Who Subscribes for Colenso', in Trollope's *The Clergymen of the Church of England* (Leicester: Leicester University Press [first published *Pall Mall Gazette* 10 May 1865]): 119-30
1974b   'The Zulu in London', in Trollope's *The Clergymen of the Church of England* (Leicester: Leicester University Press [first published *Pall Mall Gazette* 10 May 1865]): <51-62> [page numbering here following the 1974 printing of *The Clergymen of the Church of England*].

Turner, J.B.
1863　　An Answer to the Difficulties in Bishop Colenso's Book on the Pentateuch (place and publisher unknown).

Tyler, T.
1863　　Christ the Lord the Revealer of God, and the Fulfillment of the Prophetic Name 'Jehova': with a Reply to Bishop Colenso on the Name 'Jehova' (London/Edinburgh: publisher unknown).

Unattributed
1986　　'John William Colenso', in de Kock (ed.), 1968: 177-81.

Van Zuylen, R.N.
1987　　'A Historical-Theological Study of the Concept and Role of the Laity in the Church of the Province of South Africa and their Manifestation in Natal with Special Reference to Certain Zulu and English Congregations' (unpublished Masters dissertation, Durban, University of Durban-Westville).

Varner, L.B.
1974　　The Literary Reception of Bishop Colenso: Arnold, Kingsley, Newman, and Others (Varner: Leo Bentley).

Vidler, A.R.
1961　　The Church in an Age of Revolution: 1789 to the Present Day (Middlesex: Penguin).

Warwick, G.W.
1966　　'The Contribution of Bishop Colenso to Biblical Criticism' (unpublished Masters dissertation, Pietermaritzburg, University of Natal).

Wayland, J.
1881　　The Sword and the Keys Civil and Spiritual Jurisdictions: Their Union and Difference: A Treatise Giving Some Account of Ecclesiastical Appeals in Foreign Countries… (London: English Church Union).

Webb, C.B. de, and J.B. Wright (eds.)
1976–86　　The James Stuart Archive (4 vols.; Pietermaritzburg: University of Natal Press; Durban: Killie Campbell Africana Library).

Wellington, N.M.
1980　　'John William Colenso and Early and Mid-Victorian Attitudes to Race' (unpublished Bachelors dissertation, Pietermaritzburg, University of Natal).

Werner, A.
　　'The Life and Work of Bishop Colenso' (unpublished paper).

White, P.O.G.
1962　　'The Colenso Controversy', Theology 65.508: 402-408.

Whitelaw, D.
1987　　'A Crisis of Credibility: Contemporary Dialogue with Colenso and Du Plessis', Journal of Theology for Southern Africa 60 (September): 12-27.

Wickes, W.
1863　　Moses, or the Zulu? A Detailed Reply to the Objections Contained in Parts I and II of Bishop Colenso's Work (London: Wertheim, Macintosh & Hunt).

Wilder, H.A.
1856　　Review of 'Remarks on the Proper Treatment of Cases of Polygamy, as Found Already Existing in Converts from Heathenism', by John William Colenso, D.D., Lord Bishop of Natal (Durban: publisher unknown).

Winckler, W.G.
1964   'The Life and Writings of Bishop Colenso' (unpublished Masters dissertation, Pretoria, University of South Africa).
Wirgman, A.T.
1909   *Life of James Green...Dean of Pietermaritzburg, Natal, from February, 1849, to January 1906* (2 vols.; New York: Longmans, Green).
Woolsey, T.D.
1858   'Colenso and Grout on Polygamy', *The New Englander* (4 February): 407-33.
Wright, J.B., and A. Manson
1983   *The Hlubi Chiefdom in Zululand-Natal: A History* (Ladysmith: Ladysmith Historical Society).
Young, J.R.
1865   *Modern Scepticism, Viewed in Relation to Modern Science; More Especially in Reference to the Doctrines of Colenso, Huxley, Lyell, and Darwin Respecting the Noachian Deluge, the Antiquity of Man, and the Origin of Species* (London: Saunders, Otley & Co.).

CUMULATIVE BIBLIOGRAPHY

Abbott, Evelyn, and Lewis Campbell
    1897   *The Life and Letters of Benjamin Jowett* (2 vols.; London: John Murray).
Allison, James
    1846   *Tenkatekisemi ta la Methodisti* (Platberg: Wesleyan Mission Press).
The Alternative Service Book
    1980   (Clowes: SPCK).
An Anglican Prayer Book
    1989   (London: Collins).
Anderson, Rufus
    1848   *Tract on the Control to be Exercised over Missionaries and Mission Churches
                in ABCFM Annual Report* 1848: 62-80. (Published as a pamphlet in Boston.)
    1851   *The Missionary Age: A Half-Century Sermon* (Missionary Tracts, 10; Bos-
                ton).
    1869   *Foreign Missions: Their Relations and Claims* (New York: Charles Scrib-
                ner's Sons).
    1905   *The Theory of Missions to the Heathen: A Sermon Preached at the Ordina-
                tion of Mr Edward Webb as a Missionary to the Heathen* (Boston: Press of
                Crocker & Brewster).
Anonymous
    1880   *The Natal Almanac, Directory, and Yearly Register* (Pietermaritzburg:
                P. Davis).
    1886   *Jubilee of the American Mission in Natal, 1835–1885* (Pietermaritzburg:
                Horne Brothers/'Natalian' Office).
Arnold, M.
    1895   *Letters of Matthew Arnold 1848–1888*, I (ed. G.W.E. Russell; London: Mac-
                millan).
Ashcroft, Bill, Gareth Griffiths and Helen Tiffin
    1989   *The Empire Writes Back: Theory and Practice in Post-Colonial Literatures*
                (London: Routledge).
Baeta, C.G. (ed.)
    1968   *Christianity in Tropical Africa: Studies Presented and Discussed at the
                Seventh International African Seminar, University of Ghana, April 1965*
                (Oxford: Oxford University Press).
Bailey, Randall C., and Tina Pippin
    1996   'Race, Class and the Politics of Bible Translation', *Semeia* 76: 1-6.
Bassnett-McGuire, Susan
    1980   *Translation Studies* (London: Methuen).

Bassnett, Susan, and Harish Trivedi
1999   'Introduction', in Bassnett and Trivedi (eds.) 1999: 1-18.
Bassnett, Susan, and Harish Trivedi (eds.)
1999   *Post-Colonial Translation: Theory and Practice* (London: Routledge).
Batalden, Stephen K.
1992   'The Politics of Modern Russian Biblical Translation', in Philip C. Stine
            (ed.), *Bible Translation and the Spread of the Church: The Last 200 Years*
            (Leiden: E.J. Brill): 68-80.
Beaver, R.P. (ed.)
1967   *To Advance the Gospel: Selections from the Writings of Rufus Anderson*
            (Grand Rapids: Eerdmans).
Bediako, Kwame
1994   *Theology and Identity: The Impact of Culture upon Christian Thought in the
            Second Century and in Modern Africa* (Oxford: Regnum Books).
Benham, M.S.
1896   *Henry Callaway First Bishop of Kaffraria* (London: MacMillan).
Berger, P., and T. Luckmann
1966   *The Social Construction of Reality: A Treatise in the Sociology of Know-
            ledge* (New York: Doubleday).
Berglund, A.-I.
1976   *Zulu Thought-Patterns and Symbolism* (Cape Town: David Philip).
Blaut, J.
1995   *The Colonizer's Model of the World: Geographical Diffussionism and Euro-
            centric History* (New York: The Guilford Press).
Booth, A.R. (ed.)
1967   *Journal of the Rev. George Champion, American Missionary in Zululand
            1835–9* (Cape Town: Struik).
1968   *The Journal of an American Missionary in the Cape Colony 1835* (Cape
            Town: South African Library).
Boyce, W.B.
1834   *A Grammar of the Kafir Language* (Grahamstown: Wesleyan Mission Press).
Brookes, Edgar H., and Colin B. de Webb
1965   *A History of Natal* (Pietermaritzburg: University of Natal Press).
1987   *A History of Natal* (Pietermaritzburg: University of Natal Press, 2nd edn).
Brown, W.E.
1960   *The Catholic Church in South Africa* (London: Burns & Oats).
Bryant, Alfred T.
1905   *A Zulu–English Dictionary* (Marianhill, Natal: Marianhill Mission Press).
Buis, Robert
1975   *Religious Belief and White Prejudice* (Johannesburg: Ravan).
Bundy, Colin
1988   *The Rise and Fall of the South African Peasantry* (London: James Currey
            [1979]).
Burnett, B.B.
1947   'The Missionary Work of the First Anglican Bishop of Natal, the Right Rev.
            John William Colenso, D.D.; Between the Years 1852–1873' (unpublished
            Masters dissertation, Rhodes University).

Buthelezi, Manas
1972   'An African Theology or a Black Theology', in Motlhabi (ed.), 1972: 3-9.
Callaway, G.
1926   *The Fellowship of the Veld* (London: SPCK).
Callaway, Henry
unknown   *Incwadi Yokukuleka Yabantu abaKristu, isimo amasacramento, nezimo ezinye njengokuma kweKeriki li ti 'Church of England' namaHhubo kaDavidi* (The Book of Common Prayer etc. and Psalms) (London: SPCK).
1862   *Polygamy: A Bar to Admission into the Christian Church* (Durban: John O. Browne).
1868   *Unkhulunkulu and Uthiko* (Natal: J. Blair).
1870   *The Religious System of the Amazulu* (Springvale: John Blair [The Folk-Lore Society 1884]).
Calvin, John
1856a   *Commentaries on The Epistles to Timothy, Titus, and Philemon* (Edinburgh: Calvin Translation Society).
1856b   *Harmony of the Three Gospels*, II (Edinburgh: T. & T. Clark).
1953   *Institutes of the Christian Religion* (Grand Rapids: Eerdmans).
Carpenter, Joseph Estlin
1903   *The Bible in the Nineteenth Century* (London: Longmans).
Chadwick, Owen
1970   *The Victorian Church Part II* (London: A. & C. Black).
Cheyne, T.K.
1893   *Founders of Old Testament Criticism* (London: Methuen).
Chidester, D.
1996   *Savage Systems: Colonialism and Comparative Religion in Southern Africa* (Cape Town: University of Cape Town Press).
Chidester, David *et al.*
1997   *Christianity in South Africa: An Annotated Bibliography* (London: Greenwood).
Christensen, Torben, and William Hutchinson (eds.)
1982   *Missionary Ideologies in the Imperialist Era: 1880–1920* (Struer: Christensens Bogtrykkeri).
Christoferson, Arthur Fridjof
1967   *Adventuring with God in Africa: The Story of the American Board Mission in South Africa* (Durban: Robinson & Co.).
Chronicles of Convocation
Chronicle of Convocation, Lower House, 1863 11 February: 1036, 1041, 1049-50.
Chronicle of Convocation, Lower House, 1863 19 May: 1177-81, 1184.
Chronicle of Convocation, Upper House, 1863 20 May: 1205-206, 1208.
Church of the Province of South Africa
1887   *The Constitution and Canons of the Church of the Province of South Africa as Revised, Amended and Confirmed by the Provincial Synod, Held at Capetown, 1887* (Cape Town: College Press, Zonnebloem).
Cockshut, A.O.J.
1959   *Anglican Attitudes: A Study of Victorian Religious Controversies* (London: Collins).

1966 *The Unbelievers: English Agnostic Thought 1840–1890* (New York: New York University Press, repr. [London: Collins, 1964]).

Cohen, David W.
1994 *The Combing of History* (Chicago: University of Chicago Press).

Coldham, G.E. (ed.)
1966 *A Bibliography of Scriptures in African Languages*, II (London: British and Foreign Bible Society).

Colenso, F.E.
1885 'Attacks on J. W. Colenso', *The Eagle* (St John's College, Cambridge) 13.

Comaroff, Jean, and John L. Comaroff
1991 *Of Revelation and Revolution.* I. *Christianity, Colonialism, and Consciousness in South Africa* (Chicago: University of Chicago Press).
1997 *Of Revelation and Revolution.* II. *The Dialectics of Modernity on a South African Frontier* (Chicago: University of Chicago Press).

Committee for World Evangelization
1978 *The Willowbank Report* (Lausanne: Committee for World Evangelization).

Conn, Joann W.
1995 'Dancing in the Dark: Women's Spirituality and Ministry', in Robert J. Wicks (ed.), *Handbook of Spirituality for Ministers* (Minneapolis: Paulist Press): 77-95.

Cooper, Frederick, and Ann Stoler (eds.)
1997 *Tensions of Empire: Colonial Cultures in a Bourgeois World* (Berkeley: University of California Press).

Cordeur, Basille, and Christopher Saunders
1836 *The Kitchington Papers* (Newton Adams to James Kitchington, Bethelsdorp, 3 September 1836).

Correspondence of the Most Reverend the Lord Archbishop of Canterbury *et al.*
1968 *Correspondence of the Most Reverend the Lord Archbishop of Canterbury, the Most Reverend the Lord Archbishop of York, the Right Reverend the Lord Bishop of London, with the Bishop of Capetown, Concerning the Appointment of an Orthodox Bishop to Natal* (London: Rivington's, Waterloo Place).

Cory, G.E. (ed.)
1926 *The Diary of the Rev. Francis Owen, M.A., Missionary with Dingaan in 1837–8* (Cape Town: The Van Riebeeck Society).

Cox, G.W.
1888 *The Life of John William Colenso, D.D.* (2 vols.; London: W. Ridgway).

Cross, F.L. (ed.)
1957 *The Oxford Dictionary of the Christian Church* (London: Oxford University Press).

Darby, I.D.
1981 'Soteriology of Bishop J. W. Colenso' (unpublished doctoral dissertation, University of Natal, Pietermaritzburg).

David, K.
1994 *Sacrament and Struggle* (Geneva: WCC Publications).

Davidson, A.J.
1899 *The Autobiography and Diary of Samuel Davidson* (Edinburgh: T. & T. Clark).

Davidson, R.T., and William Benham
1891   *Life of Archibald Campbell Tait, Archbishop of Canterbury* (2 vols.; London: Macmillan).
Davidson, S.
1959   *The Text of the Old Testament Considered; With a Treatise on Sacred Interpretation, and a Brief Introduction to the Old Testament Books and the Apocrypha* (London: Longman, 2nd and rev. edn).
De Gruchy, J.W.
1979   *The Church Struggle in South Africa* (Cape Town: David Philip).
De Kock, W.T. (ed.)
1976   *Suid-Afrikaanse Biografiese Woordeboek*, I (CapeTown: Tafelberg vir die Raad vir Geesteswetenskaplike Navorsing).
De Kock, W.T., and D.W. Krüger (eds.)
1972   *Suid-Afrikaanse Biografiese Woordeboek*, II (CapeTown: Tafelberg vir die Raad vir Geesteswetenskaplike Navorsing).
Deist, Ferdinand
1984   'John William Colenso: Biblical Scholar', in J.A Loader and J.H le Roux (eds.), *Old Testament Essays*, II: 98-132.
1999   'Colenso, John William (1814–83)', in J.H. Hayes (ed.), *Dictionary of Biblical Interpretation* (Nashville: Abingdon Press), I: 203-204.
Denis, Philippe
1994   *The Making of an Indigenous Clergy in Southern Africa* (Pietermaritzburg: Cluster Publications).
Desmond, Adrian
1997   *Huxley: From Devil's Disciple to the High Priest of Evolution* (London: Penguin Books [the 1997 edn was reprinted in 1998]).
Desmond, Adrian, and James Moore
1992   *Darwin* (London: Penguin [1991]).
Döhne, J.L.
1857   *Zulu–Kafir Dictionary Etymologically Explained with Copious Illustrations of the Zulu–Kafir Language* (Cape Town: Pike's Printing Office).
Doke, C.M.
1958   'Scripture Translation into Bantu Languages', *African Studies* 17/2 (Johannesburg: Witwatersrand University Press): 82-99.
Doke, C.M., D.M. Malcom, J.M.A. Sikakana and B.W. Vilakazi
1990   *English–Zulu: Zulu–English Dictionary* (Johannesburg: Witwatersrand University Press, 1990).
Doke, C.M., and B.W. Vilakazi
1948   *Zulu–English Dictionary* (Johannesburg: Witwatersrand University Press).
Draper, Jonathan A.
1998a   'Magema Fuze and the Insertion of the Subjugated Historical Subject into the Discourse of Hegemony', *Bulletin for Contextual Theology* 5/1-2: 16-26.
1998b   'Archbishop Gray and the Interpretation of the Bible', in J. Suggit and M. Goedhals (eds.), *Change and Challenge: Essays Commemorating the 150th Anniversary of Robert Gray as First Bishop of Cape Town (20 February 1848)* (Johannesburg: CPSA): 44-54.
1999   'Hermeneutical Drama on the Colonial Stage: Liminal Space and Creativity in Colenso's *Commentary on Romans*', *Journal of Theology for Southern Africa* 103: 13-32.

2000a 'The Bishop and the Bricoleur: Bishop John William Colenso's *Commentary on Romans* and Magema Fuze's *The Black People and Whence they Came*', in G.O. West and M.W. Dube (eds.), *The Bible in Africa: Transactions, Trajectories, and Trends* (Leiden: E.J. Brill): 415-54.

2000b 'Bishop John William Colenso's Interpretation to the Zulu People of the *Sola Fide* in Paul's Letter to the Romans', *Seminar Papers of the Society of Biblical Literature Annual Meeting 2000* (Atlanta: Scholars Press): 465-93.

2003 *Commentary on Romans* (edited with an Introduction by Jonathan A. Draper; Pietermaritzburg: Cluster Publications).

Driver, S.R.
1897 *An Introduction to the Literature of the Old Testament* (Edinburgh: T. & T. Clark [1891]).

Du Plessis, J.
1911 *A History of Christian Missions in South Africa* (London: Macmillan).

Dube, J.L.
1909 *The Zulu's Appeal for Light and England's Duty* (London: Longman).

Durant, J.
1984 'Darwinism and Divinity: A Century of Debate', in *idem* (ed.), *Darwinism and Divinity: Essays on Evolution and Religious Belief* (Oxford: Basil Blackwell): 9-39.

Eagleton, Terry
1992 *Literary Theory: An Introduction* (repr., Oxford: Basil Blackwell [1983]).

Edgecombe, R. (ed.)
1982 *Bringing Forth Light* (Pietermaritzburg: University of Natal Press).

Ellis, Ieuan
1980 *Seven against Christ* (Leiden: E.J. Brill).

Erlank, Natasha
1998 'Jane Philip: Partnership, Usefulness and Sexuality in the Service of God', in John de Gruchy (ed.), *The London Missionary Society in Southern Africa* (Cape Town: David Philip): 82-98.

Etherington, Norman
1970 'Errand into the Wilderness', *Church History* 39: 62-71.
1978 *Preachers, Peasants and Politics in Southeast Africa, 1835–1880: African Christian Communities in Natal, Pondoland and Zululand* (London: Royal Historical Society).
1987 'Kingdoms of This World and the Next: Christian Beginnings among Zulu and Swazi', in Richard Elphick and Rodney Davenport (eds.), *Christianity in South Africa. A Political, Social & Cultural History* (Oxford: James Currey/ Cape Town: David Philip): 89-106.
1989 'Christianity and African Society in Nineteenth-Century Natal', in Andrew Duminy and Bill Guest (eds.), *Natal and Zululand: From Earliest Times to 1910: A New History* (Pietermaritzburg: Shuter & Shooter, 1989): 275-301.
2002 'The Missionary Writing Machine and Religious Change in Nineteenth-Century KwaZulu-Natal' (unpublished paper presented at the Symposium entitled 'Religious Change and Indigenous People: Australia in an International Context', Edith Cowan University, Perth, Australia, 6-8 February 2002).

Eveleigh, W.
1920   *The Settlers and Methodism* (Cape Town: Methodist Publishing Office).
Farrar, F.W.
1988   'On the Attitude of the Clergy towards Science', in James R. Moore (ed.), *Religion in Victorian Britain*. III. *Sources* (Manchester: Manchester University Press [1868]): 437-44.
Felder, Cain Hope
1989   *Troubling Biblical Waters: Race, Class and Family* (Maryknoll, NY: Orbis Books).
1991   *Stony the Road We Trod: African American Biblical Interpretation* (Minneapolis: Fortress Press).
Fraser, B.D.
1952   *John William Colenso: A Bibliography* (University of Cape Town: School of Librarianship).
Freire, P.
1972   *Pedagogy of the Oppressed* (New York: Herder & Herder).
Fuze, Magema M.
1922   *Abantu Abamnyama, Lapa Bavela Ngakona* (Pietermaritzburg: City Printing Works) (English translation published as *The Black People and Whence they Came* [ed. A.T. Cope; trans. H.C. Lugg; Pietermaritzburg: University of Natal Press, 1979]).
1979   *The Black People and Whence They Came: A Zulu View* (trans. H.C. Lugg; ed. A.T. Cope; Pietermaritzburg: University of Natal Press; Durban: Killie Campbell Africana Library).
Gardiner, A.F.
1836   *Narrative of a Journey to the Zoolu Country in South Africa, Undertaken in 1835* (London: William Crofts [Cape Town: C. Struik, facsimile repr., 1966]).
Gordon, R.E.
1976   'Theophilus Shepstone', in de Kock (ed.), 1976, I: *s.v.*
Gray, Bishop Robert
1852   *A Journal of a Bishop's Visitation Tour through the Cape Colony, in 1850* (London: SPCK).
Greaves, Adrian (ed.)
1999   'Bishop Colenso's Speech. Preached in the Cathedral of St Peter's, Pietermaritzburg on Wednesday, March 12th 1879', *The Journal of the Anglo Zulu War Historical Society* (December): 47-51.
Griesel, G.J.
1991   'Aspekte van die Linguistiese Studie van Zulu 1849–1991: 'n Bydrae tot die Linguistiese Historiografie' (unpublished doctoral dissertation, Pietermaritzburg, University of Natal).
Grillmeier, Aloys
1975   *Christ in Christian Tradition* (trans. J. Bowden; London: Mowbrays, 2nd rev. edn).
Grote, (Miss)
1854   'H.P.S. Schreuder's Grammar of the Zulu Language, Translated for the Use of the Right Reverend the Bishop of Natal, with Notes on the Structure of the Zulu Language by Rev. John Grote' (unpublished manuscript, Cam-

bridge: Trumpington; Grey Collection, National Library of South Africa, Cape Town).

Grout, Lewis
  1864   *Zululand; or Life among the Zulu-Kafirs of Natal and Zulu-Land, South Africa* (Philadelphia: Presbyterian Publication Committee).

Grout, Lewis (Under the pseudonym, 'An American Missionary')
  1855   *A Reply to Bishop Colenso's 'Remarks on the Proper Treatment of Cases of POLYGAMY as found already existing in Converts from Heathenism'* (Pietermaritzburg: May & Davis).
  1856   *An Answer to Dr. Colenso's 'Letter' on Polygamy* (Pietermaritzburg: May & Davis).

Guy, Jeff
  1979   *The Destruction of the Zulu Kingdom: The Civil War in Zululand, 1879–1884* (Longman: London [repr. in 1982 by Ravan Press and in 1994 by the University of Natal Press]).
  1983   *The Heretic: A Study of the Life of John William Colenso 1814–1883* (Johannesburg: Ravan Press; Pietermaritzburg: University of Natal Press).
  1991   'Learning from History: Religion, Politics, and the Problem of Contextualization—The Case of J.W. Colenso', in C.F. Hallencreutz and M. Palmberg (eds.), *Religion and Politics in Southern Africa* (Uppsala: Scandinavian Institute of African Studies): 185-93.
  1997   'Class, Imperialism and Literary Criticism: William Ngidi, John Colenso and Matthew Arnold', *Journal of Southern African Studies* 23.2: 219-41.
  2001a   *The View Across the River: Harriette Colenso and the Zulu Struggle against Imperialism* (Cape Town: David Phillips; Oxford: James Currey).
  2001b   'A Paralysis of Perspective: Image and Text in the Creation of an African Chief' (unpublished paper presented at the African Studies and History Seminar, 30 May 2001).

Harris, Jonathan
  2001   *The New Art History: A Critical Introduction* (Routledge: New York)

Hart, Jenifer
  1977   'Religion and Social Control in the Mid-Nineteenth Century', in A.P. Donajgrodzki (ed.), *Social Control in Nineteenth Century Britain* (London: Croom Hel): 108-31.

Hermanson, E.A.
  1992   'The Grey Collection and the Dating of Early Scripture Publications in Zulu', *Quarterly Bulletin of the South African Library* 47.2.
  1991   'The Transliteration of New Testament Proper Names in Zulu' (unpublished Masters dissertation, University of South Africa).
  1995   'Metaphor in Zulu: Problems in the Translation of Biblical Metaphor in the Book of Amos' (unpublished doctoral dissertation, University of Stellenbosch).

Hexham, I.
  1987   *Texts on Zulu Religion: Traditional Zulu Ideas about God* (African Studies, 6; Lewiston/Queenston: Edwin Mellen).

Hick, J.
  1977   *The Myth of God Incarnate* (London: SCM Press).

Hinchliff, P.B.
1962   'John William Colenso: A Fresh Appraisal', *Journal of Ecclesiastical History* 13: 203-19.
1963   *The Anglican Church in South Africa: An Account of the History and Development of the Church of the Province of South Africa* (London: Darton, Longman & Todd).
1964   *John William Colenso Bishop of Natal* (London: Thomas Nelson).
1976   'Henry Callaway', in de Kock (ed.), 1976, I: *s.v.*
1986   'Ethics, Evolution and Biblical Criticism in the Thought of Benjamin Jowett and John William Colenso', *Journal of Ecclesiastical History* 37: 91-110.
Hofmeyer, J.W., and Gerald Pillay (eds.)
1994   *A History of Christianity in South Africa*, I (Pretoria: Haum Tertiary).
Hofmeyr, Isabel
2003   *The Portable Bunyan: A Transnational History of The Pilgrim's Progress* (Princeton: Princeton University Press).
Hooker, M.A.
1953   'The Place of Bishop J.W. Colenso in the History of South Africa' (unpublished doctoral dissertation, University of the Witwatersrand).
Houghton, Walter E. (ed.)
1979   *Wellesley Index to Victorian Periodicals* 3 (Toronto).
Houtman, C.
1993   'Die Wirkung der Arbeit Kuenens in den Niederlanden', *Oudtestamentische Studiën* 29: 29-48.
1994   *Der Pentateuch: Die Geschichte seiner Erforschung neben einer Auswertung* (Kampen: Kok Pharos).
1998   *Biografisch Lexicon voor de Geschiedenis van het Nederlandse Protestantisme*, IV (Kampen: Kok Pharos).
Hughes, Heather
1990   '"A lighthouse for African womanhood": Inanda Seminary, 1869–1945', in Cherryl Walker (ed.), *Woman and Gender in Southern Africa to 1945* (Cape Town: David Philip): 197-220
Huxley, Leonard
1899   *Life and Letters of Thomas Henry Huxley* (2 vols.; London: Macmillan).
1918   *Life and letters of Sir Joseph Dalton Hooker* (2 vols.; London: John Murray).
Irvine, William
1956   *Apes, Angels and Victorians: A Joint Biography of Darwin and Huxley* (London: Weidenfield & Nicolson).
Ive, A.
1966   *The Church of England in South Africa: A Study of its History Principles and Status* (Cape Town: Church of England Information Office).
Iversen, Joan.
1997   *The Anti-Polygamy Controversy in U.S. Women's Movements, 1880–1925: A Debate on the American Home* (New York: Garland Publishing).
Jarrett-Kerr, Martin
1989   'Victorian Certainty and Zulu Doubt: A Study in Christian Missionary Hermeneutics from Shaka to Colenso', in D. Jasper and T.R. Wright (eds.), *The Critical Spirit and The Will to Believe* (London: Macmillan): 145-57.
Jeffreys, M.D.W.
1951   'Lobolo is Child-Price', *African Studies* 10: 145-84.

Jensen, J.V.
1972   'Interrelationships within the Victorian "X Club"', *The Dalhousie Review*
            51: 539-52.
Jobling, David
1993   'Globalization in Biblical Studies/Biblical Studies in Globalization', *Biblical
            Interpretation* 1: 96-110.
Jones, T. Hughie
1987   '*Ex Africa Semper Aliquid Novi*: Colenso Revisited', *Ecclesiastical Law
            Journal* 24: 188-95.
Kempe, A.R. (ed.)
1905   *Remarks on Zulu Orthography on the Occasion of the Conference to be Held
            in Maritzburg 20-23 March 1906* (Pietermaritzburg: Ebenezer Press, Church
            of Sweden Mission).
Kline, Benjamin
1988   *Genesis of Apartheid: British African Policy in the Colony of Natal 1845–
            1893* (London: University Press of America).
Kotzé, D.J.
1986   'Allen Francis Gardiner', in de Kock and Krüger (eds.), 1972, II: 259-60.
Kotzé, D.J. (ed.)
1950   *Letters of the American Missionaries, 1835–1838* (VRS, 31; Cape Town:
            Van Riebeeck Society).
Krige, Eileen Jensen
1950   *The Social System of the Zulus* (Pietermaritzburg: Shuter & Shooter [1936]).
Kritzinger, Gerrit S.
2002   'Preface: Bible Society of South Africa', in J.A. Naude and C.H.J. van der
            Merwe (eds.), *Contemporary Translation Studies and Bible Translation: A
            South African Perspective* (Acta Theologica 2002, Supplementum 2; Bloem-
            fontein: University of the Free State).
Külling, S.R.
1964   *Zur Datierung der 'Genesis-P-Stücke'* (Kampen: Kok).
Kuenen, Abraham
1861   *Historisch-kritisch onderzoek naar het ontstaan en de verzameling van de
            boeken des Ouden Verbonds* (Leiden: P. Engels en Zoon) (English transla-
            tion published as *An Historico-Critical Inquiry into the Origin and Compo-
            sition of the Hexateuch [Pentateuch and Book of Joshua]* [trans. Philip H.
            Wicksteed; London: Macmillan, 1866]).
1865   'De Kerkelijke Beweging in England', in *De Gids*, III.1-30: 185-216.
1884   'John William Colenso', in E.D. Pijzel (ed.), *Mannen van Beteekenis in Onze
            Dagen* (Haarlem: Tjeenk Willink): 1-28.
1869–70   *De godsdienst van Israël tot den ondergang van den Joodschen staat*, I-II.
            (Haarlem) (English translation published as *The Religion of Israel to the Fall
            of the Jewish State*, I-III [trans. A. Heath May; London: Williams &
            Norgate, 1874–75]).
1870   'Critische bijdragen tot de geschiedenis van den Israëlitischen godsdienst. V.
            De Priesterlijke bestanddeelen van Pentateuch en Josua', *Theologisch
            Tijdschrift* 4: 391-426, 487-526 (398-401).
1872   'Critische bijdragen tot de geschiedenis van den Israëlitischen godsdienst.
            VII. De stam Levi', *Theologisch Tijdschrift* 6: 628-72.

1876   'Yahveh and the "Other Gods"', *The Theological Review* (July): 329-65.
Lambeth Conferences
    1878   *First Lambeth Conference 1867* (edited and published privately in an un-
                authorized version by W. Benham before the second Lambeth Conference
                [USPG-Pamphlet 10 C/AFS/8]).
    1929   *The Six Lambeth Conferences 1867–1920* (London: SPCK).
    1948   *Lambeth Conferences (1867–1930)* (London: SPCK).
    1988   *The Truth Shall Make You Free: The Lambeth Conference 1988* (London:
                Church House Publishing).
Land, J.P.N.
    1866   'Nog iets over het verhaal van Qorach, Dathan, en Abiram', *Godgeleerde
                Bijdragen* 40: 416-37.
Landau, Paul Stuart
    1995   *The Realm of the Word: Language, Gender, and Christianity in a Southern
                African Kingdom* (Cape Town: David Philip, 1995).
Larsen, Timothy
    forthcoming   'John William Colenso', in Jeffrey P. Greenman and Timothy Larsen (eds.),
                *Reading Romans: Encounters with the Epistle to the Romans through the
                Centuries*.
Le Roux, J.H.
    1993   *A Story of Two Ways: Thirty Years of Old Testament Scholarship in South
                Africa* (Pretoria: Verba Vitae).
Legge, M.
    1997   'Bricoleurs-in-Community: Reframing Theologies of Culture', *Religious
                Studies and Theology* 16: 5-21.
Lenkoe, Peter
    1994   'From Native Agents to the Search for an Authentic Spirituality', in P. Denis
                (ed.), *The Making of an Indigenous Clergy in Southern Africa* (Pietermaritz-
                burg: Cluster Publications): 78-82.
Letters from the Archbishop of Canterbury *et al.*
    1866   *Letters from the Archbishop of Canterbury, the Bishop of Capetown, and the
                Bishop of Natal: With Some Observations on the Archbishop of Canter-
                bury's Reply to the Bishop of Natal* (London: Trübner & Co.).
    1966   *Letters from the Archbishop of Canterbury, the Bishop of Capetown and the
                Bishop of Natal: With some Observations on the Archbishop of Canterbury's
                Reply to the Bishop of Natal* (London: Trübner & Co).
Leverton, B.J.T.
    1972a   'Francis Owen', in de Kock and Krüger (eds.) 1972, II: 540-41.
    1972b   'Newton Adams', in de Kock and Krüger (eds.), 1972, II: 1-2.
Lévy-Bruhl, Lucien
    1923   *Primitive Mentality* (London: George Allen & Unwin).
Lewis, C., and G.E. Edwards
    1934   *The Historical Records of the Church of the Province of South Africa*
                (London: SPCK).
Livingstone, James C.
    1974   *The Ethics of Belief: An Essay on the Victorian Religious Conscience*
                (Tallahassee, FL: American Academy of Religion).

Cumulative Bibliography   403

Lorimer, Douglas A.
1978   *Colour Class and the Victorians: English Attitudes to the Negro in the Mid-Nineteenth Century* (Leicester: Leicester University Press).
Louw, J.A.
1986   'James Perrin', in de Kock and Krüger (eds.), 1972, II: 554-55.
Lyell, K.M.
1881   *Life, Letters and Journals of Sir Charles Lyell, Bart* (2 vols.; London: John Murray).
MacCrone, I.D.
1937   *Race attitudes in South Africa* (Johannesburg: Witwatersrand University Press).
Mackenzie, A.
1859   *Journal Written While at Bishopstowe* (unpublished journal, Killie Campbell Library).
Macknight, James
unknown   *A New Literal Translation, from the Original Greek, of all the Apostolical Epistles with a Commentary* (published in numerous editions by a variety of publishers).
Macquarrie, J.
1966   *Principles of Christian Theology* (London: SCM Press).
Marks, Shula
1970   *Reluctant Rebellion: The 1906–8 Disturbances in Natal* (Oxford Studies in African Affairs; Oxford: Clarendon Press).
1986   *Ambiguities of Dependence in South Africa: Class, Nationalism, and the State in Twentieth Century Natal* (Johannesburg: Raven Press).
Marx, Karl
1976   *Capital*, I (Introduced by Ernest Mandel; Middlesex: Penguin Books [1867]).
Maurice, Frederick Denison
1840   *The Kingdom of Christ, or, Hints on the Principles, Ordinances and Constitution of the Catholic Church: In Letters to a Member of the Society of Friends* (London: Dent [1883]).
1855   *The Communion Service, From the Book of Common Prayer: With Select Readings from the Writings of F.D. Maurice* (ed. John William Colenso; London: Macmillan).
1868   *The Ground and Object of Hope for Mankind: Four Sermons Preached Before the University of Cambridge, in November 1867* (London: Macmillan).
1885   *The Life of Frederick Denison Maurice Chiefly Told in his Own Letters*, II (London: Macmillan, 4th edn).
1891   *Sermons Preached at Lincolns Inn* (4 vols.; London: Macmillan).
1975   *What is Revelation? A Series of Sermons on the Epiphany, to which are Added Letters to a Student of Theology on the Bampton Lectures of Mr Mansel* (New York: AMS Press [first published 1859]).
McGrath, A.
1993   *The Renewal of Anglicanism* (London: SPCK).
Mears, W.J. Gordon
1967   *The Rev James Allison, Missionary. Biographical Outline* (Durban: Mission and Extension Committee of the Methodist Church of South Africa).

Merwe, H.W. van der
    1975   *Looking at the Afrikaner Today* (Cape Town: Tafelberg).
Miller, Perry
    1956   *Errand into the Wilderness* (Cambridge, MA: Harvard University Press).
Milman, A.
    1899   *Henry Hart Milman, D.D. Dean of St. Paul's: A Biographical Sketch* (London: J. Murray).
Mitchell, Gordon
    1997   'A Hermeneutic of Intercultural Learning: The Writings of John Colenso', *Old Testament Essays* 10: 449-58.
Mojola, Aloo Osotsi
    2002   'Bible Translation in African Christianity: Some Preliminary Thoughts', *African Institute for Contemporary Mission and Research* 1: 1-14.
Mokoena, Hlonipha
    2003   'The Black People and Whence they Came: Christian Converts and the Production of Kholwa Histories in the Nineteenth-Century Colonial Natal—The Case of Magema Fuze' (unpublished paper presented to the Centre of African Studies, September 2003).
Moore, James R.
    1986   'Geologists and Interpreters of Genesis in the Nineteenth Century', in D.C. Lindberg and R.L. Numbers (eds.), *God and Nature: Historical Essays on the Encounter between Christianity and Science* (London: University of California Press): 322-50.
Mosothoane, Ephraim
    1991   'John William Colenso: Pioneer in the Quest for an Authentic African Christianity', *Scottish Journal of Theology* 44: 215-36.
Mostert N.
    1993   *Frontiers: The Epic of South Africa's Creation and Tragedy of the Xhosa People* (London: Pimlico).
Motlhabi, M.
    1972   *Essays in Black Theology* (Johannesburg: Ravan).
Muir, John
    1873   *Three Notices of 'the Speaker's Commentary'* (London).
Naudé, J.A., and C.H.J. van der Merwe (eds.)
    2002   *Contemporary Translation Studies and Bible Translation: A South African Perspective* (Acta Theologica 2002, Supplementum, 2; Bloemfontein: University of the Free State).
Neil, W.
    1963   'The Criticism and Theological Use of the Bible, 1700–1950', in S.L. Greenslade (ed.), *The Cambridge History of the Bible*. III. *The West from the Reformation to the Present Day* (Cambridge: Cambridge University Press): 238-93.
Ngcongwane, S.D.
    1985   *The Languages We Speak: Publications* (Series B No. 54; KwaDlangezwa: University of Zululand).
Nias, J.C.S.
    1951   *Gorham and the Bishop of Exeter* (London: SPCK).

Cumulative Bibliography

405

Nicholls, Brenda M.
1995   'The Colenso Endeavour in its Context 1887–1897' (unpublished doctoral dissertation, University of Natal).
Nicolson, R.
1990   *A Black Future? Jesus and Salvation in South Africa* (London: SCM Press).
Ntuli, D.B.Z., and M.N. Makhambeni
1998   *Izimpande: Ubucikomazwi besizulu kuze kufike ku–1993* (Pretoria: University of South Africa Press, 1998).
O'Connor, Daniel *et al.*
2000   *Three Centuries of Mission: The United Society for the Propagation of the Gospel 1701–2000* (London: Continuum).
Oort, Henricus
1865   *De dienst der Baälim in Israël. Naar aanleiding van het geschrift van Dr R. Dozy 'de Israëlieten te Mekka'* (Leiden: Akademische Boekhandel van P. Engels).
1866a   'Joël', *Godgeleerde Bijdragen* 40: 760-73.
1866b   'Numeri 16 en 17', *Godgeleerde Bijdragen* 40: 416-37.
Parsons, Gerald
1988a   'On Speaking Plainly: "Honest Doubt" and the Ethics of Belief', in Parsons (ed.), 1988: 191-219.
1988b   'Biblical Criticism in Victorian Britain: From Controversy to Acceptance?', in Parsons (ed.), 1988: 238-57.
1997   'Rethinking the Missionary Position: Bishop Colenso of Natal', in John Wolffe (ed.), *Religion in Victorian Britain. V. Culture and Empire* (Manchester: Manchester University Press): 135-75.
Parsons, Gerald (ed.)
1988   *Religion in Victorian Britain. II. Controversies* (Manchester: Manchester University Press).
Pearson, B.W.R.
1999   'Remainderless Translations? Implications of the Tradition Concerning the Translation of the LXX for Modern Translation Theory', in Porter and Hess (eds.), 1999: 63-84.
Peires, J.B.
[1981] *The House of Phalo: A History of the Xhosa People in the Days of their Independence* (Johannesburg: Ravan Press).
1989   *The Dead Will Arise: Nongqawuse and the Great Xhosa Cattle-Killing Movement of 1856-7* (Johannesburg: Raven Press).
Perowne, J.J.S. (ed.)
1877   *Remains, Literary and Theological of Connop Thirlwall* (2 vols.; London).
Perrin, James
1855a   *A Kafir–English Dictionary of the Zulu-Kafir Language, as Spoken by the Tribes of the Colony of Natal* (London: SPCK).
1855b   *An English–Kafir Dictionary of the Zulu-Kafir Language as Spoken by the Tribes of the Colony of Natal* (Pietermaritzburg: May & Davis).
Phillips, Clifton Jackson
1968   *Protestant America and the Pagan World: The First Half-Century of the American Board of Commissioners for Foreign Missions, 1810–1860* (Cambridge, MA: Harvard East Asian Monographs).

Porter, Stanley E.
1999 'The Contemporary English Version and the Ideology of Translation', in Porter and Hess (eds.), 1999: 18-45.

Porter, S.E., and R.S. Hess (eds.)
1999 *Translating the Bible: Problems and Prospects* (JSNTSup, 173; Sheffield: Sheffield Academic Press).

Poulter, C.
1980 'The Proper Study of Mankind: Anthropology in its Social Context in England in the 1860s' (unpublished doctoral dissertation, University of Cambridge).

Powell, Baden
1860 'Study of the Evidences of Christianity', in Temple *et al.* (eds.), 1860: 94-142.

Privy Council
1863 *Judgment of the Lords of the Judicial Committee of the Privy Council on the Appeal of the Rev William Long v. the Right Rev Robert Gray, D.D., Bishop of Cape Town, from the Supreme Court of the Cape of Good Hope: Delivered June 24, 1863.*

1864 *The Case of the Bishop of Natal: Judgment of the Lords of the Judicial Committee of the Privy Council upon the Petition of the Lord Bishop of Natal, referred to the Judicial Committee by her Majesty's Order in Council of the 10th June, 1864; delivered 20th March, 1865.*

Prothero, R.E.
1893 *Life and Correspondence of Arthur Penrhyn Stanley* (2 vols.; London).

Radford Ruether, R.
1974 *Faith and Fratricide* (New York: Seabury).

Rees, W. (ed.)
1958 *Colenso Letters from Natal* (Pietermaritzburg: Shuter & Shooter).

Richardson, A.
1969 *A Dictionary of Christian Theology* (London: SCM Press).

Ridge, Stanley
1994 'A Sifting Process: The Truth, Language and Bishop Colenso', *Journal of Theology for Southern Africa* 88: 21-33.

Ries, J.H.
1957 'Die Zoeloe-vertaling van die Bybel—in besonder die Evangelie na die beskrywing van Johannes, hoofstuk 1' (unpublished Masters dissertation, University of Stellenbosch).

Rogerson, J.W.
1977 *Anthropology and the Old Testament: Growing Points in Theology* (Oxford: Basil Blackwell).

1984 *Old Testament Criticism in the Nineteenth Century: England and Germany* (London: SPCK).

1985 'John William Colenso', in J.W. Rogerson (ed.), *Old Testament Criticism in the Nineteenth Century: England and Germany* (London: SPCK): 220-37.

1988 'The Old Testament', in J.W. Rogerson, C. Rowland and B. Linders (eds.), *The History of Christian Theology*. II. *The Study and Use of the Bible* (Basingstoke: Marshall Pickering; Grand Rapids: Eerdmans): 1-152.

Rogerson, J.W. (ed.)
2001   *The Oxford Illustrated History of the Bible* (Oxford: Oxford University Press).

Sanneh, Lamin
1989   *Translating the Message: The Missionary Impact on Culture* (Maryknoll, NY: Orbis Books).
1993   *Encountering the West: Christianity and the Global Cultural Process* (Maryknoll, NY: Orbis Books).

Scholder, Klaus
1990   *The Birth of Modern Critical Theology: Origins and Problems of Biblical Criticism in the Seventeenth Century* (London: SCM Press [German original 1966]).

Schreuder, H.P.S.
1850   *Grammatik for Zulu-Sproget* (Christiana: W.C. Fabritius).

Scott, Thomas
1812   *The Holy Bible, containing the Old and New Testaments, with original notes, practical observations and copious marginal references* (New York: Williams & Whiting).

Seme, Pixley
1913   'The Regeneration of Africa', in William H. Ferris (ed.), *The African Abroad on His Evolution in Western Civilization: Tracing His Development Under Caucasian Milieu* (New Haven: Tuttle, Morehouse & Taylor): 436-39.

Smend, R.
1991   *Epochen der Bibelkritik* (München: Chr. Kaiser Verlag).

Smith, Edwin W.
1949   *The Life and Times of Daniel Lindley, 1801–1880* (London: Epworth Press).

Sobel, Dava
1999   *Galileo's Daughter: A Drama of Science, Faith and Love* (London: Fourth Estate).

South African Native Affairs Commission
1905   *South African Native Affairs Commission 1903–5*. III. *Evidence* (Natal).

Spivak, G.
1999   *A Critique of Postcolonial Reason: Toward a History of the Vanishing Present* (Cambridge, MA: Harvard University Press).

Stephen, Leslie, and Sidney Lee (eds.)
1921–22   'Connop Thirlwall (1792–1875)', in Leslie Stephen and Sidney Lee (eds.), *Dictionary of National Biography* (Oxford: Oxford University Press), XIX: 618-21.

Stephenson A.M.G.
1978   *Anglicanism and the Lambeth Conferences* (London: SPCK).

Stine, Philip C.
1988   'Introduction', in Philip C. Stine (ed.), *Issues in Bible Translation* (London: United Bible Societies): vii-viii.

Stott, John (ed.)
1996   *Making Christ Known: Historic Mission Documents from the Lausanne Movement, 1974–1989* (Carlisle: Paternoster Press).

Stuart, James
1906a   *Notes on the Conjunctive and Disjunctive Methods of Writing Zulu* (Durban: Natal and Zululand Conference on Zulu Orthography).

408   *The Eye of the Storm*

1906b   'Notes on the Conjunctive and disjunctive Methods of writing Zulu' (unpublished paper prepared in connection with the Natal and Zululand Conference on Zulu Orthography, March 1906). [Housed at Killie Campbell Africana Library.]

Stuart, J. (ed.)
1907   *Zulu Orthography* (Durban: Zulu Orthography Committee).

Sugirtharajah, R.S.
2001   *The Bible and the Third World: Precolonial, Colonial and Postcolonial Encounters* (Cambridge: Cambridge University Press).

Sugirtharajah, R.S. (ed.)
1998   *The Postcolonial Bible* (The Bible and Colonialism, 1; Sheffield: Sheffield Academic Press).

Sundkler, Bengt
1948   *Bantu Prophets in South Africa* (London: Oxford University Press).

Temple, F.
1861   'The Education of the World' [1860], in F. Temple *et al.* (eds.), 1861: 1-49.

Temple, F. *et al.* (eds.)
1861 *Essays and Reviews* (London: John W. Parker & Son [1860]).

Thomson, David
1967   *England in the Nineteenth Century* (Middlesex: Penguin Books [1950]).

Thompson, R.J.
1970   *Moses and the Law in a Century of Criticism since Graf* (Leiden: E.J. Brill).

Thornton, R.J.
1983   '"This dying out race": W.H. Bleek's Approach to the Languages of Southern Africa', *Social Dynamics* 9/2: 1-10.

Towner, Philip H.
2001   'Editorial Comment', *Bible Translator* 52/1.

Trial Reports
1863   *Trial of the Bishop of Natal for Erroneous Teaching before the Metropolitan Bishop of Cape Town and the Bishops of Graham's Town and the Orange Free State as Assessors* (Cape Town: Cape Argus).

Trollope, Anthony
1974   *The Clergymen of the Church of England* (Leicester: Leicester University Press [1866]).

Tshehla, M.S.
2000   'Reading John 1:1-18 in Sesotho: An Investigation of the Issues, Meanings and Interpretations Raised by Mother Tongue Exegesis' (unpublished Masters dissertation, University of Natal).

2002   'Can Anything Good Come Out of Africa? Reflections of a South African Mosotho Reader of the Bible', *Journal of African Christian Thought* 5/1: 15-24.

forthcoming   'Translation and the Vernacular Bible in the Debate between My "Traditional" and Academic Worldviews', in Jonathan A. Draper (ed.), *Script, Subjugation And Subversion: Essays In Orality, Literacy and Colonialism in Southern Africa* (*Semeia*).

Tymoczko, Maria
1999   'Postcolonial Writing and Literary Translation', in Bassnett and Trivedi (eds.) 1999: 19-40.

Van der Walt, W.
1989 'Die Bydrae van Sendelinge tot die Vestiging van Zulu as Skryftaal' (unpublished Masters dissertation, Potchefstroom University for Higher Christian Education).

Venn, Henry
1857 'Appendix' (on the subject of Polygamy printed in Church Missionary Society), *Proceedings of the Church Missionary Society for Africa and the East.*

Vermigli, Peter
1576 *Loci Communes* (London: Kyngston).

Vidler, Alec R.
1961 *The Church in an Age of Revolution: 1789 to the Present Day* (Middlesex: Penguin Books).

Vilakazi A., B. Mthethwa and M. Mpanza
1986 *Shembe: A Revitalization of African Society* (Braamfontein: Skotaville Publishers).

Vincent, Jean Marcel
1990 *Leben und Werk des frühen Eduard Reuss: ein Beitrag zu den gestesgeschichtlichen Voraussetzungen der Bibelkritik im zweiten Viertel des 19 Jahrhunderdts* (München: Chr. Kaiser).

Wagner, W.
1923-26 'The Zulu Notion of God According to the Traditional Zulu God-Names', *Anthropos* 18–19: 656-87; 20: 558-78; 21: 351-85.

Wakefield, Gordon S.
1983 *A Dictionary of Christian Spirituality* (London: SCM Press).

Walls, A.F.
2001 'Christian Scholarship in Africa in the Twenty-first Century', *Journal of African Christian Thought* 4/2: 44-52.

Waterland, Daniel
1737 *A Review of the Doctrine of the Eucharist as Laid Down in Scripture and Antiquity* (London: W. Innys & R. Manby).

Webster, J.B.
1968 'Attitudes and Policies of the Yoruba African Churches Towards Polygamy', in B.C. Baeta (ed.), *Christianity in Tropical Africa: Studies Presented and Discussed at the Seventh International African Seminar, University of Ghana, April 1965* (Oxford: Oxford University Press).

Wellhausen, Julius
1927 *Prolegomena zur Geschichte Israels* (Berlin/Leipzig: G. Reimer, 6th edn).

Welsh, David
1971 *The Roots of Segregation: Native Policy in Natal (1845–1910)* (Cape Town: Oxford University Press).

Werner, Alice
unknown 'Recollections of H.E. Colenso' (unpublished paper housed at Killie Campbell Africana Library).

Wesley, John
unknown *Explanatory Notes upon the New Testament* (published in numerous editions by a variety of publishers).

West, Gerald O.
 1997   'On the Eve of an African Biblical Studies: Trajectories and Trends', *Journal
           of Theology for Southern Africa* 99: 99-115.
Whang, Y.C.
 1999   'To whom is a Translator Responsible—Reader or Author?', in Porter and
           Hess (eds.), 1999: 46-62.
Whitby, Daniel
 1804   *A Paraphrase and Commentary on the New Testament in Two Volumes*
           (London: James Mayes, repr.).
Wilder, Hyman, A.
 1856   Review of *'Remarks on the Proper Treatment of Cases of Polygamy, as found
           already existing in Converts from Heathenism' by John William Colenso
           D.D. Lord Bishop of Natal* (Durban: no details of publication available).
Williams, D.
 1978   *Umfundisi: A Biography of Tiyo Soga 1829–1871* (Alice: Lovedale Press).
Williams, Rowland
 1860   'Bunsen's Biblical Researches', in Temple *et al.* (eds.), 1860: 50-83.
Wilson, H.B.
 1860   'Séances historiques de Genève. The National Church', in Temple *et al.*
           (eds.), 1860: 130-86.
Wilson, Linda
 2000   *Constrained by Zeal: Female Spirituality among Non-conformists 1825–
           1875* (Carlisle: Paternoster Press).
Winckler, W.G.
 1964   'The Life and Writings of Bishop Colenso' (unpublished Masters
           dissertation, University of South Africa).
Wirgman, A.T.
 1909   *Life of James Green* (2 vols.; London: Longmans, Green & Co.).
Woolsey, Theodore Dwight
 1858   'Colenso and Grout on Polygamy', *The New Englander* (4 February): 407-33.
Wordsworth, C.
 1866   *Genesis and Exodus; with Notes and Introductions* (London: Rivingtons).
Young, J.R.
 1865   *Modern Scepticism, Viewed in Relation to Modern Science; More Especially
           in Reference to the Doctrines of Colenso, Huxley, Lyell, and Darwin Respect-
           ing the Noachian Deluge, the Antiquity of Man, and the Origin of Species*
           (London: Saunders, Otley & Co.).
Ziervogel, D.
 1950   'A Swazi Translation of 1846', *African Studies* (published by Witwatersrand
           University Press) (December).

INDEX OF AUTHORS

INDEX OF SUBJECTS